Teacher's day

Now Playing

수능 날 1시 10분,

그 1시간 10분을 너의 시간으로

01:10   11:16

3편

EBS 수능특강 영어 주제 소재편 20~31강

2024학년도 수능·내신대비교재

EBS 수능특강 영어 「1시 10분」

스승의날
Teachers Day Publisher

머리말

대한민국 고3 필수관문, EBS 수능특강 영어!
2024학년도에 더 멋진 모습으로 돌아온 스승의날 분석서, 1시 10분입니다.

여러분은 이 책을 '왜' 구매하셨나요?
상반기에 남은 '인생 마지막 내신'을 성공적으로 준비하기 위해?
그렇다면 잘 선택하셨습니다!
이 책은 선생님들께는 수업 준비와 연구용으로, 학생들에게는 친절한 분석과 풍부한 문제들로 <내신 대비>에 아주 탁월하거든요.

그러나 우리는 알고 있어요.
고3이라면 내신도 챙겨야 함은 물론, 수능 날을 위해 더 많은 걸 준비해야 한다는 사실을요.
스승의날은 많은 고민을 했답니다. 이 책이 자문을 암기시켜 학교 시험을 잘 보게 하는 것을 넘어서, 궁극적인 학생들의 <영어 실력>을 올려줄 수 있을까? 비록 1년도 채 되지 않는 시간만이 남았더라도 말입니다.

내신 시험이 암기를 요구하는 시험이라면, 수능 시험은 글의 흐름을 빠르게 간파하고 맞는 선지를 고를 수 있는 '독해력과 사고력'이 필요한 시험일 거예요. 이러한 측면을 고려해 「1시 10분」은 자문의 흐름을 정리해주고 주제문을 도출해주는 <개요도>, 자문 속 내용적, 문법적 출제 포인트를 꼼꼼하게 짚어주는 <손필가분석지> 등 '글을 읽는 훈련'을 함께할 수 있는 콘텐츠들로 준비했어요. 이 책을 만나, 그동안 기계적인 문제풀이나 지루한 암기에 지쳤던 학생 여러분께서 '지금까지와 다른 학습'에 눈이 번쩍 뜨이기를 기대하고 있답니다!

「1시 10분」 수능 영어 시작 시간!
1시 10분에 시작하여 1시간 10분 동안 진행되는 그 떨리는 시간을 스승의날이 함께 하겠습니다.
너덜너덜해진 이 책이 수능 날 그 순간, 여러분의 실력을 꽃피우는 데에 많은 도움이 되길 희망합니다.

2023년 2월
스승의날 영어연구소 선생님 일동

contents
목차

이 책의 구성

Part1 손필기분석지 & Ⓢhorts

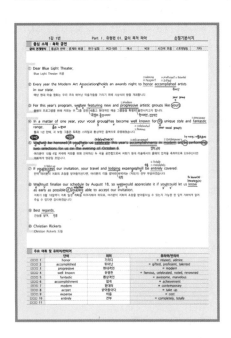

- ### 손필기분석지 & Words
  - 마치 과외를 받는 듯한 <u>친근하고 예쁜 손필기 비주얼!</u>
  - <u>글의 핵심을 담은 주제문장</u>(문장번호가 있어 기억하기도 쉬워요!)
  - <u>문법+내용 기준</u>으로 선별한 <u>주요문장</u>(=서술형)
  - 주요어휘 표시는 기본! 패러프레이징을 대비하는 <u>풍부한 동/유의어까지</u>
  - 주요어법 표시는 기본! 병렬, 도치, 생략된 관/대, 대명사의 지칭, 후치수식 등 <u>문장성분을 꼼꼼히 분석</u>
  - <u>구조화를 돕는 단락 나눔 표시</u>
  - 지문 핵심-연관 키워드의 연결(패러프레이징되는 명사(구) 색칠)
  - 빈칸/삽입 출제 예상 포인트도 참고!
  - 학교 선생님은 절대 지문 그대로 단어를 주지 않아요. <u>패러프레이징 대비 동/유의어 정리도 친절하게 알려줄게요!</u>

Ⓢhorts 흐름/내용일치/문법

- ### Ⓢhorts Ⓕlow : 글의 개요도 완성하기
  - 지문 분석을 자세히 파고들다 보면, 정작 필자가 무슨 말을 하려 하는지 놓칠 수 있어요!
  - 직접 서론-본론-결론을 연결 지으며 스스로 개요도를 완성해보세요. 수능을 위해서도 글의 흐름 파악 훈련은 필수입니다.

- ### Ⓢhorts Ⓞverview : 글의 주제 및 제목 작성하기
  - 우리말 주제, 제목을 읽고 직접 영어 문장을 완성해보세요. 지문 전체를 아우르는 주제 및 제목을 친절히 도출해주니까, 더욱 부담 없는 서술형 Warming-Up!

- ### Ⓢhorts Ⓓetail : 영어 내용 일치/불일치 문제
  - 전국 내신 트렌드에 맞게, 꼭 필요한 유형 힘차게 등장!
  - 문제(영문)를 읽고, 공부한 지문의 내용을 토대로 답을 고르세요. 영문 내용 일치 문제는 동일한 내용의 어휘/구문이 어떻게 변형될 수 있는지(패러프레이징, 서술형) 공부하기에도 큰 도움이 돼요!

- ### Ⓢhorts Ⓖrammar 어법 선택 문제
  - 분석지를 공부하고 지문을 파악했다면, 빠르게 문법 문제로 간단 몸풀기!
  - 몇 가지 대표적인 내신 문법 출제 의도를 담았어요. 수일치, 시제 파악, 품사 문제 등 기본적으로 출제될 수 있는 포인트들이니 꼭 맞히고 다음 단계로 넘어갑시다!

Part II 컴팩트

- 지문별 한 페이지로 끝내는 <u>All in One식 구성</u>
- 100점 만점으로 구성되어, <u>나의 학습 현황을 점수화</u>할 수 있어요!
- 거의 모든 문장에서 <u>출제 예상 포인트를 잡아주어</u>(연결어, 어법, 어휘), 지문 어느 부분에서 내신이 출제되어도 <u>두렵지 않아요!</u>
- 양자택일? 3자, 4자택일까지 주어져, 많~이 고민하며 풀어야 해요. 그만큼 <u>뇌리에 깊게 박히고</u>, 틀린 선택지까지 광범위하게 공부할 수 있겠죠?
- 스승의날의 정체성, <u>완벽 정리 개요도!</u> 내신시험 임박 시, <u>빠른 내용 정리와 암기에도 탁월!</u>
- 이외 요약문 등 내신 대비 <u>모든 포인트가 집약된 완전체</u>
- <u>한눈에 보는 정답지, 탄생!</u> 정답확인도 쉽고 빠르게!

[총점 : 100점]
[1] 밑줄에 알맞은 어휘를 채우며, [대괄호] 안에서 알맞은 표현을 고르고 문법 출제의도를 쓰세요.
　　(각 3점씩 20문제, 총 60점)
[2] 우리말과 일치하도록 주어진 단어를 바르게 배열하여 〈주제 및 제목〉을 작성하세요.
　　(각 10점씩 2문제, 총 20점)
[3] 위 지문에 있는 단어만을 활용하여 다음 〈요약문〉을 완성하시오(어형 변형 가능).
　　(총 20점)

Part III 변형문제

- **밑줄 없이 틀린 어법 찾아 고치기 (고난도)**
  - 앞서 분석지와 컴팩트에서 공부한 문법 포인트들을 토대로, 선택지(밑줄)의 도움 없이 스스로 틀린 부분을 찾아보세요.

- **요약문/주제/제목 서술형 (고난도)**
  - 우리말로 제시된 요약문/주제/제목을 토대로, 조건(혹은 보기)에 맞게 영작하세요.
  - 문제를 푸는 데에 그치지 않고, 문제에서 알려주는 요약문/주제/제목이 어떻게 도출되었는지 살펴보고 스스로 할 수 있도록 훈련해봅시다.
  - 〈조건〉에서 알려주는 문법/단어/용법이 곧 주요 출제 포인트가 된다는 것을 잊지 마세요!

- **주요문장 조건 영작 서술형 (고난도)**
  - 내신 시험 전, 지문별 주요 문장 정리는 필수! 연구진 선생님들이 출제 예상 〈문법+내용〉 포인트를 꼼아 꼼꼼하게 선별했어요.
  - 〈조건〉에서 알려주는 문법/단어/용법이 곧 주요 출제 포인트가 된다는 것을 잊지 마세요!

memo

Part I
손필기분석지 & Ⓢhorts

중심 소재 : 동화 작가이자 삽화가인 Leo Lionni

글의 전개방식	통념과 반박	문제와 해결	연구·실험	비교·대조	예시	비유	시간적 흐름	스토리텔링	기타

① Leo Lionni, an internationally known designer, illustrator, and graphic artist, was born in Holland and lived in Italy until he came to the United States in 1939.
=renowned =famous
국제적으로 알려진 디자이너이자 삽화가이자 그래픽 아티스트였던 Leo Lionni는 네덜란드에서 태어나 1939년 미국에 올 때까지 이탈리아에서 살았다.

② As a little boy, he would go into the museums in Amsterdam, and that's how he taught himself how to draw.
~하곤 했었다
어린 소년이었을 때 그는 암스테르담의 박물관에 들어가곤 했는데, 그것이 그가 그림 그리는 법을 독학한 방법이다.
teach oneself: 독학하다
how to +v : ~하는 법
=he ~Amsterdam

③ He got into writing and illustrating children's books almost by accident.
=by chance =accidentally =unintentionally
그는 거의 우연히 아동 도서를 쓰고 그것에 삽화를 그리게 되었다.
우연히

④ Lionni tore out bits of paper from a magazine and used them as characters and made up a story to entertain his grandchildren on a train ride.
=rip off =piece =create(invent) a story
bits ~magazine
Lionni는 기차를 타고 가면서 손주들을 즐겁게 하기 위해 잡지에서 종잇조각들을 뜯어내어 그것을 캐릭터로 사용하고 이야기를 구성했다.
즐겁게 해주다
=amuse =delight =please

⑤ This story became what we now know as the children's book titled Little Blue and Little Yellow.
목적격 관·대 서술형
titling(x)
이 이야기가 우리가 현재 Little Blue and Little Yellow라는 제목의 아동 도서로 알고 있는 것이 되었다.

⑥ He became the first children's author/ illustrator to use collage as the main medium for his illustrations.
=dominant =primary
그는 자신의 삽화의 주요 표현 수단으로 콜라주를 사용한 최초의 아동 도서 작가이자 삽화가가 되었다.
삽화

⑦ Lionni wrote and illustrated more than 40 children's books.
Lionni는 40권이 넘는 아동 도서를 쓰고 삽화를 그렸다.

⑧ In 1982, Lionni was diagnosed with Parkinson's disease, but he kept working in drawing, illustrating and teaching.
서술형 계속해서 ~하다
keep ~ing=continue=go on
진단하다
1982년, Lionni는 파킨슨병을 진단받았지만, 그는 그리기, 삽화 그리기, 그리고 가르치는 일을 계속했다.

⑨ He passed away in October 1999 in Italy.
=die
그는 1999년 10월 이탈리아에서 사망했다.

주요 어휘 및 유의어/반의어			
	단어	의미	유의어/반의어
□□□ 1	known	알려진	= famous, renowned
□□□ 2	by accident	우연히	= by chance, accidently, unintentionally
□□□ 3	tear out	뜯어내다	= rip off
□□□ 4	bit	조각	= piece
□□□ 5	make up a story	이야기를 구성하다	= create(invent) a story
□□□ 6	entertain	즐겁게 해 주다	= amuse, delight, please
□□□ 7	main	주요한	= primary, dominant
□□□ 8	keep -ing	계속해서 ~하다	= continue, go on
□□□ 9	pass away	사망하다	= die
□□□ 10			
□□□ 11			

Ⓢhorts Ⓕlow 제시된 [A], [B], [C]를 서론, 본론, 결론의 순서로 연결해보고, 단락별 내용의 흐름을 정리해보세요.		

	서론 (~)	본론 (~)	결론 (~)
개요도	·	·	·
	·	·	·

Ⓢhorts Ⓞverview 글의 〈주제 및 제목〉을 쓰시오.

주제	한글	
	영어	
	정답	
제목	한글	
	영어	
	정답	

Ⓢhorts Ⓓetails 글의 내용과 일치하면 T에, 일치하지 않으면 F에 동그라미 표기를 하세요.

① It was not until 1939 that Leo Lionni first lived in a country other than the Netherlands.　　　[T / F]

② While on the train, Lionni improvised a story using pieces of paper for its characters to entertain his grandchildren.　　　[T / F]

③ Prior to Lionni, no one was named a children's book writer / illustrator using collages.　　　[T / F]

④ Parkinson's disease kept Lionni from drawing and teaching.　　　[T / F]

Ⓢhorts Ⓖrammar 각 문장에서 어법상 가장 적절한 것을 고르시오.

① Leo Lionni, an internationally known designer, illustrator, and graphic artist, [was / being] born in Holland and lived in Italy until he came to the United States in 1939.
② As a little boy, he would go into the museums in Amsterdam, and that's how he [taught / was taught] himself how to draw.
③ He got into writing and illustrating children's books almost by accident.
④ Lionni tore out bits of paper from a magazine and used [it / them] as characters and made up a story to entertain his grandchildren on a train ride.
⑤ This story became [that / what] we now know as the children's book titled Little Blue and Little Yellow.
⑥ He became the first children's author/ illustrator to use collage as the main medium for his illustrations.
⑦ Lionni wrote and illustrated more than 40 children's books.
⑧ In 1982, Lionni was diagnosed with Parkinson's disease, but he kept [work / to work / working] in drawing, illustrating and teaching.
⑨ He passed away in October 1999 in Italy.

중심 소재 : 이탈리아 쌀을 미국에 도입하려는 Jefferson의 노력

글의 전개방식	통념과 반박	문제와 해결	연구·실험	비교·대조	예시	비유	시간적 흐름	스토리텔링	기타

주제문

(all things agricultural)
= enthusiasm = craving
= genuinely
= sincerely

① Thomas Jefferson's knowledge of and passion for all things agricultural//were truly extraordinary.

농업적인 모든 것에 대한 Thomas Jefferson의 지식과 열정은 정말 대단했다.
대단한 = impressive = outstanding

(Being) = motivated = inspired
freeing(x)　= dependence　서술형

② Driven by a desire to see the South freed from its reliance on cotton, he//was always on the lookout for crops that could replace it =cotton
의존
~을 (찾기 위해) 세심히 살피다

면화에 대한 의존에서 해방되는 (미국) 남부를 보고 싶은 욕망에 이끌려, 그는 늘 그것을 대체할 수 있는 농작물을 찾고 있었다.

(he was)
prefer A to B : A를 B보다 더 선호하다
A be preferred to B : A가 B보다 더 선호
접속사

③ While touring the south of France in 1787, Jefferson//discovered that Italian rice//was preferred to the American import grown in the Carolinas.

1787년에 프랑스 남부 지역을 여행하던 중, Jefferson은 이탈리아 쌀이 Carolina의 두 주(South Carolina 와 North Carolina)에서 재배되는 미국산 수입품보다 더 선호된다는 것을 발견했다.

(Being) = absorbed in = keen on
= eager for　의문사　Italian ~ Carolians

④ Intent on discovering why this//might be so, he//took a detour into the Italian region of Lombardy on a ~에 전념하여 mission of rice reconnaissance (a journey that (because it//required crossing the Alps)//was extremely 주격관·대 dangerous at the time).
= highly

이것이 왜 그런지 밝히려는 일념으로, 그는 (알프스산맥을 넘어야 했기 때문에, 그 당시 매우 위험했던 여정인) 쌀 정찰 임무를 띠고 이탈리아 Lombardy 지역으로 우회해서 갔다.

접속사　=people　= excellent = superb　= kind = sort　서술형　소유격 관·대

⑤ There he//discovered that the good folks of Lombardy//were growing a superior strain of crop — whose export for planting outside of Italy//was a crime punishable by death.

그곳에서 그는 Lombardy의 선량한 사람들이 우수한 품종의 농작물을 재배하고 있고, 이탈리아 이외의 지역에서 재배하기 위한 수출은 사형에 처할 수 있는 범죄라는 것을 알게 되었다.

(Being) = undeterred
분사구문

⑥ Undaunted, Jefferson//sent a small packet of the rice grain to his good friend James Madison and members of the South Carolina delegation. 대표단

굴하지 않고 Jefferson은 자신의 친한 친구 James Madison과 South Carolina 대표단원들에게 작은 벼 낟알 꾸러미를 보냈다.

= fill

⑦ Later, he//stuffed his pockets with some of the rice grains, and "walked it" out of the country.

나중에 그는 자신의 주머니에 얼마간의 벼 낟알을 채워 그 나라로부터 '그것을 멋대로 가져갔다'.

⑧ The rice//is grown in parts of the United States to this day.

그 벼는 오늘날까지도 미국의 일부 지역에서 재배되고 있다.

* reconnaissance: 정찰 ** strain: 품종 *** undaunted: 굴하지 않는

주요 어휘 및 유의어/반의어

	단어	의미	유의어/반의어
□□□ 1	passion	열정	= enthusiasm, craving
□□□ 2	truly	정말	= sincerely, genuinely
□□□ 3	extraordinary	대단한	= impressive, outstanding
□□□ 4	driven	이끌린	= motivated, inspired
□□□ 5	reliance	의존	= dependence
□□□ 6	intent on	~에 열중한	= absorbed in, keen on, eager for
□□□ 7	extremely	매우	= highly, greatly, severely
□□□ 8	folks	사람들	= people
□□□ 9	superior	우수한	= excellent, superb
□□□ 10	strain	품종	= kind, sort
□□□ 11	undaunted	의연한	= undeterred

	ⓢhorts ⓕlow 제시된 [A], [B], [C]를 서론, 본론, 결론의 순서로 연결해보고, 단락별 내용의 흐름을 정리해보세요.		
	서론 (①) ·	본론 (② ~ ⑤) ·	결론 (⑥ ~ ⑧) ·
개요도	· [A] 글감 제시 Jefferson의 농업에 대한 지식과 열정은 실로 대단했다.	· [B] 서사 전개 남프랑스를 여행하며 그는 캐롤리나에서 자라는 미국 쌀보다 이탈리아산 쌀이 선호되는 것을 발견했다.	· [C] 서사 종결 그는 처벌의 위험을 무릅쓰고 쌀을 반출했고, 지금도 미국에서 재배된다.

ⓢhorts ⓞverview 글의 〈주제 및 제목〉을 쓰시오.

주제	한글	Jefferson과 이탈리아 쌀 이야기
	영어	of / story / the / Italian / rice / and / Jefferson
	정답	
제목	한글	이탈리아 쌀을 위한 Jefferson의 노력
	영어	for / Italian / Rice / Jefferson's / Efforts
	정답	

ⓢhorts ⓓetails 글의 내용과 일치하면 T에, 일치하지 않으면 F에 동그라미 표기를 하세요.

① Desiring the southern part of the United States to be independent of resorting to one crop, Jefferson was always looking for alternative crops. [T / F]

② Jefferson decided to conduct a survey on rice in the region of Lombardy after discovering that no rice was preferred to that grown in the Carolinas during his trip to France. [T / F]

③ Knowing that it was illegal to export superior varieties of crops in the Lombardy to other countries, Jefferson eventually found a way not to export them illegally and was able to bring them to his country. [T / F]

ⓢhorts ⓖrammar 각 문장에서 어법상 가장 적절한 것을 고르시오.

① Thomas Jefferson's knowledge of and passion for all things agricultural [being / were] truly extraordinary.

② [Driving / Driven] by a desire to see the South freed from its reliance on cotton, he was always on the lookout for crops that could replace [it / them].

③ While touring the south of France in 1787, Jefferson discovered that Italian rice was preferred to the American import grown in the Carolinas.

④ Intent on discovering why this might be so, he took a detour into the Italian region of Lombardy on a mission of rice reconnaissance (a journey that, because it required crossing the Alps, was extremely dangerous at the time).

⑤ There he discovered that the good folks of Lombardy were growing a superior strain of crop — [which / what / whose] export for planting outside of Italy was a crime punishable by death.

⑥ Undaunted, Jefferson sent a small packet of the rice grain to his good friend James Madison and members of the South Carolina delegation.

⑦ Later, he [stuffed / was stuffed] his pockets with some of the rice grains, and "walked it" out of the country.

⑧ The rice is grown in parts of the United States to this day.

중심 소재 : Joseph Lister가 개발한 소독 방법

글의 전개방식	통념과 반박	문제와 해결	연구·실험	비교·대조	예시	비유	시간적 흐름	스토리텔링	기타

① It's the late 1800s.
1800년대 후반이다.

② Anesthesia has just been introduced. (introduced(x))
마취법이 막 도입되었다.

③ Surgeries are on the rise, but a disturbing number of patients are dying due to infection. (감염)
(=on the increase =increasing) (=overwhelming =vast =alarming) (is(x))
수술은 증가 추세이지만, 충격적인 수의 환자들이 감염으로 사망하고 있다.

(주제문) ④ Joseph Lister is determined to figure out why and what can be done about it
(=resolved) (=discover =find out) (충격적인 의문사) (패러프레이징 a disturbing ~ infection)
Joseph Lister는 그 원인과 대처 방안을 알아내기로 결심한다.
(~을 알아내다) (접속사)

⑤ (C) After much research and thought, he concludes that Pasteur's controversial germ theory holds the key to the mystery.
(=contentious 논란이 많은)
(C) 많은 연구와 생각 끝에, 그는 논란이 많은 Pasteur의 세균설이 미스터리의 열쇠를 쥐고 있다고 결론 내린다.

⑥ Killing germs in wounds with heat isn't an option, however — a completely new method is required.
(동명사) (=entirely =fully) (=necessary =needed)
그러나 열로 상처의 세균을 죽이는 것은 선택 사항이 아니라서 완전히 새로운 방법이 필요하다.

⑦ (B) Lister guesses that there may be a chemical solution, and later that year, he reads (in a newspaper) that the treatment of sewage with a chemical called carbolic acid reduced the incidence of disease among the people and cattle of a nearby small English town.
(접속사) (접속사) (하수) (=close-by =neighboring) (발병률)
(B) Lister는 화학적 해결책이 있을 수도 있다고 추측하고, 그해 말, 석탄산이라고 불리는 화학 물질로 하수를 처리한 것이 근처의 작은 영국 마을의 사람들과 소들 사이에서 질병 발생률을 감소시켰다는 것을 신문에서 읽는다.

⑧ Lister follows the lead and, in 1865, develops a successful method of applying carbolic acid to wounds to prevent infection.
(=spread) (상처)
Lister는 그 선례를 따라 1865년에 감염을 막기 위해 상처에 석탄산을 바르는 성공적인 방법을 개발한다.

⑨ (A) He continues to work along this line and establishes antisepsis as a basic principle of surgery.
(A) 그는 이 계통으로 계속 연구하여 소독을 수술의 기본 원칙으로 확립한다. (확립하다)

⑩ Thanks to his discoveries and innovations, amputations become less frequent, deaths due to infection drop sharply, and new surgeries previously considered impossible are being routinely planned and executed. (서술형)
(=suddenly) (considering(x)) (=commonly)
그의 발견과 혁신 덕분에, 절단 수술의 횟수가 줄어들고, 감염으로 인한 사망이 급격히 감소하며, 이전에는 불가능하다고 여겨졌던 새로운 수술들이 일상적으로 계획되고 실행되고 있다.
(이전에)

* anesthesia: 마취(법) ** antisepsis: 소독(법) *** amputation: 절단 (수술)

주요 어휘 및 유의어/반의어

	단어	의미	유의어/반의어
☐☐☐ 1	on the rise	증가하는	= increasing, on the increase
☐☐☐ 2	disturbing	충격적인	= vast, alarming, overwhelming
☐☐☐ 3	determined	단단히 결심한	= resolved
☐☐☐ 4	figure out	알아내다	= find out, discover
☐☐☐ 5	controversial	논란이 많은	= contentious
☐☐☐ 6	completely	완전히	= entirely, fully
☐☐☐ 7	required	필수의	= needed, necessary
☐☐☐☐ 8	nearby	근처의	= close-by, neighboring, adjacent
☐☐☐ 9	apply	바르다	= spread
☐☐☐ 10	sharply	급격히	= suddenly, abruptly
☐☐☐ 11	routinely	일상적으로	= commonly

ⓈhortsⒻlow 제시된 [A], [B], [C]를 서론, 본론, 결론의 순서로 연결해보고, 단락별 내용의 흐름을 정리해보세요.

	서론 (① ~ ④)	본론 (⑤ ~ ⑧)	결론 (⑨ ~ ⑩)
	•	•	•
개요도	• [A] 배경 제시 마취법이 막 도입된 1800년대 후반 감염으로 죽는 환자가 많았고, Lister는 이유와 방안을 고민했다.	• [B] 결과 소개 덕분에 감염으로 인한 사망은 급격히 줄었고, 과거 불가능하다고 생각한 수술이 진행되었다.	• [C] 논의 전개 그는 석탄산이라는 화학 물질의 쓰임을 확인하고, 이를 활용하여 상처의 감염을 막는 방법을 개발했다.

ⓈhortsⓄverview 글의 〈주제 및 제목〉을 쓰시오.

주제	한글	수술을 위한 석탄산의 개발	
	영어	of / for / surgeries / carbolic / acid / development	
	정답		
제목	한글	소독법에 석탄산을 사용하는 것에 대한 Joseph Lister의 통찰	
	영어	Insight / Lister's / for / Antisepsis / Carbolic / Into / Acid / Joesph / Using	
	정답		

ⓈhortsⒹetails 글의 내용과 일치하면 T에, 일치하지 않으면 F에 동그라미 표기를 하세요.

① With the introduction of anesthesia in the late 1800s, the number of surgeries hardly increased, and many patients died of infection.　[T / F]

② Lister developed his own disinfection method after reading an article that a chemical reduced the disease called carbolic acid, which was prevalent among the people of a nearby small English village.　[T / F]

③ The decrease in the number of amputations caused by infection derives from the addition of antisepsis as a basic principle to surgery.　[T / F]

ⓈhortsⒼrammar 각 문장에서 어법상 가장 적절한 것을 고르시오.

① It's the late 1800s.

② Anesthesia has just been introduced.

③ Surgeries are on the rise, but a disturbing number of patients are dying [**because / due to**] infection.

④ Joseph Lister is determined to figure out why and [**that / what**] can be done about it.

⑤ (C) After much research and thought, he concludes that Pasteur's controversial germ theory holds the key to the mystery.

⑥ Killing germs in wounds with heat isn't an option, however — a completely new method is [**requiring / required**].

⑦ (B) Lister guesses that there may be a chemical solution, and later that year, he reads in a newspaper that the treatment of sewage with a chemical called carbolic acid reduced the incidence of disease among the people and cattle of a nearby small English town.

⑧ Lister follows the lead and, in 1865, develops a successful method of applying carbolic acid to wounds to [**prevent / preventing**] infection.

⑨ (A) He continues to work along this line and establishes antisepsis as a basic principle of surgery.

⑩ Thanks to his discoveries and innovations, amputations become less frequent, deaths due to infection drop [**sharp / sharply**], and new surgeries previously considered impossible [**being / are being**] routinely planned and executed.

| 중심 소재 : 국가주의와 관련한 역사학과 지리학의 상대적 위치 |||||||||

| 글의 전개방식 | 통념과 반박 | 문제와 해결 | 연구·실험 | 비교·대조 | 예시 | 비유 | 시간적 흐름 | 스토리텔링 | 기타 |

축제문

=be useful
=be helpful
↔absolute

① While both history and geography// could serve to develop nationalistic sentiments, the relative position
of these two subjects in the educational system// largely came to depend on the degree to which either
// seemed more useful in building up the idea of a national identity.
=generally =mostly 국가주의적인 ~에 달려있다 / ~에 의해 불성되다 / 전치사+관·대

~에 달려있다
~에 의해 불성되다
come to v : ~하게 되다

역사학과 지리학 모두 국가주의적 정서를 발달시키는 데 도움이 될 수 있었지만, 교육 제도에서 이 두 과목의 상대적 위치는 국가 정체성의
개념을 형성하는 데 어느 쪽이 더 유용해 보이는지의 정도에 따라 대체로 달라지게 되었다.

in ~ing
: ~하는 데에 있어서

서술형

② In Germany, with its long history of shifting borders and divisions into small states, geographical
patterns associated with the German-speaking lands// seemed very ❶ significant, and so geography// was
seen as very important.
=related to = involved in / =crucial =important / 패러프레이징

독일에서는, 변경되는 국경과 소국으로 분할되는 오랜 역사를 가지고 있어, 독일어권 영토와 관련된 지리적 양상이 매우 중요해 보였고, 따라서
지리학이 매우 중요하게 여겨졌다.

See A as B : A를 B로 여기다
A is seen as B : A는 B로 여겨지다
=consider
=regard

③ Norway, on the other hand// had developed its educational system during the union of the crowns
with Sweden (1814-1905) and it// had no ❷ disputed borders.

반면, 노르웨이는 스웨덴과의 왕위 통합 기간(1814~1905년) 동안 교육 제도를 발전시켜 왔고, 분쟁 중인 국경이 없었다.

분쟁을 벌이다

④ Under these circumstances, Norway's national awakening// was fostered by teaching about the glorious
history of Viking times and about the precious liberal constitution of 1814.
=condition =situation / =encourage =promote / by ~ing : ~함으로써 / =magnificent

이러한 상황에서 노르웨이의 국가적 자각은 바이킹 시대의 영광스러운 역사와 1814년의 고귀한 자유 헌법에 대한 교육에 의해 촉진되었다.

⑤ Hence, history// ❸ predominated over geography.

그리하여 역사학이 지리학보다 우위를 차지했다.

서술형 주격 관·대

⑥ Finland, however, which had also experienced a union of crowns (in this case with Tsarist Russia)//
❹ possessed lacked a clearly discernible glorious past and so geography// developed as a relatively more
important subject.
v'=distinguishable

그러나 마찬가지로 왕위 통합(이 경우에는 제정 러시아와의)을 경험했던 핀란드는 명백하게 뚜렷한 영광스러운 과거를 가지고 있었고
(→ 가지지 못했고), 그래서 지리학이 상대적으로 더 중요한 과목으로 발전했다.

=innovative =groundbreaking

⑦ A pioneering research work of great political importance in the Finnish liberation process// the Atlas of
Finland// ❺ stressed the uniqueness of the Finnish lands.
=emphasize / 해방 / =

핀란드의 해방 과정에서 정치적으로 매우 중요한 선구적 연구 저술인 Atlas of Finland는 핀란드 땅의 고유성을 강조했다.

* Tsarist Russia: 제정 러시아 ** discernible: 뚜렷한, 분간할 만한

| 주요 어휘 및 유의어/반의어 ||||

	단어	의미	유의어/반의어
☐☐☐ 1	serve	도움이 되다	= be helpful, be useful
☐☐☐ 2	relative	상대적인	↔ absolute
☐☐☐ 3	largely	대체로	= generally, mostly
☐☐☐ 4	associated with	~와 관련된	= related to, involved in
☐☐☐ 5	significant	중요한	= important, crucial
☐☐☐ 6	see	여기다	= consider, regard
☐☐☐ 7	circumstance	상황	= condition, situation
☐☐☐ 8	foster	촉진하다	= promote, encourage, stimulate
☐☐☐ 9	glorious	영광스러운	= splendid, magnificent
☐☐☐ 10	discernible	뚜렷한	= distinguishable
☐☐☐ 11	pioneering	선구적인	= innovative, groundbreaking

⑤horts Ⓕlow 제시된 [A], [B], [C]를 서론, 본론, 결론의 순서로 연결해보고, 단락별 내용의 흐름을 정리해보세요.

	서론 (①)	본론 (② ~ ⑤)	결론 (⑥ ~ ⑦)
	•	•	•
개요도	• [A] 사례 제시 독일의 경우 지리가, 노르웨이의 경우에는 역사가 국가주의적 정서 형성에 강조된다.	• [B] 글감의 집약적 제시 역사와 지리 모두 국가주의적 정서를 개발하지만, 교육에서 둘의 상대적 위치는 유용성에 달려있다.	• [C] 논의 확장 핀란드는 노르웨이와 유사한 역사를 가졌지만 지리가 교육에서 강조되는 특이한 경우가 있다.

⑤horts Ⓞverview 글의 <주제 및 제목>을 쓰시오.

주제	한글	국가 정체성을 발전시키기 위한 교육에서 역사와 지리의 상대적 위치
	영어	relative / history / of / and / developing / geography / in / education / identity / for / position / national
	정답	
제목	한글	민족주의 정서 형성을 위한 역사와 지리에 대한 강조의 지역적 차이 탐색
	영어	History / Regional / Differences / for / Building / Exploring / Emphasis / of / on / Geography / Nationalistic / and / Sentiment
	정답	

⑤horts Ⓓetails 글의 내용과 일치하면 T에, 일치하지 않으면 F에 동그라미 표기를 하세요.

① History and geography were not always considered equally important in shaping the concept of national identity in the educational system. [T / F]

② Since Germany and Norway had different characteristics of history, geography occupied an important position in the former education and history did in the latter one. [T / F]

③ Finland had a history of the same nature as Norway in terms of the union of crowns, but unlike Norway, geography developed into a more important subject than history in Finland. [T / F]

⑤horts Ⓖrammar 각 문장에서 어법상 가장 적절한 것을 고르시오.

① [While / During] both history and geography could serve to develop nationalistic sentiments, the relative position of these two subjects in the educational system largely came to depend on the degree [which / what / to which] either seemed more [useful / usefully] in building up the idea of a national identity.

② In Germany, with its long history of shifting borders and divisions into small states, geographical patterns associated with the German-speaking lands seemed very significant, and so geography was seen as very important.

③ Norway, on the other hand, had developed its educational system during the union of the crowns with Sweden (1814-1905) and it had no disputed borders.

④ Under these circumstances, Norway's national awakening was [fostering / fostered] by teaching about the glorious history of Viking times and about the precious liberal constitution of 1814.

⑤ Hence, history predominated over geography.

⑥ Finland, however, which [had / was] also experienced a union of crowns (in this case with Tsarist Russia), lacked a clearly discernible glorious past and so geography developed as a relatively more important subject.

⑦ A pioneering research work of great political importance in the Finnish liberation process, the Atlas of Finland, stressed the uniqueness of the Finnish lands.

중심 소재 : 종교와 관련한 윤리의 자율성

| 글의 전개방식 | 통념과 반박 | 문제와 해결 | 연구·실험 | 비교·대조 | 예시 | 비유 | 시간적 흐름 | 스토리텔링 | 기타 |

주제문
① One dimension of ethical theory that needs mentioning is the issue of autonomy of ethics in relation to religion.
= aspect
측면, 자원
= regarding
= in connection w
언급할 필요가 있는 윤리 이론의 한 가지 측면은 종교와 관련한 윤리의 자율성 문제이다.

② Many ethical works are written from a religious point of view, and many concrete moral judgments are influenced by religion.
= view = perspective
= viewpoint
= affect = impact
현실의, 구체적인
많은 윤리학 저술이 종교적 관점에서 쓰이고, 현실의 많은 도덕적 판단이 종교의 영향을 받는다.

③ A question in ethical theory is whether ethics has some kind of evidential dependence on religion.
서술형 = if
have(x)
= reliance
윤리 이론에서의 한 가지 문제는, 윤리가 종교에 대해 일종의 증거적 의존성을 가지고 있느냐이다. 증거적

④ Consider the question whether moral knowledge — say, that lying is (with certain exceptions) wrong — requires knowing any religious truth.
~인지 아닌지에 대한 문제
동격 접속사
예를 들어, 거짓말하는 것은(특정한 예외는 있지만) 잘못된 것이라는 도덕적 지식이 어떤 종교적 진리든 알아야 할 필요가 있는지의 문제를 생각해 보라.

⑤ This does not seem so.
= appear
이것은 그렇게 보이지 않는다.

⑥ To say this is not to claim (as some would) that we can know moral truths even if there are no theological or religious truths.
= assert
= insist
접속사
= though
= although
= even though
이렇게 말하는 것은 비록 신학적 또는 종교적 진리가 '존재하지' 않더라도 우리가 도덕적 진리를 알 수 있다고 (누군가는 그렇게 하겠지만) 주장하는 것은 아니다.

⑦ The point is theologically neutral on this matter.
= impartial
= unbiased
핵심 내용은 이 문제에 관해 신학적인 것에 얽매이지 않는다는 것이다.
중립적인

⑧ It is that knowledge of moral truths does not depend on knowledge of God or of religious truths.
접속사
= rely on
그것은 도덕적 진리에 관한 '지식'이 신이나 종교적 진리에 관한 '지식'에 의존하지 않는다는 것이다.

⑨ This view that moral knowledge is possible independently of religion is not antireligious, and indeed it has often been held by religiously committed philosophers and by theologians.
서술형
동격 접속사
= irrespective of
= regardless of
종교에 반하는
= dedicated
= devoted
헌신적인
도덕적 지식은 종교와 관계없이 가능하다는 이 견해는 종교에 반하는 것이 아니며, 사실상 그것은 종교적으로 헌신적인 철학자들과 신학자들이 흔히 품어 왔던 것이었다.

* theological: 신학적인

주요 어휘 및 유의어/반의어

	단어	의미	유의어/반의어
☐☐☐ 1	dimension	측면	= aspect
☐☐☐ 2	in relation to	~와 관련된	= regarding, with respect to, in connection with
☐☐☐ 3	point of view	관점	= view, viewpoint, perspective
☐☐☐ 4	influence	영향을 주다	= affect, impact
☐☐☐ 5	whether	~인지 아닌지	= if
☐☐☐ 6	dependence	의존성	= reliance
☐☐☐ 7	seem	~처럼 보이다	= appear
☐☐☐ 8	claim	주장하다	= insist, assert
☐☐☐ 9	neutral	얽매이지 않는	= unbiased, impartial
☐☐☐ 10	depend on	의존하다	= rely on
☐☐☐ 11	independently	~와 관계없이	= regardless of, irrespective of

⑤horts ⑤low 제시된 [A], [B], [C]를 서론, 본론, 결론의 순서로 연결해보고, 단락별 내용의 흐름을 정리해주세요.

	서론 (①)	본론 (② ~ ⑦)	결론 (⑧ ~ ⑨)
	•	•	•
개요도	• [A] 재진술 도덕적 진리에 대한 진실은 신이나 종교적 진리의 지식에 달려있지 않다.	• [B] 논의 풀이 도덕적 지식에 관한 질문에 종교적 지식이 필요 없다는 말은, 신학적으로 중립적이라는 것이 핵심이다.	• [C] 글감의 집약적 제시 종교와 관련한 윤리의 자율성 문제를 언급할 필요가 있다.

⑤horts ⑤verview 글의 〈주제 및 제목〉을 쓰시오.

주제	한글	신학적 진실과 도덕적 지식의 중립성
	영어	truth / neutrality / of / moral / and / theological / knowledge
	정답	
제목	한글	도덕적 진실을 찾기 위해 우리는 종교적이어야 할까?
	영어	Should / Find / To / Moral / Religious / We / Be / Truths
	정답	

⑤horts ⑤etails 글의 내용과 일치하면 T에, 일치하지 않으면 F에 동그라미 표기를 하세요.

①	The writer agrees with the idea that religion is the basis for many moral judgments such as lying.	[T / F]
②	The writer says no theologian has claimed that moral knowledge is possible regardless of religion.	[T / F]

⑤horts ⑤rammar 각 문장에서 어법상 가장 적절한 것을 고르시오.

① One dimension of ethical theory that needs mentioning [is / are / being] the issue of autonomy of ethics in relation to religion.

② Many ethical works are written from a religious point of view, and many concrete moral judgments are influenced by religion.

③ A question in ethical theory is [what / whether] ethics has some kind of evidential dependence on religion.

④ Consider the question whether moral knowledge — say, that lying is (with certain exceptions) wrong — [require / requires / requiring] knowing any religious truth.

⑤ This does not seem so.

⑥ To say this is not to claim (as some would) that we can know moral truths [as if / even if] there are no theological or religious truths.

⑦ The point is theologically neutral on this matter.

⑧ It is that knowledge of moral truths does not depend on knowledge of God or of religious truths.

⑨ This view that moral knowledge is possible [independent / independently] of religion is not antireligious, and indeed it has often been [holding / held] by religiously committed philosophers and by theologians.

중심 소재 : 도덕적 정체성 발달에 영향을 미치는 요인								
글의 전개방식	통념과 반박	문제와 해결	연구·실험	비교·대조	예시	비유	시간적 흐름	스토리텔링	기타

주제문

① Several factors//have been identified as influences on the development of moral identity, some individual and some contextual. 상황적인;문맥상의
=effect =impact
여러 가지 요인들이 도덕적 정체성 발달에 영향을 미치는 것으로 밝혀졌는데, 어떤 것은 개인적이고, 어떤 것은 상황적이다.

② (❶) At the individual level, things such as personality, cognitive development, attitudes and values, and broader self and identity development//can impact moral identity development.
=character　인지의
개인적 차원에서는, 성격, 인지 발달, 태도와 가치관, 그리고 더 폭넓은 자아 및 정체성 발달 같은 것들이 도덕적 정체성 발달에 영향을 미칠 수 있다.

③ (❷) For example, those more advanced in cognitive and identity development//have greater capacities for moral identity development.
=For instance 서술형　=progressive　=capability =ability
예를 들어, 인지 및 정체성 발달에서 더 뛰어난 사람들은 도덕적 정체성 발달에 대한 능력이 더 뛰어나다.

④ (❸) Also greater appreciation for moral values//might facilitate their subsequent integration into identity.
=awareness of =understanding of　패러프레이징　=ease　moral values =following 통합
또한, 도덕적 가치관에 대한 더 많은 이해는 이후에 그것(도덕적 가치관)이 정체성으로 통합되는 것을 촉진할 수도 있다. 촉진하다

⑤ (❹ At the contextual level, one important factor//is the person's social structure, including neighborhood, school, family, and institutions such as religious, youth, or community organizations.)
↔excluding 분사구문
상황적 차원에서는, 한 가지 중요한 요소가 이웃, 학교, 가족, 그리고 종교 단체, 청소년 단체 또는 지역 사회 단체와 같은 기관을 포함하는, 그 개인이 속한 사회 구조이다. 패러프레이징　기관

⑥ For example a caring and supportive family environment//can facilitate the development of morality and identity, as well as the integration of the two into moral identity.
= thoughtful =considerate　=morality and identity
예를 들어, 배려하고 도와주는 가정 환경은 도덕성과 정체성 발달을 촉진할 수 있고, 그뿐만 아니라 그 두 가지(도덕성과 정체성)가 도덕적 정체성으로 통합되는 것도 촉진할 수 있다.

⑦ (❺) Additionally, involvement in religious and youth organizations//can provide not only moral beliefs systems but also opportunities to act on those beliefs (e.g., through community involvement), which can aid their integration into identity.
=furthermore =in addition =moreover　B as well as A :A뿐만 아니라 B도　~에 따라 행동하다　주격관·대
게다가, 종교 단체 및 청소년 단체에 참여하는 것은 도덕적 신념 체계뿐만 아니라, (예를 들어, 지역 사회 참여를 통해) 그러한 신념에 따라 행동할 기회도 제공할 수 있으며, 이는 그것이 정체성으로 통합되는 것을 도울 수 있다.
not only A but also B : A뿐만 아니라 B도

주요 어휘 및 유의어/반의어			
	단어	의미	유의어/반의어
☐☐☐ 1	influence	영향	= effect, impact
☐☐☐ 2	personality	성격	= character
☐☐☐ 3	for example	예를 들어	= for instance
☐☐☐ 4	advanced	뛰어난	= progressive
☐☐☐ 5	capacity	능력	= ability, capability
☐☐☐ 6	appreciation for	~에 대한 이해	= understanding of, awareness of
☐☐☐ 7	facilitate	촉진하다	= ease
☐☐☐ 8	subsequent	이후의	= following
☐☐☐ 9	including	포함하는	↔ excluding
☐☐☐ 10	caring	배려하는	= considerate, thoughtful
☐☐☐ 11	additionally	게다가	= in addition, moreover, furthermore

⑤horts Ⓕlow 제시된 [A], [B], [C]를 서론, 본론, 결론의 순서로 연결해보고, 단락별 내용의 흐름을 정리해보세요.

	서론 (①)	본론 (② ~ ④)	결론 (⑤ ~ ⑦)
	•	•	•
개요도	•	•	•
	[A] 병렬적 논의 전개 B 상황적 수준에서는 이웃, 학교, 가족 등과 같은 사회적 구조가 중요한 요소이다.	[B] 병렬적 논의 전개 A 개인적 수준에서, 성격이나 인지 발달, 태도와 가치 등이 영향을 미친다.	[C] 글감 제시 도덕적 정체성 발달에 영향을 미치는 것으로 밝혀진 몇 가지 요소 중 일부는 개인적이고, 일부는 상황적이다.

⑤horts Ⓞverview 글의 <주제 및 제목>을 쓰시오.

주제	한글	도덕적 정체성의 발달을 위한 개인적이고 맥락적인 요소들
	영어	of / identity / the / contextual / moral / for / factors / development / individual / and
	정답	
제목	한글	도덕적 정체성 발달에 영향을 미치는 요인의 분류
	영어	of / Identity / the / Influential / Moral / for / Factors / Development / Categorization / of
	정답	

⑤horts Ⓓetails 글의 내용과 일치하면 T에, 일치하지 않으면 F에 동그라미 표기를 하세요.

① It is not factors at the individual level that can affect the development of moral identity, but factors at the situational one. [T / F]

② The greater the cognitive and identity development is, the better the ability to develop moral identity becomes. [T / F]

③ Understanding moral values has been shown to make it better possible for moral values to be integrated into identity. [T / F]

④ Participation in the social structure to which an individual belongs can only provide opportunities to act according to beliefs, not moral belief systems. [T / F]

⑤horts Ⓖrammar 각 문장에서 어법상 가장 적절한 것을 고르시오.

① Several factors have [identified / been identified] as influences on the development of moral identity, some individual and some contextual.
② (❶) At the individual level, things such as personality, cognitive development, attitudes and values, and broader self and identity development can impact moral identity development.
③ (❷) For example, those more advanced in cognitive and identity development have greater capacities for moral identity development.
④ (❸) Also, greater appreciation for moral values might facilitate their subsequent integration into identity.
⑤ (❹ At the contextual level, one important factor is the person's social structure, [includes / include / including] neighborhood, school, family, and institutions such as religious, youth, or community organizations.)
⑥ For example, a caring and supportive family environment can facilitate the development of morality and identity, as well as the integration of the two into moral identity.
⑦ (❺) Additionally, involvement in religious and youth organizations can provide not only moral beliefs systems but also opportunities to act on those beliefs (e.g., through community involvement), [what / that / which] can aid their integration into identity.

중심 소재 : 종이 재활용의 필요성

글의 전개방식	통념과 반박	문제와 해결	연구·실험	비교·대조	예시	비유	시간적 흐름	스토리텔링	기타

① Today we are using some 400 million plus tonnes of paper per annum in a global population of about seven billion, but if we look at the anticipated population figure in 2045 of nine billion, just on that basis alone paper production will need to increase by 30 per cent.   서술형

오늘날 우리는 약 70억 명의 전 세계 인구 내에서 1년에 약 4억 톤 이상의 종이를 사용하고 있지만, 만약 우리가 2045년에 90억명으로 예상되는 인구 수치를 본다면, 단지 그것에만 근거해도 종이 생산량을 30퍼센트 늘려야 할 것이다.

② On top of that within our current population not everybody is able to get a newspaper or has a book to read, or has enough exercise books to write on at school.

게다가 현재 우리의 인구 내에서 모든 사람이 신문을 구할 수 있거나 읽을 책을 가지고 있거나, 학교에서 쓸 수 있는 충분한 연습장을 가지고 있는 것은 아니다.

③ As their percentage increases the demand for paper will also increase.

그들의 비율이 늘어남에 따라 종이에 대한 수요 역시 늘어날 것이다.

④ We have limited land and a limited number of trees, and if we don't recycle we will not be able to supply the 400 million tonnes we need today or meet the demands of an increasing population.

우리는 제한된 땅과 제한된 수의 나무를 가지고 있으며, 만약 우리가 재활용을 하지 않는다면 우리는 오늘날 필요로 하는 4억 톤의 종이를 공급하거나 늘어나는 인구의 수요를 충족시킬 수 없을 것이다.

⑤ Remember of course that within the 400 million tonnes we use today about 200 million tonnes of waste paper is used in its manufacturing; 200 million tonnes of waste paper generates roughly 160 million tonnes of recycled paper.

오늘날 우리가 사용하는 4억 톤의 종이 내에서 그것을 제조하는 데 약 2억 톤의 폐지가 사용되는데, 2억 톤의 폐지는 대략 1억 6천만 톤의 재생지를 만들어 낸다는 것을 물론 명심하라.

⑥ Therefore if we didn't recycle we would only have 240 million tonnes of paper so there would be a shortfall or we would have to use more pulp.

그러므로 만약 우리가 재활용을 하지 않는다면 우리는 2억 4천만 톤의 종이만 가지게 될 것이므로, 부족분이 생길 것인데, 다시 말하면, 우리가 더 많은 펄프를 사용해야 할 것이다.

* per annum: 1년에

주요 어휘 및 유의어/반의어

	단어	의미	유의어/반의어
□□□ 1	some	약, 대략	= about, approximately, roughly
□□□ 2	per annum	1년에	= a year
□□□ 3	anticipate	예상하다	= expect, predict
□□□ 4	on top of	~뿐 아니라	= besides, other than
□□□ 5	current	현재의	= present
□□□ 6	meet	충족하다	= satisfy
□□□ 7	generate	만들어 내다	= produce
□□□ 8	therefore	그러므로	= thus, hence
□□□ 9	shortfall	부족	= shortage
□□□ 10			
□□□ 11			

Ⓢhorts Ⓕlow 제시된 [A], [B], [C]를 서론, 본론, 결론의 순서로 연결해보고, 단락별 내용의 흐름을 정리해보세요.		
서론 (①) •	본론 (② ~ ④) •	결론 (⑤ ~ ⑥) •
개요도　　• [A] 상황 제시 우리는 연간 4억 톤 가량의 종이를 사용하는데, 인구 증가에 따라 그 수요는 더 증가할 것이다.	• [B] 논점 제시 상당수의 종이가 재활용되고 있음을 인식해야 한다.	• [C] 문제 제기 우리 중 일부는 읽을 책이 없거나 학교에서 사용할 교과서가 없을 것이 다.

Ⓢhorts Ⓞverview 글의 〈주제 및 제목〉을 쓰시오.

	한글	증가하는 수요에 대한 종이 재활용의 중요성
주제	영어	of / paper / demand / increasing / recycling / the / for / importance / the
	정답	
제목	한글	비상: 종이가 부족할 수 있다
	영어	May / Out / We / Of / Paper / Run / Emergency:
	정답	

Ⓢhorts Ⓓetails 글의 내용과 일치하면 T에, 일치하지 않으면 F에 동그라미 표기를 하세요.

① If the world's population reaches 9 billion by 2045, it is estimated that about 520 million tonnes of paper will be used per year. [T / F]

② The more people buy and own books or newspapers, the more demand for paper will increase. [T / F]

③ According to the article, we can say that we need about 500 million tonnes of waste paper to make 400 million tonnes of recycled paper. [T / F]

Ⓢhorts Ⓖrammar 각 문장에서 어법상 가장 적절한 것을 고르시오.

① Today we are using some 400 million plus tonnes of paper per annum in a global population of about seven billion, but [if / unless] we look at the anticipated population figure in 2045 of nine billion, just on that basis alone paper production will need to increase by 30 per cent.

② On top of that within our current population not everybody [is / are / being] able to get a newspaper or has a book to read, or has enough exercise books to write on at school.

③ As their percentage increases the demand for paper will also increase.

④ We have [limited / been limited] land and a limited number of trees, and if we don't recycle we will not be able to supply the 400 million tonnes we need today or meet the demands of an increasing population.

⑤ Remember of course [which / what / that] within the 400 million tonnes we use today about 200 million tonnes of waste paper is used in [its / their] manufacturing; 200 million tonnes of waste paper generates roughly 160 million tonnes of recycled paper.

⑥ Therefore if we didn't recycle we would only have 240 million tonnes of paper so there would be a shortfall or we would have to [use / using] more pulp.

중심 소재 : 희금속을 확보하기 위한 기업과 국가의 노력

글의 전개방식	통념과 반박	문제와 해결	연구·실험	비교·대조	예시	비유	시간적 흐름	스토리텔링	기타

주제문

① For years, companies and countries//took their rare metal supply lines for granted, unaware of the material makeup of their products.

수년간, 기업과 국가들은 자신들이 만드는 제품의 재료 구성을 알지 못한 채, 자신들의 희금속 공급선을 당연하게 여겼다.

② In fact, in 2011, Congress//forced the U.S. military to research its supply chains because the Pentagon //was having difficulty determining ❶ which advanced metals it//needed.

실은, 2011년, 미 의회는 미국 군대에 그것의 공급망을 연구하도록 강제했는데, 그 이유는 펜타곤(미국 국방부)이 그것에 어떤 첨단 금속이 필요한지 결정하는 데 어려움을 겪고 있었기 때문이다.

③ As the materials that make up product components//❷ to have become have become more varied and complex, those who rely on sophisticated hardware//can no longer afford to remain in the dark.

제품의 부품을 구성하는 재료가 더 다양해지고 복잡해짐에 따라 정교한 하드웨어에 의존하는 사람들은 더 이상 아무것도 모르는 상태로 있을 여유가 없다.

④ Now, corporate and government leaders//are realizing how ❸ important rare metals//are.

이제, 기업과 정부 지도자들은 희금속이 얼마나 중요한지 깨닫고 있다.

⑤ Indeed, efforts to secure rare metals//have sparked a war over the periodic table.

실제로, 희금속을 확보하기 위한 노력은 주기율표를 둘러싼 전쟁을 촉발시켰다.

⑥ In offices from Tokyo to Washington, D.C., in research and development labs from Cambridge, Massachusetts, to Baotou, China, and in strategic command centers the world over, new policies and the launching of research programs//are ensuring ❹ that nations//have access.

도쿄에서 Washington, D.C.까지의 관청에서, 매사추세츠주의 Cambridge에서 중국의 Baotou까지의 연구 개발 실험실에서, 그리고 전 세계의 전략 지휘 본부에서, 새로운 정책과 연구 프로그램의 착수는 국가가 반드시 (희금속에 대해) 접근할 수 있도록 하고 있다.

⑦ The struggle for minor metals//isn't imminent; it's already here and is shaping the relationship between countries as conflicts over other resources ❺ did in the past.

비주류 금속을 위한 경쟁은 곧 닥쳐올 듯한 것이 아니라 이미 여기 있으며, 과거에 다른 자원을 둘러싼 분쟁이 그랬던 것처럼 국가 간의 관계를 형성하고 있다.

* the Pentagon: 펜타곤 (미국 국방부로, 국방부 건물이 5각형 모양인 데서 유래)

** imminent: 곧 닥쳐올 듯한, 임박한

주요 어휘 및 유의어/반의어

	단어	의미	유의어/반의어
□□□ 1	unaware	알지 못하는	= ignorant, oblivious
□□□ 2	in fact	사실	= as a matter of fact, actually
□□□ 3	force	강제하다, 강요하다	= push, compel
□□□ 4	make up	~을 구성하다	= compose, constitute
□□□ 5	complex	복잡한	= complicated
□□□ 6	rely on	~에 의존하다	= depend on, count on
□□□ 7	sophisticated	정교한	= highly developed
□□□ 8	secure	확보하다	= obtain, gain
□□□ 9	spark	촉발하다	= trigger, provoke
□□□ 10	ensure	보장하다	= make sure
□□□ 11	imminent	임박한	= impending, forthcoming

Ⓢhorts Ⓕlow 제시된 [A], [B], [C]를 서론, 본론, 결론의 순서로 연결해보고, 단락별 내용의 흐름을 정리해보세요.

	서론 (①)	본론 (② ~ ③)	결론 (④ ~ ⑦)
	•	•	•
개요도	•	•	•
	[A] 논의 전개	[B] 문제상황 제시	[C] 부연 설명
	제품의 구성이 더 복잡해지면서, 정교한 하드웨어에 의존하는 사람들이 더 이상 무지할 여유가 없다.	수년간 기업과 국가는 제품의 재료 구성을 알지 못한 채 희금속의 공급선을 당연시했다.	기업과 정부는 희금속의 중요성을 인지하고, 이를 수호하려는 노력을 이어가고 있다.

Ⓢhorts Ⓞverview 글의 〈주제 및 제목〉을 쓰시오.

주제	한글	기업과 정부의 희귀 금속 확보 노력
	영어	and / companies / secure / rare / efforts / governments / to / by / metals
	정답	
제목	한글	희귀 금속 공급선 문제화 및 확보
	영어	Rare / for / Metals / Lines / Problematizing / Supply / Securing / and
	정답	

Ⓢhorts Ⓓetails 글의 내용과 일치하면 T에, 일치하지 않으면 F에 동그라미 표기를 하세요.

① As the materials that constitute a product have become more diverse, people who resort to advanced hardware no longer need to know the material composition of the product. 　[T / F]

② Given the recent war over securing rare metals, it is possible that countries have realized the importance of rare metals. 　[T / F]

③ Competition for rare metals is not around the corner, but a problem that will be experienced in the distant future. 　[T / F]

Ⓢhorts Ⓖrammar 각 문장에서 어법상 가장 적절한 것을 고르시오.

① For years, companies and countries took their rare metal supply lines for granted, unaware of the material makeup of their products.

② In fact, in 2011, Congress forced the U.S. military to research its supply chains [**because / due to**] the Pentagon was having difficulty [**determine / to determine / determining**] which advanced metals [**did it need / it needed**].

③ As the materials that make up product components [**to have become / have become**] more varied and complex, those who rely on sophisticated hardware can no longer afford to remain in the dark.

④ Now, corporate and government leaders are realizing how [**important / importantly**] rare metals are.

⑤ Indeed, efforts to secure rare metals have [**sparked / been sparked**] a war over the periodic table.

⑥ In offices from Tokyo to Washington, D.C., in research and development labs from Cambridge, Massachusetts, to Baotou, China, and in strategic command centers the world over, new policies and the launching of research programs are ensuring that nations have access.

⑦ The struggle for minor metals isn't imminent; it's already here and is shaping the relationship between countries as conflicts over other resources [**did / were**] in the past.

중심 소재 : 기후 정의(climate justice)

글의 전개방식	통념과 반박	문제와 해결	연구·실험	비교·대조	예시	비유	시간적 흐름	스토리텔링	기타

① The effects of climate change//will fall most heavily upon the poor of the world.
= impact = influence   = extremely = greatly

기후 변화의 영향은 세계의 가난한 사람들을 가장 크게 덮칠 것이다.

② (❶) Regions such as Africa//could face severely compromised food production and water shortages, while coastal areas in South, East, and Southeast Asia//will be at great risk of flooding.
= confront   = terribly = badly = awfully   훼손된   홍수   부족

아프리카와 같은 지역들은 심각하게 훼손된 식량 생산과 물 부족에 직면할 수 있는 동시에 남아시아, 동아시아, 동남아시아의 해안 지역은 홍수의 큰 위험에 처할 것이다.
at risk of ~ : ~의 위험에 처한

③ (❷) Tropical Latin America//will see damage to forests and agricultural areas due to drier climate, while (in South America) changes in precipitation patterns and the disappearance of glaciers//will significantly affect water availability.
= because of   = considerably = greatly = substantially   소멸, 사라짐   이용 가능성

열대 라틴 아메리카는 더 건조한 기후로 인해 숲과 농업 지역에 피해를 보는 동시에 남아메리카에서는 강우 패턴의 변화와 빙하의 소멸이 물의 이용 가능성에 큰 영향을 미칠 것이다.

④ (❸ While the richer countries//may have the economic resources to adapt to many of the effects of climate change, (without significant aid) poorer countries//will be unable to implement preventive measures, especially those that rely on the newest technologies.)
= adjust to = accommodate to = get used to   = carry out = execute = conduct   시행하다   예방   서술형   주격 관·대

더 부유한 나라들은 기후 변화의 많은 영향에 적응하기 위한 경제적 자원을 가지고 있을 수도 있지만, 상당한 원조가 없을 경우 더 가난한 나라들은 예방조치, 특히 최신 기술에 의존하는 조치를 시행할 수 없을 것이다.

⑤ This//raises fundamental issues of environmental justice in relation to the impact of economic and political power on environmental policy on a global scale.
= bring up   = basic = essential   = the measures   서술형   = regarding = with respect to   근본적인   the impact of A on B : A가 B에 미치는 영향

이는 세계적인 규모로 경제력 및 정치력이 환경 정책에 미치는 영향과 관련하여 환경 정의라는 근본적인 문제를 제기한다.

⑥ (❹) The concept of climate justice//is a term used for framing global warming as an ethical and political issue, rather than one that is purely environmental or physical in nature.
만들어내다   주격   = only   = issue

기후 정의라는 개념은 지구 온난화를 본질적으로 순전히 환경적이거나 물리적인 것이라기보다는, 윤리적이고 정치적인 문제로 만들기 위해 사용되는 용어이다.

⑦ (❺) The principles of climate justice//imply an equitable sharing both of the burdens of climate change and the costs of developing policy responses.
= mean   = just = fair

기후 정의의 원칙은 기후 변화의 부담과 정책 대응을 개발하는 비용 양쪽을 공평하게 분담하는 것을 의미한다.

* precipitation: 강우 ** equitable: 공평한

	주요 어휘 및 유의어/반의어		
	단어	**의미**	**유의어/반의어**
□□□ 1	effect	영향	= impact, influence
□□□ 2	heavily	크게	= greatly, extremely
□□□ 3	face	직면하다	= confront
□□□ 4	severely	심각하게	= awfully, terribly, badly
□□□ 5	due to	~ 때문에	= because of
□□□ 6	significantly	크게	= considerably, substantially, greatly
□□□ 7	adapt to	~에 적응하다	= adjust to, accommodate to, get used to
□□□ 8	implement	시행하다	= carry out, put ~ into action
□□□ 9	raise	제기하다	= bring up
□□□ 10	fundamental	근본적인	= basic, essential
□□□ 11	in relation to	~와 관련하여	= regarding, with respect to

ⓢhorts Ⓕlow 제시된 [A], [B], [C]를 서론, 본론, 결론의 순서로 연결해보고, 단락별 내용의 흐름을 정리해보세요.

	서론 (① ~ ④)	본론 (⑤ ~ ⑥)	결론 (⑦)
개요도	•	•	•
	•	•	•
	[A] 부연 설명	[B] 개념 제시	[C] 주장 제시
	기후 정의의 원리는 기후 변화의 부담과 정책 대응 설계의 비용을 공평하게 나누는 것을 함의한다.	기후 정의는 지구 온난화를 환경이나 물리가 아닌, 윤리적이고 정치적인 문제로 만드는 용어이다.	기후 변화의 효과는 가난한 세계에 더 크게 나타날 것이며, 부유한 나라는 경제력을 이용해 영향에 적응할 것이다.

ⓢhorts Ⓞverview 글의 <주제 및 제목>을 쓰시오.

주제	한글	기후 변화의 불균일한 영향과 환경 정의
	영어	change / of / uneven / and / effect / climate / justice / environmental
	정답	
제목	한글	기후 정의: 지구 온난화에 대한 윤리적, 정치적 접근법
	영어	and / an / Ethical / Climate / Justice: / Global / to / Warming / Approach / Political
	정답	

ⓢhorts Ⓓetails 글의 내용과 일치하면 T에, 일치하지 않으면 F에 동그라미 표기를 하세요.

① The harmful effects of climate change are not the same size for both the poor and the rich.   [T / F]

② It is how rich the country is that the ability to implement the latest technology-dependent precautions to adapt to the effects of climate change could depend on.   [T / F]

③ The concept of climate justice is to make global warming purely environmental, that is, politically neutral.   [T / F]

ⓢhorts Ⓖrammar 각 문장에서 어법상 가장 적절한 것을 고르시오.

① The effects of climate change will fall most [heavy / heavily] upon the poor of the world.
② (❶) Regions such as Africa could face severely compromised food production and water shortages, while coastal areas in South, East, and Southeast Asia will be at great risk of flooding.
③ (❷) Tropical Latin America will see damage to forests and agricultural areas [because / due to] drier climate, while in South America changes in precipitation patterns and the disappearance of glaciers will significantly affect water availability.
④ (❸ While the richer countries may have the economic resources to adapt to many of the effects of climate change, without significant aid poorer countries will be unable to implement preventive measures, especially those that rely on the newest technologies.)
⑤ This [rises / raises] fundamental issues of environmental justice in relation to the impact of economic and political power on environmental policy on a global scale.
⑥ (❹) The concept of climate justice is a term used for framing global warming as an ethical and political issue, rather than one that is [pure / purely] environmental or physical in nature.
⑦ (❺) The principles of climate justice imply an equitable sharing both of the burdens of climate change and the costs of developing policy responses.

중심 소재 : 유기 화학(organic chemistry)

글의 전개방식	통념과 반박	문제와 해결	연구·실험	비교·대조	예시	비유	시간적 흐름	스토리텔링	기타

주제문

① Organic chemistry is the part of chemistry that is concerned with the compounds of carbon. (=involved)
'유기 화학'은 탄소 화합물과 관련이 있는 화학의 일부이다. 주격관·대 ~에 관련이 있다 화합물

서술형 접속사 명사절

② That one element can command a whole division is evidence of carbon's pregnant mediocrity. (= abundant)
하나의 원소가 한 분야 전체를 차지할 수 있다는 사실은 탄소의 풍요한 범용성에 대한 증거이다. 중요한·중만한
자지하다·장악하다

③ Carbon lies at the midpoint of the Periodic Table =the chemist's map of chemical properties of the elements, and is largely indifferent to the relationships it enters into. (=unconcerned)(= carbon)
탄소는 원소들의 화학적 성질에 대한 (화학자의 지도인 '주기율표')의 중간 지점에 있으며, 대개 그것이 관여하는 관계에 개의치 않는다.
개의치 않는·무관심한   (that) 목적격 관·대   ~에 관여하다

④ In particular, it is content to bond to itself. (carbon)
특히, 그것은 기꺼이 자신과 결합한다.

⑤ As a result of its mild and unaggressive character, it is able to form chains and rings of startling complexity. (carbon)(=docile)(↔ aggressive)(= build =produce)
순하고 유화적인 성격으로 인해, 그것은 놀라울 정도의 복잡성을 가진 사슬과 고리를 형성할 수 있다. O2 패러프레이징

서술형

⑥ Startling complexity is exactly what organisms need if they are to be regarded as being alive, and thus the compounds of carbon are the structural and reactive infrastructure of life. (that(x))(=life form =living things)(간접의문문)(~로 여겨지다)
놀라울 정도의 복잡성은 바로 유기체가 살아 있는 것으로 여겨지려면 필요로 하는 것이고, 따라서 탄소 화합물은 생명체의 구조적이고 반응적인 하부 구조이다. 하부 구조

보어 강조 - 형용사 도치

⑦ So extensive are the compounds of carbon, currently numbering in the millions, that it is not surprising that a whole branch of chemistry has evolved for their study and has developed special techniques, systems of nomenclature, and attitudes. (=broad =comprehensive)(형용사)(=progress)(so~that 구문)(가S)(진S) **서술형**
현재 그 수가 수백만 개에 달하는 탄소 화합물은 매우 광범위해서, 화학의 한 분야 전체가 그것의 연구를 위해 발전해 왔고 특별한 기술, 명명법의 체계, 사고방식을 발전시켜 온 것은 놀라운 일이 아니다.

* mediocrity: 범용성 ** nomenclature: (학술적) 명명법

주요 어휘 및 유의어/반의어			
	단어	의미	유의어/반의어
□□□ 1	concerned	~에 관련이 있는	= involved
□□□ 2	pregnant	풍부한	= abundant
□□□ 3	indifferent	개의치 않는	= unconcerned
□□□ 4	mild	순한	= docile
□□□ 5	unaggressive	유화적인	↔ aggressive
□□□ 6	form	형성하다	= produce, build
□□□ 7	organism	유기체	= living things, life form
□□□ 8	extensive	광범위한	= broad, comprehensive, considerable
□□□ 9	evolve	발전하다	= progress
□□□ 10			
□□□ 11			

Ⓢhorts Ⓕlow 제시된 [A], [B], [C]를 서론, 본론, 결론의 순서로 연결해보고, 단락별 내용의 흐름을 정리해보세요.

	서론 (①) ·	본론 (② ~ ⑥) ·	결론 (⑦) ·
개요도	· [A] 개념 제시 유기 화학은 탄소 화합물과 관련 있는 화학의 갈래이다.	· [B] 특성 소개 탄소는 풍부한 범용성이 있는데, 놀라울 정도로 복잡한 사슬과 고리를 만들 수 있다.	· [C] 논의 마무리 탄소 화합물은 매우 광범위해서, 화학의 한 분야로서 발전한 것은 놀라운 일도 아니다.

Ⓢhorts Ⓞverview 글의 <주제 및 제목>을 쓰시오.

주제	한글	유기화학과 탄소화합물의 평범함
	영어	and / of / the / chemistry / mediocrity / carbonic / organic / compounds
	정답	
제목	한글	유기화학: 개념과 설명
	영어	and / Organic / Concept / Chemistry: / Explanation
	정답	

Ⓢhorts Ⓓetails 글의 내용과 일치하면 T에, 일치하지 않으면 F에 동그라미 표기를 하세요.

① The fact that organic chemistry is the field related to carbon compounds shows how widely carbon can be used. [T / F]

② If carbon cannot form chains with remarkable complexity, a carbon compound cannot be said to be a substructure of life. [T / F]

③ Carbon compounds are too broad for a whole branch of chemistry to be developed for their research. [T / F]

Ⓢhorts Ⓖrammar 각 문장에서 어법상 가장 적절한 것을 고르시오.

① Organic chemistry is the part of chemistry [what / that] is concerned with the compounds of carbon.

② That one element can command a whole division [is / are / being] evidence of carbon's pregnant mediocrity.

③ Carbon lies at the midpoint of the Periodic Table, the chemist's map of chemical properties of the elements, and is largely indifferent to the relationships it enters into.

④ In particular, it is content to bond to [it / itself].

⑤ As a result of its mild and unaggressive character, it is able to form chains and rings of startling complexity.

⑥ Startling complexity is exactly [which / that / what] organisms need if they are to [regard / be regarded] as being alive, and thus the compounds of carbon are the structural and reactive infrastructure of life.

⑦ So [extensive / extensively] are the compounds of carbon, currently numbering in the millions, that it is not surprising that a whole branch of chemistry has [evolved / evolving] for their study and has developed special techniques, systems of nomenclature, and attitudes.

중심 소재 : 붕사(硼砂)(borax)

글의 전개방식	통념과 반박	문제와 해결	연구·실험	비교·대조	예시	비유	시간적 흐름	스토리텔링	기타

① Humans//have used borax for more than four thousand years.

인간은 4천 년이 넘는 기간 동안 붕사(硼砂)를 사용해 왔다.

주제문

② Since the 1800s, it//has been mined near Death Valley, California.

1800년대 이후로, 그것은 캘리포니아주의 Death Valley 인근에서 채굴되었다.

(Being) 분사구문

③ Dirt cheap, borax//has many industrial uses, but in the home it//is used as a natural laundry-cleaning booster, multipurpose cleaner, fungicide, herbicide, and disinfectant.

붕사는 값이 매우 싸므로, 공업용으로 많이 사용되지만, 가정에서 그것은 천연 세탁 촉진제, 다목적 세제, 곰팡이 제거제, 제초제, 소독제로 사용된다.
= sterilize = germicide = sanitizer

④ Off-white, odorless, and alkaline, borax crystals//can be mixed with other cleaning agents for added power.

회색을 띤 백색이고 냄새가 없으며, 알칼리성인 붕사 결정은 효능을 더하기 위해 다른 세정제와 혼합될 수 있다.

=harmless

⑤ Although you certainly//wouldn't want to eat it, borax//is relatively safe and is quite effective without being toxic.

틀림없이 여러분이 그것을 먹는 것은 좋은 생각이 아니지만, 붕사는 비교적 안전하고 독성이 없이 꽤 효과적이다.

=sterilize =sanitize

⑥ It//is useful in a lot of the ways that baking soda//is, but it//s stronger and disinfects more, so it//s good for mold, mildew, and deeper dirt.

그것은 베이킹 소다가 유용하게 사용되는 방식 중의 많은 방식에서 유용하지만, 더 강력하고 더 많이 소독되므로 곰팡이, 흰곰팡이, 찌든 때에 효과적이다.

⑦ In general, use baking soda first and use borax only in situations (where something stronger//is needed.)

일반적으로, 베이킹 소다를 먼저 사용하고, 더 강한 것이 필요한 상황에서만 붕사를 사용하라.

서술형　enable A to B : A가 B를 가능하게 하다

⑧ It//will enable you to get (even stubborn stains) clean without resorting to toxic chemicals.

그것으로 독성이 있는 화학 물질에 의존하지 않고 지우기 힘든 얼룩까지도 깨끗하게 할 수 있을 것이다.

⑨ Borax//should not be used (where) it//might get into food, and it//should be safely stored out of the reach of children and pets.

붕사는 음식에 들어갈 수도 있는 곳에서 사용해서는 안 되며, 어린이와 반려동물의 손이 닿지 않는 곳에 안전하게 보관되어야 한다.

* disinfectant: 소독제 ** mildew: 흰곰팡이

주요 어휘 및 유의어/반의어

	단어	의미	유의어/반의어
□□□ 1	disinfectant	소독제	= sterilizer, germicide sanitizer
□□□ 2	safe	안전한	= harmless
□□□ 3	disinfect	소독하다	= sanitize, sterilize
□□□ 4			
□□□ 5			
□□□ 6			
□□□ 7			
□□□ 8			
□□□ 9			
□□□ 10			
□□□ 11			

⑤horts Ⓕlow 제시된 [A], [B], [C]를 서론, 본론, 결론의 순서로 연결해보고, 단락별 내용의 흐름을 정리해보세요.

개요도	서론 (~)	본론 (~)	결론 (~)
	·	·	·
	·	·	·

⑤horts Ⓞverview 글의 〈주제 및 제목〉을 쓰시오.

주제	한글	주제 없음
	영어	
	정답	
제목	한글	제목 없음
	영어	
	정답	

⑤horts Ⓓetails 글의 내용과 일치하면 T에, 일치하지 않으면 F에 동그라미 표기를 하세요.

① Borax is widely used for industrial use due to its economic advantage, but it is also used in various ways at home. [T / F]

② Combining borax crystals with other cleaning agents leads to weakening the function of the cleaning agent. [T / F]

③ If using baking soda does not remove stains easily, using borax can be helpful, which can be attributed to its toxic chemicals. [T / F]

⑤horts Ⓖrammar 각 문장에서 어법상 가장 적절한 것을 고르시오.

① Humans have used borax for more than four thousand years.

② Since the 1800s, it has [**mined / been mined**] near Death Valley, California.

③ Dirt cheap, borax has many industrial uses, but in the home it is used as a natural laundry-cleaning booster, multipurpose cleaner, fungicide, herbicide, and disinfectant.

④ Off-white, odorless, and alkaline, borax crystals can be mixed with other cleaning agents for added power.

⑤ Although you certainly wouldn't want to eat [**it / them**], borax is relatively safe and is quite [**effective / effectively**] without being toxic.

⑥ It is useful in a lot of the ways that baking soda [**is / does**], but it's stronger and disinfects more, so it's good for mold, mildew, and deeper dirt.

⑦ In general, use baking soda first and use borax only in situations [**what / which / where**] something stronger is needed.

⑧ It will enable you [**get / getting / to get**] even stubborn stains clean without resorting to toxic chemicals.

⑨ Borax should not be used where it might get into food, and it should be safely [**storing / stored**] out of the reach of children and pets.

중심 소재 : 무인 우주 탐사선의 플라이바이 (근접 비행)

글의 전개방식	통념과 반박	문제와 해결	연구·실험	비교·대조	예시	비유	시간적 흐름	스토리텔링	기타

주제문

① There would be//much less to say were//it not for space probes that have visited the giant planets and their moons.

가정법 도치(if 생략) : if it were not for   = enormous = colossal

만약 거대 행성과 그것들의 위성을 방문한 무인 우주 탐사선이 없다면 할 말이 훨씬 더 적을 것이다.

② ❶ Exploration began with fly-bys (missions that flew past the planet) but has moved on to the stage of orbital tours in the case of Jupiter and Saturn, which have each had a mission that orbited the planet for several years and that was able to make repeated close fly-bys of at least the regular satellites.

= revolve

탐사는 플라이바이(행성의 옆을 지나가는 우주 비행)로 시작되었지만, 목성과 토성의 경우 궤도 선회의 단계로 넘어갔는데, 각각의 궤도 선회에는 수년 동안 행성의 궤도를 돌며 적어도 규칙 위성에 대한 가까운 플라이바이를 반복적으로 할 수 있는 우주 비행이 있었다.

③ ❷ Close fly-bys of moons//enable detailed imaging, and usually take the probe close enough to see how the moon affects the strong magnetic field surrounding the planet and to detect whether the moon also has its own magnetic field.

= precise = definite = specific
= influence = change   surrounded (X)   = discover = find
enable A to B : A에게 B를 가능하게 하다   탐지하다
= the moon

위성에 대한 가까운 플라이바이는 상세한 영상 촬영을 가능하게 하며, 일반적으로, 위성이 행성을 둘러싸고 있는 강한 자기장에 어떤 영향을 미치는지 보고 그리고 그 위성 또한 자체의 자기장을 가지는지 탐지할 만큼 가깝게 무인 우주 탐사선을 접근시킨다.

④ ❸ ~~Most irregular satellites, as well as having inclined orbits, travel round their orbits in the direction opposite to their planet's spin.~~

기울어진

대부분의 불규칙 위성은, 기울어진 궤도를 가지고 있을 뿐만 아니라, 행성의 자전 방향과 반대 방향으로 궤도를 돈다.

⑤ ❹ The size of the slight deflection to a probe's trajectory as it//passes close to a moon//enables the moon's mass to be determined.

determine (X)   = figure out = detect = discover

무인 우주 탐사선이 위성에 근접하여 지날 때의 그 궤적에 대한 극미한 편차의 크기로 위성의 질량을 알아낼 수 있다.

서술형 분사구문

⑥ ❺ Knowing the moon's size, it//is then easy to work out its density.

가S   진S   밀도

위성의 크기를 알면, 그것의 밀도를 쉽게 계산할 수 있다.

* probe: 무인 우주 탐사선 ** deflection: 편차, 굴절 *** trajectory: 궤적

주요 어휘 및 유의어/반의어

	단어	의미	유의어/반의어
□□□ 1	giant	거대한	= colossal, enormous
□□□ 2	orbit	궤도를 돌다	= revolve around
□□□ 3	repeated	반복되는	= recurrent, continual
□□□ 4	detailed	상세한	= specific, precise, definite
□□□ 5	affect	영향을 미치다	= influence, change
□□□ 6	detect	탐지하다	= discover, find, identify
□□□ 7	determine	알아내다, 밝히다	= figure out, detect, discover
□□□ 8			
□□□ 9			
□□□ 10			
□□□ 11			

Ⓢhorts Ⓕlow 제시된 [A], [B], [C]를 서론, 본론, 결론의 순서로 연결해보고, 단락별 내용의 흐름을 정리해보세요.

개요도	서론 (①)	본론 (②)	결론 (③ ~ ⑥)
	·	·	·
	·	·	·
	[A] 역사 설명	[B] 역할 설명	[C] 글감 제시
	플라이바이 탐사로 시작해 궤도 선회의 단계로 넘어가며, 우주 비행은 발전해 왔다.	가까운 플라이바이는 상세한 영사 촬영, 자기장의 탐지, 질량 측정 등의 역할을 수행한다.	거대 행성과 위성을 방문한 탐사선이 없다면 할 말이 훨씬 적을 것이다 (= 아는 것이 적을 것이다).

Ⓢhorts Ⓞverview 글의 〈주제 및 제목〉을 쓰시오.

주제	한글	거대 행성과 그 위성 탐사를 위한 플라이바이 (근접 비행)
	영어	explorations / for / of / fly-bys / giant / their / and / moons / planets
	정답	
제목	한글	플라이바이를 통한 다른 행성으로의 탐험
	영어	Expedition / to / Fly-Bys / Other / Planets / Via / An
	정답	

Ⓢhorts Ⓓetails 글의 내용과 일치하면 T에, 일치하지 않으면 F에 동그라미 표기를 하세요.

① It was not until the phase of orbital tours of Jupiter that space exploration could begin fly-bys. **[T / F]**

② Taking the probe close to moons can reveal the impact of the moon on the magnetic field surrounding other planets, but it does not obtain information on the moon's own magnetic field. **[T / F]**

③ There is a way to measure the mass of a moon without a space probe's having to land directly on the moon. **[T / F]**

Ⓢhorts Ⓖrammar 각 문장에서 어법상 가장 적절한 것을 고르시오.

① There would be [**very / much**] less to say [**did / were**] it not for space probes that [**were / have**] visited the giant planets and their moons.

② ❶ Exploration began with fly-bys (missions that flew past the planet) but has moved on to the stage of orbital tours in the case of Jupiter and Saturn, [**which / what / that**] have each had a mission that orbited the planet for several years and that was able to make repeated close fly-bys of at least the regular satellites.

③ ❷ Close fly-bys of moons enable detailed imaging, and usually take the probe [**enough close / close enough**] to see how the moon affects the strong magnetic field surrounding the planet and to detect whether the moon also has its own magnetic field.

④ ❸ The size of the slight deflection to a probe's trajectory as it passes close to a moon enables the moon's mass to [**determine / be determined**].

⑤ ❹ Knowing the moon's size, it is then easy to work out its density.

중심 소재 : 공유 자원과 지속 가능한 관광

글의 전개방식	통념과 반박	문제와 해결	연구·실험	비교·대조	예시	비유	시간적 흐름	스토리텔링	기타

① The term *common pool resources* refers to resources that are available to all, but owned by no one.
'공유 자원'이라는 용어는 모든 사람이 사용할 수 있지만, 아무도 소유하지는 않은 자원을 말한다.
공유 자원

② Nature-based examples include forests, oceans, and vistas, whereas common pool ❶ cultural resources can include a community's song, dance, and traditions.
자연에 기반을 둔 예로는 숲, 해양, 경치가 포함되지만, 문화 공유 자원에는 한 지역 사회의 노래, 춤, 전통이 포함될 수 있다.

③ Many tourism products and experiences rely on common pool resources.
많은 관광 상품과 체험은 공유 자원에 의존한다.

④ The extent and ❷ accessibility of these resources has led McKean to suggest that common pool resources, (in addition to being available to anyone,) are difficult to protect and easy to deplete.
lead A to B : A가 B하게 이끌다
이러한 자원의 규모와 이용 가능성으로 인해, McKean은 공유 자원은 누구라도 이용 가능한 것에 덧붙여 보호하기는 어렵고 고갈시키기는 쉽다고 말했다.

⑤ Hardin presented the initial illustration of this concept in his influential article titled "The Tragedy of the Commons."
Hardin은 '공유지의 비극'이라는 제목의 자신의 영향력 있는 논문에서 이 개념을 처음으로 설명했다.

⑥ In this article, he described a community that thrives on the ❸ growth of its cattle, which graze on communal pastureland.
이 논문에서, 그는 소의 증가를 바탕으로 번창하는 어느 지역 사회를 묘사했는데, 그 소들은 공동 방목지에서 풀을 뜯어 먹는다.

⑦ As demand grows, residents are inclined to ❹ ~~minimize~~ maximize their benefits by ignoring the cumulative effect of each person grazing an additional head of cattle on the communal lands.
수요가 늘면서, 주민들은 각자가 공유지에서 소 한 마리씩을 추가로 방목하는 행위의 누적 결과를 무시함으로써 자신들의 이익을 최소화하고 (→ 극대화하고) 싶어 한다.

⑧ Hardin asserted that the ❺ ignorance of individuals (using common pool resources) will lead to eventual depletion of the resource.
Hardin은 개인들이 공유 자원을 사용하는 것에 대한 무지는 결국 자원의 고갈을 초래하게 된다고 주장했다.

⑨ The potential combined impact of (individual use of common pool resources) is an important element of tourism's sustainable development.
공유 자원의 개별 사용이 끼치는 잠재적인 통합 영향은 관광의 지속 가능한 발전의 중요한 요소이다.
지속 가능한

* deplete: 고갈시키다 ** cumulative: 누적하는 *** communal: 공동의

주요 어휘 및 유의어/반의어			
	단어	의미	유의어/반의어
□□□ 1	available	사용 가능한	= accessible
□□□ 2	protect	보호하다	= conserve, save, preserve, secure
□□□ 3	deplete	고갈시키다	= consume, exhaust ↔ augment
□□□ 4	illustration	설명	= explanation
□□□ 5	thrives	번창하다	= prosper, flourish, burgeon
□□□ 6	growth	증가	= increase ↔ decline
□□□ 7	graze	풀을 뜯다	= feed
□□□ 8	communal	공동의	= common
□□□ 9	inclined	~하고 싶어 하는	= disposed
□□□ 10	maximize	극대화하다	= boost, magnify, inflate
□□□ 11	benefit	이익	= profit, favor

ⓢhorts Ⓕlow 제시된 [A], [B], [C]를 서론, 본론, 결론의 순서로 연결해보고, 단락별 내용의 흐름을 정리해보세요.

	서론 (① ~ ④)	본론 (⑤ ~ ⑧)	결론 (⑨)
	·	·	·
개요도	·	·	·
	[A] 용어 소개	[B] 개념화	[C] 함의 설명
	공유 자원이란 모두가 사용할 수 있지만 소유자는 없는 자원을 말하는데, 자연이나 문화 등 영역이 있다.	공유지의 비극이란 개인의 공유 자원 사용에 대한 무지가 결국 자원 고갈을 초래하는 상황을 말한다.	공유 자원의 사용이 미치는 잠재적 영향은 관광의 지속 가능성에 중요한 요소이다.

ⓢhorts Ⓞverview 글의 〈주제 및 제목〉을 쓰시오.

주제	한글	공유 자원의 개념과 공유지의 비극
	영어	the / resources / commons / tragedy / common / and / of / pool / the / of / concept
	정답	
제목	한글	공유지의 자원이 고갈되는 방식
	영어	Commons / End / Up / the / Resources / of / How / Depleted
	정답	

ⓢhorts Ⓓetails 글의 내용과 일치하면 T에, 일치하지 않으면 F에 동그라미 표기를 하세요.

① Many tourism products resort to common pool resources that are owned by everyone but not available to anyone. [T / F]

② Because common pool resources are available to anyone, everyone can protect them, which maximizes their sustainability. [T / F]

③ Hardin pointed out that people's desire to maximize their profits may result from the depletion of communal resources. [T / F]

ⓢhorts Ⓖrammar 각 문장에서 어법상 가장 적절한 것을 고르시오.

① The term common pool resources refers to resources that are available to all, but [owning / owned] by no one.

② Nature-based examples include forests, oceans, and vistas, whereas common pool cultural resources can include a community's song, dance, and traditions.

③ Many tourism products and experiences rely on common pool resources.

④ The extent and accessibility of these resources has led McKean to suggest that common pool resources, in addition to [be / being] available to anyone, [is / are / being] difficult to protect and easy to deplete.

⑤ Hardin presented the initial illustration of this concept in his influential article titled "The Tragedy of the Commons."

⑥ In this article, he described a community that thrives on the growth of its cattle, [what / to which / which] graze on communal pastureland.

⑦ As demand grows, residents are inclined to maximize their benefits by ignoring the cumulative effect of each person [grazes / grazing / grazed] an additional head of cattle on the communal lands.

⑧ Hardin asserted that the ignorance of individuals using common pool resources will lead to eventual depletion of the resource.

⑨ The potential combined impact of individual use of common pool resources [is / are / being] an important element of tourism's sustainable development.

중심 소재 : 관광상품의 진정성상실								
글의 전개방식	통념과 반박	문제와 해결	연구·실험	비교·대조	예시	비유	시간적 흐름	스토리텔링	기타

주제문

① If part of the attraction (=appeal =charm) 매력 of the community to outsiders// is its cultural heritage and traditions, that// will likely change over time and frequently not for the better.

part of the attraction

외부인에게 지역 사회의 매력 중 일부가 그것의 문화적 유산과 전통이라면, 그것은 아마도 시간이 지남에 따라 변할 것인데, 흔히 더 나은 방향은 아닐 것이다.

② Symbols of a historic culture// may be pervasive (=common =general =widespread), but only in a make-believe form.

유서 깊은 문화의 상징물이 넘칠지 모르나, 단지 진짜가 아닌 형태로만 그럴 뿐이다.

패러프레이징

③ Tourist shops on small Pacific islands// may sell replicas (=imitation) of native (=indigenous) art — all turned out in huge quantities by manufacturers in other parts of the world.

태평양의 작은 섬들에 있는 관광 상점들은 모두 세계 다른 지역의 제조업자들에 의해 대량으로 만들어진 원주민 예술의 복제품을 팔지도 모른다. 제조업자

④ Plastic Black Forest clocks and Swiss music boxes// are offered to tourists (that are mass-produced in Taiwan or China).

수동 / 주격관·대 / 수동

대만이나 중국에서 대량 생산되는 플라스틱으로 만든 Black Forest 시계와 Swiss 뮤직 박스가 관광객들에게 판매된다.

⑤ A commitment (=responsibility =obligation) to craftsmanship (=artistry) and true local heritage (=inheritance =legacy)// vanishes (=disappear =fade).

장인 정신과 진정한 현지 유산에 대한 책무는 사라진다. 사라지다

서술형

⑥ These false (=untrue =artificial =forged) symbols of earlier times// contribute to (~에 기여하다) an overly commercial (=profit-making) feeling at destinations and a sense that nothing// seems real now, and perhaps never was (real).

꽉무·약속 / 동격 / 진정한 =genuine =sincere / 여행지

이러한 이전 시대의 가짜 상징물은 여행지에서의 지나치게 상업적인 느낌과, 이제는 어떤 것도 진짜처럼 보이지 않고 아마도 진짜인 적도 없었다는 느낌의 원인이 된다.

서술형

⑦ A danger// lies in (~에 놓여있다) the loss of a sense of personal identity by residents and a feeling of being disconnected (=separated) from their past.

위험은 주민들의 개인 정체성 상실과 자신들의 과거로부터 단절됐다는 느낌에 있다.

⑧ Their heritage and culture now// seem less significant or important.

그들의 유산과 문화는 이제 덜 의미 있거나 덜 중요해 보인다.

서술형

⑨ It// serves primarily as (serve as ~ : ~의 역할을 하다) a commercial front for visitors who buy cheap trinkets and watch professionally staged shows that attempt to recreate cultural practices or historic events.

주격 관·대 / 주격 관·대

그것은 값싼 장신구를 구매하고 문화적 관습이나 역사적 사건을 재현하려는 전문적으로 연출된 쇼를 보는 방문객들에게 주로 상업의 첨병 역할을 한다. 연출된

* pervasive: 넘치는 ** replica: 복제품 *** trinket: (값싼) 장신구

주요 어휘 및 유의어/반의어			
	단어	**의미**	**유의어/반의어**
☐☐☐ 1	attraction	매력	= appeal, charm
☐☐☐ 2	pervasive	만연한	= widespread, common, general
☐☐☐ 3	replica	복제품	= imitation
☐☐☐ 4	native	원주민의	= indigenous
☐☐☐ 5	commitment	전념, 책임	= responsibility, obligation
☐☐☐ 6	craftsmanship	손재주, 솜씨	= artistry
☐☐☐ 7	true	진정한	= genuine, authentic
☐☐☐ 8	heritage	유산	= legacy, inheritance
☐☐☐ 9	vanish	사라지다	= fade, disappear
☐☐☐ 10	false	가짜의	= untrue, artificial, forged
☐☐☐ 11	commercial	상업적인	= profit-making

Ⓢhorts Ⓕlow 제시된 [A], [B], [C]를 서론, 본론, 결론의 순서로 연결해보고, 단락별 내용의 흐름을 정리해보세요.

개요도	서론 (① ~ ②)	본론 (③ ~ ⑥)	결론 (⑦ ~ ⑨)
	•	•	•
	•	•	•
	[A] 재진술	[B] 문제 제기	[C] 글감의 집약적 제시
	주민들의 정체성 상실이나 과거와의 단절을 경험하는 등 과도한 상업화의 위험이 따른다.	관광 상점들은 대만이나 중국 등에서 대량생산된 예술 복제품을 팔며 상업적인 느낌을 낸다.	지역 사회의 매력 중 일부가 문화적 유산이나 전통이라면, 그것은 시간이 지남에 따라 변할 것이다.

Ⓢhorts Ⓞverview 글의 〈주제 및 제목〉을 쓰시오.

주제	한글	전통 유산의 상업화와 그 위협
	영어	commercialization / threat / heritage / traditional / of / its / and
	정답	
제목	한글	관광의 역학: 문화유산과 전통이 바뀔 수 있는 방식
	영어	Can / Heritage / Cultural / of / Dynamics / Changed / Be / and / How / Tourism: / Tradition
	정답	

Ⓢhorts Ⓓetails 글의 내용과 일치하면 T에, 일치하지 않으면 F에 동그라미 표기를 하세요.

① When tourists are attracted to the cultural heritage of the attractions, the quantitative aspect of historical cultural symbols tends to grow while the qualitative aspect tends to deteriorate. [T / F]

② Travelers' feeling that everything they see at their destination is not real results in an overflow of fake symbols from the pre-destination era. [T / F]

③ As fake symbols related to the culture of the destination are pervasive, people living there are more likely to feel their identity loss and disconnection from the past. [T / F]

Ⓢhorts Ⓖrammar 각 문장에서 어법상 가장 적절한 것을 고르시오.

① If part of the attraction of the community to outsiders [is / are / being] its cultural heritage and traditions, that will likely change over time and [frequent / frequently] not for the better.

② Symbols of a historic culture may be pervasive, but only in a make-believe form.

③ Tourist shops on small Pacific islands may sell replicas of native art — all turned out in huge quantities by manufacturers in other parts of the world.

④ Plastic Black Forest clocks and Swiss music boxes are offered to tourists [what / that] are mass-produced in Taiwan or China.

⑤ A commitment to craftsmanship and true local heritage vanishes.

⑥ These false symbols of earlier times contribute to an overly commercial feeling at destinations and a sense that nothing seems real now, and perhaps never [was / did].

⑦ A danger lies in the loss of a sense of personal identity by residents and a feeling of being disconnected from their past.

⑧ Their heritage and culture now seem less [significant / significantly] or important.

⑨ It serves [primary / primarily] as a commercial front for visitors [with whom / what / who] buy cheap trinkets and watch professionally staged shows that attempt to recreate cultural practices or historic events.

중심 소재 : (고대) 그리스 체육 대회와 경기의 사회적 기능									
글의 전개방식	통념과 반박	문제와 해결	연구·실험	비교·대조	예시	비유	시간적 흐름	스토리텔링	기타

① Physical contests and games in Greek culture // influenced(=affect) art, philosophy and the everyday lives of people wealthy enough to train, hire professionals and travel to events. 철학

그리스 문화에서 체육 대회와 경기는 예술과 철학, 그리고 훈련하고 전문 선수를 고용하며 경기를 보러 갈 수 있을 정도로 충분히 부유한 사람들의 일상에 영향을 미쳤다.

= well-off = well-to-do
= affluent = prosperous　서술형

② However, Greek contests and games // were different from the organized competitive sports of today. 체계적인

그러나 그리스의 대회와 경기는 오늘날의 체계화된 경쟁 스포츠와는 달랐다.

Greek contests and games

③ First, they // were grounded in religion; second, they // lacked complex administrative structures; third, they // did not involve (measurements and record keeping) from event to (event). 관리의

첫째, 그것은 종교에 기반을 두고 있었고, 둘째, 그것은 복합적 관리 체계가 없었으며, 셋째, 그것은 매 경기의 측정과 기록 관리를 포함하지 않았다. 측정

주제문

= replicate = mirror　= governing
= recreate　　　 = ruling

④ However, there is // one major similarity: they often // reproduced dominant patterns of social relations in society as a whole.

그러나 한 가지 주요한 유사점이 있다. 즉 그것은 흔히 사회 전반의 사회적 관계의 지배적인 패턴을 재현했다.

패러프레이징

⑤ The power and advantages (that // went with being wealthy, male, young and able-bodied in Greek society // shaped the games and contests in ways (that limited the participation of most people. =restrict =curb　서술형

그리스 사회에서 부유하고, 남성이며, 젊고 신체 건강한 것과 병행하는 권력과 이점은 대부분의 사람들의 참여를 제한하는 방식으로 경기와 대회의 모습을 만들었다.

= form = make
= produce

evaluating(x)
= assess = appraise

= potential = competence
= capability

⑥ Even the definitions of excellence used to evaluate performance // reflected the abilities of young males.

심지어 경기력을 평가하기 위해 사용된 탁월함의 정의도 젊은 남성의 능력을 반영했다. 탁월함

접속사

⑦ This // meant that the abilities of others // were substandard by definition — if you // could not do it as a young, able-bodied Greek man // did it, you // were doing it the wrong way.

이것은 그 밖의 다른 사람들의 능력은 당연히 수준 이하라는 것, 즉 젊고 신체 건강한 그리스 남성이 하는 것처럼 그것을 할 수 없다면, 그것을 잘못된 방식으로 하고 있다는 것을 의미했다.

= authorize　= defend　= benefit
= validate　= conserve　= advantage　enjoying(x)　= choice　서술형

⑧ This // legitimized and preserved the privilege enjoyed by a select group of men in Greek society.

이것은 그리스 사회에서 선택된 남성 집단이 누리는 특권을 정당화하고 보호했다.

* legitimize: 정당화하다

주요 어휘 및 유의어/반의어			
	단어	의미	유의어/반의어
☐☐☐ 1	influence	영향을 미치다	= affect
☐☐☐ 2	wealthy	부유한	= well-off, well-to-do, affluent, prosperous
☐☐☐ 3	reproduce	재현하다	= recreate, replicate, mirror
☐☐☐ 4	dominant	지배적인	= ruling, governing
☐☐☐ 5	shape	만들다	= form, make, produce, create
☐☐☐ 6	limit	제한하다	= restrict, curb, hinder
☐☐☐ 7	evaluate	평가하다	= appraise, assess
☐☐☐ 8	ability	능력	= capability, potential, competence
☐☐☐ 9	legitimize	정당화하다	= validate, authorize
☐☐☐ 10	preserve	보호하다	= conserve, defend
☐☐☐ 11	privilege	특권	= advantage, benefit

⑤horts ⑤low 제시된 [A], [B], [C]를 서론, 본론, 결론의 순서로 연결해보고, 단락별 내용의 흐름을 정리해보세요.

	서론 (①)	본론 (② ~ ③)	결론 (④ ~ ⑧)
	·	·	·
개요도	·	·	·
	[A] 대조를 통한 논의 진행 그리스의 대회와 경기는 오늘날 경쟁 스포츠와는 세 가지 측면에서 다르다.	[B] 논점 제시 그러나 사회 전반에 있는 사회적 관계의 지배적인 패턴을 재현한다는 공통점이 있다.	[C] 글감 제시 그리스 문화에서 체육은 예술과 철학, 그리고 부유한 사람들의 일상에 영향을 미쳤다.

⑤horts ⑤verview 글의 〈주제 및 제목〉을 쓰시오.

주제	한글	다양한 시간 설정에서 스포츠의 기능에 대한 교차 조사
	영어	on / of / settings / in / time / different / functions / cross-examination / sports
	정답	
제목	한글	그리스 문화의 체육 대회와 오늘날 스포츠의 비교
	영어	Culture / Today / Contests / Comparing / Physical / Greek / in / of / Sports / with
	정답	

⑤horts ⑤etails 글의 내용과 일치하면 T에, 일치하지 않으면 F에 동그라미 표기를 하세요.

① It cannot be said that athletic competitions in ancient Greece were more organized than those of today. [T / F]

② Many of the features found in ancient Greek athletics were compatible with those of society's overall structure at that time. [T / F]

③ Judging from the fact that the definition of excellence in athletic sports in ancient Greece reflected the ability of young men, it can be showed that young men must have had many advantages in society at that time. [T / F]

⑤horts ⑤rammar 각 문장에서 어법상 가장 적절한 것을 고르시오.

① Physical contests and games in Greek culture influenced art, philosophy and the everyday lives of people [**enough wealthy / wealthy enough**] to train, hire professionals and travel to events.

② However, Greek contests and games were different from the organized competitive sports of today.

③ First, they were grounded in religion; second, they lacked complex administrative structures; third, they did not involve measurements and record keeping from event to.

④ However, there is one major similarity: they often reproduced dominant patterns of social relations in society as a whole.

⑤ The power and advantages that went with being wealthy, male, young and able-bodied in Greek society shaped the games and contests in ways [**that / what**] limited the participation of most people.

⑥ Even the definitions of excellence used to evaluate performance reflected the abilities of young males.

⑦ This meant that the abilities of others were substandard by definition — if you could not do [**it / them**] as a young, able-bodied Greek man did it, you were doing it the wrong way.

⑧ This legitimized and preserved the privilege enjoyed by a select group of men in Greek society.

중심 소재 : 음악적 능력에 관한 양분된 생각								
글의 전개방식	통념과 반박	문제와 해결	연구·실험	비교·대조	예시	비유	시간적 흐름	스토리텔링	기타

주제문
① In the field of musical expertise, there is a dichotomy of thinking.
　　 음악적 전문 지식 분야에서는 생각이 양분되어 있다.

② On the one hand, there is a widespread perception in the general population that expert musicians have innate talent, or giftedness, beyond ordinary abilities.
　　 한편으로는, 음악의 대가는 보통의 능력을 넘는 타고난 재능, 즉 영재성이 있다는 인식이 일반 대중에 널리 퍼져 있다.

서술형
③ Talent, as part of the vernacular in the field of music is usually ❶ assumed to be a stable trait — one is either born with musical talent or not (born with musical talent).
　　 재능은, 음악 분야에서 사용되는 말의 일부로, 주로 불변의 특성으로 간주되는데, 사람은 음악적 재능을 타고났거나, 그렇지 않다는 것이다.

either A or B : A, B 둘 중 하나
(which are)

④ Music aptitude tests ❷ popular in the early to mid-twentieth century, such as the *Seashore Tests of Musical Talent* and *the Music Aptitude Profile* attempted to find children (who had this musical talent).
　　 Seashore Tests of Musical Talent와 the Music Aptitude Profile과 같은 20세기 초중반에 유행한 음악 적성 검사는 이러한 음악적 재능이 있는 어린이들을 찾으려고 했다.

⑤ On the other hand, there is a very real feeling ❸ that ability in music comes from a disciplined work ethic.
　　 다른 한편으로는, 음악에서의 능력은 훈련된 근면 정신에서 비롯되는 것이라는 매우 현실적인 생각이 있다.

가S　서술형
⑥ It would be unacceptable, even for those considered talented, not ❹ to practice.
　　 재능이 있다고 여겨지는 사람들에게 조차도 연습하지 않는 것은 용납될 수 없을 것이다.

서술형
⑦ In fact, those (who are considered talented) ❺ being are expected to practice all the more.
　　 사실상, 재능이 있다고 여겨지는 사람들은 그만큼 더 연습해야 한다.

* dichotomy: (의견 따위의) 양분. 이분 ** vernacular: (특정 지역·집단이 쓰는) 말

주요 어휘 및 유의어/반의어			
	단어	**의미**	**유의어/반의어**
□□□ 1	expertise	전문 지식	= skill, knowledge
□□□ 2	dichotomy	양분	= division, separation
□□□ 3	perception	인식	= awareness, understanding
□□□ 4	general	일반적인	= common
□□□ 5	expert	전문적인	= professional
□□□ 6	innate	타고난	= inborn, natural, ingrained
□□□ 7	ordinary	보통의	= typical, normal
□□□ 8	vernacular	(특정 지역·집단이 쓰는) 말	= jargon
□□□ 9	stable	불변의	= permanent, solid
□□□ 10	trait	특성	= attribute, feature
□□□ 11	talent	재능	= gift, capability, aptness

⑤horts ⒻLow 제시된 [A], [B], [C]를 서론, 본론, 결론의 순서로 연결해보고, 단락별 내용의 흐름을 정리해보세요.

	서론 (①)	본론 (② ~ ④)	결론 (⑤ ~ ⑦)
	·	·	·
개요도	·	·	·
	[A] 병렬적 논의 전개 A	[B] 글감 제시	[C] 병렬적 논의 전개 B
	한편으로는 음악의 대가들이 타고난 재능이나 영재성이 있다고 믿는다.	음악적 전문 분야에서는 생각이 양분되어 있다.	다른 한편으로, 음악에서 능력은 훈련과 연습에서 온다고 여겨지곤 한다.

⑤horts ⒪verview 글의 〈주제 및 제목〉을 쓰시오.

주제	한글	음악 분야에서의 사고의 이분법
	영어	of / in / thinking / of / music / the / field / dichotomy / the
	정답	
제목	한글	타고난 재능 또는 훈련된 관행: 음악 속 흑백 사고에 대해 배우기
	영어	Thinking / Music / in / Disciplined / or / Innate / About / Talent / Black-and-White / the / Learning / Practice:
	정답	

⑤horts ⒟etails 글의 내용과 일치하면 T에, 일치하지 않으면 F에 동그라미 표기를 하세요.

① In the field of music, it is only the idea that natural talent is more important than any other ability that is accepted as true. [T / F]

② In the argument that talent is important in music, talent is considered to be available to anyone who wants it. [T / F]

③ The argument that ability in music comes from hard effort says that the more talented people are, the more they should practice. [T / F]

⑤horts ⒢rammar 각 문장에서 어법상 가장 적절한 것을 고르시오.

① In the field of musical expertise, there is a dichotomy of thinking.

② On the one hand, there is a widespread perception in the general population [what / that] expert musicians have innate talent, or giftedness, beyond ordinary abilities.

③ Talent, as part of the vernacular in the field of music, is usually [assuming / assumed] to be a stable trait — one is either born with musical talent or not.

④ Music aptitude tests [popular / popularly] in the early to mid-twentieth century, such as the Seashore Tests of Musical Talent and the Music Aptitude Profile, [attempted / attempting] to find children who had this musical talent.

⑤ On the other hand, there is a very real feeling [that / which / what] ability in music comes from a disciplined work ethic.

⑥ It would be unacceptable, even for those considered talented, not [practiced / to practice].

⑦ In fact, those who are considered talented [being / is / are] expected to practice all the more.

중심 소재 : 사진의 유용함								
글의 전개방식	통념과 반박	문제와 해결	연구·실험	비교·대조	예시	비유	시간적 흐름	스토리텔링	기타

① For a long time photographs//were understood to be visible traces, as irrefutable evidence of the existence of the presented, its "it has been."

= seeable = apparent　= evidence　= undeniable = indisputable

보이는　명백함.증거

오랫동안 사진은, 제시된 것의 존재에 대한 반박할 수 없는 명백함, 곧 그것의 "그것이 있었다"로서, 눈에 보이는 흔적인 것으로 이해되었다.

② (B) Therefore, photographs//were initially classified as documents, whether used in the media, in the family album, in books, archives or collections.

(they were)

분류하다, 구분하다

(B) 따라서, 사진은 매체, 가족 앨범, 서적, 기록, 수집품 어느 것에 쓰이든 간에, 처음에는 문서로 분류되었다.

③ As digitization//began to feed into the realm of photography, and the end of the photographic era //was proclaimed, it//was its documentary qualities, its "ontology" as a chemical-physical symbol, that suddenly lost its persuasive powers. 서술형

= domain　= demise

it ~ that 강조

디지털화가 사진 영역에 영향을 미치기 시작하고, 사진 시대의 끝이 선포되었을 때, 돌연 그것의 설득력을 잃은 것은 바로 그것의 사실을 기록하는 본질, 즉 화학적, 물리적 상징으로서의 그것의 '존재론'이었다.

= declare = announce

주제문　패러프레이징

④ (A) But even if the sting of digital doubt//seems deeply ingrained within the photographic authenticity and evidence, many of its tasks and uses//have hardly changed.

= brick = pain　= deep-rooted

깊이 배어든　신뢰성

has(x)

(A) 그러나 비록 디지털 불신의 아픔이 사진의 신뢰성과 명백함 속에 깊이 배어든 것 같지만, 사진의 임무와 용도 가운데 많은 것들은 거의 변한 적이 없다.

부분 of 명사　= scarcely = rarely

수일치

⑤ When we//look at a family album created with digital images, closely inspect the X-rays of a broken foot together with the doctor, or view the image of the finish of the 100-meter finals at the Olympic Games, our trust in photography//remains.

= continue = survive = stay

면밀하게 살피다

디지털 화상으로 만들어진 가족 앨범을 보거나, 골절된 발의 엑스선 사진을 의사와 함께 면밀하게 살피거나, 혹은 올림픽 경기에서 100m 결승전의 결승선 사진을 볼 때, 사진에 대한 우리의 신뢰는 남아 있다.

⑥ (C) If we//trust the use of the images, or more precisely if we//assign them persuasive powers via their use, it//does not matter whether they//are analog or digital. 서술형

관접 접속사　I.O　D.O

설득하는

(C) 우리가 이미지의 사용을 신뢰하거나, 더 정확하게는, 우리가 그것의 사용을 통해 그것에 설득력을 부여한다면, 그것이 아날로그인지, 디지털인지는 중요하지 않다.

⑦ In other words: We//doubt photography, but still use certain photographs to dispel doubt and produce evidence.

= suspect = distrust　서술형　= eliminate = dismiss　= demonstration = proof

다시 말해서, 우리는 사진을 불신하지만, 불신을 떨쳐 버리고 명백성을 제시하기 위해 특정한 사진을 여전히 사용한다.

* irrefutable: 반박할 수 없는 ** ontology: 존재론 *** dispel: 떨쳐 버리다

주요 어휘 및 유의어/반의어			
	단어	의미	유의어/반의어
□□□ 1	visible	보이는	= apparent, seeable
□□□ 2	trace	흔적	= evidence
□□□ 3	irrefutable	반박할 수 없는	= indisputable, undeniable
□□□ 4	realm	영역	= domain
□□□ 5	end	끝, 종말	= demise
□□□ 6	proclaim	선포하다	= declare, announce
□□□ 7	sting	아픔	= prick, pain
□□□ 8	ingrained	깊이 밴	= deep-seated, fixed, deep-rooted
□□□ 9	remain	남아 있다	= continue, survive, stay
□□□ 10	doubt	불신하다	= distrust, suspect
□□□ 11	dispel	떨치다	= dismiss, eliminate

Ⓢhorts Ⓕlow 제시된 [A], [B], [C]를 서론, 본론, 결론의 순서로 연결해보고, 단락별 내용의 흐름을 정리해보세요.

개요도	서론 (① ~ ③)	본론 (④ ~ ⑤)	결론 (⑥ ~ ⑦)
	·	·	·
	·	·	·
	[A] 부연 설명 우리가 사진에 설득력을 부여한다면, 그것이 아날로그인지 디지털인지는 중요치 않다.	[B] 변화상 제시 사진은 눈에 보이는 흔적으로 이해되었지만, 디지털화로 인해 사실을 기록하는 본질을 잃어버렸다.	[C] 주장 제시 디지털 불신의 아픔이 사진의 신뢰성을 해친 것 같지만, 사진의 용도 중 많은 것은 거의 변함이 없다.

Ⓢhorts Ⓞverview 글의 〈주제 및 제목〉을 쓰시오.

주제	한글	디지털화 및 사진에 대한 인식 변화
	영어	photographs / digitization / on / and / perception / changing
	정답	
제목	한글	사진의 증거력은 여전히 강력하다
	영어	of / Photographs / Still / Evidential / Strong / The / Power / Remains
	정답	

Ⓢhorts Ⓓetails 글의 내용과 일치하면 T에, 일치하지 않으면 F에 동그라미 표기를 하세요.

① Before digitization affected the photographic domain, the documentary qualities of photography were emphasized to the extent that photographs were classified as documents. [T / F]

② With the digitization of photographs and the destruction of photography's credibility occurring, almost all of the photography's tasks and uses are becoming different from before. [T / F]

③ Whether a photo is digital or analog is irrelevant as long as it is trusted for its persuasive abilities. [T / F]

Ⓢhorts Ⓖrammar 각 문장에서 어법상 가장 적절한 것을 고르시오.

① For a long time photographs were [**understanding / understood**] to be visible traces, as irrefutable evidence of the existence of the presented, its "it has been."

② (B) Therefore, photographs were [**initial / initially**] classified as documents, whether used in the media, in the family album, in books, archives or collections.

③ As digitization began to feed into the realm of photography, and the end of the photographic era [**was / were**] proclaimed, it was its documentary qualities, its "ontology" as a chemical-physical symbol, that suddenly lost its persuasive powers.

④ (A) But [**even if / as if**] the sting of digital doubt seems [**deep / deeply**] ingrained within the photographic authenticity and evidence, many of its tasks and uses have hardly changed.

⑤ When we look at a family album created with digital images, closely [**inspect / inspecting**] the X-rays of a broken foot together with the doctor, or view the image of the finish of the 100-meter finals at the Olympic Games, our trust in photography remains.

⑥ (C) If we trust the use of the images, or more [**precise / precisely**], if we assign [**it / them**] persuasive powers via their use, it does not matter whether they are analog or digital.

⑦ In other words: We doubt photography, but still use certain photographs to dispel doubt and produce evidence.

중심 소재 : 영화의 성공

글의 전개방식	통념과 반박	문제와 해결	연구·실험	비교·대조	예시	비유	시간적 흐름	스토리텔링	기타

=anticipate
접속사

① <u>Predicting</u> (whether) a movie//will be a success//is perhaps the "Holy Grail" of most film-makers and especially the big movie studios.

영화가 성공작이 될지를 예측하는 것은 아마도 대부분의 영화 제작자와 특히 대규모 영화 제작소의 '성배(간절히 원하는 것)'일 것이다.

↔blame, criticism
=praise

② While critical <u>acclaim</u>//is always welcome, in the end it//is important that a movie//makes money. 서술형

비평가의 찬사는 늘 반가운 것이지만, 결국 영화는 돈을 버는 것이 중요하다.

패러프레이징

③ For the big studios — now increasingly owned by massive global corporations — making movies (that) //<u>deliver</u> wide profit margins//is the ultimate metric of performance.
=bring
주격 관·대

대규모 영화사의 경우, 지금은 점점 더 대규모의 글로벌 기업이 소유하고 있는데, 많은 수익을 내는 영화를 제작하는 것이 성과의 궁극적인 측정 기준이다.
수익　　　　　　궁극적인, 최종의

주제문
= profit = gain
= income = return

④ Movies increasingly//depend on non-theatrical sources for <u>revenues</u>.

영화는 점점 더 영화관 외의 수입원에 의존한다.
수입, 수익

=decline =lessen
=decrease =shrink

⑤ This fact//does not <u>diminish</u> the continuing significance of solid box office performance.

이러한 사실이 견실한 박스 오피스 성과의 지속적인 중요성을 깎아내리지는 않는다. 견실한

서술형
부정어 도치
is(x)

⑥ When a movie//hits top spot at the box office, not only <u>does</u> this deliver direct revenue yield, it//can further <u>promote</u> other income sources over time.

영화가 박스 오피스에서 정상을 차지하면, 이것은 직접적인 수익 산출을 낼 뿐만 아니라, 시간이 지나면서 다른 수입원을 더욱더 활성화할 수 있다.
=reproduce

접속사

⑦ A high public profile//means not only (that) its potential as an attractive choice for repeat viewing on other platforms//increases but (that) its potential to yield sequels//might increase, too. 서술형
접속사

높은 대중의 관심은 다른 플랫폼에서 반복 시청을 위한 매력적인 선택으로서 그것의 잠재적 가능성이 증가한다는 것뿐만 아니라, 속편을 제작할 가능성도 증가할 수 있다는 것을 의미한다.

not only A but also B
= B as well as A
A뿐 아니라 B도

⑧ In the end, nothing//breeds success like success.

결국, 성공만큼 성공을 낳는 것은 아무것도 없다.

=adage
=motto
관계부사

⑨ This <u>maxim</u>//is probably the main reason (why) the major movie studios really//like making <u>sequels</u> to highly successful movies and really like to <u>hire</u> star actors with a track record of appearing in blockbuster films (that) generally do well at the box office.
=employ =engage
속편 들
주격 관·대

이 격언이 아마도 주요 영화 제작소가 매우 성공적인 영화의 속편을 진정 만들고 싶어 하고 박스 오피스에서 전반적으로 성공하는 블록버스터 영화에 나오는 실적이 있는 인기 배우를 진정으로 캐스팅하고 싶어 하는 주요 이유일 것이다.

* Holy Grail: 성배 (간절히 원하는 것)　** acclaim: 찬사. 호평　*** metric: 측정 기준

주요 어휘 및 유의어/반의어

	단어	의미	유의어/반의어
□□□ 1	predict	예측하다	= anticipate
□□□ 2	acclaim	찬사	= praise ↔ blame, criticism
□□□ 3	deliver	(수익 등을) 내다	= bring
□□□ 4	revenue	수입	= income, return, profit, gain
□□□ 5	diminish	깎아내리다	= decrease, decline, lessen, shrink
□□□ 6	promote	활성화하다	= encourage, support, advance, forward
□□□ 7	potential	가능성	= possibility
□□□ 8	yield	제작하다	= produce, provide
□□□ 9	breed	낳다	= reproduce
□□□ 10	maxim	격언	= adage, motto
□□□ 11	hire	캐스팅하다	= employ, engage

---

⑤horts Ⓕlow 제시된 [A], [B], [C]를 서론, 본론, 결론의 순서로 연결해보고, 단락별 내용의 흐름을 정리해보세요.

	서론 (① ~ ③)	본론 (④ ~ ⑦)	결론 (⑧ ~ ⑨)
개요도	· · [A] 논의 진행 영화는 점점 영화관 외의 수입원에 의존하는데, 그럼에도 박스오피스 성과의 중요성은 여전하다.	· · [B] 논점 함축 성공만큼 성공을 낳는 것은 없는데, 이 때문에 인기 배우를 캐스팅하고 싶어 할 것이다.	· · [C] 글감 제시 영화가 성공작이 될지 예측하는 것은 대부분 제작자와 영화 제작소의 성배 같은 일이다.

---

⑤horts Ⓞverview 글의 〈주제 및 제목〉을 쓰시오.

주제	한글	큰 수익률을 위한 매표소 흥행의 중요성
	영어	profit / importance / office / success / for / the / box / margin / of / wide
	정답	
제목	한글	성공은 성공을 가져온다: 영화산업의 성공을 위해 박스오피스가 중심이 되는 이유
	영어	Brings / Success: / Centered / Why / Is / of / Office / Industry / Success / the / Movie / For / Box / Success
	정답	

---

⑤horts Ⓓetails 글의 내용과 일치하면 T에, 일치하지 않으면 F에 동그라미 표기를 하세요.

① Even though movies are increasingly generating revenue from non-theatrical sources, a solid performance at the box office remains critical. [T / F]

② Although receiving positive reviews from critics is invaluable, the most important factor for a movie's success is its profitability. [T / F]

③ When a movie becomes the top-grossing film at the box office, it not only generates direct revenue but can also lead to more revenue over time by increasing its popularity on other platforms and the potential for sequels. [T / F]

---

⑤horts Ⓖrammar 각 문장에서 어법상 가장 적절한 것을 고르시오.

① Predicting whether a movie will be a success **[is / being]** perhaps the "Holy Grail" of most film-makers and especially the big movie studios.

② While critical acclaim is always welcome, in the end it is important that a movie makes money.

③ For the big studios — now **[increasing / increasingly]** owned by massive global corporations — making movies that deliver wide profit margins **[is / are]** the ultimate metric of performance.

④ Movies increasingly depend on non-theatrical sources for revenues.

⑤ This fact does not diminish the continuing significance of solid box office performance.

⑥ When a movie hits top spot at the box office, not only **[is / does]** this deliver direct revenue yield, it can further promote other income sources over time.

⑦ A high public profile means not only that its potential as an attractive choice for repeat viewing on other platforms increases but that its potential to yield sequels might increase, too.

⑧ In the end, nothing breeds success like success.

⑨ This maxim is probably the main reason **[what / why]** the major movie studios really like making sequels to **[high / highly]** successful movies and really like to hire star actors with a track record of appearing in blockbuster films that generally do **[good / well]** at the box office.

중심 소재 : 귀인 (歸因) 효과 향상

글의 전개방식	통념과 반박	문제와 해결	연구·실험	비교·대조	예시	비유	시간적 흐름	스토리텔링	기타

주제문

=strengthen
=enhance

① Learners//can improve the effectiveness of their attributions through training.
학습자는 훈련을 통해 자기의 귀인 효과를 향상할 수 있다.
효과

provide A with B : A에게 B를 제공하다

② In a pioneering study, Carol Susan Dweck, an American psychologist, //provided students (who
=display=show　선구적인　　　　　　　　　　　　　　=failing=unfruitful　　서술형　　주격 관.대
demonstrated learned helplessness) with both successful and unsuccessful experiences. 서술형
선구적인 한 연구에서, 미국 심리학자인 Carol Susan Dweck은 학습된 무력감을 보이는 학생들에게 성공한 경험과 성공하지 못한 경험 모두를 제공했다.
보여주다　　　　　　　　　　　　　both A and B : A, B 모두　　　　　접속사　　=produce
　　　　　　　　　　　　　　　　　　　　　　　　　　　　　　　　　　　　　　=bring about

③ When the students//were unsuccessful, the experimenter specifically//stated that the failure//was caused
　　　　　　　s'　　v'=useless=futile　　　　　　　s　　　　　　　v　　　　　　s'　　v'
by lack of effort ∆ ineffective strategies.
학생들이 성공하지 못했을 때, 실험자는 그 실패가 노력의 부족이나 비효과적인 전략 때문에 일어났다고 명확하게 말했다.

giving(x)　　　　　　　패러프레이징　(they were given)
④ Comparable students//were given similar experiences but no training.
　　　　　　　　s'　　v'
비교 가능한 학생들에게 유사한 경험이 주어졌지만, 훈련은 전혀 주어지지 않았다.
패러프레이징

주격 관.대
⑤ After 25 sessions, the learners (who were counseled about their effort and strategies)//responded more
=properly=suitably　　　s　　　v'　　상담하다　　　　　전략　　　　　responding(x)
appropriately to failure (by persisting longer and adapting their strategies more effectively.
25회의 실험 활동 이후에, 자신의 노력과 전략에 관해 상담받은 학습자들은 더 오래 끈기 있게 지속하고 자신의 전략을 더 효과적으로
조정함으로써 실패에 더 적절하게 대응했다.　　=adjust=modify　　effective(x)
by~ing : ~함으로써　　　　　=accommodate

=validate=verify=back up
⑥ Additional research//has corroborated Dweck's findings.
　　　　　　s　　　v
추가적인 연구를 통해 Dweck의 연구 결과가 입증되었다.

서술형

주격 관.대　　접속사
⑦ Strategy instruction//was most effective for students (who believed that they//were already trying hard)
전략 교육은 이미 자신이 열심히 노력하고 있다고 믿는 학생들에게 가장 효과적이었다.
서술형　교육　　접속사　　=escalate　　　　　　　　　　　　teach A B : A에게 B를 가르치다
　　　　　　　　　　　　　　　　=enhance=boost
⑧ This research//suggests that teachers//can increase students' motivation to learn (by teaching) them
　　　　s　　v　　　　　　　s　　　v　　　　　　　　　　　　　　　　　　　　　　　　　　　v
learning strategies and encouraging them to attribute successes (to effort.
이 연구는 교사들이 학생들에게 학습 전략을 가르치고 성공을 노력 덕분으로 생각하도록 고무함으로써 학생들의 학습 동기를 향상할 수 있다는
것을 보여준다.　　　　　　　　　　　　　attribute A to B　　　　by~ing : ~함으로써
　　　　　　　　　　　　　　　　　　　　: A를 B 덕분이라고 여기다

* attribution: 귀인 (歸因, 성공이나 실패의 원인을 찾는 행위)　** corroborate: 입증하다

주요 어휘 및 유의어/반의어

	단어	의미	유의어/반의어
□□□ 1	improve	향상하다	= enhance, strengthen
□□□ 2	demonstrate	보여주다	= show, display
□□□ 3	unsuccessful	성공하지 못한	= failing, unfruitful
□□□ 4	cause	야기하다, 초래하다	= bring about, produce
□□□ 5	ineffective	비효과적인	= futile, useless
□□□ 6	appropriately	적절하게	= properly, suitably
□□□ 7	adapt	조정하다	= adjust, modify, accommodate
□□□ 8	corroborate	입증하다	= validate, verify, back up
□□□ 9	increase	향상하다	= boost, enhance, escalate
□□□ 10			
□□□ 11			

Ⓢhorts Ⓕlow 제시된 [A], [B], [C]를 서론, 본론, 결론의 순서로 연결해보고, 단락별 내용의 흐름을 정리해보세요.

	서론 (①)	본론 (② ~ ⑦)	결론 (⑧)
	•	•	•
개요도	•	•	•
	[A] 주장 제시	[B] 함의 제시	[C] 연구 소개
	학습자는 훈련을 통해 자기 귀인 효과를 향상할 수 있다.	교사들이 학생들에게 성공을 노력 덕분으로 생각하도록 유도하여, 학습 동기를 향상할 수 있다.	연구에서 Dweck은 25회의 실험 이후 자신의 노력에 대해 상담받은 학습자들이 실패에 더 적절하게 대응함을 발견했다.

Ⓢhorts Ⓞverview 글의 〈주제 및 제목〉을 쓰시오.

주제	한글	학습자의 귀인의 효과성 향상
	영어	effectiveness / improving / learner's / the / attribution / of
	정답	
제목	한글	귀인효과를 통한 학생의 학습동기 부여
	영어	Through / Learning / Motivating / Effect / Attribution / Student's
	정답	

Ⓢhorts Ⓓetails 글의 내용과 일치하면 T에, 일치하지 않으면 F에 동그라미 표기를 하세요.

① Additional studies have confirmed Dweck's findings on the impact of strategy instruction, which was most successful for students who were already putting in significant effort. [T / F]

② Learners who received no training had the same response to failure as those who received training. [T / F]

③ The effectiveness of strategy instruction in improving learners' attributions was found to be unrelated to their belief about how hard they were trying. [T / F]

Ⓢhorts Ⓖrammar 각 문장에서 어법상 가장 적절한 것을 고르시오.

① Learners can improve the effectiveness of their attributions through training.

② In a pioneering study, Carol Susan Dweck, an American psychologist, [**provided** / providing] students who demonstrated learned helplessness with both successful and unsuccessful experiences.

③ When the students were unsuccessful, the experimenter specifically stated [which / what / **that**] the failure was caused by lack of effort or ineffective strategies.

④ Comparable students were [giving / **given**] similar experiences but no training.

⑤ After 25 sessions, the learners who were counseled about their effort and strategies responded more [appropriate / **appropriately**] to failure by persisting longer and adapting their strategies more effectively.

⑥ Additional research has corroborated Dweck's findings.

⑦ Strategy instruction was most effective for students who believed that they were already trying [**hard** / hardly].

⑧ This research suggests that teachers can increase students' motivation to learn by teaching them learning strategies and encouraging them [attribute / **to attribute**] successes to effort.

중심 소재 : 직접 참여를 통한 학습								
글의 전개방식	통념과 반박	문제와 해결	연구·실험	비교·대조	예시	비유	시간적 흐름	스토리텔링	기타

서술형

주격 관·대
= cause = prompt = lasting
= bring about = constant

① A lot of research//discusses what leads to relatively permanent acquisition of new knowledge or skills.
   S   V
많은 연구는 무엇이 새로운 지식이나 기술을 비교적 영구적으로 습득할 수 있게 하는가에 관해 논한다.
                       비교적   습득

주제문
                          접속사

② You//won't be surprised to hear that active learning//works far better than passive learning.
   S   V   S'   V'
여러분은 '능동적인 학습'이 수동적인 학습보다 훨씬 효과가 있다는 말을 들어도 놀라지 않을 것이다.
                                      비교급 강조 (even, much, still, a lot)

패러프레이징

③ In other words, sitting still in a classroom for more than a half hour at a time (no matter how interesting the material)//isn't nearly as potent as having opportunities (to engage actively with the concepts through discussion, group interaction, practice, immersion, △ some other form of direct experience.
                                 1   2   3   4   5
다시 말해, 교실에서 한 번에 30분이 넘게 가만히 앉아 있는 것은 (그 자료가 얼마나 흥미롭든지 간에) 토론, 집단 상호 작용, 연습, 몰입, 또는 어떤 다른 형태의 직접 경험을 통해 개념을 적극적으로 다룰 기회를 얻는 것만큼 결코 효과적이지 않다.

서술형 가S
= unquestionally = vital = significant
= certainly = crucial

진S

④ Likewise, it is absolutely critical for retaining new knowledge and skills that all your senses//are engaged.
                                                           S'   V'
마찬가지로, 새로운 지식과 기술을 유지하기 위해서는 여러분의 '모든' 감각이 관여하는 것이 절대적으로 중요하다.
                             유지하다, 보유하다

가S   진S   involving (x)   **패러프레이징**

⑤ It is great to simulate your intellect, but even better if you//can become involved emotionally, physically, and interpersonally.
                    지력   S' V'
여러분의 지력을 모의실험하는 것도 좋지만, 여러분이 감정적으로, 신체적으로, 그리고 사람과 사람 사이에서 참여할 수 있게 된다면 훨씬 더 좋다.

서술형 가S   진S   to talk (x)

⑥ In other words, it isn't enough to merely read this material in a book △ hear an instructor talk about it in class.
                                        1   2
다시 말해서, 단순히 책에 있는 이 자료를 읽거나 수업 시간에 교사가 그것에 관해 말하는 것을 듣는 것만으로는 충분하지 않다.
                                             교사, 강사

⑦ You//must also have opportunities (to practice the skills and make the ideas your own)
   S   V   1   2
여러분은 또한 기술을 연습하고 아이디어를 여러분 자신의 것으로 만들 기회를 가져야 한다.

* immersion: 몰입

	주요 어휘 및 유의어/반의어		
	단어	**의미**	**유의어/반의어**
☐☐☐ 1	lead to	~로 이어지다	= bring about, cause, prompt
☐☐☐ 2	permanent	영구적인	= constant, lasting
☐☐☐ 3	absolutely	절대적으로	= certainly, unquestionably
☐☐☐ 4	critical	중요한	= crucial, vital, significant
☐☐☐ 5	retain	유지하다	= hold, keep, maintain
☐☐☐ 6			
☐☐☐ 7			
☐☐☐ 8			
☐☐☐ 9			
☐☐☐ 10			
☐☐☐ 11			

Ⓢhorts Ⓕlow 제시된 [A], [B], [C]를 서론, 본론, 결론의 순서로 연결해보고, 단락별 내용의 흐름을 정리해보세요.

	서론 (① ~ ②)	본론 (③ ~ ⑤)	결론 (⑥ ~ ⑦)
	•	•	•
개요도	•	•	•
	[A] 주장 제시	[B] 논의 전개	[C] 재진술
	능동적인 학습이 수동적 학습보다 효과가 있다는 말은 그리 놀랍지도 않다.	교실에 가만히 앉아있는 것보다 토론, 상호 작용, 몰입, 직접 경험 등이 더 뛰어난 학습 효과를 가져온다.	단순히 책에 있는 자료를 읽는 것은 부족하고, 분명히 아이디어를 자신의 것으로 만들 기회가 필요하다.

Ⓢhorts Ⓞverview 글의 〈주제 및 제목〉을 쓰시오.

주제	한글	지식 습득을 위한 능동적 학습의 효과
	영어	the / active / of / for / of / effectiveness / acquisition / learning / knowledge
	정답	
제목	한글	능동적 학습의 힘
	영어	Power / The / Learning / Active / of
	정답	

Ⓢhorts Ⓓetails 글의 내용과 일치하면 T에, 일치하지 않으면 F에 동그라미 표기를 하세요.

① Unisensory learning, which involves relying on a single sensory modality, is sufficient for consolidating new knowledge and enhancing retention. [T / F]

② Active learning modalities, which require learners to engage with and reflect on the material, lead to significantly better outcomes than passive learning approaches that involve minimal engagement with the material. [T / F]

③ It is essential to have opportunities to practice skills and make ideas one's own to retain new knowledge and skills effectively. [T / F]

Ⓢhorts Ⓖrammar 각 문장에서 어법상 가장 적절한 것을 고르시오.

① A lot of research discusses [that / what] leads to relatively permanent acquisition of new knowledge or skills.
② You won't be [surprising / surprised] to hear that active learning works [very / far] better than passive learning.
③ In other words, sitting still in a classroom for more than a half hour at a time (no matter how interesting the material) isn't nearly as potent as having opportunities to engage [active / actively] with the concepts through discussion, group interaction, practice, immersion, or some other form of direct experience.
④ Likewise, it is absolutely critical for retaining new knowledge and skills that all your senses are [engaging / engaged].
⑤ It is great to simulate your intellect, but even better if you can become involved emotionally, physically, and interpersonally.
⑥ In other words, it isn't enough to merely read this material in a book or hear an instructor talk about it in class.
⑦ You must also have opportunities to practice the skills and make the ideas your own.

중심 소재 : Piaget의 균형 상태 이론								
글의 전개방식	통념과 반박	문제와 해결	연구·실험	비교·대조	예시	비유	시간적 흐름	스토리텔링	기타

주제문

① According to Piaget, organizing, assimilating, and accommodating can be viewed as a kind of complex balancing act.
= adapt = adjust = modify　viewing(x)　= recognize = perceive
조직하다　조절

Piaget에 따르면, 조직하기, 동화하기, 그리고 조절하기는 일종의 복잡한 균형 잡기 행위로 여겨질 수 있다.

② (❶) In his theory, the actual changes in thinking take place through the process of equilibration — the act of searching for a balance.
= happen = occur

그의 이론에서, 사고의 실제 변화는 평형의 과정, 즉 균형을 찾는 행위를 통해 일어난다.

③ (❷) Piaget assumed that people continually test the adequacy of their thinking processes in order to achieve that balance.
접속사　끊임없이　적절성　= reach = obtain = attain

Piaget는 사람들이 그 균형을 이루기 위해 자신의 사고 과정의 적절성을 끊임없이 시험한다고 가정했다.

④ (❸) Briefly, the process of equilibration works like this: If we apply a particular scheme to an event or situation and the scheme works, then equilibrium exists.
간단히 말해서　apply A to B : A를 B에 적용하다

간단히 말해서, 평형 과정은 다음과 같이 작동한다. 만약 우리가 어떤 사건이나 상황에 특정한 도식을 적용하고 그 도식이 작동하면 평형이 나타난다.

⑤ (❹) If the scheme does not produce a satisfying result, then disequilibrium exists, and we become uncomfortable.
= yield = create = generate　불편한

그 도식이 만족스러운 결과를 낳지 못하면, 비평형 상태가 생기고, 우리는 불편해진다.

⑥ (❺ This motivates us to keep searching for a solution through assimilation and accommodation, and thus our thinking changes and moves ahead.)
동기를 부여하다

이것은 우리가 동화와 조절을 통해 해결책을 계속 찾도록 동기를 부여하고, 따라서 우리의 사고는 변화하며 앞으로 나아간다.

⑦ Of course, the level of disequilibrium must be just right optimal — too little and we aren't interested in changing, too much and we may be discouraged or anxious and not change.
interesting(x)　= afraid = concerned = worried

물론 비평형의 수준은 딱 적당하거나 최적이어야 하는데, 너무 적으면 우리는 변화에 관심이 없고, 너무 많으면 우리는 낙담하거나 불안해하며 변화하지 않을 수도 있다.

* assimilation: 동화

	주요 어휘 및 유의어/반의어		
	단어	**의미**	**유의어/반의어**
□□□ 1	accommodate	조절하다	= adapt, adjust, modify
□□□ 2	view	여기다	= recognize, perceive
□□□ 3	take place	일어나다	= happen, occur
□□□ 4	achieve	이루다	= reach, obtain, attain
□□□ 5	produce	(결과를) 낳다	= generate, yield, create
□□□ 6	anxious	불안한	= afraid, concerned, worried
□□□ 7			
□□□ 8			
□□□ 9			
□□□ 10			
□□□ 11			

Ⓢhorts Ⓕlow 제시된 [A], [B], [C]를 서론, 본론, 결론의 순서로 연결해보고, 단락별 내용의 흐름을 정리해보세요.

	서론 (① ~ ②)	본론 (③ ~ ⑤)	결론 (⑥ ~ ⑦)
	•	•	•
개요도	•	•	•
	[A] 부연 설명	[B] 논의 전개	[C] 견해 소개
	이는 해결책을 찾을 동기를 부여하고, 우리의 사고는 변화하며 앞으로 나아간다.	어떤 사건에 대해 특정 도식을 적용하여, 그 결과에 따라 평형이나 비평형 상태가 나타난다.	Piaget에 따르면 조직, 동화, 조절은 복잡한 균형잡기 행위와 같다.

Ⓢhorts Ⓞverview 글의 〈주제 및 제목〉을 쓰시오.

주제	한글	균형을 찾는 과정으로서의 사고
	영어	of / a / thinking / equilibrium / finding / process / as
	정답	
제목	한글	생각이 변화하고 앞으로 나아가는 방식에 대한 Piaget의 설명
	영어	Piaget's / and / Moves / Ahead / Thinking / How / on / Changes / Account
	정답	

Ⓢhorts Ⓓetails 글의 내용과 일치하면 T에, 일치하지 않으면 F에 동그라미 표기를 하세요.

① In Piaget's theory, cognitive conflict in the process of equilibration occurs when new information challenges existing cognitive structures and motivates learners to seek resolution through adaptation. [T / F]

② Equilibration is a static and fixed state that does not involve ongoing adaptation or transformation of cognitive structures. [T / F]

③ The process of equilibration, which involves seeking cognitive balance through adaptation, can be conceptualized as a cyclical and iterative process that operates at multiple levels of cognitive development. [T / F]

Ⓢhorts Ⓖrammar 각 문장에서 어법상 가장 적절한 것을 고르시오.

① According to Piaget, organizing, assimilating, and accommodating can [viewed / be viewed] as a kind of complex balancing act.

② (❶) In his theory, the actual changes in thinking take place through the process of equilibration — the act of searching for a balance.

③ (❷) Piaget assumed [what / which / that] people continually test the adequacy of their thinking processes in order to achieve that balance.

④ (❸) Briefly, the process of equilibration works like this: If we apply a particular scheme to an event or situation and the scheme works, then equilibrium [exist / exists / existing].

⑤ (❹) If the scheme does not produce a satisfying result, then disequilibrium exists, and we become [uncomfortable / uncomfortably].

⑥ (❺ This motivates us to keep [searched / searching] for a solution through assimilation and accommodation, and thus our thinking changes and moves ahead.)

⑦ Of course, the level of disequilibrium must be just right or optimal — too little and we aren't interested in changing, too much and we may be discouraged or anxious and not change.

중심 소재 : 메시지 전달 기술을 통한 의사소통에서의 오해

글의 전개방식	통념과 반박	문제와 해결	연구·실험	비교·대조	예시	비유	시간적 흐름	스토리텔링	기타

서술형
imagine + V ing : ~하는 것을 상상하다

① In many ways it's difficult to imagine communicating without any emotion whatsoever.
to communicate(x)

여러 가지 면에서 전혀 아무 감정도 없이 의사소통하는 것은 상상하기 어렵다. 전혀

서술형
= factor
= part = element

② What would communication (stripped of its nonverbal components) even look like?
stripping(x) 비언어적인

비언어적 요소가 제거된 의사소통은 심지어 어떤 모습일까?

= hint = cue

③ Perhaps messaging technology // can give us a clue.

아마도 메시지 전달 기술이 우리에게 단서를 줄 수 있을 것이다.

= go through
= undergo 　　패러프레이징 　　 문사구문 　　 = swap
exchanged(x)

④ After all, who // hasn't experienced a misunderstanding with someone when exchanging text messages?

어쨌든 간에, 문자 메시지를 주고받을 때 누군가와의 오해를 경험하지 않은 사람이 누가 있겠는가?
오해 　　앞문장

주제문
= absence
= deficien~
= shortage

⑤ While there can be a number of reasons for (this) many misinterpretations // are in fact due to the lack of nonverbal cues and tone of voice in these communications.

여기에는 여러 가지 이유가 있을 수 있지만, 많은 오해는 사실 이러한 의사소통에서 비언어적 단서와 목소리의 어조가 부족하기 때문이다.

= plentiful = abundant 　　　　앞문장

⑥ Numerous studies of text messaging and email // support (this).

문자 메시지와 이메일에 대한 수많은 연구가 이를 뒷받침한다.
수많은

⑦ A 2005 paper, "Egocentrism Over E-Mail: Can We Communicate as Well as We Think?" // cites studies (that) showed participants // had a 50 percent chance of correctly distinguishing (whether) the tone in an email // was sarcastic or not.
주격 관.CH (that)접속사 　　　　　　　　　= figure out = differentiate 　 구별하다 　　if

2005년 논문 '이메일상에서의 자기중심성: 우리가 생각하는 것 만큼 의사소통을 잘 할 수 있을까?'는 참가자들이 이메일의 어조가 비꼬는 것인지 아닌지를 정확하게 구별할 수 있는 가능성이 50퍼센트라는 것을 보여 주는 연구를 인용한다.

서술형
가S

⑧ If our ability (to correctly deduce such information) // is no better than chance, (it's small wonder texting often // leads to misunderstandings.
(that)접속사 　 진S

만약 그러한 정보를 정확하게 추론하는 우리의 능력이 우연보다 나을 것이 없다면, 문자 메시지가 자주 오해를 불러일으키는 것은 별로 놀라운 일이 아니다.

* egocentrism: 자기중심성 ** sarcastic: 비꼬는 *** deduce: 추론하다

주요 어휘 및 유의어/반의어

	단어	의미	유의어/반의어
☐☐☐ 1	component	요소	= part, element, factor
☐☐☐ 2	clue	단서	= hint, cue
☐☐☐ 3	experience	경험하다	= go through, undergo
☐☐☐ 4	exchange	주고받다	= swap
☐☐☐ 5	lack	부족	= deficiency, shortage, absence
☐☐☐ 6	numerous	수많은	= plentiful, abundant
☐☐☐ 7	support	뒷받침하다	= uphold
☐☐☐ 8	distinguish	구별하다	= figure out, differentiate
☐☐☐ 9			
☐☐☐ 10			
☐☐☐ 11			

⑤horts Ⓕlow 제시된 [A], [B], [C]를 서론, 본론, 결론의 순서로 연결해보고, 단락별 내용의 흐름을 정리해보세요.

	서론 (① ~ ②)	본론 (③ ~ ⑤)	결론 (⑥ ~ ⑧)
	·	·	·
개요도	·	·	·
	[A] 글감 제시	[B] 연구 결과	[C] 의문 제기
	문자를 통한 소통에서 대부분의 오해는 비언어적 신호와 목소리 어조가 없기 때문이다.	연구에 따르면, 이메일이 비꼬는 내용인지 아닌지 정확히 추론하는 가능성이 50%였다.	비언어적 요소가 제거된 소통은 어떤 모습일까?

⑤horts Ⓞverview 글의 〈주제 및 제목〉을 쓰시오.

주제	한글	오해 없는 의사소통을 위한 비언어적 신호의 중요성
	영어	without / misunderstanding / communication / importance / cues / the / of / for / nonverbal
	정답	
제목	한글	우리가 가끔 문자 메시지를 잘못 해석하는 이유
	영어	Messages / Text / We / Misinterpret / Why / Sometimes
	정답	

⑤horts Ⓓetails 글의 내용과 일치하면 T에, 일치하지 않으면 F에 동그라미 표기를 하세요.

① The lack of nonverbal cues in electronic communication makes it difficult to convey emotions and contextual information.　[T / F]

② Electronic communication is always more efficient and effective than in-person communication due to the ability to know if the tone is sarcastic or not.　[T / F]

⑤horts Ⓖrammar 각 문장에서 어법상 가장 적절한 것을 고르시오.

① In many ways it's difficult to imagine communicating without any emotion whatsoever.

② What would communication stripped of [its / their] nonverbal components even look like?

③ Perhaps messaging technology can [give / give to] us a clue.

④ After all, who hasn't experienced a misunderstanding with someone when [exchanged / exchanging] text messages?

⑤ While there can be a number of reasons for this, many misinterpretations are in fact [due to / because] the lack of nonverbal cues and tone of voice in these communications.

⑥ Numerous studies of text messaging and email support this.

⑦ A 2005 paper, "Egocentrism Over E-Mail: Can We Communicate as Well as We Think?" cites studies that showed participants had a 50 percent chance of correctly distinguishing whether the tone in an email [was / were / being] sarcastic or not.

⑧ If our ability to correctly deduce such information is no better than chance, it's small wonder texting often [leads / leading] to misunderstandings.

중심 소재 : 사회적 확인

글의 전개방식	통념과 반박	문제와 해결	연구·실험	비교·대조	예시	비유	시간적 흐름	스토리텔링	기타

서술형

① Social validation means that certain beliefs and values are confirmed only by the shared social experience of a group.

'사회적 확인'이란 특정 신념과 가치가 한 집단의 공유된 사회적 경험에 의해서만 확인된다는 것을 의미한다.

② For example, any given culture cannot prove that its religion and moral system are superior to another culture's religion and moral system, but if the members reinforce each other's beliefs and values, they come to be taken for granted. take for granted : 당연시하다

예를 들자면, 어떤 특정 문화도 자신의 종교와 도덕 체계가 다른 문화의 종교와 도덕 체계보다 우월하다는 것을 증명할 수는 없지만, 구성원들이 서로의 신념과 가치를 강화한다면, 그것들은 당연하게 받아들여지게 된다.

③ ❶ Those who fail to accept such beliefs and values run the risk of "excommunication," of being thrown out of the group.

그러한 신념과 가치를 받아들이지 못하는 사람들은 '제명', 즉 집단에서 쫓겨나는 위험에 처하게 된다.

서술형

④ ❷ The test of whether they work or not is how comfortable and anxiety-free members are when they abide by them. = beliefs and values

그것들(신념과 가치)이 효과가 있는지 없는지에 대한 시험은 구성원들이 그것들을 준수할 때 얼마나 편안하고 불안함이 없는가 하는 것이다.

⑤ ❸ In these realms, the group learns that certain beliefs and values, as initially promulgated by prophets, founders, and leaders, "work" in the sense of reducing uncertainty in critical areas of the group's functioning.

이러한 영역에서 그 집단은 예언자, 설립자, 지도자에 의해 처음 전파된 대로의 특정 신념과 가치가 집단의 기능 중 중요한 영역에서 불확실성을 감소시킨다는 의미에서 '효과가 있다'는 것을 배운다.

⑥ ❹ Accepted beliefs and values often make large areas of behavior unexplained, leaving people with a suspicious feeling that they still do not have the entire culture in hand.

받아들여진 신념과 가치는 흔히 행동의 넓은 영역을 설명하지 못하여, 사람들이 여전히 문화 전체를 장악하지 못하고 있다는 의구심을 그들에게 남긴다.

⑦ ❺ Moreover, as they continue to provide meaning and comfort to group members, they also become transformed into non-discussible assumptions even though they may not be correlated with actual performance.

더욱이, 그것들이 집단 구성원들에게 의미와 편안함을 계속 제공함에 따라, 그것들은 또한 실제의 행위와 서로 상관관계가 없을 수 있을지라도 논할 수 없는 전제로 변형된다.

abide by: 준수하다 ** promulgate: 전파하다

주요 어휘 및 유의어/반의어			
	단어	의미	유의어/반의어
□□□ 1	confirm	확인하다	= validate, affirm
□□□ 2	prove	증명하다	= verify, substantiate
□□□ 3	accept	받아들이다	= approve, acknowledge
□□□ 4	abide by	준수하다	= follow, comply with
□□□ 5	promulgate	전파하다	= promote, declare
□□□ 6	reduce	감소시키다	= diminish, lower, curtail
□□□ 7	transform	변형되다	= convert
□□□ 8	correlated with	~와 관련 있는	= associate with, linked to
□□□ 9			
□□□ 10			
□□□ 11			

ⓈhortsⒻlow 제시된 [A], [B], [C]를 서론, 본론, 결론의 순서로 연결해보고, 단락별 내용의 흐름을 정리해보세요.

	서론 (① ~ ②)	본론 (③ ~ ④)	결론 (⑤ ~ ⑦)
	•	•	•
개요도	• [A] 부연 설명 집단은 그 특정 신념이나 가치가 불확실성을 감소시킨다는 의미에서 효과가 있다고 배운다.	• [B] 개념 설명 사회적 확인이란 특정 신념이나 가치가 공유된 사회적 경험에 의해서만 확인된다는 것을 말한다.	• [C] 논의 진행 신념과 가치를 받아들이지 못하는 사람들은 집단에서 쫓겨나는 위험에 처하게 된다.

ⓈhortsⓄverview 글의 〈주제 및 제목〉을 쓰시오.

주제	한글	사회적 검증의 개념과 작동 방식
	영어	concept / and / validation / social / works / the / of / how / it
	정답	
제목	한글	사회적 확인: 특정 신념이 그룹 내에서 확인되는 방식
	영어	Confirmed / Group / Beliefs / How / Within / Are / A / Social / Validation: / Certain
	정답	

ⓈhortsⒹetails 글의 내용과 일치하면 T에, 일치하지 않으면 F에 동그라미 표기를 하세요.

① It is possible for different cultures to demonstrate the superiority of their religion and moral system over others. [T / F]

② Certain beliefs and values, which were originally introduced by prophets, founders, and leaders, are effective in lessening doubt in crucial aspects of the group's operation. [T / F]

③ Social validation is a process that fosters doubt and skepticism among members of a group regarding their beliefs and values. [T / F]

ⓈhortsⒼrammar 각 문장에서 어법상 가장 적절한 것을 고르시오.

① Social validation means that certain beliefs and values are [confirming / confirmed] only by the shared social experience of a group.

② For example, any given culture cannot prove that its religion and moral system are superior to another culture's religion and moral system, but if the members reinforce each other's beliefs and values, they come to [take / be taken] for granted.

③ ❶ Those who fail to accept such beliefs and values run the risk of "excommunication," of being thrown out of the group.

④ ❷ The test of whether they work or not [is / are / being] how comfortable and anxiety-free members are when they abide by [it / them].

⑤ ❸ In these realms, the group learns that certain beliefs and values, as initially promulgated by prophets, founders, and leaders, "work" in the sense of reducing uncertainty in critical areas of the group's functioning.

⑥ ❹ Moreover, as they continue to provide meaning and comfort to group members, they also become [transforming / transformed] into non-discussible assumptions even though they may not be correlated with actual performance.

중심 소재 : 정보 교환을 통해 발생되는 사회문화적 행동

글의 전개방식	통념과 반박	문제와 해결	연구·실험	비교·대조	예시	비유	시간적 흐름	스토리텔링	기타

① Socio-cultural behaviors arise from the exchange of information between individuals and, therefore, they are closely linked to how the information flows among the population.

사회문화적 행동은 개인 간의 정보 교환에서 발생하며, 따라서 정보가 사람들 사이에서 어떻게 흐르는지와 밀접하게 연관되어 있다.

② In particular, the social ties built and maintained in the local neighborhood are useful for solving concrete local problems and affect the spread of information and behaviors, playing a key role in integrating social groups at higher scales.

특히 지역 사회에서 구축되고 유지되는 사회적 유대는 구체적인 지역 문제를 해결하는 데 유용하며 정보와 행동의 확산에 영향을 미쳐, 더 높은 수준에서 사회 집단을 통합하는 데 핵심적인 역할을 한다.

③ Residential segregation directly impacts how these social ties of physical nearness are displayed, drawing boundaries on the structure of information flows.

거주지 분리는 이러한 물리적 근접성의 사회적 유대가 어떻게 나타나는지에 직접적인 영향을 미쳐, 정보 흐름의 구조에 경계를 짓는다.

④ We can think of the segregation process as a dynamical formation of echo-chambers: social fragmentation over the residential space encourages individual within a group to interact only with their peers.

우리는 분리 과정을 반향실의 역학적인 형성 과정으로 생각할 수 있다. 즉, 거주 공간에 대한 사회적 균열은 집단 내의 개인들이 자신들의 동료들과만 상호 작용을 하도록 조장한다.

⑤ In this case, the collective behaviors of the socio-cultural space that emerge could clash at higher scales, as polarized positions may arise.

이러한 경우에, 새로이 생겨나는, 사회문화적 공간의 집단행동이 더 높은 수준에서 충돌할 수도 있을 터인데, 이는 양극화된 입장이 생길 수도 있기 때문이다.

* segregation: 분리 ** echo-chamber: 반향실(특정한 정보에 갇혀 새로운 정보를 받아들이지 못하는 환경)

*** fragmentation: 균열

주요 어휘 및 유의어/반의어

	단어	의미	유의어/반의어
□□□ 1	arise	발생하다	= appear, originate
□□□ 2	affect	영향을 미치다	= influence
□□□ 3	spread	확산	= transmission, dissemination
□□□ 4	segregation	분리	= separation
□□□ 5	display	나타내다, 드러내다	= exhibit, demonstrate
□□□ 6	clash	충돌하다	= collide
□□□ 7			
□□□ 8			
□□□ 9			
□□□ 10			
□□□ 11			

⑤horts Ⓕlow 제시된 [A], [B], [C]를 서론, 본론, 결론의 순서로 연결해보고, 단락별 내용의 흐름을 정리해보세요.

	서론 (① ~ ②)	본론 (③ ~ ④)	결론 (⑤)
	·	·	·
개요도	·	·	·
	[A] 상황 제시	[B] 글감 제시	[C] 논의 구체화
	거주지 분리는 사회적 유대 발생 방식에 직접적 영향을 미쳐 정보 흐름의 구조에 경계를 짓는다.	사회문화적 행동은 개인 간의 정보 교환에서 발생하는데, 따라서 사회적 유대는 사회 집단을 통합하는 데 핵심적 역할을 한다.	거주지 분리로 사회문화적 공간의 집단행동이 더 높은 수준에서 충돌할 수 있다.

⑤horts Ⓞverview 글의 〈주제 및 제목〉을 쓰시오.

주제	한글	개인 간의 정보 교환이 사회 문화적 행동에 미치는 영향
	영어	between / behaviors / socio-cultural / individuals / of / influence / the / exchanges / of / information / on
	정답	
제목	한글	정보 흐름의 구조와 사회문화적 행동
	영어	of / Structure / Information / Behaviors / and / Sociocultural / Flows
	정답	

⑤horts Ⓓetails 글의 내용과 일치하면 T에, 일치하지 않으면 F에 동그라미 표기를 하세요.

① Socio-cultural behaviors are completely independent of the exchange of information between individuals. [T / F]

② Community social bonds help solve local problems, which leads to a higher level of social integration. [T / F]

③ Social division within a residential area can prompt people to associate merely with those who are similar to them, resulting in the formation of isolated groups with strongly held opinions. [T / F]

⑤horts Ⓖrammar 각 문장에서 어법상 가장 적절한 것을 고르시오.

① Socio-cultural behaviors arise from the exchange of information between individuals and, therefore, they are [close / closely] linked to how the information flows among the population.

② In particular, the social ties built and maintained in the local neighborhood are useful for solving concrete local problems and affect the spread of information and behaviors, [play / playing] a key role in integrating social groups at higher scales.

③ Residential segregation directly impacts [what / how] these social ties of physical nearness are displayed, drawing boundaries on the structure of information flows.

④ We can think of the segregation process as a dynamical formation of echo-chambers: social fragmentation over the residential space encourages individual within a group to interact only with their peers.

⑤ In this case, the collective behaviors of the socio-cultural space that emerge could clash at higher scales, as polarized positions may [arise / be arisen].

중심 소재 : 인공위성을 통한 인터넷 제공								
글의 전개방식	통념과 반박	문제와 해결	연구·실험	비교·대조	예시	비유	시간적 흐름	스토리텔링	기타

① Connecting the current offline population//will be a difficult undertaking.
=attempt = task
일.과업
현재 인터넷에 연결되지 않는 인구를 연결하는 것은 힘든 일일 것이다.

② Many of the remaining unserved areas//are geographically challenging to reach due to rough terrain or
=tough =difficult
remote location, thus raising providers' costs and pushing broadband services further out of reach of
외딴   분사구문
low-income households.

(인터넷) 서비스가 여전히 제공되지 않는 지역들 중 많은 곳은 험한 지형이나 외딴 위치 때문에 지리적으로 도달하기 어려우며, 따라서 공급자의
비용을 높여 저소득 가구가 광대역 서비스를 더욱더 이용할 수 없게 한다.

주제문

③ However, more affordable and accessible Internet//is becoming a reality in parts of the world, thanks to
=inexpensive
=economical
저렴한
satellite technologies(emerging as an alternative to expanding access at lower costs to remote locations
=distant =faraway
대안
across the planet)

그러나 지구 도처의 외딴 지역에 더 저렴한 비용으로 (인터넷) 접속을 확장하는 것에 대한 대안으로 떠오르고 있는 인공위성 기술 덕분에 더
저렴하고 더 이용하기 쉬운 인터넷이 세계 여러 지역에서 현실이 되고 있다.
패러프레이징

서술형

④ For example, a network of orbital satellites(operated by an American spacecraft manufacturer)//has
=run = manage
launched 1,735 satellites into orbit since 2019.

예를 들어, 한 미국 우주선 제조업체가 운영하는 궤도 위성망은 2019년 이래로 1,735개의 인공위성을 궤도로 쏘아 올려 왔다.

서술형
⑤ According to the company: "The satellite network//is ideally suited for areas of the globe where
=suitable   관계부사
=appropriate
connectivity//has typically been a challenge.
접속성
그 회사에 따르면 "그 위성망은 (인터넷) 접속성이 대체로 난제였던 지구의 여러 지역에 이상적으로 적합합니다.
패러프레이징
서술형
⑥ Unbounded by traditional ground infrastructure, the network//can deliver high-speed broadband Internet
구애되지 않는
to locations where access//has been unreliable or completely unavailable."
완부사   믿을 수 없는
그 위성망은, 기존의 지상 기반 시설에 구애되지 않으므로, (인터넷) 접속을 믿을 수 없었거나 전적으로 이용할 수 없었던 지역에 고속 광대역
인터넷을 제공할 수 있습니다."

* terrain: 지형, 지역 ** broadband: 광대역, 고속 데이터 통신망

	주요 어휘 및 유의어/반의어		
	단어	의미	유의어/반의어
□□□ 1	undertaking	일	= task, attempt
□□□ 2	challenging	어려운	= difficult, tough
□□□ 3	affordable	저렴한	= inexpensive, economical
□□□ 4	remote	외딴	= distant, faraway
□□□ 5	operate	운영하다	= run, manage
□□□ 6	suited	적합한	= appropriate, suitable
□□□ 7			
□□□ 8			
□□□ 9			
□□□ 10			
□□□ 11			

⑤horts Ⓕlow 제시된 [A], [B], [C]를 서론, 본론, 결론의 순서로 연결해보고, 단락별 내용의 흐름을 정리해보세요.

	서론 (① ~ ②)	본론 (③)	결론 (④ ~ ⑥)
	•	•	•
개요도	• [A] 대안 제시 인공위성 기술 덕분에 더 저렴하고 이용하기 쉬운 인터넷이 현실화되고 있다.	• [B] 글감 제시 지형이나 외딴 위치 때문에 인터넷 서비스를 제공받지 못하는 곳이 있다.	• [C] 사례 제시 한 미국 우주선 제조업체의 궤도 위성망은 여러 지역에 이상적으로 적합하다.

⑤horts Ⓞverview 글의 <주제 및 제목>을 쓰시오.

주제	한글	지리적으로 어려운 지역에 인터넷 서비스를 제공하는 위성 기술
	영어	challenging / service / for / technology / to / supplying / areas / satellite / geographically / internet
	정답	
제목	한글	세계를 연결하는 궤도 위성들
	영어	World / For / Satellites / the / Orbital / Connecting
	정답	

⑤horts Ⓓetails 글의 내용과 일치하면 T에, 일치하지 않으면 F에 동그라미 표기를 하세요.

① Unserved areas are geographically easy to reach, making it possible to expand broadband services to low-income households at a low cost. [T / F]

② Despite the challenges, there are some areas where internet access is becoming more affordable and available thanks to advancements in satellite technology. [T / F]

③ An American spacecraft manufacturer has launched 1,735 orbital satellites since 2019 to create a network that can deliver high-speed broadband internet to areas where it was once difficult to obtain. [T / F]

⑤horts Ⓖrammar 각 문장에서 어법상 가장 적절한 것을 고르시오.

① Connecting the current offline population will be a difficult undertaking.

② Many of the remaining unserved areas are geographically challenging to reach [because / due to] rough terrain or remote location, thus raising providers' costs and pushing broadband services further out of reach of low-income households.

③ However, more affordable and accessible Internet is becoming a reality in parts of the world, thanks to satellite technologies [emerging / emerged] as an alternative to expanding access at lower costs to remote locations across the planet.

④ For example, a network of orbital satellites operated by an American spacecraft manufacturer [was / has / had] launched 1,735 satellites into orbit since 2019.

⑤ According to the company: "The satellite network is ideally suited for areas of the globe [which / what / where] connectivity has typically been a challenge.

⑥ Unbounded by traditional ground infrastructure, the network can deliver high-speed broadband Internet to locations where access has been unreliable or [complete / completely] unavailable."

중심 소재 : 엄청나게 증가하는 데이터양								
글의 전개방식	통념과 반박	문제와 해결	연구·실험	비교·대조	예시	비유	시간적 흐름	스토리텔링	기타

① Data will be generated from everywhere.
= produce = create
데이터는 어디에서나 생겨날 것이다.
패러프레이징

② Cars, smartphones, bodies, minds, homes, and cities will be sources of massive amounts of information
= immense = enormous / 거대한
that will grow exponentially and flow at an unprecedented speed over the internet.
자동차, 스마트폰, 몸, 마음, 집, 도시는, 인터넷상에서 기하급수적으로 증가하고 전례 없는 속도로 유통될 거대한 양의 정보의 원천이 될 것이다.
전례 없는

③ In the years ahead, the expression "less is more" will have a greater level of importance as to how you
= significance / 서술형 / 간접의문문
= combine = accommodate
integrate the ocean of insights coming your way and will aid you to understand the world around you.
= figure out = grasp
앞으로는 "더 적은 것이 더 많은 것이다"라는 표현이 여러분이 어떻게 자신에게 닥쳐오는 수많은 식견을 통합하는지에 관해 더 큰 정도의 중요성을 가질 것이고, 여러분이 주변 세상을 이해하도록 도움을 줄 것이다.
통합하다

④ The amount of information and media surrounding us will be impracticable to process and retrieve;
= the amount ~ us / 실행이 불가능한 / = handle = deal with
패러프레이징
you can leave that for the machines, which can process data faster and more accurately than we can.
= precisely = correctly
우리를 둘러싸고 있는 정보와 매체의 양은 처리하고 기억하기가 거의 불가능할 것이어서, 여러분은 그것을 기계에 맡길 수 있는데, 그것 (기계)은 우리가 할 수 있는 것보다 더 빠르고 더 정확하게 데이터를 처리할 수 있다.

⑤ Your job will be to focus on what matters most to you.
수격 관.대
여러분이 할 일은 여러분에게 가장 중요한 것에 집중하는 것일 것이다.

주제문
⑥ The key to an easy digital future is not so much accessing a tsunami of data but how you
not so much A but B : A보다는 B / 간접의문문
= turn = convert
comprehend and translate it into new contexts, scenarios, and ideas.
안락한 디지털 미래의 비결은 쓰나미처럼 밀려오는 데이터에 접근하는 것이라기보다는 오히려 어떻게 그것을 이해해서 새로운 맥락, 시나리오, 아이디어로 바꾸는가이다.
= understand 이해하다 / = grasp / = a tsunami of data

* exponentially: 기하급수적으로 ** retrieve: 기억하다, 상기하다

주요 어휘 및 유의어/반의어			
	단어	의미	유의어/반의어
□□□ 1	generate	생겨나다	= produce, create
□□□ 2	massive	거대한	= enormous, immense
□□□ 3	importance	중요성	= significance
□□□ 4	integrate	통합하다	= combine, accommodate
□□□ 5	understand	이해하다	= figure out, grasp
□□□ 6	process	처리하다	= handle, deal with
□□□ 7	accurately	정확하게	= precisely, correctly
□□□ 8	comprehend	이해하다	= understand, grasp
□□□ 9	translate	바꾸다	= turn, convert
□□□ 10			
□□□ 11			

ⓢhorts Ⓕlow 제시된 [A], [B], [C]를 서론, 본론, 결론의 순서로 연결해보고, 단락별 내용의 흐름을 정리해보세요.

	서론 (① ~ ②)	본론 (③ ~ ④)	결론 (⑤ ~ ⑥)
	•	•	•
개요도	• [A] 논의 추상화 "더 적은 것이 더 많은 것이다"라는 표현이 닥쳐오는 수많은 식견을 통합하는 방식에 대해 더 큰 중요성을 가진다.	• [B] 주장 제시 우리의 일은 가장 중요한 것에 집중하는 것이고, 데이터를 이해해서 아이디어로 바꾸는 것이다.	• [C] 배경 제시 데이터는 어디에서나 생겨날 것이고 전례 없는 속도로 유통될 것이다.

ⓢhorts Ⓞverview 글의 <주제 및 제목>을 쓰시오.

주제	한글	늘어나는 데이터와 인간의 역할
	영어	and / of / amount / job / growing / data / human's / the
	정답	
제목	한글	데이터 쓰나미 속에서 헤엄치기 위해 해야 할 일
	영어	Tsunami / of / Should / In / To / Swim / Be / What / The / Done / Data
	정답	

ⓢhorts Ⓓetails 글의 내용과 일치하면 T에, 일치하지 않으면 F에 동그라미 표기를 하세요.

① The volume of data will make it impractical for humans to process and retrieve, which is where machines come in handy.   [T / F]

② It is important to process all available data, regardless of relevance.   [T / F]

③ Machines are better than humans in processing data quickly and accurately.   [T / F]

ⓢhorts Ⓖrammar 각 문장에서 어법상 가장 적절한 것을 고르시오.

① Data will [generate / be generated] from everywhere.

② Cars, smartphones, bodies, minds, homes, and cities will be sources of massive amounts of information [what / that] will grow exponentially and flow at an unprecedented speed over the internet.

③ In the years ahead, the expression "less is more" will have a greater level of importance as to how you integrate the ocean of insights [coming / come] your way and will aid you to understand the world around you.

④ The amount of information and media surrounding us will be impracticable to process and retrieve; you can leave that for the machines, [which / what / where] can process data faster and more accurately than we can.

⑤ Your job will be to focus on what matters most to you.

⑥ The key to an easy digital future is not so much accessing a tsunami of data but how you comprehend and translate [it / them] into new contexts, scenarios, and ideas.

중심 소재 : '속박감'의 문제								
글의 전개방식	통념과 반박	문제와 해결	연구·실험	비교·대조	예시	비유	시간적 흐름	스토리텔링	기타

① Unless you're one of those lucky people (who) only drive new cars,) on at least one occasion you've probably experienced the painful realization (that) your car is too old and no longer worth repairing any more.

주격 관.대
= distressing = grievous
통념

여러분이 새 차만 운전하는 운이 좋은 그런 사람들 중 한명이 아니라면, 아마도 여러분의 차가 너무 낡아서 이제 더는 수리할 가치가 없다고 고통스럽게 깨달았던 경험을 한 경우가 적어도 한 번은 있었을 것이다.

worth + ~ing
: ~ing 만한 가치가 있는

② As a car ages, more and more things can go wrong and need fixing.

차가 노후화되면서, 점점 더 많은 것들이 고장 나서 수리가 필요할 수 있다.

③ At some point, the owner needs to decide: is it worth getting this latest issue looked at or is it time to give up on this car and find another?

서술형
to get(x)
(to be)
get + O + O.C

어떤 시점에서는, 소유자가 결정을 내려야 하는데, 이 최근 문제를 살펴보게 하는 것이 가치가 있는가, 아니면 이 차를 포기하고 다른 차를 구해서 얻을 때인가?

④ The problem is that a lot of money has already been spent on the car, and scrapping it makes it seem as if that money has just been wasted, which makes it very difficult to choose the best option.

접속사
= expend
= pay out
= ditch
= discard
서술형
주격 관.대 가목
진목
O.C
낭비

문제는 이미 그 차에 많은 돈이 들어갔고 폐차하는 것이 그 돈이 그저 헛되이 쓰인 것처럼 보이게 하는데, 그것이 선택할 수 있는 최선의 것을 고르는 것을 매우 어렵게 만든다는 것이다.

⑤ It's a problem known as entrapment, when a person gets trapped into making the wrong decision just because they've previously invested so much.

주제문
= ratch
= snare
속박감

그것은 '속박감'이라고 알려진 문제인데, 어떤 사람이 단지 이전에 매우 많이 투자했다는 이유만으로 잘못된 결정을 내리는 함정에 빠지는 경우이다.

* scrap: 폐기하다

주요 어휘 및 유의어/반의어			
	단어	의미	유의어/반의어
□□□ 1	painful	고통스러운	= distressing, grievous
□□□ 2	spend	쓰다	= pay out, expand
□□□ 3	scrap	폐기하다	= discard, ditch
□□□ 4	trap	함정에 빠뜨리다, 잡다	= catch, snare
□□□ 5			
□□□ 6			
□□□ 7			
□□□ 8			
□□□ 9			
□□□ 10			
□□□ 11			

⑤horts Ⓕlow 제시된 [A], [B], [C]를 서론, 본론, 결론의 순서로 연결해보고, 단락별 내용의 흐름을 정리해보세요.

	서론 (① ~ ②)	본론 (③ ~ ④)	결론 (⑤)
개요도	•	•	•
	•	•	•
	[A] 배경 제시	[B] 개념 도입	[C] 상황 제시
	새 차만 운전할 것이 아니라면, 언젠가는 차가 너무 오래되었고 더 수리할 가치를 못 느낄 수 있다.	속박감이라고 알려진 문제인데, 이전에 많이 투자했다는 이유만으로 잘못된 선택을 내리는 것을 말한다.	문제를 살펴볼 것인지 다른 차를 구할지 고민에 빠지게 되는데, 기존에 투자한 돈을 고려하게 된다.

⑤horts Ⓞverview 글의 〈주제 및 제목〉을 쓰시오.

주제	한글	속박감의 개념과 사례
	영어	case / of / entrapment / an / example / the / concept / and
	정답	
제목	한글	속박감: 당신이 여전히 매몰 비용을 신경쓰는 이유
	영어	Why / About / Sunk / Entrapment: / Cost / Care / You / the / Still
	정답	

⑤horts Ⓓetails 글의 내용과 일치하면 T에, 일치하지 않으면 F에 동그라미 표기를 하세요.

① The sunk costs of previous repairs can make it harder to choose the best course of action.　　　[T / F]

② It's always easy to decide whether to keep repairing an old car or to buy a new one.　　　[T / F]

⑤horts Ⓖrammar 각 문장에서 어법상 가장 적절한 것을 고르시오.

① [If / Unless] you're one of those lucky people who only drive new cars, on at least one occasion you've probably experienced the painful realization that your car is too old and no longer worth [repair / repairing / repaired] any more.

② As a car ages, more and more things can go wrong and need fixing.

③ At some point, the owner needs to decide: is it worth getting this latest issue looked at or is it time to give up on this car and find another?

④ The problem is [what / which / that] a lot of money has already [spent / been spent] on the car, and scrapping it makes it seem [as if / even if] that money has just been wasted, which makes it very difficult to choose the best option.

⑤ It's a problem known [as / for] entrapment, when a person gets [trapping / trap / trapped] into making the wrong decision just because they've previously [invested / been invested] so much.

중심 소재 : 동조를 얻기 위한 리더의 노력

글의 전개방식	통념과 반박	문제와 해결	연구·실험	비교·대조	예시	비유	시간적 흐름	스토리텔링	기타

① Teams and organizations//also have a 'mental life'.
　팀과 조직에도 또한 '정신적 삶'이 있다.

② Most leaders//work hard to get alignment — getting everybody on the same thinking wavelength. (to be)
　대부분의 리더는 (사고의) 일치를 얻기 위하여 열심히 노력하는데, 그것은 모든 사람을 동일한 '사고' 주파수에 맞추는 것이다.　주파수. 파장

주제문
③ But to help organizations and teams ❶ to flourish, leaders//must also work equally hard on getting attunement — getting people on the same feeling wavelength, getting the purpose of the organization and the meaning of the work to resonate with people in a felt way. flourishing(x) 번창하다 (to be) =affect =appeal to
　그러나 조직과 팀이 번창하도록 도우려면 리더는 또한 동조를 얻는 데에도 똑같이 열심히 노력해야 하는데, 그것은 사람들을 동일한 '감정' 주파수에 맞추는 것, 조직의 목적과 업무의 의미가 (감정적으로) 느껴지는 방식으로 사람들에게 반향을 불러일으키도록 하는 것이다.

④ 'Felt'//is the important word here.
　여기서는 '느껴지는'이란 말이 중요한 말이다.

서술형
⑤ ❷ It//is relatively easy to explain the purpose and goals of an organization in a cognitive way. 가S 진S
　조직의 목적과 목표를 인지적인 방식으로 설명하는 것은 비교적 쉽다.　비교적　인지적인

서술형
⑥ But to function at our best, we//have to feel the connection (between) ❸ that what we are being asked to do (and) some larger purpose of the group.
　하지만 우리가 최상의 상태에서 기능하기 위해서, 우리는 하라는 요구를 받고 있는 것과 집단의 어떤 더 큰 목적 사이의 연관성을 '느껴야' 한다.

=prosperous =thriving
⑦ Leaders of flourishing organizations//succeed in (making strong feeling connections (between) the personal goals and values of the people (working there) and ❹ those of the organization, or even the larger society.
　번창하는 조직의 리더는 그곳에서 일하는 사람들의 개인적인 목표와 가치, 그리고 조직, 혹은 심지어 더 큰 집단의 그것들(목표와 가치)을 서로 강력하게 감정적으로 연관 짓는 데 성공한다.　=goals and values

서술형 =secure =firm =fast
⑧ The tighter the links in the chain, the happier the people and ❺ the better the results. (are) (are) (are)
　그 사슬의 고리가 단단할수록, 그 (조직의) 사람들은 더 행복하고, 결과는 더 좋다.

* alignment: 일치 ** attunement: 동조. 감정 맞추기
*** restate with: ~에게 반향을 불러일으키다

주요 어휘 및 유의어/반의어

	단어	의미	유의어/반의어
□□□ 1	attunement	동조	= sympathy
□□□ 2	resonate with	~에 반향을 불러일으키다	= affect, appeal to
□□□ 3	flourishing	번창하는	= prosperous, thriving
□□□ 4	tight	단단한	= firm, fast, secure
□□□ 5			
□□□ 6			
□□□ 7			
□□□ 8			
□□□ 9			
□□□ 10			
□□□ 11			

⑤horts Ⓕlow 제시된 [A], [B], [C]를 서론, 본론, 결론의 순서로 연결해보고, 단락별 내용의 흐름을 정리해보세요.		
서론 (① ~ ③)	본론 (④ ~ ⑥)	결론 (⑦ ~ ⑧)
ㆍ	ㆍ	ㆍ

개요도	ㆍ	ㆍ	ㆍ
	[A] 강조점 지적	[B] 논점 제시	[C] 부연 설명
	"느껴지는"이라는 말이 중요한데, 인지적인 방식의 설명은 쉽지만 연관성을 느끼게 하는 것은 까다롭다.	팀과 조직에도 정신적 삶이 있는데, 사람들을 동일한 감정 주파수에 맞추는 것은 중요하다.	성공적인 조직의 리더는 개인의 목표와 조직의 가치를 감정적으로 연관 짓는 데 성공한다.

⑤horts Ⓞverview 글의 〈주제 및 제목〉을 쓰시오.

주제	한글	리더가 그룹 구성원들 사이에서 (감정적)조화를 이루는 것의 중요성
	영어	leader's / significance / getting / members / the / of / within / group / attunement
	정답	
제목	한글	조직의 성공 비결: 사람들의 마음을 조율하기
	영어	A / Organization's / an / Key / People / Getting / Attuned / Success: / to
	정답	

⑤horts Ⓓetails 글의 내용과 일치하면 T에, 일치하지 않으면 F에 동그라미 표기를 하세요.

① Successful leaders not only strive for cognitive alignment but also emotional attunement among team members, fostering a sense of resonance between individuals and the organization's mission. **[T / F]**

② A more fragmented sense of purpose and values in an organization will lead to a happier and more productive workforce. **[T / F]**

③ Organizations that prioritize strong feeling connections between their employees' personal goals and values and those of the organization achieve higher employee satisfaction and better outcomes. **[T / F]**

⑤horts Ⓖrammar 각 문장에서 어법상 가장 적절한 것을 고르시오.

① Teams and organizations also have a 'mental life'.

② Most leaders work hard to get alignment — getting everybody on the same thinking wavelength.

③ But to help organizations and teams to flourish, leaders must also work [**equal / equally**] hard on getting attunement ── getting people on the same feeling wavelength, getting the purpose of the organization and the meaning of the work to resonate with people in a felt way.

④ 'Felt' is the important word here.

⑤ It is relatively easy [**explain / to explain**] the purpose and goals of an organization in a cognitive way.

⑥ But to function at our best, we have to feel the connection between what we are [**asking / being asked**] to do and some larger purpose of the group.

⑦ Leaders of flourishing organizations succeed in making strong feeling connections between the personal goals and values of the people working there and those of the organization, or even the larger society.

⑧ [**The / A**] tighter the links in the chain, the happier the people and the better the results.

중심 소재 : 면전에서 문 닫기 기법								
글의 전개방식	통념과 반박	문제와 해결	연구·실험	비교·대조	예시	비유	시간적 흐름	스토리텔링	기타

① In the door-in-the-face technique, a large, unreasonable request is made, which is turned down; this is followed by a smaller more reasonable request.
= illogical = irrational　*불합리한*　*수적 관·대*　*= reject = refuse*　*= a large, unreasonable request*　*↔ precede*

'면전에서 문 닫기 기법'에서는, 크고 불합리한 요청이 이루어지고, 그것이 거절되며, 이것이 더 작으면서 더 합리적인 요청으로 이어진다.

② (❶) People are more likely to agree to this smaller second request when it is placed in the context of the more unreasonable request than if it had been placed at the outset.
= start　*서술형*

사람들은 이 더 작은 두 번째 요청이 처음부터 이루어진 경우보다 더 불합리한 요청이라는 맥락 속에서 이루어질 때 그것에 동의할 가능성이 더 크다.

③ (❷) The success of this technique may be related to the reciprocity social norm, the rule that we should pay back in kind what we receive from others.
= mutual benefit　*호혜*　*동격 접속사*

이 기법의 성공은 '호혜적 사회 규범', 즉 우리가 다른 사람들로부터 받는 것을 동일하게 갚아야 한다는 규칙과 관련이 있을 것이다.

④ (❸) The person asking for our support or assistance appears to have made a concession by giving up their initial request, for a much smaller one.
서술형　*= Compromise*　*도움·원조*　*seem to*

우리의 지원이나 도움을 요청하는 사람은 훨씬 더 작은 요청을 위해 자신의 처음 요청을 포기함으로써 양보를 한 것처럼 보인다.

⑤ (❹ As a result, we feel compelled to reciprocate and agree to the smaller request.)
= oblige = impel = force　*= react to = requite = request*

그 결과, 우리는 더 작은 요청에 화답하고 동의해야 한다고 느낀다.

⑥ A common application of door-in-the-face is when teens ask their parents for a large request (attending an out-of-town concert) and then when the permission is denied, asking them for something smaller (attending a local concert).
= consent = approval　*허락*　*거부하다*　*분사구문*　*their parents*

면전에서 문 닫기 기법이 흔히 응용되는 것은 십 대들이 자기 부모에게 큰 요청(다른 도시에서 하는 콘서트에 참석하기)을 한 뒤 허락이 거부되면 그들에게 더 작은 것(지역 콘서트에 참석하기)을 요청하는 경우이다.

⑦ (❺) Having denied the larger request increases the likelihood that parents will acquiesce in the later, smaller request.
서술형　*동격 접속사*　*= allow = permit = consent to*

더 큰 요청을 거부한 것은 부모가 그 뒤의 더 작은 요청을 묵인할 가능성을 높인다.

* reciprocate: 화답하다 ** concession: 양보 *** acquiesce: 묵인하다

주요 어휘 및 유의어/반의어			
	단어	**의미**	**유의어/반의어**
□□□ 1	unreasonable	불합리한	= irrational, illogical
□□□ 2	turn down	거절하다	= deny, reject, refuse
□□□ 3	follow	이어지다	↔ precede
□□□ 4	outset	처음	= start, beginning
□□□ 5	reciprocity	호혜	= mutual benefit
□□□ 6	concession	양보	= compromise
□□□ 7	compel	강요하다	= force, oblige, impel
□□□ 8	reciprocate	화답하다	= requite, react to, respond to
□□□ 9	permission	허락	= consent, approval, assent
□□□ 10	acquiesce	묵인하다	= consent to, allow, permit
□□□ 11			

ⓢhorts Ⓕlow 제시된 [A], [B], [C]를 서론, 본론, 결론의 순서로 연결해보고, 단락별 내용의 흐름을 정리해보세요.

	서론 (① ~ ②)	본론 (③ ~ ⑤)	결론 (⑥ ~ ⑦)
	•	•	•
개요도	•	•	•
	[A] 글감 제시	[B] 사례 제시	[C] 분석 진행
	면전에서 문 닫기 기법에서는 크고 불합리한 제안 후, 작고 합리적인 요청을 내미는 것을 말한다.	십 대들이 큰 요청을 한 뒤 거부되면 더 작은 요청을 연달아 하는 상황을 떠올릴 수 있다.	호혜적 사회 규범 덕에 이 기법이 성공하는데, 마치 처음 요청을 포기함으로써 '양보'를 한 것처럼 보이기 때문이다.

ⓢhorts Ⓞverview 글의 〈주제 및 제목〉을 쓰시오.

주제	한글	면전에서 문 닫기 기법이 작동하는 방식
	영어	door-in-the-face / works / how / technique / the
	정답	
제목	한글	규범적 측면에서의 면전에서 문 닫기 기법
	영어	From / Technique / Door-In-The-Face / A / Perspective / The / Normative
	정답	

ⓢhorts Ⓓetails 글의 내용과 일치하면 T에, 일치하지 않으면 F에 동그라미 표기를 하세요.

① The door-in-the-face technique is a social influence method whereby a substantial and unreasonable request is first made, which is then rejected, and later followed by a smaller, more sensible request. 　[T / F]

② Individuals who use the door-in-the-face technique often give up on their smaller request when they don't get a positive response, making the recipient feel less compelled to reciprocate. 　[T / F]

③ The efficacy of this method may be attributed to the reciprocity social norm, which mandates that we should return the favor in the same manner as we receive it from others. 　[T / F]

ⓢhorts Ⓖrammar 각 문장에서 어법상 가장 적절한 것을 고르시오.

① In the door-in-the-face technique, a large, unreasonable request is made, [what / which] is turned down; this is followed by a smaller more reasonable request.

② (❶) People are more likely to [agree / agreeing] to this smaller second request when it is placed in the context of the more unreasonable request than if it [was / had been] placed at the outset.

③ (❷) The success of this technique may be related to the reciprocity social norm, the rule that we should pay back in kind what we receive from [other / others].

④ (❸) The person asking for our support or assistance, appears to [had made / have made] a concession by giving up their initial request, for a much smaller one.

⑤ (❹ As a result, we feel [compelling / compelled] to reciprocate and agree to the smaller request.)

⑥ A common application of door-in-the-face is when teens ask their parents for a large request (attending an out-of-town concert) and then when the permission is denied, [asks / asking / asked] them for something smaller (attending a local concert).

⑦ (❺) Having [denied / been denied] the larger request increases the likelihood that parents will acquiesce in the later, smaller request.

중심 소재 : 자본주의 체제에서의 기업의 책임								
글의 전개방식	통념과 반박	문제와 해결	연구·실험	비교·대조	예시	비유	시간적 흐름	스토리텔링	기타

① "Capitalism" is generally understood as a market-based, economic system governed by capital — that is, the wealth of an individual or an establishment accumulated by or employed in (its business activities.)

일반적으로 '자본주의'는 자본, 즉 사업 활동에 의해 축적되거나 그에 사용되는 개인이나 회사의 재산에 의해 지배되는 시장 기반의 경제 체제로 이해된다.

② Entrepreneurs and the institutions (they create) generate the capital with which businesses provide goods, services, and payments to workers.

기업가와 그들이 만드는 기관은 기업이 상품, 서비스, 노동자의 임금을 제공하는 데 사용하는 자본을 창출한다.

③ Defenders of capitalism argue that this system maximally distributes social freedoms and desirable resources, resulting in the best economic outcomes for everyone in society.

자본주의 옹호자들은 이 체제가 사회적 자유와 가치 있는 자원을 최대한 배분하여 사회의 모든 사람에게 최상의 경제적 결과를 낸다고 주장한다.

④ On this view, business's only social responsibilities are to maximize legally generated profits.

이러한 관점에서는, 기업의 유일한 사회적 책임은 합법적으로 창출되는 이윤을 최대화하는 것이다.

⑤ However, over the past several decades there has been a significant reaction against this view.

그러나 지난 수십 년간에 걸쳐 이 견해에 대한 상당한 반발이 있었다.

⑥ It is argued that businesses have responsibilities far beyond following the law and profit making.

기업은 법을 따르고 이윤을 창출하는 것을 훨씬 넘어서는 그 이상의 책임이 있다는 주장이 제기된다.

⑦ When society accepts capitalism, (this view holds) it need not also accept the view that economic freedom always has priority over competing conceptions of the collection and distribution of social goods, or of other responsibilities owed to employees, customers, society, and the environment.

이 견해가 주장하는 바는, 사회가 자본주의를 받아들일 때 경제적 자유가 사회적 재화의 축적과 분배, 혹은 직원, 고객, 사회, 그리고 환경에 빚진 여타의 책임이라는 대립하는 개념보다 항상 우선한다는 관점 또한 받아들일 필요는 없다는 것이다.

* entrepreneur: 기업가

주요 어휘 및 유의어/반의어		

	단어	의미	유의어/반의어
☐☐☐ 1	govern	지배하다	= rule, control, handle
☐☐☐ 2	establishment	회사	= organization, company, firm, institution
☐☐☐ 3	accumulate	축적하다	= amass, build up, increase
☐☐☐ 4	defender	옹호자	= advocate, supporter
☐☐☐ 5	result in	결과를 내다	= lead to, cause
☐☐☐ 6	maximize	최대화하다	↔ minimize
☐☐☐ 7	profit	이윤	= revenue, earnings
☐☐☐ 8	significant	상당한	= important, serious
☐☐☐ 9	against	~에 반대하여	↔ for
☐☐☐ 10	competing	대립하는	= conflicting, opposing
☐☐☐ 11			

Ⓢhorts Ⓕlow 제시된 [A], [B], [C]를 서론, 본론, 결론의 순서로 연결해보고, 단락별 내용의 흐름을 정리해보세요.

개요도	서론 (① ~ ②) ·	본론 (③ ~ ④) ·	결론 (⑤ ~ ⑦) ·
	·	·	·
	[A] 개념 소개	[B] 상반되는 견해 소개	[C] 견해 소개
	자본주의란 자본에 의해 운영되는 시장 기반 경제 체제로 이해된다.	사업은 단순히 법을 지켜 이윤을 만드는 것이 아니라, 특정 사회적 책임이 있다는 견해도 존재한다.	찬성론자들은 최상의 경제 결과가 모두에게 나온다는 점을 강조한다.

Ⓢhorts Ⓞverview 글의 〈주제 및 제목〉을 쓰시오.

주제	한글	자본주의를 둘러싼 상반된 관점들
	영어	perspectives / surrounding / capitalism / contrasting
	정답	
제목	한글	자본주의와 기업의 사회적 책임
	영어	Responsibilities / of / Capitalism / and / Businesses / Social
	정답	

Ⓢhorts Ⓓetails 글의 내용과 일치하면 T에, 일치하지 않으면 F에 동그라미 표기를 하세요.

① Proponents of capitalism contend that it offers the most effective distribution of social freedoms and resources, leading to the best possible economic outcomes for society as a whole. [T / F]

② The argument that the only social responsibility of a company maximizes legally generated profits is evaluated as complete so far. [T / F]

③ Society's acceptance of capitalism always implies a prioritization of economic freedom over all other social goods. [T / F]

Ⓢhorts Ⓖrammar 각 문장에서 어법상 가장 적절한 것을 고르시오.

① "Capitalism" is generally understood as a market-based, economic system [governing / governed] by capital — that is, the wealth of an individual or an establishment accumulated by or employed in its business activities.

② Entrepreneurs and the institutions they create [generate / generating] the capital [which / what / whose / with which] businesses provide goods, services, and payments to workers.

③ Defenders of capitalism argue that this system maximally distributes social freedoms and desirable resources, [results / resulting] in the best economic outcomes for everyone in society.

④ On this view, business's only social responsibilities are to maximize [legal / legally] generated profits.

⑤ However, over the past several decades there has been a significant reaction against this view.

⑥ It is argued [which / what / that] businesses have responsibilities far beyond following the law and profit making.

⑦ When society accepts capitalism, this view holds, it need not also [accept / accepted] the view that economic freedom always has priority over competing conceptions of the collection and distribution of social goods, or of other responsibilities owed to employees, customers, society, and the environment.

중심 소재 : 위기와 사회 변화의 관계								
글의 전개방식	통념과 반박	문제와 해결	연구·실험	비교·대조	예시	비유	시간적 흐름	스토리텔링	기타

주제문

= predicament
= plight

① The relationship between crisis and social change is a bit like the relationship between a rainstorm and a mudslide.

위기와 사회 변화의 관계는 호우와 진흙 사태의 관계와 다소 비슷하다.

rain　　　the mudslide　　　패러프레이징

② The rain doesn't give the mudslide its power — that comes from the weight of earth, built up over decades.

비가 진흙 사태에 그것의 힘을 가하는 것이 아니라, 그것은 수십 년 동안 쌓인 흙의 무게에서 비롯되는 것이다.

서술형

(to) = unloose = separate
= detach　　분사구문

③ What the rain can do is loosen things up, creating the conditions for change.

비가 '할 수' 있는 것은 상태를 느슨하게 만들어, 변화를 위한 여건을 만드는 것이다.

= settle　　　　　= deal with
= handle

④ Britain's post-Second World War settlement didn't solve the problems of the war: it addressed the pent-up problems of the 1930s, and its intellectual ingredients dated back further, to the opening years of the 1900s.

= suppressed = repressed
Britain's ~ settlement　합의, 협정　요소, 성분

영국의 제2차 세계 대전 이후 합의는 전쟁의 문제들을 해결한 것이 아니었다. 그것은 1930년대의 억눌려 있던 문제를 다루었고, 그것의 지적 요소들은 역사가 1900년대 초반까지 더 거슬러 올라갔다.

= cause = bring about
= result in　　목적격 관·대 (that)　서술형

⑤ Likewise, America's New Deal of the 1930s was triggered by the Great Depression, but the issues (it addressed) and the approaches (it applied) emerged decades before, in the progressive and populist movements of the 1890s and 1900s.

마찬가지로, 1930년대의 미국의 뉴딜 정책은 대공황에 의해 촉발되었지만, 그것이 다룬 문제와 그것이 사용한 접근 방식은 수십 년 전, 1890년대와 1900년대의 진보 운동과 인민주의 운동에서 나타났다.

서술형　　패러프레이징

강조 do

⑥ So, if the 2020 pandemic does lead to a radical social renewal, then the main elements of that renewal will be visible already today.

따라서 만약 2020년의 전 세계적인 유행병이 진정 급격한 사회 개선을 가져온다면, 그러면 그 개선의 주요 요소들은 오늘날 이미 눈에 보일 것이다.

개선, 재생

* pent-up: 억눌려 있는

주요 어휘 및 유의어/반의어			
	단어	**의미**	**유의어/반의어**
□□□ 1	crisis	위기	= plight, predicament
□□□ 2	loosen	느슨하게 하다	= detach, unloose, separate
□□□ 3	solve	해결하다	= settle
□□□ 4	address	다루다	= handle, deal with
□□□ 5	pent-up	억눌려 있는	= suppressed, repressed
□□□ 6	trigger	촉발하다	= cause, provoke, bring about
□□□ 7	lead to	초래하다	= result in, cause, bring about
□□□ 8			
□□□ 9			
□□□ 10			
□□□ 11			

⑤horts Ⓕlow 제시된 [A], [B], [C]를 서론, 본론, 결론의 순서로 연결해보고, 단락별 내용의 흐름을 정리해보세요.

	서론 (① ~ ③)	본론 (④ ~ ⑤)	결론 (⑥)
	•	•	•
개요도	• [A] 부연 설명 마찬가지로 2020년 판데믹 위기가 사회적 변화를 이끈다면, 그 사회적 변화의 구성요소는 이미 눈에 보일 것이다.	• [B] 주장의 집약적 제시 위기와 사회적 변화 사이의 관계는 호우와 진흙 사태의 관계와 비슷하다.	• [C] 사례 제시 영국의 제2차대전 후 합의와 뉴딜 정책은 모두 위기가 사회적 변화에 대한 여건을 만든다는 것을 보여준다.

⑤horts Ⓞverview 글의 <주제 및 제목>을 쓰시오.

주제	한글	위기가 사회 변화에 미치는 영향
	영어	on / influence / of / crisis / change / social / the
	정답	
제목	한글	위기가 사회 변화에 실제로 미치는 영향에 대한 통찰
	영어	For / On / Actually / An / Does / Insight / Social / Change / What / A / Crisis / A
	정답	

⑤horts Ⓓetails 글의 내용과 일치하면 T에, 일치하지 않으면 F에 동그라미 표기를 하세요.

①	The main elements of social renewal after the 2020 pandemic will only be visible after the pandemic ends.	[T / F]
②	The roots of many social and political movements can be traced back to earlier periods of history.	[T / F]
③	The New Deal and post-World War II settlement were entirely disconnected from some movements of the early 20th century.	[T / F]

⑤horts Ⓖrammar 각 문장에서 어법상 가장 적절한 것을 고르시오.

① The relationship between crisis and social change is a bit like the relationship between a rainstorm and a mudslide.

② The rain doesn't give the mudslide its power — that comes from the weight of earth, [building / built] up over decades.

③ What the rain can do [is / are / being] loosen things up, creating the conditions for change.

④ Britain's post-Second World War settlement didn't solve the problems of the war: it addressed the pent-up problems of the 1930s, and its intellectual ingredients dated back further, to the opening years of the 1900s.

⑤ Likewise, America's New Deal of the 1930s was triggered by the Great Depression, but the issues [it / they] addressed and the approaches it applied [emerging / emerged / were emerged] decades before, in the progressive and populist movements of the 1890s and 1900s.

⑥ So, if the 2020 pandemic does lead to a radical social renewal, then the main elements of that renewal will be [visibly / visible] already today.

중심 소재 : 농업 사회가 성장 둔화를 보인 이유								
글의 전개방식	통념과 반박	문제와 해결	연구·실험	비교·대조	예시	비유	시간적 흐름	스토리텔링	기타

an agricultural society

① The characteristics of an agricultural society//affected its long-run growth pattern prior to the Industrial Revolution, while self-sufficiency and land dependency//limited the motivation to increase the yield.

=before =ahead of
~이전에
=production =crop

농업 사회의 특징은 산업 혁명 이전에 그것의 장기적인 성장 패턴에 영향을 미친 한편, 자급자족과 토지 의존은 수확량을 증가시키려는 의욕을 제한했다.

의욕.욕구.동기

패러프레이징　서술형

② ❶ Even though some attempts//were made to reform agricultural production, the low level of technologies available//could not capitalize on the effect of those attempts.

reform(x)
=utilize =use

비록 농업 생산을 개혁하려는 몇차례의 시도가 있었지만, 가용할 수 있는 기술 수준이 낮아 그러한 시도의 효과를 이용할 수 없었다.

~를 이용하다
=insecurity
=difference = gap
서술형　패러프레이징

③ ❷ Moreover, inelasticity (in demand) instability (in supply) and price divergence//prevented the capital accumulation needed for reinvestment in agricultural technologies.

needing(x)

게다가, 수요의 비탄력성, 공급의 불안정성, 그리고 가격 격차는 농업 기술 재투자에 필요한 자본의 축적을 방해했다.

축적

서술형 =virtuous
so that

④ ❸ All of these factors//created a vicious circle such that agricultural production//could not boom.

이 모든 요인들이 악순환을 만들어 농업 생산은 크게 증가할 수 없었다.

⑤ ❹ Increasing agricultural production to feed a growing world population while at the same time conserving resources for future generations has led to a search for 'sustainable' agricultural methods.

증가하는 세계 인구에게 먹을 것을 제공하기 위해 농업 생산을 늘리는 한편, 동시에 미래 세대를 위한 자원을 보존하는 것은 '지속 가능한' 농법을 추구하게 만들었다.

보존하다

⑥ ❺ As a result, the agricultural society//showed a long-term decelerating growth pattern in history.

결과적으로, 농업 사회는 역사적으로 장기간 둔화하는 성장 패턴을 보였다.

* inelasticity: 비탄력성 ** divergence: 격차, 차이 *** decelerate: 둔화하다

	주요 어휘 및 유의어/반의어		
	단어	의미	유의어/반의어
□□□ 1	prior	이전의	= before, ahead of
□□□ 2	yield	수확량	= production, crop
□□□ 3	capitalize on	이용하다	= take advantage of, utilize, use
□□□ 4	instability	불안정성	= insecurity, unsteadiness
□□□ 5	divergence	격차	= difference, gap
□□□ 6	vicious	악성의	↔ virtuous
□□□ 7			
□□□ 8			
□□□ 9			
□□□ 10			
□□□ 11			

⑤horts Ⓕlow 제시된 [A], [B], [C]를 서론, 본론, 결론의 순서로 연결해보고, 단락별 내용의 흐름을 정리해보세요.

개요도	서론 (①)	본론 (② ~ ⑤)	결론 (⑥)
	•	•	•
	•	•	•
	[A] 글감 제시 농경 사회의 특성은 그것의 장기적 성장 패턴에 영향을 주었다.	[B] 분석 진행 낮은 수준의 기술, 수요의 비탄력성, 공급 불안정성 등은 자본의 축적을 막아 악순환을 만들었다.	[C] 논의 마무리 농경 사회는 장기적으로 둔화하는 성장 패턴을 보인다.

⑤horts Ⓞverview 글의 〈주제 및 제목〉을 쓰시오.

주제	한글	장기적인 성장을 방해하는 농업 사회의 특성
	영어	long-term / society / of / that / agricultural / characteristics / prevent / growth
	정답	
제목	한글	농업사회의 감속성장 패턴에 관한 분석
	영어	Pattern / of / Analysis / Society / Decelerated / Agricultural / on / Growth / An
	정답	

⑤horts Ⓓetails 글의 내용과 일치하면 T에, 일치하지 않으면 F에 동그라미 표기를 하세요.

① The long-term growth pattern of agricultural societies prior to the Industrial Revolution was decelerating. [T / F]

② Agricultural societies had a strong motivation to increase yield despite their self-sufficiency and land dependency. [T / F]

③ Agricultural technologies were highly advanced and therefore capital accumulation was not needed for reinvestment. [T / F]

⑤horts Ⓖrammar 각 문장에서 어법상 가장 적절한 것을 고르시오.

① The characteristics of an agricultural society affected its long-run growth pattern prior to the Industrial Revolution, [while / during] self-sufficiency and land dependency limited the motivation to increase the yield.

② ❶ Even though some attempts were [making / made] to reform agricultural production, the low level of technologies available could not capitalize on the effect of those attempts.

③ ❷ Moreover, inelasticity in demand, instability in supply, and price divergence prevented the capital accumulation needed for reinvestment in agricultural technologies.

④ ❸ All of these factors [created / were created] a vicious circle such that agricultural production could not boom.

⑤ ❹ As a result, the agricultural society showed a long-term decelerating growth pattern in history.

중심 소재 : 자존감이 건강에 미치는 영향								
글의 전개방식	통념과 반박	문제와 해결	연구·실험	비교·대조	예시	비유	시간적 흐름	스토리텔링	기타

주제문

= momentous
= astonishing = remarkable

① It//is evident that self-esteem//has a significant effect on health — both directly and indirectly.
자존감이 건강에 큰 영향을 미치는 것은 분명한데, 직접적으로든 간접적으로든 모두 그렇다.
자존감

② For instance, self-esteem//is typically considered a key feature of mental health and therefore worth pursuing in its own right.
worth -ing
: -ing 할 만한 가치가 있는
예를 들면, 자존감은 일반적으로 정신 건강의 주요 특징으로 여겨지므로 그 자체만으로 추구할 가치가 있다.

self-esteem
= enter into
= launch = start

③ It//may also have an indirect influence through its ❶ contribution to intentions to undertake healthy or unhealthy actions.
원인 제공
시도하다, 착수하다
그것은 또한 건강에 좋거나 건강에 좋지 않은 행동을 시도하려는 의도에 원인을 제공함으로써 간접적인 영향을 미칠 수도 있다.

목적 관.대

④ For instance, at a commonsense level, individuals (who respect and value themselves) will, [other things being equal,] seek to look after themselves by ❷ adopting courses of action (that prevent disease.)
equally(x) = try to = attempt to　them(x)
예를 들면, 상식적인 수준에서 자신을 존중하고 중시하는 사람은 다른 것이 같은 조건이라면, 질병을 막는 행동 방침을 채택함으로써 자신을 돌보려고 할 것이다.
by ~ing : ~함으로써

서술형
동격 접속사
↔ unwilling

⑤ Less obviously perhaps, there is//strong evidence (that people (enjoying high self-esteem) are less willing to tolerate dissonance and more likely to take rational action to ❸ reduce that dissonance, by, for example, rejecting unhealthy behaviour.
= incongruity
= refuse = deny
아마 덜 분명하기는 하겠지만, 높은 자존감을 누리는 사람은 부조화를 덜 용인하려 하고 그러한 부조화를 줄이기 위해, 예컨대 건강에 좋지 않은 행동을 거부함으로써, 이성적인 행동을 할 가능성이 더 크다는 강력한 증거가 있다.
용인하다, 참다

서술형
= comply

⑥ Those (having low self-esteem)//are more likely to ❹ ~~object~~ conform to interpersonal pressures than those (enjoying high self-esteem) with unfortunate consequences when such social pressure//results in 'unhealthy behaviour'.
= lead to = cause
자존감이 낮은 사람들은 높은 자존감을 누리는 사람들보다 대인 관계에서 오는 압박에 반대하여 (→ 순응하여) 그러한 사회적 압박이 '건강에 좋지 않은 행동'으로 귀결될 때의 불행한 결과를 맞이할 가능성이 더 크다.

= give in
= submit

⑦ In terms of empowerment, though, any unthinking yielding to social pressure//would be considered ❺ unhealthy!
하지만 자율권의 측면에서는 사회적 압박에 경솔하게 굴복하는 것은 무엇이든 건강에 좋지 않은 것으로 여겨질 것이다!
경솔한, 분별없는

* dissonance: 부조화 ** empowerment: 자율권

주요 어휘 및 유의어/반의어			
	단어	의미	유의어/반의어
□□□ 1	significant	큰, 주목할 만한	= astonishing, remarkable, momentous
□□□ 2	undertake	시도하다	= launch, start, enter into
□□□ 3	seek to	~하려고 하다	= try to, attempt to, struggle to
□□□ 4	willing	기꺼이 하는	↔ reluctant, unwilling
□□□ 5	dissonance	부조화	= incongruity, discrepancy
□□□ 6	reject	거부하다	= refuse, deny
□□□ 7	conform	순응하다	= comply
□□□ 8	result in	(결과를) 낳다	= lead to, cause, bring about
□□□ 9	yield	굴복하다	= submit, give in
□□□ 10			
□□□ 11			

⑤horts ⑤low 제시된 [A], [B], [C]를 서론, 본론, 결론의 순서로 연결해보고, 단락별 내용의 흐름을 정리해보세요.

개요도	서론 (①)	본론 (② ~ ④)	결론 (⑤ ~ ⑦)
	•	•	•
	•	•	•
	[A] 근거 확장	[B] 주장 제시	[C] 근거 제시
	높은 자존감을 가진 사람은 부조화를 줄이기 위해 이성적인 행동을 할 가능성이 더 크다.	자존감이 건강에 큰 영향을 미치는 것은 분명한데, 직/간접적으로 모두 그렇다.	자존감은 정신 건강의 주요 특징이므로 그 자체만으로 건강과 관련 있다.

⑤horts ⑩verview 글의 <주제 및 제목>을 쓰시오.

주제	한글	건강에 대한 자존감의 영향
	영어	health / self-esteem / the / on / influence / of
	정답	
제목	한글	자존감이 건강에 미치는 직간접적 영향
	영어	of / on / Indirect / Direct / Health / and / Effects / Self-Esteem
	정답	

⑤horts ⑩etails 글의 내용과 일치하면 T에, 일치하지 않으면 F에 동그라미 표기를 하세요.

① Individuals with low self-esteem are more likely to resist social pressures and engage in healthy behavior. [T / F]

② People with high self-esteem are less tolerant of dissonance and more likely to take rational action to minimize it. [T / F]

③ The more you respect and value yourself, the less likely you are to take action to prevent disease. [T / F]

⑤horts ⑥rammar 각 문장에서 어법상 가장 적절한 것을 고르시오.

① It is evident [**which** / **what** / **that**] self-esteem has a significant effect on health — both directly and indirectly.

② For instance, self-esteem is [**typical** / **typically**] considered a key feature of mental health and therefore worth [**pursuing** / **pursue** / **to pursue**] in its own right.

③ It may also have an indirect influence through [**its** / **their**] contribution to intentions to undertake healthy or unhealthy actions.

④ For instance, at a commonsense level, individuals who respect and value themselves will, other things [**are** / **being**] equal, seek to look after themselves by adopting courses of action that prevent disease.

⑤ Less obviously perhaps, there is strong evidence that people enjoying high self-esteem are less willing to [**tolerate** / **tolerating**] dissonance and more likely to take rational action to reduce that dissonance, by, for example, rejecting unhealthy behaviour.

⑥ Those having low self-esteem are more likely to conform to interpersonal pressures than those enjoying high self-esteem with unfortunate consequences when such social pressure results [**from** / **in**] 'unhealthy behaviour'.

⑦ In terms of empowerment, [**despite** / **though**], any unthinking yielding to social pressure would be considered unhealthy!

중심 소재 : 사춘기에 일어나는 뇌의 변화								
글의 전개방식	통념과 반박	문제와 해결	연구·실험	비교·대조	예시	비유	시간적 흐름	스토리텔링	기타

① In recent years, researchers//have been trying to understand the changes that occur in the brain during adolescence.
= strive to = seek to = struggle to　주격 관·대
최근 몇 년 동안, 연구자들은 사춘기에 뇌에서 일어나는 변화를 알기 위해 노력해 오고 있다.

주제문
② Structural brain imaging studies over the past decade//have challenged the belief that structural brain development//ends in early childhood, revealing that changes//occur through early adulthood.
= tackle = dispute = question　접속사　=unveil = show
구조의·구조적인
지난 십 년에 걸친 뇌 구조 영상 연구는 뇌 구조 발달이 유아기에 끝난다는 믿음에 이의를 제기하며 변화는 성인기 초기 내내 일어난다는 것을 밝혔다.

③ In addition, these studies//provide an insight into the biological basis for understanding adolescent thinking and behavior.
통찰·이해
그뿐만 아니라, 이러한 연구들은 사춘기의 사고와 행동을 이해하기 위한 생물학적 근거에 대한 통찰을 제공한다.

④ For example, the ventromedial prefrontal cortex of the brain//is responsible for evaluating risk and reward to help guide the person to make a decision.
서술형
예를 들면, 뇌의 복내측 시상하핵 전전두엽 피질은 사람이 결정을 내리도록 이끄는 데 도움이 되도록 위험과 보상을 평가하는 것을 담당한다.

⑤ Imaging studies//have shown that this part of the brain//is the last to mature in adolescents, which //supports behavioral studies that//show adolescents take greater risks than adults in activities such as substance abuse.
접속사　서술형 주격 관·대　주격 관·대　발달하다 (do) take
영상 연구는 뇌의 이 부분이 청소년에게 있어서 가장 마지막으로 발달한다는 것을 보여 주었는데, 이것은 성인보다 청소년이 약물 남용과 같은 행동에서 더 큰 위험을 감수한다는 것을 보여 주는 행동 연구들을 뒷받침한다.

⑥ Adolescents//tend to engage in more reckless behaviors because the area of the brain that assesses risk and benefits//has not completely developed yet.
= take part in = be involved in = careless　패러프레이징　주격 관·대　평가하다
청소년은 더 무모한 행동을 하는 경향이 있는데, 위험과 이득을 평가하는 뇌의 영역이 아직 완전히 발달하지는 않았기 때문이다.

⑦ These findings, (along with other studies examining the maturation of other regions of the prefrontal cortex during adolescence)//suggest that the spontaneity, short-sightedness, and risk-taking behaviors (associated with adolescence) could be partially biological in nature.
another(x)　examined(x)　=progress =development =growth　접속사　=actually =in reality
사춘기의 전전두엽 피질의 다른 부위의 발달을 조사하는 다른 연구와 함께, 이러한 연구 결과는 청소년기와 연관된 즉흥성, 짧은 생각 및 모험을 감수하는 행동이 사실상 부분적으로 생물학적일 수 있다는 것을 시사한다.

* ventromedial prefrontal cortex: 복내측시상하핵 전전두엽 피질
** reckless: 무모한. 무분별한 *** spontaneity: 즉흥성

주요 어휘 및 유의어/반의어			
	단어	의미	유의어/반의어
□□□ 1	try to	노력하다	= struggle to, strive to, seek to
□□□ 2	challenge	이의를 제기하다	= dispute, question, tackle
□□□ 3	reveal	밝히다	= unveil, show
□□□ 4	engage in	~에 관여하다	= be involved in, take part in
□□□ 5	reckless	무모한	= careless
□□□ 6	maturation	발달	= development, growth, progress
□□□ 7	in nature	사실상	= actually, in reality
□□□ 8			
□□□ 9			
□□□ 10			
□□□ 11			

⑤horts ⒡low 제시된 [A], [B], [C]를 서론, 본론, 결론의 순서로 연결해보고, 단락별 내용의 흐름을 정리해보세요.

	서론 (① ~ ②)	본론 (③ ~ ⑥)	결론 (⑦)
	•	•	•
개요도	• [A] 글감 제시 뇌 구조 영상 연구를 통해 뇌 구조 발달이 성인기 초기 내내 일어난다는 것을 밝혔다.	• [B] 함의 제시 연구 결과는 즉흥성이 사실상 부분적으로 생물학적인 이유가 있음을 시사한다.	• [C] 연구 소개 복내측시상하핵 전전도엽 피질이 덜 발달하여, 청소년은 더 무모하고 위험한 행동을 한다는 연구가 있다.

⑤horts ⓞverview 글의 <주제 및 제목>을 쓰시오.

주제	한글	뇌의 발달 구조에 대한 분석
	영어	analysis / the / developmental / the / brain / structure / of / an / on
	정답	
제목	한글	청소년들이 위험을 감수하는 이유에 대한 생물학적 접근
	영어	Biological / Risk-Takers / Adolescents / Why / Are / to / Approach
	정답	

⑤horts ⒟etails 글의 내용과 일치하면 T에, 일치하지 않으면 F에 동그라미 표기를 하세요.

① Imaging studies have demonstrated that the prefrontal cortex continues to develop into early adulthood, suggesting that young adults may not yet have fully matured decision-making abilities. [T / F]

② Studies have found that adolescents' risk-taking behavior can be attributed solely to environmental factors, such as peer pressure and social norms. [T / F]

⑤horts ⒢rammar 각 문장에서 어법상 가장 적절한 것을 고르시오.

① In recent years, researchers have been trying to understand the changes [what / that] occur in the brain during adolescence.

② Structural brain imaging studies over the past decade have [challenged / been challenged] the belief that structural brain development ends in early childhood, [revealing / revealed / reveals] that changes occur through early adulthood.

③ In addition, these studies provide an insight into the biological basis for understanding adolescent thinking and behavior.

④ For example, the ventromedial prefrontal cortex of the brain is responsible for evaluating risk and reward to help [guide / guided] the person to make a decision.

⑤ Imaging studies have [shown / been shown] that this part of the brain is the last to mature in adolescents, [what / when / which / that] supports behavioral studies that show adolescents take greater risks than adults in activities such as substance abuse.

⑥ Adolescents tend to engage in more reckless behaviors [because / because of] the area of the brain that assesses risk and benefits has not completely developed yet.

⑦ These findings, along with other studies examining the maturation of other regions of the prefrontal cortex during adolescence, suggest that the spontaneity, short-sightedness, and risk-taking behaviors associated with adolescence could be partially [biological / biologically] in nature.

중심 소재 : 통제 대상에서 벗어난 건강 보조 식품

글의 전개방식	통념과 반박	문제와 해결	연구·실험	비교·대조	예시	비유	시간적 흐름	스토리텔링	기타

서술형 be subject to N

분사구문 (=, which incl

① Both prescription and over-the-counter drugs//are subject to strict control by the FDA, including the
=requisite
regulation of manufacturing processes, specific requirements for the demonstration of safety and
=effectiveness　　　　　　　　　　　제고
efficacy, as well as well-defined limits on advertising and labeling claims.
입증,증명

처방이 필요한 약과 처방전 없이 살 수 있는 약 모두 FDA의 엄격한 통제를 받는데, 광고와 라벨의 설명 문구에 대한 명확한 제한과 아울러,
제조 과정의 규제, 안전과 효능의 입증에 대한 특정 요건이 포함된다.

B as well as A　　명확한
=not only A but also B　　=guarantee =promise =conviction

② (C) Such controls//provide assurances to consumers and health care professionals about the quality of
확신
the products and contribute to their acceptance as "legitimate" treatments.

(C) 그러한 통제는 소비자와 보건 전문가에게 제품의 질에 대한 확신을 주며, '적법한' 치료제로 그것을 받아들이는 데 기여한다.
= the products

주제문

③ The exemption of dietary supplements from these specific regulatory controls//may impact their
=valid =justifiable =authentic
consideration as "legitimate".

건강 보조 식품에서 이러한 특정한 규제적 통제를 면제하는 것은 그것이 '적법한' 것으로 여겨지는 데 영향을 줄 수도 있다.

접속사

④ (B) If health care professionals//feel that the quality of dietary supplement products//is lacking, and if
they//consider dietary supplements outside the scope of "prevailing" medical pharmacy practice, then
지배적인
physicians and pharmacists//will have a low level of confidence in recommending these products to
=suggest
their patients for fear of legal action.

(B) 보건 전문가가 건강 보조 식품의 질이 부족하다고 느낀다면, 그리고 그들이 건강 보조 식품을 '널리 행하여지는' 의료나 약제 업무 영역을
벗어난다고 간주한다면, 그러면 의사와 약사는 소송을 두려워해서 이러한 제품을 자신의 환자에게 추천하는 데 낮은 수준의 확신을 가질 것이다.

서술형

⑤ (A) Physicians and pharmacists//cannot, however, separate themselves from the use of dietary supplements.

(A) 그러나 의사와 약사는 건강 보조 식품의 사용에서 자신을 떼어 놓고 생각할 수 없다.

⑥ With more than 29,000 dietary supplements on the market, consumers//have broad access to and are
using these products.

29,000개가 넘는 건강 보조 식품이 시장에 나와 있으며, 소비자들은 이러한 제품에 폭넓게 접근할 수 있고 이용하고 있다.

접속사 =roughly

⑦ In fact, a survey of consumers//has suggested that approximately 42% of American consumers//were
대략　　 used(x)
using complementary and alternative therapies, with 24% of consumers using plant-based dietary
보완적인　　　　　　부대상황 분사구문
supplements on a regular basis. 서술형

사실, 소비자 설문 조사는 미국 소비자의 대략 42퍼센트가 보완 요법과 대체 요법을 이용하고 있고, 소비자의 24퍼센트는 정기적으로 식물성
건강 보조 식품을 이용하고 있다는 것을 보여주었다.

* efficacy: 효능, 효험 ** legitimate: 적법한. 정당한 *** exemption: 면제

주요 어휘 및 유의어/반의어			
	단어	의미	유의어/반의어
☐☐☐ 1	requirement	요건	= requisite
☐☐☐ 2	efficacy	효능	= effectiveness
☐☐☐ 3	well-defined	명확한	↔ ill-defined
☐☐☐ 4	assurance	확신, 보장	= guarantee, promise, conviction
☐☐☐ 5	legitimate	적법한	= valid, justifiable, authentic
☐☐☐ 6	exemption	면제	= exception, exclusion
☐☐☐ 7	prevailing	널리 행해지는	= widespread, predominant
☐☐☐ 8	recommend	추천하다	= suggest
☐☐☐ 9	broad	폭넓은	= wide
☐☐☐ 10	approximately	대략	= roughly
☐☐☐ 11			

⑤horts Ⓕlow 제시된 [A], [B], [C]를 서론, 본론, 결론의 순서로 연결해보고, 단락별 내용의 흐름을 정리해보세요.

	서론 (① ~ ②) •	본론 (③ ~ ④) •	결론 (⑤ ~ ⑦) •
개요도	• [A] 부연 설명 의사와 약사는 건강 보조 식품과 떼어낼 수 없고, 시중에 많은 종류의 건강 보조 식품과 소비자가 있다.	• [B] 문제 제기 건강 보조 식품에서 특정 규제를 면제하는 것은 적법성 문제에 영향을 줄 수 있다.	• [C] 배경 제시 의약품은 모두 FDA의 엄격한 통제를 받는데, 제조 과정은 물론 광고나 설명 문구 등 전반을 포함한다.

⑤horts Ⓞverview 글의 〈주제 및 제목〉을 쓰시오.

주제	한글	규제를 벗어난 건강 보조 식품
	영어	of / out / regulatory / supplements / dietary / control
	정답	
제목	한글	건강보조식품에 대한 확고한 규제 부재의 문제화
	영어	Absence / Problematizing / Dietary / of / Regulation / on / Firm / Supplements / The
	정답	

⑤horts Ⓓetails 글의 내용과 일치하면 T에, 일치하지 않으면 F에 동그라미 표기를 하세요.

① Healthcare professionals may have a low level of confidence in recommending dietary supplements to their patients due to the lack of regulatory controls.　[T / F]

② Dietary supplements are subject to more rigorous regulatory controls than prescription and over-the-counter drugs.　[T / F]

⑤horts Ⓖrammar 각 문장에서 어법상 가장 적절한 것을 고르시오.

① Both prescription and over-the-counter drugs are subject to strict control by the FDA, [including / includes] the regulation of manufacturing processes, specific requirements for the demonstration of safety and efficacy, as well as well-defined limits on advertising and labeling claims.

② (C) Such controls provide assurances to consumers and health care professionals about the quality of the products and contribute to their acceptance as "legitimate" treatments.

③ The exemption of dietary supplements from these specific regulatory controls may impact their consideration as "legitimate".

④ (B) If health care professionals feel that the quality of dietary supplement products [is / are / being] lacking, and if they consider dietary supplements outside the scope of "prevailing" medical or pharmacy practice, then physicians and pharmacists will have a low level of confidence in recommending these products to their patients for fear of legal action.

⑤ (A) Physicians and pharmacists cannot, however, separate [them / themselves] from the use of dietary supplements.

⑥ With more than 29,000 dietary supplements on the market, consumers have broad access to and are [using / used] these products.

⑦ In fact, a survey of consumers has suggested that approximately 42% of American consumers [being / were] using complementary and alternative therapies, with 24% of consumers using plant-based dietary supplements on a regular basis.

memo

Part II
컴팩트

[1] 밑줄에 알맞은 어휘를 채우며, [대괄호] 안에서 알맞은 표현을 고르고 문법 출제의도를 쓰세요. (각 3점씩 20문제, 총 60점)

① Leo Lionni, an internationally 1) [knowing / known] designer, 2) i_____, and graphic artist, 3) [being / was] born in Holland and lived in Italy 4) [until / during] he came to the United States in 1939.
국제적으로 알려진 디자이너이자 삽화가이자 그래픽 아티스트였던 Leo Lionni는 네덜란드에서 태어나 1939년 미국에 올 때까지 이탈리아에서 살았다.

② As a little boy, he would go into the museums in Amsterdam, and that's 5) [what / that / how] he 6) [taught / was taught] himself how to draw.
어린 소년이었을 때 그는 암스테르담의 박물관에 들어가곤 했는데, 그것이 그가 그림 그리는 법을 독학한 방법이다.

③ He got into writing and illustrating children's books almost by 7) a_____.
그는 거의 우연히 아동 도서를 쓰고 그것에 삽화를 그리게 되었다.

④ Lionni tore out bits of paper from a magazine and used 8) [it / them] as characters and made up a story to 9) e_____ his grandchildren on a train ride.
Lionni는 기차를 타고 가면서 손주들을 즐겁게 하기 위해 잡지에서 종잇조각들을 뜯어내어 그것을 캐릭터로 사용하고 이야기를 구성했다.

⑤ This story became 10) [that / what] we now 11) [know / knowing] as the children's book 12) [titling / titled] Little Blue and Little Yellow.
이 이야기가 우리가 현재 Little Blue and Little Yellow라는 제목의 아동 도서로 알고 있는 것이 되었다.

⑥ He became the first children's author/ illustrator to 13) [use / using] 14) c_____ as the main 15) m_____ for his illustrations.
그는 자신의 삽화의 주요 표현 수단으로 콜라주를 사용한 최초의 아동 도서 작가이자 삽화가가 되었다.

⑦ Lionni wrote and illustrated 16) [more / less] than 40 children's books.
Lionni는 40권이 넘는 아동 도서를 쓰고 삽화를 그렸다.

⑧ In 1982, Lionni was 17) [diagnosing / diagnosed] with Parkinson's 18) d_____, but he kept 19) [to work / worked / working] in drawing, illustrating and teaching.
1982년, Lionni는 파킨슨병을 진단받았지만, 그는 그리기, 삽화 그리기, 그리고 가르치는 일을 계속했다.

⑨ He 20) p_____ed away in October 1999 in Italy.
그는 1999년 10월 이탈리아에서 사망했다.

글의 전개방식	통념과 반박	문제와 해결	연구·실험	비교·대조	예시	비유	시간적 흐름	스토리텔링	기타

	서론	본론	결론
개요도		storytelling	

[2] 우리말과 일치하도록 주어진 단어를 바르게 배열하여 <주제 및 제목>을 쓰시오. (각 10점씩 2문제, 총 20점)

한글	
영어	
정답	storytelling
한글	
영어	
정답	

[3] 위 지문에 있는 단어만을 활용하여 다음 <요약문>을 완성하시오(어형 변형 가능). (총 20점)

요약문 없음

[1] 밑줄에 알맞은 어휘를 채우며, [대괄호] 안에서 알맞은 표현을 고르고 문법 출제의도를 쓰세요. (각 3점씩 20문제, 총 60점)

① Thomas Jefferson's knowledge of and 1) p_____ for all things 2) a_____ 3) [were / being] truly 4) e_____.
농업적인 모든 것에 대한 Thomas Jefferson의 지식과 열정은 정말 대단했다.

② 5) [Driving / Driven] by a desire to see the South freed from its 6) r_____ on cotton, he was always on the lookout for crops 7) [what / that] could replace 8) [it / them].
면화에 대한 의존에서 해방되는 (미국) 남부를 보고 싶은 욕망에 이끌려, 그는 늘 그것을 대체할 수 있는 농작물을 찾고 있었다.

③ While touring the south of France in 1787, Jefferson discovered 9) [what / which / that] Italian rice was preferred 10) [to / than] the American import grown in the Carolinas.
1787년에 프랑스 남부 지역을 여행하던 중, Jefferson은 이탈리아 쌀이 Carolina의 두 주(South Carolina 와 North Carolina)에서 재배되는 미국산 수입품보다 더 선호된다는 것을 발견했다.

④ Intent on discovering why this might 11) [do / be] so, he took a 12) d_____ into the Italian region of Lombardy on a mission of rice reconnaissance (a journey that, because it required crossing the Alps, was 13) [extreme / extremely] dangerous at the time).
이것이 왜 그런지 밝히려는 일념으로, 그는 (알프스산맥을 넘어야 했기 때문에, 그 당시 매우 위험했던 여정인) 쌀 정찰 임무를 띠고 이탈리아 Lombardy 지역으로 우회해서 갔다.

⑤ There he discovered 14) [which / what / that] the good folks of Lombardy were growing a 15) [superior / inferior] strain of crop — 16) [whose / which / what] export for planting outside of Italy was a crime 17) p_____ by death.
그곳에서 그는 Lombardy의 선량한 사람들이 우수한 품종의 농작물을 재배하고 있고, 이탈리아 이외의 지역에서 재배하기 위한 수출은 사형에 처할 수 있는 범죄라는 것을 알게 되었다.

⑥ Undaunted, Jefferson sent a small packet of the rice grain to his good friend James Madison and members of the South Carolina 18) d_____.
굴하지 않고 Jefferson은 자신의 친한 친구 James Madison과 South Carolina 대표단원들에게 작은 벼 낟알 꾸러미를 보냈다.

⑦ Later, he 19) [stuffed / was stuffed] his pockets with some of the rice grains, and "walked it" out of the country.
나중에 그는 자신의 주머니에 얼마간의 벼 낟알을 채워 그 나라로부터 '그것을 멋대로 가져갔다'.

⑧ The rice is 20) [growing / grown] in parts of the United States to this day.
그 벼는 오늘날까지도 미국의 일부 지역에서 재배되고 있다.

* reconnaissance: 정찰 ** strain: 품종 *** undaunted: 굴하지 않는

글의 전개방식	통념과 반박	문제와 해결	연구·실험	비교·대조	예시	비유	시간적 흐름	스토리텔링	기타

개요도	서론		본론	결론
	글감 제시		서사 전개	서사 종결
	Jefferson의 농업에 대한 지식과 열정은 실로 대단했다.		남프랑스를 여행하며 그는 캐롤리나에서 자라는 미국 쌀보다 이탈리아산 쌀이 선호되는 것을 발견했다.	그는 처벌의 위험을 무릅쓰고 쌀을 반출했고, 지금도 미국에서 재배된다.

[2] 우리말과 일치하도록 주어진 단어를 바르게 배열하여 〈주제 및 제목〉을 쓰시오. (각 10점씩 2문제, 총 20점)

한글	Jefferson과 이탈리아 쌀 이야기
영어	of / story / the / Italian / rice / and / Jefferson
정답	
한글	이탈리아 쌀을 위한 Jefferson의 노력
영어	for / Italian / Rice / Jefferson's / Efforts
정답	

[3] 위 지문에 있는 단어만을 활용하여 다음 〈요약문〉을 완성하시오(어형 변형 가능). (총 20점)

By introducing Italian rice to his home country, Thomas Jefferson ran the risk of facing the _____ penalty in order to _____ a better strain.

[1] 밑줄에 알맞은 어휘를 채우며, [대괄호] 안에서 알맞은 표현을 고르고 문법 출제의도를 쓰세요. (각 3점씩 20문제, 총 60점)

① It's the late 1800s. ② Anesthesia has just 1) [introduced / been introduced].
1800년대 후반이다. 마취법이 막 도입되었다.

③ Surgeries are on the 2) [rise / fall], but a disturbing number of patients are dying 3) [because / due to] 4) i_____.
수술은 증가 추세이지만, 충격적인 수의 환자들이 감염으로 사망하고 있다.

④ Joseph Lister is determined 5) [figuring / to figure] out why and 6) [that / what] can be done about 7) [it / them].
Joseph Lister는 그 원인과 대처 방안을 알아내기로 결심한다.

⑤ (C) After much research and thought, he concludes that Pasteur's 8) c_____ germ theory 9) [holds / holding] the key to the mystery.
(C) 많은 연구와 생각 끝에, 그는 논란이 많은 Pasteur의 세균설이 미스터리의 열쇠를 쥐고 있다고 결론 내린다.

⑥ Killing germs in wounds with heat isn't an option, however — a completely new method is 10) [requiring / required].
그러나 열로 상처의 세균을 죽이는 것은 선택 사항이 아니라서 완전히 새로운 방법이 필요하다.

⑦ (B) Lister guesses 11) [which / what / that] there may be a chemical solution, and later that year, he reads in a newspaper that the treatment of 12) s_____ with a 13) c_____ called carbolic acid reduced the 14) i_____ of disease among the people and cattle of a nearby small English town.
(B) Lister는 화학적 해결책이 있을 수도 있다고 추측하고, 그해 말, 석탄산이라고 불리는 화학 물질로 하수를 처리한 것이 근처의 작은 영국 마을의 사람들과 소들 사이에서 질병 발생률을 감소시켰다는 것을 신문에서 읽는다.

⑧ Lister follows the lead and, in 1865, develops a 15) [successful / successive] method of applying carbolic acid to wounds to prevent infection.
Lister는 그 선례를 따라 1865년에 감염을 막기 위해 상처에 석탄산을 바르는 성공적인 방법을 개발한다.

⑨ (A) He continues to work along this line and establishes antisepsis as a basic 16) [principal / principle] of surgery.
(A) 그는 이 계통으로 계속 연구하여 소독을 수술의 기본 원칙으로 확립한다.

⑩ Thanks to his discoveries and 17) i_____s, amputations become 18) [more / less] frequent, deaths due to infection drop 19) [sharp / sharply], and new surgeries previously considered impossible 20) [being / are being] routinely planned and executed.
그의 발견과 혁신 덕분에, 절단 수술의 횟수가 줄어들고, 감염으로 인한 사망이 급격히 감소하며, 이전에는 불가능하다고 여겨졌던 새로운 수술들이 일상적으로 계획되고 실행되고 있다.

* anesthesia: 마취(법) ** antisepsis: 소독(법) *** amputation: 절단 (수술)

글의 전개방식	통념과 반박	문제와 해결	연구·실험	비교·대조	예시	비유	시간적 흐름	스토리텔링	기타

개요도	서론		본론		결론	
	배경 제시		논의 전개		결과 소개	
	마취법이 막 도입된 1800년대 후반 감염으로 죽는 환자가 많았고, Lister는 이유와 방안을 고민했다.		그는 석탄산이라는 화학 물질의 쓰임을 확인하고, 이를 활용하여 상처의 감염을 막는 방법을 개발했다.		덕분에 감염으로 인한 사망은 급격히 줄었고, 과거 불가능하다고 생각한 수술이 진행되었다.	

[2] 우리말과 일치하도록 주어진 단어를 바르게 배열하여 〈주제 및 제목〉을 쓰시오. (각 10점씩 2문제, 총 20점)

한글	수술을 위해 석탄산을 사용하는 방법의 개발
영어	surgeries / carbolic / for / acid / method / applying / of / a / developing
정답	
한글	소독법에 석탄산을 사용하는 것에 대한 Joseph Lister의 통찰
영어	Insight / Lister's / for / Antisepsis / Carbolic / Into / Acid / Joseph / Using
정답	

[3] 위 지문에 있는 단어만을 활용하여 다음 〈요약문〉을 완성하시오(어형 변형 가능). (총 20점)

Since many people were dying due to _____, Joseph Lister came up with an _____ idea of using carbolic acid to establish antisepsis.

[1] 밑줄에 알맞은 어휘를 채우며, [대괄호] 안에서 알맞은 표현을 고르고 문법 출제의도를 쓰세요. (각 3점씩 20문제, 총 60점)

① **1)** [While / During] both history and geography could serve to develop **2)** n_____ sentiments, the relative position of these two subjects in the educational system largely came to depend on the degree **3)** [to which / which / what] either seemed more **4)** [useful / usefully] in building up the idea of a national identity.

역사학과 지리학 모두 국가주의적 정서를 발달시키는 데 도움이 될 수 있었지만, 교육 제도에서 이 두 과목의 상대적 위치는 국가 정체성의 개념을 형성하는 데 어느 쪽이 더 유용해 보이는지의 정도에 따라 대체로 달라지게 되었다.

② In Germany, with its long history of shifting borders and **5)** d_____s into small states, geographical patterns **6)** [associating / associated] with the German-speaking lands seemed very significant, and so geography was seen as very **7)** [important / importantly].

독일에서는, 변경되는 국경과 소국으로 분할되는 오랜 역사를 가지고 있어, 독일어권 영토와 관련된 지리적 양상이 매우 중요해 보였고, 따라서 지리학이 매우 중요하게 여겨졌다.

③ Norway, **8)** [besides / likewise / on the other hand], **9)** [had / was] developed its educational system during the union of the crowns with Sweden (1814-1905) and it had no disputed borders.

반면, 노르웨이는 스웨덴과의 왕위 통합 기간(1814~1905년) 동안 교육 제도를 발전시켜 왔고, 분쟁 중인 국경이 없었다.

④ Under these **10)** c_____s, Norway's national awakening was **11)** [fostering / fostered] by teaching about the **12)** g_____ history of Viking times and about the precious liberal **13)** c_____ of 1814.

이러한 상황에서 노르웨이의 국가적 자각은 바이킹 시대의 영광스러운 역사와 1814년의 고귀한 자유 헌법에 대한 교육에 의해 촉진되었다.

⑤ Hence, history **14)** p_____d over geography.

그리하여 역사학이 지리학보다 우위를 차지했다.

⑥ Finland, **15)** [however / furthermore / for example], which **16)** [was / had] also experienced a union of crowns (in this case with Tsarist Russia), **17)** [possessed / lacked] a clearly discernible glorious past and so geography developed as a relatively **18)** [more / less] important subject.

그러나 마찬가지로 왕위 통합(이 경우에는 제정 러시아와의)을 경험했었던 핀란드는 명백하게 뚜렷한 영광스러운 과거를 가지고 있었고 (→ 가지지 못했고), 그래서 지리학이 상대적으로 더 중요한 과목으로 발전했다.

⑦ A **19)** p_____ research work of great political importance in the Finnish liberation process, the Atlas of Finland, stressed the **20)** u_____ of the Finnish lands.

핀란드의 해방 과정에서 정치적으로 매우 중요한 선구적 연구 저술인 Atlas of Finland는 핀란드 땅의 고유성을 강조했다.

* Tsarist Russia: 제정 러시아 ** discernible: 뚜렷한, 분간할 만한

글의 전개방식	통념과 반박	문제와 해결	연구·실험	비교·대조	예시	비유	시간적 흐름	스토리텔링	기타

	서론	본론	결론
	글감의 집약적 제시	사례 제시	논의 확장
개요도	역사와 지리 모두 국가주의적 정서를 개발하지만, 교육에서 둘의 상대적 위치는 유용성에 달려있다.	독일의 경우 지리가, 노르웨이의 경우에는 역사가 국가주의적 정서 형성에 강조된다.	핀란드는 노르웨이와 유사한 역사를 가졌지만 지리가 교육에서 강조되는 특이한 경우가 있다.

[2] 우리말과 일치하도록 주어진 단어를 바르게 배열하여 〈주제 및 제목〉을 쓰시오. (각 10점씩 2문제, 총 20점)

한글	국가 정체성을 발전시키기 위한 교육에서 역사와 지리의 상대적 위치
영어	relative / history / of / and / developing / geography / in / education / identity / for / position / national
정답	
한글	민족주의 정서 형성을 위한 역사와 지리에 대한 강조의 지역적 차이 탐색
영어	History / Regional / Differences / for / Building / Exploring / Emphasis / of / on / Geography / Nationalistic / and / Sentiment
정답	

[3] 위 지문에 있는 단어만을 활용하여 다음 〈요약문〉을 완성하시오(어형 변형 가능). (총 20점)

Both history and geography in the _____ system serve to build nationalistic _____, whose relative position may change according to their _____.

[1] 밑줄에 알맞은 어휘를 채우며, [대괄호] 안에서 알맞은 표현을 고르고 문법 출제의도를 쓰세요. (각 3점씩 20문제, 총 60점)

① One **1)** d_____ of ethical theory that needs mentioning **2)** [**is / are / being**] the issue of **3)** a_____ of ethics in relation to religion.
언급할 필요가 있는 윤리 이론의 한 가지 측면은 종교와 관련한 윤리의 자율성 문제이다.

② Many **4)** e_____ works are **5)** [**writing / written**] from a religious point of view, and many **6)** c_____ moral judgments are influenced by religion.
많은 윤리학 저술이 종교적 관점에서 쓰이고, 현실의 많은 도덕적 판단이 종교의 영향을 받는다.

③ A question in ethical theory is **7)** [**what / whether**] ethics **8)** [**have / has**] some kind of evidential **9)** d_____ on religion.
윤리 이론에서의 한 가지 문제는, 윤리가 종교에 대해 일종의 증거적 의존성을 가지고 있느냐이다.

④ **10)** [**Considering / Consider**] the question **11)** [**that / whether**] moral knowledge — say, that lying is (with certain exceptions) wrong — **12)** [**require / requires / requiring**] knowing any religious truth.
예를 들어, 거짓말하는 것은(특정한 예외는 있지만) 잘못된 것이라는 도덕적 지식이 어떤 종교적 진리든 알아야 할 필요가 있는지의 문제를 생각해 보라.

⑤ This does not seem so.
이것은 그렇게 보이지 않는다.

⑥ To say this is not to claim (as some would) that we can know **13)** m_____ truths **14)** [**as if / even if**] there are no **15)** t_____ or religious truths.
이렇게 말하는 것은 비록 신학적 또는 종교적 진리가 '존재하지' 않더라도 우리가 도덕적 진리를 알 수 있다고 (누군가는 그렇게 하겠지만) 주장하는 것은 아니다.

⑦ The point is theologically **16)** n_____ on this matter.
핵심 내용은 이 문제에 관해 신학적인 것에 얽매이지 않는다는 것이다.

⑧ It is **17)** [**what / which / that**] knowledge of moral truths does not depend on knowledge of God or of religious truths.
그것은 도덕적 진리에 관한 '지식'이 신이나 종교적 진리에 관한 '지식'에 의존하지 않는다는 것이다.

⑨ This view that moral knowledge **18)** [**is / being**] possible **19)** [**independent / independently**] of religion is not antireligious, and indeed it has often been **20)** [**holding / held**] by religiously committed philosophers and by theologians.
도덕적 지식은 종교와 관계없이 가능하다는 이 견해는 종교에 반하는 것이 아니며, 사실상 그것은 종교적으로 헌신적인 철학자들과 신학자들이 흔히 품어 왔던 것이었다.

* theological: 신학적인

글의 전개방식	통념과 반박	문제와 해결	연구·실험	비교·대조	예시	비유	시간적 흐름	스토리텔링	기타

개요도	서론	본론	결론
	글감의 집약적 제시	논의 풀이	재진술
	종교와 관련한 윤리의 자율성 문제를 언급할 필요가 있다.	도덕적 지식에 관한 질문에 종교적 지식이 필요 없다는 말은, 신학적으로 중립적이라는 것이 핵심이다.	도덕적 진리에 대한 진실은 신이나 종교적 진리의 지식에 달려있지 않다.

[2] 우리말과 일치하도록 주어진 단어를 바르게 배열하여 〈주제 및 제목〉을 쓰시오. (각 10점씩 2문제, 총 20점)

한글	신학적 진실과 도덕적 지식의 중립성
영어	truth / neutrality / of / moral / and / theological / knowledge
정답	
한글	도덕적 진실을 찾기 위해 우리는 종교적이어야 할까?
영어	Should / Find / To / Moral / Religious / We / Be / Truths
정답	

[3] 위 지문에 있는 단어만을 활용하여 다음 〈요약문〉을 완성하시오(어형 변형 가능). (총 20점)

Though many ethical works are written from a _____ perspective, it seems that knowledge of moral truth is _____ of _____ truth.

[1] 밑줄에 알맞은 어휘를 채우며, [대괄호] 안에서 알맞은 표현을 고르고 문법 출제의도를 쓰세요. (각 3점씩 20문제, 총 60점)

① Several factors have 1) [identified / been identified] as influences on the development of moral 2) i_____, some individual and some contextual.

여러 가지 요인들이 도덕적 정체성 발달에 영향을 미치는 것으로 밝혀졌는데, 어떤 것은 개인적이고, 어떤 것은 상황적이다.

② (❶) At the individual level, things such as personality, 3) c_____ development, attitudes and values, and broader self and identity development can impact moral identity development.

개인적 차원에서는, 성격, 인지 발달, 태도와 가치관, 그리고 더 폭넓은 자아 및 정체성 발달 같은 것들이 도덕적 정체성 발달에 영향을 미칠 수 있다.

③ (❷) 4) [Nevertheless / For example / Though], those 5) [more / less] advanced in cognitive and identity development have greater capacities for moral identity development.

예를 들어, 인지 및 정체성 발달에서 더 뛰어난 사람들은 도덕적 정체성 발달에 대한 능력이 더 뛰어나다.

④ (❸) Also, greater 6) a_____ for moral values might 7) f_____ their 8) [consequent / subsequent] 9) i_____ into identity.

또한, 도덕적 가치관에 대한 더 많은 이해는 이후에 그것(도덕적 가치관)이 정체성으로 통합되는 것을 촉진할 수도 있다.

⑤ (❹ At the contextual level, one important factor is the person's social 10) s_____, 11) [include / includes / including] neighborhood, school, family, and institutions such as religious, youth, or community organizations.)

상황적 차원에서는, 한 가지 중요한 요소가 이웃, 학교, 가족, 그리고 종교 단체, 청소년 단체 또는 지역 사회 단체와 같은 기관을 포함하는, 그 개인이 속한 사회 구조이다.

⑥ 12) [However / Unfortunately / For example], a caring and 13) s_____ family environment can 14) [facilitate / be facilitated] the development of 15) m_____ and identity, 16) [as well / as well as] the integration of the two into moral identity.

예를 들어, 배려하고 도와주는 가정 환경은 도덕성과 정체성 발달을 촉진할 수 있고, 그뿐만 아니라 그 두 가지(도덕성과 정체성)가 도덕적 정체성으로 통합되는 것도 촉진할 수 있다.

⑦ (❺) Additionally, 17) i_____ in religious and youth organizations can provide not only moral beliefs systems but also opportunities to 18) [act / be acted] on those 19) b_____s (e.g., through community involvement), 20) [that / what / which] can aid their integration into identity.

게다가, 종교 단체 및 청소년 단체에 참여하는 것은 도덕적 신념 체계뿐만 아니라, (예를 들어, 지역 사회 참여를 통해) 그러한 신념에 따라 행동할 기회도 제공할 수 있으며, 이는 그것이 정체성으로 통합되는 것을 도울 수 있다.

글의 전개방식	통념과 반박	문제와 해결	연구·실험	비교·대조	예시	비유	시간적 흐름	스토리텔링	기타

개요도	서론	본론	결론
	글감 제시	병렬적 논의 전개 A	병렬적 논의 전개 B
	도덕적 정체성 발달에 영향을 미치는 것으로 밝혀진 몇 가지 요소 중 일부는 개인적이고, 일부는 상황적이다.	개인적 수준에서, 성격이나 인지 발달, 태도와 가치 등이 영향을 미친다.	상황적 수준에서는 이웃, 학교, 가족 등과 같은 사회적 구조가 중요한 요소이다.

[2] 우리말과 일치하도록 주어진 단어를 바르게 배열하여 <주제 및 제목>을 쓰시오. (각 10점씩 2문제, 총 20점)

한글	도덕적 정체성의 발달을 위한 개인적이고 맥락적인 요소들
영어	of / identity / the / contextual / moral / for / factors / development / individual / and
정답	

한글	도덕적 정체성 발달에 영향을 미치는 요인의 분류
영어	of / Identity / the / Influential / Moral / for / Factors / Development / Categorization / of
정답	

[3] 위 지문에 있는 단어만을 활용하여 다음 <요약문>을 완성하시오(어형 변형 가능). (총 20점)

Several _____ influence the development of moral _____, some of which are individual while others are _____.

[1] 밑줄에 알맞은 어휘를 채우며, [대괄호] 안에서 알맞은 표현을 고르고 문법 출제의도를 쓰세요. (각 3점씩 20문제, 총 60점)

① Today we are using some 400 million plus tonnes of paper per annum in a global population of about seven billion, but 1) [if / unless] we look at the 2) a_____d population figure in 2045 of nine billion, just on that basis alone paper 3) p_____ will need to 4) [increase / decrease] by 30 per cent.

오늘날 우리는 약 70억 명의 전 세계 인구 내에서 1년에 약 4억 톤 이상의 종이를 사용하고 있지만, 만약 우리가 2045년에 90억명으로 예상되는 인구 수치를 본다면, 단지 그것에만 근거해도 종이 생산량을 30퍼센트 늘려야 할 것이다.

② On top of that within our current population not everybody 5) [is / are / being] able to 6) [get / getting] a newspaper or has a book to read, or has enough exercise books to write on at school.

게다가 현재 우리의 인구 내에서 모든 사람이 신문을 구할 수 있거나 읽을 책을 가지고 있거나, 학교에서 쓸 수 있는 충분한 연습장을 가지고 있는 것은 아니다.

③ As their percentage 7) [increases / decreases] the demand for paper will also increase.

그들의 비율이 늘어남에 따라 종이에 대한 수요 역시 늘어날 것이다.

④ We have 8) [limited / been limited] land and a limited number of trees, and if we don't recycle we will not be able to 9) s_____ the 400 million tonnes we need today or meet the 10) d_____s of an increasing population.

우리는 제한된 땅과 제한된 수의 나무를 가지고 있으며, 만약 우리가 재활용을 하지 않는다면 우리는 오늘날 필요로 하는 4억 톤의 종이를 공급하거나 늘어나는 인구의 수요를 충족시킬 수 없을 것이다.

⑤ 11) [Remember / Remembering] of course 12) [what / which / that] within the 400 million tonnes we 13) [use / using] today about 200 million tonnes of waste paper is used in 14) [its / their] manufacturing; 200 million tonnes of waste paper 15) [generates / is generated] 16) [rough / roughly] 160 million tonnes of recycled paper.

오늘날 우리가 사용하는 4억 톤의 종이 내에서 그것을 제조하는 데 약 2억 톤의 폐지가 사용되는데, 2억 톤의 폐지는 대략 1억 6천만 톤의 재생지를 만들어 낸다는 것을 물론 명심하라.

⑥ Therefore 17) [if / unless] we didn't 18) r_____ we would only have 240 million tonnes of paper so there would be a 19) s_____ or we would have to 20) [use / using] more pulp.

그러므로 만약 우리가 재활용을 하지 않는다면 우리는 2억 4천만 톤의 종이만 가지게 될 것이므로, 부족분이 생길 것인데, 다시 말하면, 우리가 더 많은 펄프를 사용해야 할 것이다.

* per annum: 1년에

글의 전개방식	통념과 반박	문제와 해결	연구·실험	비교·대조	예시	비유	시간적 흐름	스토리텔링	기타

개요도	서론	본론	결론
	상황 제시	문제 제기	논점 제시
	우리는 연간 4억 톤 가량의 종이를 사용하는데, 인구 증가에 따라 그 수요는 더 증가할 것이다.	우리 중 일부는 읽을 책이 없거나 학교에서 사용할 교과서가 없을 것이다.	상당수의 종이가 재활용되고 있음을 인식해야 한다.

[2] 우리말과 일치하도록 주어진 단어를 바르게 배열하여 〈주제 및 제목〉을 쓰시오. (각 10점씩 2문제, 총 20점)

한글	증가하는 수요에 대한 종이 재활용의 중요성
영어	of / paper / demand / increasing / recycling / the / for / importance / the
정답	
한글	비상: 종이가 부족할 수 있다
영어	May / Out / We / Of / Paper / Run / Emergency:
정답	

[3] 위 지문에 있는 단어만을 활용하여 다음 〈요약문〉을 완성하시오(어형 변형 가능). (총 20점)

If we do not _____ paper, the demand for paper may not be satisfied in the near future considering the growing size of the _____.

[1] 밑줄에 알맞은 어휘를 채우며, [대괄호] 안에서 알맞은 표현을 고르고 문법 출제의도를 쓰세요. (각 3점씩 20문제, 총 60점)

① For years, companies and countries took their rare metal supply lines for granted, 1) [aware / unaware] of the material 2) m_____ of their products.

　수년간, 기업과 국가들은 자신들이 만드는 제품의 재료 구성을 알지 못한 채, 자신들의 희금속 공급선을 당연하게 여겼다.

② In fact, in 2011, Congress forced the U.S. military to research 3) [its / their] supply chains 4) [because / due to] the Pentagon was having difficulty 5) [determine / to determine / determining] 6) [what / whose / which] advanced metals 7) [did it need / it needed].

　실은, 2011년, 미 의회는 미국 군대에 그것의 공급망을 연구하도록 강제했는데, 그 이유는 펜타곤(미국 국방부)이 그것에 어떤 첨단 금속이 필요한지 결정하는 데 어려움을 겪고 있었기 때문이다.

③ As the materials that make up product 8) c_____s 9) [to have become / have become] more varied and complex, those who rely on 10) s_____ hardware can no longer afford 11) [remaining / to remain] in the dark.

　제품의 부품을 구성하는 재료가 더 다양해지고 복잡해짐에 따라, 정교한 하드웨어에 의존하는 사람들은 더 이상 아무것도 모르는 상태로 있을 여유가 없다.

④ Now, 12) c_____ and government leaders are realizing how 13) [important / importantly] rare metals are.

　이제, 기업과 정부 지도자들은 희금속이 얼마나 중요한지 깨닫고 있다.

⑤ Indeed, efforts to secure rare metals have 14) [sparked / been sparked] a war over the periodic table.

　실제로, 희금속을 확보하기 위한 노력은 주기율표를 둘러싼 전쟁을 촉발시켰다.

⑥ In offices from Tokyo to Washington, D.C., in research and development labs from Cambridge, Massachusetts, to Baotou, China, and in 15) s_____ command centers the world over, new policies and the launching of research programs are ensuring 16) [that / what / in which] nations have access.

　도쿄에서 Washington, D.C.까지의 관청에서, 매사추세츠주의 Cambridge에서 중국의 Baotou까지의 연구 개발 실험실에서, 그리고 전 세계의 전략 지휘 본부에서, 새로운 정책과 연구 프로그램의 착수는 국가가 반드시 (희금속에 대해) 접근할 수 있도록 하고 있다.

⑦ The 17) s_____ for minor metals isn't imminent; it's already here and is 18) [shaping / shaped] the relationship between countries as 19) c_____s over other resources 20) [were / did] in the past.

　비주류 금속을 위한 경쟁은 곧 닥쳐올 듯한 것이 아니라 이미 여기 있으며, 과거에 다른 자원을 둘러싼 분쟁이 그랬던 것처럼 국가 간의 관계를 형성하고 있다.

* the Pentagon: 펜타곤 (미국 국방부로, 국방부 건물이 5각형 모양인 데서 유래)
** imminent: 곧 닥쳐올 듯한, 임박한

글의 전개방식	통념과 반박	문제와 해결	연구·실험	비교·대조	예시	비유	시간적 흐름	스토리텔링	기타

개요도	서론	본론	결론
	문제상황 제시	논의 전개	부연 설명
	수년간 기업과 국가는 제품의 재료 구성을 알지 못한 채 희금속의 공급선을 당연시했다.	제품의 구성이 더 복잡해지면서, 정교한 하드웨어에 의존하는 사람들이 더 이상 무지할 여유가 없다.	기업과 정부는 희금속의 중요성을 인지하고, 이를 수호하려는 노력을 이어가고 있다.

[2] 우리말과 일치하도록 주어진 단어를 바르게 배열하여 〈주제 및 제목〉을 쓰시오. (각 10점씩 2문제, 총 20점)

한글	기업과 정부의 희귀 금속 확보 노력
영어	and / companies / secure / rare / efforts / governments / to / by / metals
정답	
한글	희귀 금속 공급선 문제화 및 확보
영어	Rare / for / Metals / Lines / Problematizing / Supply / Securing / and
정답	

[3] 위 지문에 있는 단어만을 활용하여 다음 〈요약문〉을 완성하시오(어형 변형 가능). (총 20점)

Companies and countries _____ that rare metal supply lines that they _____ _____ _____ for several years should now be firmly secured.

[1] 밑줄에 알맞은 어휘를 채우며, [대괄호] 안에서 알맞은 표현을 고르고 문법 출제의도를 쓰세요. (각 3점씩 20문제, 총 60점)

① The effects of climate change will **1)** [rise / fall] most **2)** [heavy / heavily] upon the poor of the world.
　기후 변화의 영향은 세계의 가난한 사람들을 가장 크게 덮칠 것이다.

② (❶) Regions such as Africa could face **3)** [severe / severely] compromised food production and water **4)** s_____s, while coastal areas in South, East, and Southeast Asia will be at great risk of flooding.
　아프리카와 같은 지역들은 심각하게 훼손된 식량 생산과 물 부족에 직면할 수 있는 동시에 남아시아, 동아시아, 동남아시아의 해안 지역은 홍수의 큰 위험에 처할 것이다.

③ (❷) Tropical Latin America will see damage to forests and **5)** a_____ areas **6)** [because / due to] drier climate, **7)** [while / during] in South America changes in precipitation patterns and the **8)** d_____ of glaciers will significantly **9)** [affect / be affected] water **10)** a_____.
　열대 라틴 아메리카는 더 건조한 기후로 인해 숲과 농업 지역에 피해를 보는 동시에 남아메리카에서는 강우 패턴의 변화와 빙하의 소멸이 물의 이용 가능성에 큰 영향을 미칠 것이다.

④ (❸ While the richer countries may have the economic resources to adapt to many of the effects of climate change, without significant aid poorer countries will be **11)** [able / unable] to **12)** i_____ preventive measures, especially those that rely on the newest technologies.)
　더 부유한 나라들은 기후 변화의 많은 영향에 적응하기 위한 경제적 자원을 가지고 있을 수도 있지만, 상당한 원조가 없을 경우 더 가난한 나라들은 예방조치, 특히 최신 기술에 의존하는 조치를 시행할 수 없을 것이다.

⑤ This **13)** [rises / raises] fundamental issues of environmental justice in **14)** r_____ to the impact of economic and political power on environmental policy on a global **15)** s_____.
　이는 세계적인 규모로 경제력 및 정치력이 환경 정책에 미치는 영향과 관련하여 환경 정의라는 근본적인 문제를 제기한다.

⑥ (❹) The concept of climate justice is a term **16)** [using / used] for framing global warming as an ethical and political issue, rather than one that is **17)** [pure / purely] environmental or physical in nature.
　기후 정의라는 개념은 지구 온난화를 본질적으로 순전히 환경적이거나 물리적인 것이라기보다는, 윤리적이고 정치적인 문제로 만들기 위해 사용되는 용어이다.

⑦ (❺) The principles of climate justice **18)** [imply / implying] an **19)** [equitable / inequitable] sharing both of the **20)** b_____s of climate change and the costs of developing policy responses.
　기후 정의의 원칙은 기후 변화의 부담과 정책 대응을 개발하는 비용 양쪽을 공평하게 분담하는 것을 의미한다.

* precipitation: 강우 ** equitable: 공평한

글의 전개방식	통념과 반박	문제와 해결	연구·실험	비교·대조	예시	비유	시간적 흐름	스토리텔링	기타

개요도	서론	본론	결론
	주장 제시	개념 제시	부연 설명
	기후 변화의 효과는 가난한 세계에 더 크게 나타날 것이며, 부유한 나라는 경제력을 이용해 영향에 적응할 것이다.	기후 정의는 지구 온난화를 환경이나 물리가 아닌, 윤리적이고 정치적인 문제로 만드는 용어이다.	기후 정의의 원리는 기후 변화의 부담과 정책 대응 설계의 비용을 공평하게 나누는 것을 함의한다.

[2] 우리말과 일치하도록 주어진 단어를 바르게 배열하여 〈주제 및 제목〉을 쓰시오. (각 10점씩 2문제, 총 20점)

한글	기후 변화의 불균일한 영향과 환경 정의
영어	change / of / uneven / and / effect / climate / justice / environmental
정답	
한글	기후 정의: 지구 온난화에 대한 윤리적, 정치적 접근법
영어	and / an / Ethical / Climate / Justice: / Global / to / Warming / Approach / Political
정답	

[3] 위 지문에 있는 단어만을 활용하여 다음 〈요약문〉을 완성하시오(어형 변형 가능). (총 20점)

The concept of climate _____ is concerned with _____ an environmental problem as an _____ and political concern, in order to address equity issues.

[1] 밑줄에 알맞은 어휘를 채우며, [대괄호] 안에서 알맞은 표현을 고르고 문법 출제의도를 쓰세요. (각 3점씩 20문제, 총 60점)

① Organic chemistry is the part of chemistry **1)** [what / that] is **2)** [concerning / concerned] with the **3)** c_____s of carbon.

　'유기 화학'은 탄소 화합물과 관련이 있는 화학의 일부이다.

② That one element can **4)** c_____ a whole division **5)** [is / are / being] evidence of carbon's pregnant mediocrity.

　하나의 원소가 한 분야 전체를 차지할 수 있다는 사실은 탄소의 풍요한 범용성에 대한 증거이다.

③ Carbon lies at the midpoint of the Periodic Table, the chemist's map of chemical properties of the elements, and is largely **6)** i_____ to the relationships **7)** [it enters / they enter] into.

　탄소는 원소들의 화학적 성질에 대한 화학자의 지도인 '주기율표'의 중간 지점에 있으며, 대개 그것이 관여하는 관계에 개의치 않는다.

④ In particular, it is **8)** c_____ to bond to **9)** [it / itself].

　특히, 그것은 기꺼이 자신과 결합한다.

⑤ As a result of its mild and **10)** [aggressive / unaggressive] character, it is able to form chains and rings of startling **11)** c_____.

　순하고 유화적인 성격으로 인해, 그것은 놀라울 정도의 복잡성을 가진 사슬과 고리를 형성할 수 있다.

⑥ Startling complexity is exactly **12)** [that / which / what] organisms need **13)** [if / unless] they are to **14)** [regard / be regarded] as being alive, and thus the compounds of carbon are the structural and **15)** r_____ infrastructure of life.

　놀라울 정도의 복잡성은 바로 유기체가 살아 있는 것으로 여겨지려면 필요로 하는 것이고, 따라서 탄소 화합물은 생명체의 구조적이고 반응적인 하부 구조이다.

⑦ So **16)** [extensive / extensively] are the compounds of carbon, **17)** [current / currently] numbering in the millions, that it is not **18)** [surprising / surprised] that a whole branch of chemistry has **19)** [evolved / evolving] for their study and has developed special **20)** t_____s, systems of nomenclature, and attitudes.

　현재 그 수가 수백만 개에 달하는 탄소 화합물은 매우 광범위해서, 화학의 한 분야 전체가 그것의 연구를 위해 발전해 왔고 특별한 기술, 명명법의 체계, 사고방식을 발전시켜 온 것은 놀라운 일이 아니다.

　　　　　　　　　　　　　　　　　　* mediocrity: 범용성　** nomenclature: (학술적) 명명법

글의 전개방식	통념과 반박	문제와 해결	연구·실험	비교·대조	예시	비유	시간적 흐름	스토리텔링	기타

개요도	서론	본론	결론
	개념 제시	특성 소개	논의 마무리
	유기 화학은 탄소 화합물과 관련 있는 화학의 갈래이다.	탄소는 풍부한 범용성이 있는데, 놀라울 정도로 복잡한 사슬과 고리를 만들 수 있다.	탄소 화합물은 매우 광범위해서, 화학의 한 분야로서 발전한 것은 놀라운 일도 아니다.

[2] 우리말과 일치하도록 주어진 단어를 바르게 배열하여 〈주제 및 제목〉을 쓰시오. (각 10점씩 2문제, 총 20점)

한글	유기화학과 탄소화합물의 평범함
영어	and / of / the / chemistry / mediocrity / carbonic / organic / compounds
정답	
한글	유기화학: 개념과 설명
영어	and / Organic / Concept / Chemistry: / Explanation
정답	

[3] 위 지문에 있는 단어만을 활용하여 다음 〈요약문〉을 완성하시오(어형 변형 가능). (총 20점)

As a branch of chemistry, organic chemistry studies various _____ of carbon, whose mild _____ allows for the formation of _____ chains.

[1] 밑줄에 알맞은 어휘를 채우며, [대괄호] 안에서 알맞은 표현을 고르고 문법 출제의도를 쓰세요. (각 3점씩 20문제, 총 60점)

① Humans have 1) [used / been used] borax for more than four thousand years.
인간은 4천 년이 넘는 기간 동안 붕사(硼砂)를 사용해 왔다.

② Since the 1800s, it has 2) [mined / been mined] near Death Valley, California.
1800년대 이후로, 그것은 캘리포니아주의 Death Valley 인근에서 채굴되었다.

③ Dirt cheap, borax has many 3) i_____ uses, but in the home it is 4) [using / used] as a natural laundry-cleaning booster, multipurpose cleaner, fungicide, herbicide, and disinfectant.
붕사는 값이 매우 싸므로, 공업용으로 많이 사용되지만, 가정에서 그것은 천연 세탁 촉진제, 다목적 세정제, 곰팡이 제거제, 제초제, 소독제로 사용된다.

④ Off-white, odorless, and alkaline, borax crystals can 5) [mix / be mixed] with other cleaning agents for added power.
회색을 띤 백색이고, 냄새가 없으며, 알칼리성인 붕사 결정은 효능을 더하기 위해 다른 세정제와 혼합될 수 있다.

⑤ 6) [Although / In spite of] you certainly wouldn't want to eat 7) [it / them], borax is relatively safe and is quite 8) [effective / effectively] 9) [with / without] being toxic.
틀림없이 여러분이 그것을 먹는 것은 좋은 생각이 아니지만, 붕사는 비교적 안전하고 독성이 없이 꽤 효과적이다.

⑥ It is 10) [useful / useless] in a lot of the ways that baking soda 11) [is / does], but it's stronger and disinfects more, so it's good for mold, mildew, and deeper dirt.
그것은 베이킹 소다가 유용하게 사용되는 방식 중의 많은 방식에서 유용하지만, 더 강력하고 더 많이 소독되므로 곰팡이, 흰곰팡이, 찌든 때에 효과적이다.

⑦ In general, use baking soda first and use borax only in 12) s_____s 13) [what / which / where] something stronger is needed.
일반적으로, 베이킹 소다를 먼저 사용하고, 더 강한 것이 필요한 상황에서만 붕사를 사용하라.

⑧ It will enable you 14) [to get / get / getting] even 15) s_____ stains clean without 16) r_____ing to toxic chemicals.
그것으로 독성이 있는 화학 물질에 의존하지 않고 지우기 힘든 얼룩까지도 깨끗하게 할 수 있을 것이다.

⑨ Borax should not be used 17) [what / in what / which / where] it might get into food, and it should be 18) [safe / safely] 19) [storing / stored] out of the 20) r_____ of children and pets.
붕사는 음식에 들어갈 수도 있는 곳에서 사용해서는 안 되며, 어린이와 반려동물의 손이 닿지 않는 곳에 안전하게 보관되어야 한다.

* disinfectant: 소독제 ** mildew: 흰곰팡이

글의 전개방식	통념과 반박	문제와 해결	연구·실험	비교·대조	예시	비유	시간적 흐름	스토리텔링	기타
	서론			본론				결론	
개요도				붕사에 대한 설명					

[2] 우리말과 일치하도록 주어진 단어를 바르게 배열하여 <주제 및 제목>을 쓰시오. (각 10점씩 2문제, 총 20점)

한글	
영어	
정답	붕사에 대한 설명
한글	
영어	
정답	

[3] 위 지문에 있는 단어만을 활용하여 다음 <요약문>을 완성하시오(어형 변형 가능). (총 20점)

요약문 없음

[1] 밑줄에 알맞은 어휘를 채우며, [대괄호] 안에서 알맞은 표현을 고르고 문법 출제의도를 쓰세요. (각 3점씩 20문제, 총 60점)

① There would be 1) [very / much] less to say 2) [did / were] it not for space probes that have 3) [visited / been visited] the giant planets and their moons.
만약 거대 행성과 그것들의 위성을 방문한 무인 우주 탐사선이 없다면 할 말이 훨씬 더 적을 것이다.

② ❶ 4) E_____ began with fly-bys (missions that flew past the planet) but has moved on to the stage of orbital tours in the case of Jupiter and Saturn, 5) [which / what / that] have each had a 6) m_____ that orbited the planet for several years and that was able to make repeated close fly-bys of at least the regular satellites.
탐사는 플라이바이(행성의 옆을 지나가는 우주 비행)로 시작되었지만, 목성과 토성의 경우 궤도 선회의 단계로 넘어갔는데, 각각의 궤도 선회에는 수년 동안 행성의 궤도를 돌며 적어도 규칙 위성에 대한 가까운 플라이바이를 반복적으로 할 수 있는 우주 비행이 있었다.

③ ❷ Close fly-bys of moons enable detailed imaging, and usually take the probe 7) [close enough / enough close] to see 8) [where / when / how] the moon affects the strong 9) m_____ field 10) [surrounds / surrounding] the planet and to 11) d_____ 12) [that / whether] the moon also has 13) [its / their] own magnetic field.
위성에 대한 가까운 플라이바이는 상세한 영상 촬영을 가능하게 하며, 일반적으로, 위성이 행성을 둘러싸고 있는 강한 자기장에 어떤 영향을 미치는지 보고 그리고 그 위성 또한 자체의 자기장을 가지는지 탐지할 만큼 가깝게 무인 우주 탐사선을 접근시킨다.

④ ❸ The size of the 14) s_____ deflection to a probe's trajectory as it 15) [passes / passing] close to a moon enables the moon's 16) [mass / mess] to 17) [determine / be determined].
무인 우주 탐사선이 위성에 근접하여 지날 때의 그 궤적에 대한 극미한 편차의 크기로 위성의 질량을 알아낼 수 있다.

⑤ ❹ 18) [Knowing / Known] the moon's size, it is then easy 19) [to work / work] out its 20) d_____.
위성의 크기를 알면, 그것의 밀도를 쉽게 계산할 수 있다.

* probe: 무인 우주 탐사선 ** deflection: 편차, 굴절 *** trajectory: 궤적

글의 전개방식	통념과 반박	문제와 해결	연구·실험	비교·대조	예시	비유	시간적 흐름	스토리텔링	기타
	서론			본론			결론		
개요도	글감 제시			역사 설명			역할 설명		
	거대 행성과 위성을 방문한 탐사선이 없다면 할 말이 훨씬 적을 것이다 (=아는 것이 적을 것이다).			플라이바이 탐사로 시작해 궤도 선회의 단계로 넘어가며, 우주 비행은 발전해 왔다.			가까운 플라이바이는 상세한 영사 촬영, 자기장의 탐지, 질량 측정 등의 역할을 수행한다.		

[2] 우리말과 일치하도록 주어진 단어를 바르게 배열하여 〈주제 및 제목〉을 쓰시오. (각 10점씩 2문제, 총 20점)

한글	거대 행성과 그 위성 탐사를 위한 플라이바이 (근접 비행)
영어	giant / planets / of / moons / and / explorations / for / their / fly-bys
정답	
한글	플라이바이를 통한 다른 행성으로의 탐험
영어	Planets / to / An / Fly-Bys / Via / Other / Expedition
정답	

[3] 위 지문에 있는 단어만을 활용하여 다음 〈요약문〉을 완성하시오(어형 변형 가능). (총 20점)

_____ allowed people to have detailed images of giant planets and their _____, detect magnetic fields, and measure the size and _____ of planets.

[1] 밑줄에 알맞은 어휘를 채우며, [대괄호] 안에서 알맞은 표현을 고르고 문법 출제의도를 쓰세요. (각 3점씩 20문제, 총 60점)

① The term *common pool resources* refers to resources that are 1) [available / unavailable] to all, but 2) [owning / owned] by no one.
'공유 자원'이라는 용어는 모든 사람이 사용할 수 있지만, 아무도 소유하지는 않은 자원을 말한다.

② Nature-based examples include forests, oceans, and vistas, whereas common pool 3) c_____ resources can include a community's song, dance, and traditions.
자연에 기반을 둔 예로는 숲, 해양, 경치가 포함되지만, 문화 공유 자원에는 한 지역 사회의 노래, 춤, 전통이 포함될 수 있다.

③ Many tourism products and experiences rely on common pool resources.
많은 관광 상품과 체험은 공유 자원에 의존한다.

④ The extent and 4) a_____ of these resources has 5) [led / been led] McKean to 6) [suggest / suggesting] that common pool resources, in addition to 7) [be / being] available to anyone, 8) [is / are / being] difficult to protect and easy to deplete.
이러한 자원의 규모와 이용 가능성으로 인해, McKean은 공유 자원은 누구라도 이용 가능한 것에 덧붙여 보호하기는 어렵고 고갈시키기는 쉽다고 말했다.

⑤ Hardin presented the 9) i_____ illustration of this concept in his influential article titled "The Tragedy of the Commons."
Hardin은 '공유지의 비극'이라는 제목의 자신의 영향력 있는 논문에서 이 개념을 처음으로 설명했다.

⑥ In this article, he described a 10) c_____ that thrives on the growth of its cattle, 11) [what / to which / which] graze on communal pastureland.
이 논문에서, 그는 소의 증가를 바탕으로 번창하는 어느 지역 사회를 묘사했는데, 그 소들은 공동 방목지에서 풀을 뜯어 먹는다.

⑦ As demand grows, residents are inclined to 12) [maximize / minimize] their benefits by ignoring the cumulative effect of each person 13) [grazes / grazing / grazed] an additional head of cattle on the communal lands.
수요가 늘면서, 주민들은 각자가 공유지에서 소 한 마리씩을 추가로 방목하는 행위의 누적 결과를 무시함으로써 자신들의 이익을 최소화하고 (→ 극대화하고) 싶어 한다.

⑧ Hardin asserted 14) [that / what / which] the 15) i_____ of individuals 16) [using / used] common pool resources will lead to eventual 17) d_____ of the resource.
Hardin은 개인들이 공유 자원을 사용하는 것에 대한 무지는 결국 자원의 고갈을 초래하게 된다고 주장했다.

⑨ The 18) p_____ combined impact of individual use of common pool resources 19) [is / are / being] an important element of tourism's 20) s_____ development.
공유 자원의 개별 사용이 끼치는 잠재적인 통합 영향은 관광의 지속 가능한 발전의 중요한 요소이다.

* deplete: 고갈시키다 ** cumulative: 누적하는 *** communal: 공동의

글의 전개방식	통념과 반박	문제와 해결	연구·실험	비교·대조	예시	비유	시간적 흐름	스토리텔링	기타

개요도	서론		본론		결론	
	용어 소개		개념화		함의 설명	
	공유 자원이란 모두가 사용할 수 있지만 소유자는 없는 자원을 말하는데, 자연이나 문화 등 영역이 있다.		공유지의 비극이란 개인의 공유 자원 사용에 대한 무지가 결국 자원 고갈을 초래하는 상황을 말한다.		공유 자원의 사용이 미치는 잠재적 영향은 관광의 지속 가능성에 중요한 요소이다.	

[2] 우리말과 일치하도록 주어진 단어를 바르게 배열하여 〈주제 및 제목〉을 쓰시오. (각 10점씩 2문제, 총 20점)

한글	공유 자원의 개념과 공유지의 비극
영어	tragedy / the / the / pool / commons / of / and / resources / common / of / concept
정답	
한글	공유지의 자원이 고갈되는 방식
영어	How / Up / the / of / End / Commons / Depleted / Resources
정답	

[3] 위 지문에 있는 단어만을 활용하여 다음 〈요약문〉을 완성하시오(어형 변형 가능). (총 20점)

As Hardin famously conceptualized, resources that are _____ to everyone but owned by no one can be easily depleted because of _____ of the _____ influence of each use.

[1] 밑줄에 알맞은 어휘를 채우며, [대괄호] 안에서 알맞은 표현을 고르고 문법 출제의도를 쓰세요. (각 3점씩 20문제, 총 60점)

① If part of the attraction of the community to outsiders 1) [is / are / being] its cultural heritage and traditions, that will likely 2) [change / changing] over time and 3) [frequent / frequently] not for the better.
외부인에게 지역 사회의 매력 중 일부가 그것의 문화적 유산과 전통이라면, 그것은 아마도 시간이 지남에 따라 변할 것인데, 흔히 더 나은 방향은 아닐 것이다.

② Symbols of a historic culture may be 4) p_____, but only in a make-believe form.
유서 깊은 문화의 상징물이 넘칠지 모르나, 단지 진짜가 아닌 형태로만 그럴 뿐이다.

③ Tourist shops on small Pacific islands may sell replicas of native art — all 5) [turned / turning] out in huge quantities by manufacturers in other parts of the world.
태평양의 작은 섬들에 있는 관광 상점들은 모두 세계 다른 지역의 제조업자들에 의해 대량으로 만들어진 원주민 예술의 복제품을 팔지도 모른다.

④ Plastic Black Forest clocks and Swiss music boxes are 6) [offering / offered] to tourists 7) [that / what] are mass-produced in Taiwan or China.
대만이나 중국에서 대량 생산되는 플라스틱으로 만든 Black Forest 시계와 Swiss 뮤직 박스가 관광객들에게 판매된다.

⑤ A 8) c_____ to craftsmanship and true local 9) h_____ 10) [vanish / vanishes / vanishing].
장인 정신과 진정한 현지 유산에 대한 책무는 사라진다.

⑥ These false symbols of earlier times contribute to an overly commercial feeling at 11) d_____s and a sense that nothing seems real now, and perhaps never 12) [was / did].
이러한 이전 시대의 가짜 상징물은 여행지에서의 지나치게 상업적인 느낌과, 이제는 어떤 것도 진짜처럼 보이지 않고 아마도 진짜인 적도 없었다는 느낌의 원인이 된다.

⑦ A danger lies in the loss of a sense of personal identity by 13) r_____s and a feeling of 14) [disconnecting / being disconnected] from their past.
위험은 주민들의 개인 정체성 상실과 자신들의 과거로부터 단절됐다는 느낌에 있다.

⑧ Their heritage and culture now seem 15) [more / less] 16) [significant / significantly] or important.
그들의 유산과 문화는 이제 덜 의미 있거나 덜 중요해 보인다.

⑨ It serves 17) [primary / primarily] as a 18) c_____ front for visitors 19) [who / with whom / what] buy cheap trinkets and watch professionally staged shows that attempt 20) [recreating / to recreate] cultural practices or historic events.
그것은 값싼 장신구를 구매하고 문화적 관습이나 역사적 사건을 재현하려는 전문적으로 연출된 쇼를 보는 방문객들에게 주로 상업의 첨병 역할을 한다.

* pervasive: 넘치는 ** replica: 복제품 *** trinket: (값싼) 장신구

글의 전개방식	통념과 반박	문제와 해결	연구·실험	비교·대조	예시	비유	시간적 흐름	스토리텔링	기타
	서론			본론			결론		
	글감의 집약적 제시			문제 제기			재진술		
개요도	지역 사회의 매력 중 일부가 문화적 유산이나 전통이라면, 그것은 시간이 지남에 따라 변할 것이다.			관광 상점들은 대만이나 중국 등에서 대량생산된 예술 복제품을 팔며 상업적인 느낌을 낸다.			주민들의 정체성 상실이나 과거와의 단절을 경험하는 등 과도한 상업화의 위험이 따른다.		

[2] 우리말과 일치하도록 주어진 단어를 바르게 배열하여 〈주제 및 제목〉을 쓰시오. (각 10점씩 2문제, 총 20점)

한글	전통 유산의 상업화와 그 위협
영어	its / of / and / heritage / threat / traditional / commercialization
정답	
한글	관광의 역학: 문화유산과 전통이 바뀔 수 있는 방식
영어	Tourism: / and / Cultural / Dynamics / Tradition / Changed / Can / of / Heritage / How / Be
정답	

[3] 위 지문에 있는 단어만을 활용하여 다음 〈요약문〉을 완성하시오(어형 변형 가능). (총 20점)

Mass production and _____ sentiment can greatly change the cultural _____ and tradition of a tourist spot, which can lead to the loss of _____.

[1] 밑줄에 알맞은 어휘를 채우며, [대괄호] 안에서 알맞은 표현을 고르고 문법 출제의도를 쓰세요. (각 3점씩 20문제, 총 60점)

① Physical contests and games in Greek culture influenced art, 1) p_____ and the everyday lives of people 2) [wealthy enough / enough wealthy] to train, 3) [hire / hiring] professionals and travel to events.
　그리스 문화에서 체육 대회와 경기는 예술과 철학, 그리고 훈련하고 전문 선수를 고용하며 경기를 보러 갈 수 있을 정도로 충분히 부유한 사람들의 일상에 영향을 미쳤다.

② 4) [Therefore / However / In addition], Greek contests and games were different from the organized 5) c_____ sports of today.
　그러나 그리스의 대회와 경기는 오늘날의 체계화된 경쟁 스포츠와는 달랐다.

③ First, they were grounded in religion; second, they lacked complex 6) a_____ structures; third, they did not involve 7) m_____s and record keeping from event to.
　첫째, 그것은 종교에 기반을 두고 있었고, 둘째, 그것은 복합적 관리 체계가 없었으며, 셋째, 그것은 매 경기의 측정과 기록 관리를 포함하지 않았다.

④ 8) [However / In other words], there is one major 9) [similarity / difference]: they often reproduced 10) d_____ patterns of social relations in society as a whole.
　그러나 한 가지 주요한 유사점이 있다. 즉 그것은 흔히 사회 전반의 사회적 관계의 지배적인 패턴을 재현했다.

⑤ The power and advantages 11) [that / what] went with being wealthy, male, young and able-bodied in Greek society shaped the games and contests in ways 12) [that / what] 13) [limited / are limited] the 14) p_____ of most people.
　그리스 사회에서 부유하고, 남성이며, 젊고 신체 건강한 것과 병행하는 권력과 이점은 대부분의 사람들의 참여를 제한하는 방식으로 경기와 대회의 모습을 만들었다.

⑥ Even the definitions of excellence 15) [using / used] to 16) e_____ performance reflected the abilities of young males.
　심지어 경기력을 평가하기 위해 사용된 탁월함의 정의도 젊은 남성의 능력을 반영했다.

⑦ This meant 17) [that / which / what] the abilities of others were substandard by definition — if you could not do 18) [it / them] as a young, able-bodied Greek man did it, you were doing it the wrong way.
　이것은 그 밖의 다른 사람들의 능력은 당연히 수준 이하라는 것, 즉 젊고 신체 건강한 그리스 남성이 하는 것처럼 그것을 할 수 없다면, 그것을 잘못된 방식으로 하고 있다는 것을 의미했다.

⑧ This legitimized and 19) p_____d the 20) p_____ enjoyed by a select group of men in Greek society.
　이것은 그리스 사회에서 선택된 남성 집단이 누리는 특권을 정당화하고 보호했다.

* legitimize: 정당화하다

글의 전개방식	통념과 반박	문제와 해결	연구·실험	비교·대조	예시	비유	시간적 흐름	스토리텔링	기타

	서론	본론	결론
	글감 제시	대조를 통한 논의 진행	논점 제시
개요도	그리스 문화에서 체육은 예술과 철학, 그리고 부유한 사람들의 일상에 영향을 미쳤다.	그리스의 대회와 경기는 오늘날 경쟁 스포츠와는 세 가지 측면에서 다르다.	그러나 사회 전반에 있는 사회적 관계의 지배적인 패턴을 재현한다는 공통점이 있다.

[2] 우리말과 일치하도록 주어진 단어를 바르게 배열하여 〈주제 및 제목〉을 쓰시오. (각 10점씩 2문제, 총 20점)

한글	다양한 시간 설정에서 스포츠의 기능에 대한 교차 조사
영어	time / different / sports / functions / on / of / cross-examination / settings / in
정답	
한글	그리스 문화의 체육 대회와 오늘날 스포츠의 비교
영어	Culture / Today / with / Sports / of / Comparing / Contests / Greek / in / Physical
정답	

[3] 위 지문에 있는 단어만을 활용하여 다음 〈요약문〉을 완성하시오(어형 변형 가능). (총 20점)

One major _____ between physical contests in Greek culture and sports of today is the function of reproducing _____ patterns of social relations.

[1] 밑줄에 알맞은 어휘를 채우며, [대괄호] 안에서 알맞은 표현을 고르고 문법 출제의도를 쓰세요. (각 3점씩 20문제, 총 60점)

① In the field of musical 1) e_____, there is a dichotomy of thinking.
음악적 전문 지식 분야에서는 생각이 양분되어 있다.

② 2) [On the one hand / For example / Nevertheless], there is a widespread 3) p_____ in the general population 4) [that / which / what] expert musicians have 5) i_____ talent, or giftedness, beyond 6) o_____ abilities.
한편으로는, 음악의 대가는 보통의 능력을 넘는 타고난 재능, 즉 영재성이 있다는 인식이 일반 대중에 널리 퍼져 있다.

③ 7) T_____, as part of the vernacular in the field of music, is usually 8) [assuming / assumed] to be a stable 9) t_____ — one is 10) [either / neither] born with musical talent or not.
재능은, 음악 분야에서 사용되는 말의 일부로, 주로 불변의 특성으로 간주되는데, 사람은 음악적 재능을 타고났거나, 그렇지 않다는 것이다.

④ Music aptitude tests 11) [popular / popularly] in the early to mid-twentieth century, such as the *Seashore Tests of Musical Talent and the Music Aptitude Profile*, 12) [attempting / attempted] to find children who had this musical talent.
Seashore Tests of Musical Talent와 the Music Aptitude Profile과 같은 20세기 초중반에 유행한 음악 적성 검사는 이러한 음악적 재능이 있는 어린이들을 찾으려고 했다.

⑤ On the other hand, there is a very real feeling 13) [that / which / what] ability in music comes from a disciplined work ethic.
다른 한편으로는, 음악에서의 능력은 훈련된 근면 정신에서 비롯되는 것이라는 매우 현실적인 생각이 있다.

⑥ It would be 14) [acceptable / unacceptable], even for 15) [that / those] considered talented, not 16) [to practice / practiced].
재능이 있다고 여겨지는 사람들에게 조차도 연습하지 않는 것은 용납될 수 없을 것이다.

⑦ 17) [In fact / However / Nevertheless], those who are 18) [considering / considered] talented 19) [being / is / are] expected 20) [to practice / practicing] all the more.
사실상, 재능이 있다고 여겨지는 사람들은 그만큼 더 연습해야 한다.

* dichotomy: (의견 따위의) 양분. 이분 ** vernacular: (특정 지역 · 집단이 쓰는) 말

글의 전개방식	통념과 반박	문제와 해결	연구·실험	비교·대조	예시	비유	시간적 흐름	스토리텔링	기타

개요도	서론	본론	결론
	글감 제시	병렬적 논의 전개 A	병렬적 논의 전개 B
	음악적 전문 분야에서는 생각이 양분되어 있다.	한편으로는 음악의 대가들이 타고난 재능이나 영재성이 있다고 믿는다.	다른 한편으로, 음악에서 능력은 훈련과 연습에서 온다고 여겨지곤 한다.

[2] 우리말과 일치하도록 주어진 단어를 바르게 배열하여 〈주제 및 제목〉을 쓰시오. (각 10점씩 2문제, 총 20점)

한글	음악 분야에서의 사고의 이분법
영어	thinking / field / music / in / of / of / dichotomy / the / the
정답	
한글	타고난 재능 또는 훈련된 관행: 음악 속 흑백 사고에 대해 배우기
영어	Innate / About / in / or / Disciplined / Learning / Black-and-White / Talent / Practice: / Thinking / the / Music
정답	

[3] 위 지문에 있는 단어만을 활용하여 다음 〈요약문〉을 완성하시오(어형 변형 가능). (총 20점)

There is a _____ of thinking in the field of music, in which people attribute great musical _____ to either an innate _____ or a disciplined work ethic.

[1] 밑줄에 알맞은 어휘를 채우며, [대괄호] 안에서 알맞은 표현을 고르고 문법 출제의도를 쓰세요. (각 3점씩 20문제, 총 60점)

① For a long time photographs were 1) [understanding / understood] to be 2) [visible / invisible] traces, as irrefutable evidence of the existence of the presented, its "it has been."

오랫동안 사진은, 제시된 것의 존재에 대한 반박할 수 없는 명백함, 곧 그것의 "그것이 있었다"로서, 눈에 보이는 흔적인 것으로 이해되었다.

② (B) Therefore, photographs were 3) [initial / initially] classified as documents, whether 4) [using / used] in the media, in the family album, in books, archives or collections.

(B) 따라서, 사진은 매체, 가족 앨범, 서적, 기록, 수집품 어느 것에 쓰이든 간에, 처음에는 문서로 분류되었다.

③ As digitization began to feed into the 5) r_____ of photography, and the end of the photographic era 6) [was / being] proclaimed, it was its documentary qualities, its "ontology" as a chemical-physical symbol, that suddenly lost 7) [its / their] persuasive powers.

디지털화가 사진 영역에 영향을 미치기 시작하고, 사진 시대의 끝이 선포되었을 때, 돌연 그것의 설득력을 잃은 것은 바로 그것의 사실을 기록하는 본질, 즉 화학적, 물리적 상징으로서의 그것의 '존재론'이었다.

④ (A) But 8) [as if / even if] the sting of digital doubt seems 9) [deep / deeply] ingrained within the photographic 10) a_____ and evidence, many of its tasks and uses have 11) [hard / hardly] changed.

(A) 그러나 비록 디지털 불신의 아픔이 사진의 신뢰성과 명백함 속에 깊이 배어든 것 같지만, 사진의 임무와 용도 가운데 많은 것들은 거의 변한 적이 없다.

⑤ When we look at a family album 12) [creating / created] with digital images, 13) [close / closely] 14) [inspect / inspecting] the X-rays of a broken foot together with the doctor, or view the image of the finish of the 100-meter finals at the Olympic Games, our trust in photography 15) [remains / remaining].

디지털 화상으로 만들어진 가족 앨범을 보거나, 골절된 발의 엑스선 사진을 의사와 함께 면밀하게 살피거나, 혹은 올림픽 경기에서 100m 결승전의 결승선 사진을 볼 때, 사진에 대한 우리의 신뢰는 남아 있다.

⑥ (C) If we trust the use of the images, or more 16) [precise / precisely], if we 17) a_____ 18) [it / them] persuasive powers via their use, it does not matter 19) [whether / that] they are analog or digital.

(C) 우리가 이미지의 사용을 신뢰하거나, 더 정확하게는, 우리가 그것의 사용을 통해 그것에 설득력을 부여한다면, 그것이 아날로그인지, 디지털인지는 중요하지 않다.

⑦ In other words: We doubt photography, but still use certain photographs to dispel doubt and produce 20) e_____.

다시 말해서, 우리는 사진을 불신하지만, 불신을 떨쳐 버리고 명백성을 제시하기 위해 특정한 사진을 여전히 사용한다.

* irrefutable: 반박할 수 없는 ** ontology: 존재론 *** dispel: 떨쳐 버리다

글의 전개방식	통념과 반박	문제와 해결	연구·실험	비교·대조	예시	비유	시간적 흐름	스토리텔링	기타

	서론	본론	결론
개요도	변화상 제시	주장 제시	부연 설명
	사진은 눈에 보이는 흔적으로 이해되었지만, 디지털화로 인해 사실을 기록하는 본질을 잃어버렸다.	디지털 불신의 아픔이 사진의 신뢰성을 해친 것 같지만, 사진의 용도 중 많은 것은 거의 변함이 없다.	우리가 사진에 설득력을 부여한다면, 그것이 아날로그인지 디지털인지는 중요치 않다.

[2] 우리말과 일치하도록 주어진 단어를 바르게 배열하여 〈주제 및 제목〉을 쓰시오. (각 10점씩 2문제, 총 20점)

한글	디지털화 및 사진에 대한 인식 변화
영어	perception / changing / on / digitization / and / photographs
정답	
한글	사진의 증거력은 여전히 강력하다
영어	Still / of / Power / Strong / Evidential / Photographs / Remains / The
정답	

[3] 위 지문에 있는 단어만을 활용하여 다음 〈요약문〉을 완성하시오(어형 변형 가능). (총 20점)

Though digitization may seem as if it marked the end of the _____ era, we still endow certain functions and values on photographs as a source of _____ and _____.

[1] 밑줄에 알맞은 어휘를 채우며, [대괄호] 안에서 알맞은 표현을 고르고 문법 출제의도를 쓰세요. (각 3점씩 20문제, 총 60점)

① Predicting whether a movie will be a success 1) [is / being] perhaps the "Holy Grail" of most film-makers and especially the big movie studios.
영화가 성공작이 될지를 예측하는 것은 아마도 대부분의 영화 제작자와 특히 대규모 영화 제작소의 '성배(간절히 원하는 것)'일 것이다.

② While critical acclaim is always welcome, in the end it is important 2) [that / what] a movie makes money.
비평가의 찬사는 늘 반가운 것이지만, 결국 영화는 돈을 버는 것이 중요하다.

③ For the big studios — now 3) [increasing / increasingly] owned by 4) m_____ global corporations — making movies that deliver wide profit margins 5) [is / are / being] the ultimate metric of 6) p_____.
대규모 영화사의 경우, 지금은 점점 더 대규모의 글로벌 기업이 소유하고 있는데, 많은 수익을 내는 영화를 제작하는 것이 성과의 궁극적인 측정 기준이다.

④ Movies increasingly depend on non-theatrical sources for 7) r_____s.
영화는 점점 더 영화관 외의 수입원에 의존한다.

⑤ This fact does not 8) d_____ the continuing 9) s_____ of solid box office performance.
이러한 사실이 견실한 박스 오피스 성과의 지속적인 중요성을 깎아내리지는 않는다.

⑥ When a movie hits top spot at the box office, not only 10) [does / is] this deliver direct revenue yield, it can further 11) p_____ other income sources over time.
영화가 박스 오피스에서 정상을 차지하면, 이것은 직접적인 수익 산출을 낼 뿐만 아니라, 시간이 지나면서 다른 수입원을 더욱더 활성화할 수 있다.

⑦ A 12) [high / highly] public profile means not only that 13) [its / their] potential as an 14) a_____ choice for repeat viewing on other platforms increases but that its 15) p_____ to yield sequels might increase, too.
높은 대중의 관심은 다른 플랫폼에서 반복 시청을 위한 매력적인 선택으로서 그것의 잠재적 가능성이 증가한다는 것뿐만 아니라, 속편을 제작할 가능성도 증가할 수 있다는 것을 의미한다.

⑧ In the end, nothing 16) b_____s success like success.
결국, 성공만큼 성공을 낳는 것은 아무것도 없다.

⑨ This maxim is probably the main reason 17) [what / why] the major movie studios really like making sequels to 18) [high / highly] 19) [successful / successive] movies and really like to hire star actors with a track record of appearing in blockbuster films that generally do 20) [good / well] at the box office.
이 격언이 아마도 주요 영화 제작소가 매우 성공적인 영화의 속편을 진정 만들고 싶어 하고 박스 오피스에서 전반적으로 성공하는 블록버스터 영화에 나오는 실적이 있는 인기 배우를 진정으로 캐스팅하고 싶어 하는 주요 이유일 것이다.

* Holy Grail: 성배 (간절히 원하는 것)　** acclaim: 찬사. 호평　*** metric: 측정 기준

글의 전개방식	통념과 반박	문제와 해결	연구·실험	비교·대조	예시	비유	시간적 흐름	스토리텔링	기타

개요도	서론	본론	결론
	글감 제시	논의 진행	논점 함축
	영화가 성공작이 될지 예측하는 것은 대부분 제작자와 영화 제작소의 성배 같은 일이다.	영화는 점점 영화관 외의 수입원에 의존하는데, 그럼에도 박스오피스 성과의 중요성은 여전하다.	성공만큼 성공을 낳는 것은 없는데, 이 때문에 인기 배우를 캐스팅하고 싶어 할 것이다.

[2] 우리말과 일치하도록 주어진 단어를 바르게 배열하여 〈주제 및 제목〉을 쓰시오. (각 10점씩 2문제, 총 20점)

한글	큰 수익률을 위한 매표소 흥행의 중요성
영어	margin / of / the / success / box / for / wide / office / profit / importance
정답	
한글	성공은 성공을 가져온다: 영화산업의 성공을 위해 박스오피스가 중심이 되는 이유
영어	Industry / Brings / Why / Success / Office / Box / Is / of / For / Success / the / Success: / Movie / Centered
정답	

[3] 위 지문에 있는 단어만을 활용하여 다음 〈요약문〉을 완성하시오(어형 변형 가능). (총 20점)

Even though movie industries are increasingly utilizing non-theatrical sources for making _____, the importance of box office _____ remains _____.

[1] 밑줄에 알맞은 어휘를 채우며, [대괄호] 안에서 알맞은 표현을 고르고 문법 출제의도를 쓰세요. (각 3점씩 20문제, 총 60점)

① Learners can improve the 1) e_____ of their attributions through training.

학습자는 훈련을 통해 자기의 귀인 효과를 향상할 수 있다.

② In a pioneering study, Carol Susan Dweck, an American psychologist, 2) [provided / providing] students 3) [who / what / with whom] demonstrated learned 4) [helpfulness / helplessness] with both successful and unsuccessful experiences.

선구적인 한 연구에서, 미국 심리학자인 Carol Susan Dweck은 학습된 무력감을 보이는 학생들에게 성공한 경험과 성공하지 못한 경험 모두를 제공했다.

③ When the students were 5) [successful / unsuccessful], the experimenter specifically stated 6) [that / which / what] the failure was caused by lack of effort or 7) i_____ strategies.

학생들이 성공하지 못했을 때, 실험자는 그 실패가 노력의 부족이나 비효과적인 전략 때문에 일어났다고 명확하게 말했다.

④ 8) C_____ students were 9) [giving / given] similar experiences but no training.

비교 가능한 학생들에게 유사한 경험이 주어졌지만, 훈련은 전혀 주어지지 않았다.

⑤ After 25 sessions, the learners who were counseled about their effort and strategies responded more 10) [appropriate / appropriately] to failure by 11) p_____ing longer and 12) [adapting / adopting] their strategies more 13) [effective / effectively].

25회의 실험 활동 이후에, 자신의 노력과 전략에 관해 상담받은 학습자들은 더 오래 끈기 있게 지속하고 자신의 전략을 더 효과적으로 조정함으로써 실패에 더 적절하게 대응했다.

⑥ 14) A_____ research has corroborated Dweck's findings.

추가적인 연구를 통해 Dweck의 연구 결과가 입증되었다.

⑦ Strategy instruction was most effective for students who believed 15) [what / that] they were already trying 16) [hard / hardly].

전략 교육은 이미 자신이 열심히 노력하고 있다고 믿는 학생들에게 가장 효과적이었다.

⑧ This research suggests 17) [what / which / that] teachers can 18) [increase / decrease] students' 19) m_____ to learn by teaching them learning strategies and encouraging them 20) [to attribute / attributing / attribute] successes to effort.

이 연구는 교사들이 학생들에게 학습 전략을 가르치고 성공을 노력 덕분으로 생각하도록 고무함으로써 학생들의 학습 동기를 향상할 수 있다는 것을 보여준다.

* attribution: 귀인 (歸因, 성공이나 실패의 원인을 찾는 행위) ** corroborate: 입증하다

글의 전개방식	통념과 반박	문제와 해결	연구·실험	비교·대조	예시	비유	시간적 흐름	스토리텔링	기타

	서론	본론	결론
개요도	주장 제시	연구 소개	함의 제시
	학습자는 훈련을 통해 자기 귀인 효과를 향상할 수 있다.	연구에서 Dweck은 25회의 실험 이후 자신의 노력에 대해 상담받은 학습자들이 실패에 더 적절하게 대응함을 발견했다.	교사들이 학생들에게 성공을 노력 덕분으로 생각하도록 유도하여, 학습 동기를 향상할 수 있다.

[2] 우리말과 일치하도록 주어진 단어를 바르게 배열하여 〈주제 및 제목〉을 쓰시오. (각 10점씩 2문제, 총 20점)

한글	학습자의 귀인의 효과성 향상
영어	the / improving / attribution / effectiveness / learner's / of
정답	
한글	귀인효과를 통한 학생의 학습동기 부여
영어	Student's / Motivating / Effect / Learning / Attribution / Through
정답	

[3] 위 지문에 있는 단어만을 활용하여 다음 〈요약문〉을 완성하시오(어형 변형 가능). (총 20점)

An experiment revealed that students _____ longer and get more _____ when they _____ their learning to themselves.

[1] 밑줄에 알맞은 어휘를 채우며, [대괄호] 안에서 알맞은 표현을 고르고 문법 출제의도를 쓰세요. (각 3점씩 20문제, 총 60점)

① A lot of research discusses 1) [that / what] leads to 2) [relative / relatively] permanent 3) a＿＿＿＿＿＿ of new knowledge or skills.

많은 연구는 무엇이 새로운 지식이나 기술을 비교적 영구적으로 습득할 수 있게 하는가에 관해 논한다.

② You won't be 4) [surprising / surprised] to hear 5) [that / what / which] active learning works 6) [far / very] better than passive learning.

여러분은 '능동적인 학습'이 수동적인 학습보다 훨씬 효과가 있다는 말을 들어도 놀라지 않을 것이다.

③ 7) [In other words / For instance / Though], sitting still in a classroom for more than a half hour at a time (no matter how interesting the material) isn't nearly as 8) [potent / potently] as 9) [have / having] opportunities to engage 10) [active / actively] with the concepts through discussion, group 11) i＿＿＿＿＿＿, practice, immersion, or some other form of direct experience.

다시 말해, 교실에서 한 번에 30분이 넘게 가만히 앉아 있는 것은 (그 자료가 얼마나 흥미롭든지 간에) 토론, 집단 상호 작용, 연습, 몰입, 또는 어떤 다른 형태의 직접 경험을 통해 개념을 적극적으로 다룰 기회를 얻는 것만큼 결코 효과적이지 않다.

④ 12) [Likewise / Otherwise / In conclusion], it is absolutely critical for retaining new knowledge and skills that all your senses are 13) [engaging / engaged].

마찬가지로, 새로운 지식과 기술을 유지하기 위해서는 여러분의 '모든' 감각이 관여하는 것이 절대적으로 중요하다.

⑤ 14) [It / That / What] is great to simulate your 15) i＿＿＿＿＿＿, but even better 16) [if / unless] you can become involved 17) [emotional / emotionally], physically, and interpersonally.

여러분의 지력을 모의실험하는 것도 좋지만, 여러분이 감정적으로, 신체적으로, 그리고 사람과 사람 사이에서 참여할 수 있게 된다면 훨씬 더 좋다.

⑥ In other words, it isn't enough to 18) [mere / merely] read this material in a book or hear an instructor talk about 19) [it / them] in class.

다시 말해서, 단순히 책에 있는 이 자료를 읽거나 수업 시간에 교사가 그것에 관해 말하는 것을 듣는 것만으로는 충분하지 않다.

⑦ You must also have opportunities to 20) [practice / practicing] the skills and make the ideas your own.

여러분은 또한 기술을 연습하고 아이디어를 여러분 자신의 것으로 만들 기회를 가져야 한다.

＊ immersion: 몰입

글의 전개방식	통념과 반박	문제와 해결	연구·실험	비교·대조	예시	비유	시간적 흐름	스토리텔링	기타

개요도	서론	본론	결론
	주장 제시	논의 전개	재진술
	능동적인 학습이 수동적 학습보다 효과가 있다는 말은 그리 놀랍지도 않다.	교실에 가만히 앉아있는 것보다 토론, 상호 작용, 몰입, 직접 경험 등이 더 뛰어난 학습 효과를 가져온다.	단순히 책에 있는 자료를 읽는 것은 부족하고, 분명히 아이디어를 자신의 것으로 만들 기회가 필요하다.

[2] 우리말과 일치하도록 주어진 단어를 바르게 배열하여 〈주제 및 제목〉을 쓰시오. (각 10점씩 2문제, 총 20점)

한글	지식 습득을 위한 능동적 학습의 효과
영어	of / knowledge / active / learning / the / acquisition / of / for / effectiveness
정답	
한글	능동적 학습의 힘
영어	of / Learning / The / Active / Power
정답	

[3] 위 지문에 있는 단어만을 활용하여 다음 〈요약문〉을 완성하시오(어형 변형 가능). (총 20점)

Rather than staring at a blackboard, the learning effect is much stronger when learners actively ＿＿＿＿＿ with the material and have ＿＿＿＿＿＿＿ to make the ideas their own.

[1] 밑줄에 알맞은 어휘를 채우며, [대괄호] 안에서 알맞은 표현을 고르고 문법 출제의도를 쓰세요. (각 3점씩 20문제, 총 60점)

① According to Piaget, organizing, assimilating, and accommodating can 1) [**view / be viewed**] as a kind of 2) c_____ balancing act.

　　Piaget에 따르면, 조직하기, 동화하기, 그리고 조절하기는 일종의 복잡한 균형 잡기 행위로 여겨질 수 있다.

② (❶) In his theory, the actual changes in thinking 3) [**take / taking**] place through the 4) p_____ of equilibration — the act of searching for a balance.

　　그의 이론에서, 사고의 실제 변화는 평형의 과정, 즉 균형을 찾는 행위를 통해 일어난다.

③ (❷) Piaget 5) [**assumed / was assumed**] 6) [**which / what / that**] people continually test the 7) a_____ of their thinking processes in order to 8) [**achieve / achieving**] that balance.

　　Piaget는 사람들이 그 균형을 이루기 위해 자신의 사고 과정의 적절성을 끊임없이 시험한다고 가정했다.

④ (❸) 9) B_____, the process of equilibration works like this: If we apply a particular 10) s_____ to an event or situation and the scheme 11) [**works / working**], then equilibrium 12) [**exist / exists / existing**].

　　간단히 말해서, 평형 과정은 다음과 같이 작동한다. 만약 우리가 어떤 사건이나 상황에 특정한 도식을 적용하고 그 도식이 작동하면 평형이 나타난다.

⑤ (❹) If the scheme does not produce a 13) [**satisfying / satisfied**] result, then disequilibrium exists, and we become 14) [**uncomfortable / uncomfortably**].

　　그 도식이 만족스러운 결과를 낳지 못하면, 비평형 상태가 생기고, 우리는 불편해진다.

⑥ (❺ This motivates us to keep 15) [**searching / searched**] for a solution through assimilation and accommodation, and thus our thinking changes and moves ahead.)

　　이것은 우리가 동화와 조절을 통해 해결책을 계속 찾도록 동기를 부여하고, 따라서 우리의 사고는 변화하며 앞으로 나아간다.

⑦ Of course, the level of disequilibrium must be just right or 16) o_____ — too little and we aren't 17) [**interesting / interested**] in changing, too much and we may be 18) [**encouraged / discouraged**] or 19) [**anxious / anxiously**] and not 20) [**change / changed**].

　　물론 비평형의 수준은 딱 적당하거나 최적이어야 하는데, 너무 적으면 우리는 변화에 관심이 없고, 너무 많으면 우리는 낙담하거나 불안해하며 변화하지 않을 수도 있다.

* assimilation: 동화

글의 전개방식	통념과 반박	문제와 해결	연구·실험	비교·대조	예시	비유	시간적 흐름	스토리텔링	기타

개요도	서론	본론	결론
	견해 소개	논의 전개	부연 설명
	Piaget에 따르면 조직, 동화, 조절은 복잡한 균형잡기 행위와 같다.	어떤 사건에 대해 특정 도식을 적용하여, 그 결과에 따라 평형이나 비평형 상태가 나타난다.	이는 해결책을 찾을 동기를 부여하고, 우리의 사고는 변화하며 앞으로 나아간다.

[2] 우리말과 일치하도록 주어진 단어를 바르게 배열하여 〈주제 및 제목〉을 쓰시오. (각 10점씩 2문제, 총 20점)

한글	균형을 찾는 과정으로서의 사고
영어	of / process / a / as / equilibrium / thinking / finding
정답	
한글	생각이 변화하고 앞으로 나아가는 방식에 대한 Piaget의 설명
영어	Ahead / Thinking / on / Changes / How / Moves / Piaget's / Account / and
정답	

[3] 위 지문에 있는 단어만을 활용하여 다음 〈요약문〉을 완성하시오(어형 변형 가능). (총 20점)

Piaget believed that thinking is like the process of _____ in which a particular _____ is _____ applied to contexts and revised.

[1] 밑줄에 알맞은 어휘를 채우며, [대괄호] 안에서 알맞은 표현을 고르고 문법 출제의도를 쓰세요. (각 3점씩 20문제, 총 60점)

① In many ways it's difficult 1) [to imagine / imagining] communicating 2) [with / without] any emotion whatsoever.
여러 가지 면에서 전혀 아무 감정도 없이 의사소통하는 것은 상상하기 어렵다.

② What would communication stripped of 3) [its / their] nonverbal 4) c_____s even look like?
비언어적 요소가 제거된 의사소통은 심지어 어떤 모습일까?

③ Perhaps messaging technology can 5) [give / give to] us a 6) c_____.
아마도 메시지 전달 기술이 우리에게 단서를 줄 수 있을 것이다.

④ After all, who hasn't 7) [experienced / been experienced] a misunderstanding with someone when 8) [exchanging / exchanged] text messages?
어쨌든 간에, 문자 메시지를 주고받을 때 누군가와의 오해를 경험하지 않은 사람이 누가 있겠는가?

⑤ 9) [While / During] there can be 10) [a / the] number of reasons for this, many 11) m_____s are in fact 12) [due to / because] the lack of nonverbal cues and tone of voice in these communications.
여기에는 여러 가지 이유가 있을 수 있지만, 많은 오해는 사실 이러한 의사소통에서 비언어적 단서와 목소리의 어조가 부족하기 때문이다.

⑥ 13) N_____ studies of text messaging and email support this.
문자 메시지와 이메일에 대한 수많은 연구가 이를 뒷받침한다.

⑦ A 2005 paper, "Egocentrism Over E-Mail: Can We Communicate as Well as We Think?" cites studies 14) [that / which / what] showed participants had a 50 percent chance of 15) [correct / correctly] distinguishing whether the tone in an email 16) [was / were / being] 17) s_____ or not.
2005년 논문 '이메일상에서의 자기중심성: 우리가 생각하는 것 만큼 의사소통을 잘 할 수 있을까?'는 참가자들이 이메일의 어조가 비꼬는 것인지 아닌지를 정확하게 구별할 수 있는 가능성이 50퍼센트라는 것을 보여 주는 연구를 인용한다.

⑧ If our ability to 18) [correct / correctly] deduce such information is no better than chance, it's small wonder 19) [texting / texted] often 20) [leads / leading] to misunderstandings.
만약 그러한 정보를 정확하게 추론하는 우리의 능력이 우연보다 나을 것이 없다면, 문자 메시지가 자주 오해를 불러일으키는 것은 별로 놀라운 일이 아니다.

* egocentrism: 자기중심성 ** sarcastic: 비꼬는 *** deduce: 추론하다

글의 전개방식	통념과 반박	문제와 해결	연구·실험	비교·대조	예시	비유	시간적 흐름	스토리텔링	기타
개요도	서론			본론			결론		
	의문 제기			글감 제시			연구 결과		
	비언어적 요소가 제거된 소통은 어떤 모습일까?			문자를 통한 소통에서 대부분의 오해는 비언어적 신호와 목소리 어조가 없기 때문이다.			연구에 따르면, 이메일이 비꼬는 내용인지 아닌지 정확히 추론하는 가능성이 50%였다.		

[2] 우리말과 일치하도록 주어진 단어를 바르게 배열하여 〈주제 및 제목〉을 쓰시오. (각 10점씩 2문제, 총 20점)

한글	오해 없는 의사소통을 위한 비언어적 신호의 중요성
영어	of / for / nonverbal / without / cues / importance / the / misunderstanding / communication
정답	
한글	우리가 가끔 문자 메시지를 잘못 해석하는 이유
영어	Why / Sometimes / Misinterpret / Messages / We / Text
정답	

[3] 위 지문에 있는 단어만을 활용하여 다음 〈요약문〉을 완성하시오(어형 변형 가능). (총 20점)

Numerous studies point to the fact that the reason why we _____ text messages is due to the lack of _____ cues and tone of voice.

[1] 밑줄에 알맞은 어휘를 채우며, [대괄호] 안에서 알맞은 표현을 고르고 문법 출제의도를 쓰세요. (각 3점씩 20문제, 총 60점)

① Social 1) v_____ means that certain beliefs and values are 2) [confirming / confirmed] only by the shared social experience of a group.
'사회적 확인'이란 특정 신념과 가치가 한 집단의 공유된 사회적 경험에 의해서만 확인된다는 것을 의미한다.

② 3) [In conclusion / Otherwise / For example], any given culture cannot prove that its religion and moral system are 4) [superior / inferior] to another culture's religion and moral system, but if the members 5) r_____ each other's beliefs and values, they come to 6) [take / be taken] for granted.
예를 들자면, 어떤 특정한 문화도 자신의 종교와 도덕 체계가 다른 문화의 종교와 도덕 체계보다 우월하다는 것을 증명할 수는 없지만, 구성원들이 서로의 신념과 가치를 강화한다면, 그것들은 당연하게 받아들여지게 된다.

③ ❶ Those 7) [with whom / what / who] fail to 8) a_____ such beliefs and values run the risk of "excommunication," of 9) [throwing / being thrown] out of the group.
그러한 신념과 가치를 받아들이지 못하는 사람들은 '제명', 즉 집단에서 쫓겨나는 위험에 처하게 된다.

④ ❷ The test of whether they work or not 10) [is / are / being] how comfortable and anxiety-free members are when they 11) a_____ by 12) [it / them].
그것들(신념과 가치)이 효과가 있는지 없는지에 대한 시험은 구성원들이 그것들을 준수할 때 얼마나 편안하고 불안함이 없는가 하는 것이다.

⑤ ❸ In these realms, the group learns 13) [which / what / that] certain beliefs and values, as 14) [initial / initially] promulgated by prophets, founders, and leaders, "work" in the sense of reducing 15) [certainty / uncertainty] in 16) c_____ areas of the group's functioning.
이러한 영역에서 그 집단은 예언자, 설립자, 지도자에 의해 처음 전파된 대로의 특정 신념과 가치가 집단의 기능 중 중요한 영역에서 불확실성을 감소시킨다는 의미에서 '효과가 있다'는 것을 배운다.

⑥ ❹ 17) [However / On the one hand / Moreover], as they continue to provide meaning and comfort to group members, they also become 18) [transforming / transformed] into non-discussible assumptions 19) [even though / despite / in spite] they may not be correlated with actual 20) p_____.
더욱이, 그것들이 집단 구성원들에게 의미와 편안함을 계속 제공함에 따라, 그것들은 또한 실제의 행위와 서로 상관관계가 없을 수 있을지라도 논할 수 없는 전제로 변형된다.

abide by: 준수하다 ** promulgate: 전파하다

글의 전개방식	통념과 반박	문제와 해결	연구·실험	비교·대조	예시	비유	시간적 흐름	스토리텔링	기타

개요도	서론	본론	결론
	개념 설명	논의 진행	부연 설명
	사회적 확인이란 특정 신념이나 가치가 공유된 사회적 경험에 의해서만 확인된다는 것을 말한다.	신념과 가치를 받아들이지 못하는 사람들은 집단에서 쫓겨나는 위험에 처하게 된다.	집단은 그 특정 신념이나 가치가 불확실성을 감소시킨다는 의미에서 효과가 있다고 배운다.

[2] 우리말과 일치하도록 주어진 단어를 바르게 배열하여 〈주제 및 제목〉을 쓰시오. (각 10점씩 2문제, 총 20점)

한글	사회적 검증의 개념과 작동 방식
영어	social / it / works / validation / concept / how / of / and / the
정답	
한글	사회적 확인: 특정 신념이 그룹 내에서 확인되는 방식
영어	Are / A / How / Certain / Beliefs / Confirmed / Within / Group / Social / Validation:
정답	

[3] 위 지문에 있는 단어만을 활용하여 다음 〈요약문〉을 완성하시오(어형 변형 가능). (총 20점)

With certain beliefs and values being _____ only by the shared social _____ of a group, social validation greatly affects the course of the group's functioning.

[1] 밑줄에 알맞은 어휘를 채우며, [대괄호] 안에서 알맞은 표현을 고르고 문법 출제의도를 쓰세요. (각 3점씩 20문제, 총 60점)

① Socio-cultural behaviors arise from the **1)** e_____ of information between individuals and, **2)** [therefore / though / likewise], they are **3)** [close / closely] linked to how the information **4)** [flows / flowing] among the population.

사회문화적 행동은 개인 간의 정보 교환에서 발생하며, 따라서 정보가 사람들 사이에서 어떻게 흐르는지와 밀접하게 연관되어 있다.

② In particular, the social ties built and maintained in the local neighborhood **5)** [is / are / being] **6)** [useful / useless] for solving **7)** c_____ local problems and affect the spread of information and behaviors, **8)** [play / playing] a key role in integrating social groups at higher scales.

특히 지역 사회에서 구축되고 유지되는 사회적 유대는 구체적인 지역 문제를 해결하는 데 유용하며 정보와 행동의 확산에 영향을 미쳐, 더 높은 수준에서 사회 집단을 통합하는 데 핵심적인 역할을 한다.

③ **9)** R_____ segregation **10)** [direct / directly] impacts **11)** [what / that / how] these social ties of physical nearness are **12)** [displaying / displayed], drawing boundaries on the **13)** s_____ of information flows.

거주지 분리는 이러한 물리적 근접성의 사회적 유대가 어떻게 나타나는지에 직접적인 영향을 미쳐, 정보 흐름의 구조에 경계를 짓는다.

④ We can think of the segregation process as a **14)** d_____ formation of echo-chambers: social fragmentation over the residential space encourages individual within a group **15)** [to interact / interacting] only with their peers.

우리는 분리 과정을 반향실의 역학적인 형성 과정으로 생각할 수 있다. 즉, 거주 공간에 대한 사회적 균열은 집단 내의 개인들이 자신들의 동료들과만 상호 작용을 하도록 조장한다.

⑤ In this case, the **16)** [individual / collective] behaviors of the socio-cultural space **17)** [what / that] **18)** [emerge / are emerged] could clash at higher scales, as **19)** p_____d positions may **20)** [arise / be arisen].

이러한 경우에, 새로이 생겨나는, 사회문화적 공간의 집단행동이 더 높은 수준에서 충돌할 수도 있을 터인데, 이는 양극화된 입장이 생길 수도 있기 때문이다.

* segregation: 분리 ** echo-chamber: 반향실(특정한 정보에 갇혀 새로운 정보를 받아들이지 못하는 환경)
*** fragmentation: 균열

글의 전개방식	통념과 반박	문제와 해결	연구·실험	비교·대조	예시	비유	시간적 흐름	스토리텔링	기타
개요도	서론			본론			결론		
	글감 제시			상황 제시			논의 구체화		
	사회문화적 행동은 개인 간의 정보 교환에서 발생하는데, 따라서 사회적 유대는 사회 집단을 통합하는 데 핵심적 역할을 한다.			거주지 분리는 사회적 유대 발생 방식에 직접적 영향을 미쳐 정보 흐름의 구조에 경계를 짓는다.			거주지 분리로 사회문화적 공간의 집단행동이 더 높은 수준에서 충돌할 수 있다.		

[2] 우리말과 일치하도록 주어진 단어를 바르게 배열하여 〈주제 및 제목〉을 쓰시오. (각 10점씩 2문제, 총 20점)

한글	사회적 확인: 특정 신념이 그룹 내에서 확인되는 방식
영어	on / information / of / of / individuals / socio-cultural / between / exchanges / influence / behaviors / the
정답	
한글	정보 흐름의 구조와 사회문화적 행동
영어	Structure / Information / Behaviors / Sociocultural / and / of / Flows
정답	

[3] 위 지문에 있는 단어만을 활용하여 다음 〈요약문〉을 완성하시오(어형 변형 가능). (총 20점)

The implication of the fact that socio-cultural behaviors arise from the _____ of information between _____ is that social ties can play a key role in _____ social groups at higher scales.

[1] 밑줄에 알맞은 어휘를 채우며, [대괄호] 안에서 알맞은 표현을 고르고 문법 출제의도를 쓰세요. (각 3점씩 20문제, 총 60점)

① Connecting the current offline 1) p_____ will be a difficult undertaking.
　현재 인터넷에 연결되지 않는 인구를 연결하는 것은 힘든 일일 것이다.

② Many of the remaining unserved areas are 2) [geographic / geographically] challenging to reach 3) [because / due to] rough terrain or remote location, thus 4) [rising / raising] providers' costs and pushing broadband services further out of reach of low-income households.
　(인터넷) 서비스가 여전히 제공되지 않는 지역들 중 많은 곳은 험한 지형이니 외딴 위치 때문에 지리적으로 도달하기 어려우며, 따라서 공급자의 비용을 높여 저소득 가구가 광대역 서비스를 더욱더 이용할 수 없게 한다.

③ 5) [However / Likewise / Thus], more 6) a_____ and accessible Internet is becoming a reality in parts of the world, thanks to satellite technologies 7) [emerge / emerging / emerged] as an 8) a_____ to 9) [expand / expanding] access at lower costs to remote locations across the planet.
　그러나 지구 도처의 외딴 지역에 더 저렴한 비용으로 (인터넷) 접속을 확장하는 것에 대한 대안으로 떠오르고 있는 인공위성 기술 덕분에 더 저렴하고 더 이용하기 쉬운 인터넷이 세계 여러 지역에서 현실이 되고 있다.

④ 10) [For example / In addition / On the other hand], a network of orbital satellites operated by an American spacecraft manufacturer 11) [was / had / has] launched 1,735 satellites into orbit since 2019.
　예를 들어, 한 미국 우주선 제조업체가 운영하는 궤도 위성망은 2019년 이래로 1,735개의 인공위성을 궤도로 쏘아 올려 왔다.

⑤ According to the company: "The satellite network is ideally 12) [suiting / suited] for areas of the globe 13) [which / what / where] connectivity has 14) t_____ been a challenge.
　그 회사에 따르면 "그 위성망은 (인터넷) 접속성이 대체로 난제였던 지구의 여러 지역에 이상적으로 적합합니다.

⑥ 15) [Unbounding / Unbounded] by traditional ground infrastructure, the network can deliver high-speed broadband Internet to locations 16) [which / whose / where] access 17) [has / having] been 18) u_____ or 19) [complete / completely] 20) [available / unavailable]."
　그 위성망은, 기존의 지상 기반 시설에 구애되지 않으므로, (인터넷) 접속을 믿을 수 없었거나 전적으로 이용할 수 없었던 지역에 고속 광대역 인터넷을 제공할 수 있습니다."

　　　　　　　　　　　　　* terrain: 지형, 지역 ** broadband: 광대역, 고속 데이터 통신망

글의 전개방식	통념과 반박	문제와 해결	연구·실험	비교·대조	예시	비유	시간적 흐름	스토리텔링	기타

개요도	서론		본론		결론	
	글감 제시		대안 제시		사례 제시	
	지형이나 외딴 위치 때문에 인터넷 서비스를 제공받지 못하는 곳이 있다.		인공위성 기술 덕분에 더 저렴하고 이용하기 쉬운 인터넷이 현실화되고 있다.		한 미국 우주선 제조업체의 궤도 위성망은 여러 지역에 이상적으로 적합하다.	

[2] 우리말과 일치하도록 주어진 단어를 바르게 배열하여 〈주제 및 제목〉을 쓰시오. (각 10점씩 2문제, 총 20점)

한글	지리적으로 어려운 지역에 인터넷 서비스를 제공하는 위성 기술
영어	geographically / internet / service / challenging / technology / for / to / supplying / satellite / areas
정답	
한글	세계를 연결하는 궤도 위성들
영어	For / World / Connecting / Satellites / Orbital / the
정답	

[3] 위 지문에 있는 단어만을 활용하여 다음 〈요약문〉을 완성하시오(어형 변형 가능). (총 20점)

Thanks to _____ technologies, it became possible to provide internet service to _____ challenging areas.

[1] 밑줄에 알맞은 어휘를 채우며, [대괄호] 안에서 알맞은 표현을 고르고 문법 출제의도를 쓰세요. (각 3점씩 20문제, 총 60점)

① Data will 1) [generate / be generated] from everywhere.
데이터는 어디에서나 생겨날 것이다.

② Cars, smartphones, bodies, minds, homes, and cities will be sources of 2) m_____ amounts of information 3) [what / that] will grow exponentially and flow at an 4) u_____ speed over the internet.
자동차, 스마트폰, 몸, 마음, 집, 도시는, 인터넷상에서 기하급수적으로 증가하고 전례 없는 속도로 유통될 거대한 양의 정보의 원천이 될 것이다.

③ In the years ahead, the expression "less is 5) [more / less]" will have a greater level of 6) i_____ as to how you 7) i_____ the ocean of 8) i_____s 9) [coming / come] your way and will 10) [aid / be aided] you to understand the world around you.
앞으로는, "더 적은 것이 더 많은 것이다"라는 표현이 여러분이 어떻게 자신에게 닥쳐오는 수많은 식견을 통합하는지에 관해 더 큰 정도의 중요성을 가질 것이고, 여러분이 주변 세상을 이해하도록 도움을 줄 것이다.

④ The amount of information and media 11) [surrounding / surrounded] us will be impracticable to process and retrieve; you can leave 12) [that / those] for the machines, 13) [which / what / where] can process data faster and more 14) [accurate / accurately] than we can.
우리를 둘러싸고 있는 정보와 매체의 양은 처리하고 기억하기가 거의 불가능할 것이어서, 여러분은 그것을 기계에 맡길 수 있는데, 그것(기계)은 우리가 할 수 있는 것보다 더 빠르고 더 정확하게 데이터를 처리할 수 있다.

⑤ Your job will be to focus on 15) [that / what] matters most to you.
여러분이 할 일은 여러분에게 가장 중요한 것에 집중하는 것일 것이다.

⑥ The key to an easy digital future 16) [is / are / being] not so much 17) a_____ a tsunami of data but 18) [how / what / that] you 19) c_____ and translate 20) [it / them] into new contexts, scenarios, and ideas.
안락한 디지털 미래의 비결은 쓰나미처럼 밀려오는 데이터에 접근하는 것이라기보다는 오히려 어떻게 그것을 이해해서 새로운 맥락, 시나리오, 아이디어로 바꾸는가이다.

* exponentially: 기하급수적으로 ** retrieve: 기억하다, 상기하다

글의 전개방식	통념과 반박	문제와 해결	연구·실험	비교·대조	예시	비유	시간적 흐름	스토리텔링	기타

개요도	서론		본론		결론	
	배경 제시		논의 추상화		주장 제시	
	데이터는 어디에서나 생겨날 것이고 전례 없는 속도로 유통될 것이다.		"더 적은 것이 더 많은 것이다"라는 표현이 닥쳐오는 수많은 식견을 통합하는 방식에 대해 더 큰 중요성을 가진다.		우리의 일은 가장 중요한 것에 집중하는 것이고, 데이터를 이해해서 아이디어로 바꾸는 것이다.	

[2] 우리말과 일치하도록 주어진 단어를 바르게 배열하여 〈주제 및 제목〉을 쓰시오. (각 10점씩 2문제, 총 20점)

한글	늘어나는 데이터와 인간의 역할
영어	job / and / human's / data / the / of / amount / growing
정답	
한글	데이터 쓰나미 속에서 헤엄치기 위해 해야 할 일
영어	The / What / Done / In / of / To / Tsunami / Should / Be / Swim / Data
정답	

[3] 위 지문에 있는 단어만을 활용하여 다음 〈요약문〉을 완성하시오(어형 변형 가능). (총 20점)

Since data is _____ from everywhere and the amount grows _____, we should be able to _____ and translate data into valuable ideas.

[1] 밑줄에 알맞은 어휘를 채우며, [대괄호] 안에서 알맞은 표현을 고르고 문법 출제의도를 쓰세요. (각 3점씩 20문제, 총 60점)

① 1) [If / Unless] you're one of those lucky people 2) [who / with whom / what] only drive new cars, on at least one 3) o_____ you've probably 4) [experienced / been experienced] the painful 5) r_____ that your car is too old and no longer worth 6) [repair / repairing / repaired] any more.

여러분이 새 차만 운전하는 운이 좋은 그런 사람들 중 한명이 아니라면, 아마도 여러분의 차가 너무 낡아서 이제 더는 수리할 가치가 없다고 고통스럽게 깨달았던 경험을 한 경우가 적어도 한 번은 있었을 것이다.

② As a car ages, more and more things can go 7) [wrong / wrongly] and need fixing.

차가 노후화되면서, 점점 더 많은 것들이 고장 나서 수리가 필요할 수 있다.

③ At some point, the owner needs to decide: is it worth getting this latest issue 8) [looking / looked] at or is it time to give up on this car and find another?

어떤 시점에서는, 소유자가 결정을 내려야 하는데, 이 최근 문제를 살펴보게 하는 것이 가치가 있는가, 아니면 이 차를 포기하고 다른 차를 구해서 얻을 때인가?

④ The problem is 9) [that / what / which] a lot of money has already 10) [spent / been spent] on the car, and scrapping 11) [it / them] makes it seem 12) [as if / even if] that money has just been wasted, 13) [which / what / that] makes it very 14) d_____ to 15) [choose / choosing] the best option.

문제는 이미 그 차에 많은 돈이 들어갔고 폐차하는 것이 그 돈이 그저 헛되이 쓰인 것처럼 보이게 하는데, 그것이 선택할 수 있는 최선의 것을 고르는 것을 매우 어렵게 만든다는 것이다.

⑤ It's a problem known 16) [as / for] 17) e_____, when a person gets 18) [trapping / trapped / trap] into making the wrong 19) d_____ just because they've previously 20) [invested / been invested] so much.

그것은 '속박감'이라고 알려진 문제인데, 어떤 사람이 단지 이전에 매우 많이 투자했다는 이유만으로 잘못된 결정을 내리는 함정에 빠지는 경우이다.

* scrap: 폐기하다

글의 전개방식	통념과 반박	문제와 해결	연구·실험	비교·대조	예시	비유	시간적 흐름	스토리텔링	기타

개요도	서론	본론	결론
	배경 제시	상황 제시	개념 도입
	새 차만 운전할 것이 아니라면, 언젠가는 차가 너무 오래되었고 더 수리할 가치를 못 느낄 수 있다.	문제를 살펴볼 것인지 다른 차를 구할지 고민에 빠지게 되는데, 기존에 투자한 돈을 고려하게 된다.	속박감이라고 알려진 문제인데, 이전에 많이 투자했다는 이유만으로 잘못된 선택을 내리는 것을 말한다.

[2] 우리말과 일치하도록 주어진 단어를 바르게 배열하여 〈주제 및 제목〉을 쓰시오. (각 10점씩 2문제, 총 20점)

한글	속박감의 개념과 사례
영어	and / entrapment / the / case / of / concept / an / example
정답	
한글	속박감: 당신이 여전히 매몰 비용을 신경쓰는 이유
영어	the / Still / Entrapment: / Care / You / Cost / About / Why / Sunk
정답	

[3] 위 지문에 있는 단어만을 활용하여 다음 〈요약문〉을 완성하시오(어형 변형 가능). (총 20점)

A concept known as entrapment indicates that we sometimes make a wrong _____ just because of previous _____.

[1] 밑줄에 알맞은 어휘를 채우며, [대괄호] 안에서 알맞은 표현을 고르고 문법 출제의도를 쓰세요. (각 3점씩 20문제, 총 60점)

① Teams and **1)** o_____s also have a 'mental life'.

팀과 조직에도 또한 '정신적 삶'이 있다.

② Most leaders work **2)** [hard / hardly] to get alignment — getting everybody on the same thinking **3)** w_____.

대부분의 리더는 (사고의) 일치를 얻기 위하여 열심히 노력하는데, 그것은 모든 사람을 동일한 '사고' 주파수에 맞추는 것이다.

③ But to help organizations and teams **4)** [to flourish / flourished], leaders must also work **5)** [equal / **equally**] hard on getting attunement ⸺ getting people on the same feeling wavelength, getting the **6)** p_____ of the organization and the meaning of the work to **7)** r_____ with people in a felt way.

그러나 조직과 팀이 번창하도록 도우려면 리더는 또한 동조를 얻는 데에도 똑같이 열심히 노력해야 하는데, 그것은 사람들을 동일한 '감정' 주파수에 맞추는 것, 조직의 목적과 업무의 의미가 (감정적으로) 느껴지는 방식으로 사람들에게 반향을 불러일으키도록 하는 것이다.

④ 'Felt' is the important word here.

여기서는 '느껴지는'이란 말이 중요한 말이다.

⑤ **8)** [It / This / That] is **9)** [relative / relatively] easy **10)** [to explain / explain] the purpose and goals of an organization in a **11)** c_____ way.

조직의 목적과 목표를 인지적인 방식으로 설명하는 것은 비교적 쉽다.

⑥ But to function at our best, we have to **12)** [feel / feeling] the **13)** c_____ between **14)** [that / what] we are **15)** [asking / being asked] to do and some larger purpose of the group.

하지만 우리가 최상의 상태에서 기능하기 위해서, 우리는 하라는 요구를 받고 있는 것과 집단의 어떤 더 큰 목적 사이의 연관성을 '느껴야' 한다.

⑦ Leaders of flourishing organizations **16)** s_____ in making strong feeling connections between the **17)** p_____ goals and values of the people working there and **18)** [that / those] of the organization, or even the larger society.

번창하는 조직의 리더는 그곳에서 일하는 사람들의 개인적인 목표와 가치, 그리고 조직, 혹은 심지어 더 큰 집단의 그것들(목표와 가치)을 서로 강력하게 감정적으로 연관 짓는 데 성공한다.

⑧ The tighter the links in the **19)** c_____, the happier the people and **20)** [a / the] better the results.

그 사슬의 고리가 단단할수록, 그 (조직의) 사람들은 더 행복하고, 결과는 더 좋다.

　　　　　　　　　* alignment: 일치 ** attunement: 동조. 감정 맞추기
　　　　　　　*** restate with: ~에게 반향을 불러일으키다

글의 전개방식	통념과 반박	문제와 해결	연구·실험	비교·대조	예시	비유	시간적 흐름	스토리텔링	기타

	서론	본론	결론
	논점 제시	강조점 지적	부연 설명
개요도	팀과 조직에도 정신적 삶이 있는데, 사람들을 동일한 감정 주파수에 맞추는 것은 중요하다.	"느껴지는"이라는 말이 중요한데, 인지적인 방식의 설명은 쉽지만 연관성을 느끼게 하는 것은 까다롭다.	성공적인 조직의 리더는 개인의 목표와 조직의 가치를 감정적으로 연관 짓는 데 성공한다.

[2] 우리말과 일치하도록 주어진 단어를 바르게 배열하여 〈주제 및 제목〉을 쓰시오. (각 10점씩 2문제, 총 20점)

한글	리더가 그룹 구성원들 사이에서 (감정적)조화를 이루는 것의 중요성
영어	the / attunement / within / leader's / significance / getting / group / members / of
정답	
한글	조직의 성공 비결: 사람들의 마음을 조율하기
영어	A / Success: / Getting / an / Key / Organization's / People / Attuned / to
정답	

[3] 위 지문에 있는 단어만을 활용하여 다음 〈요약문〉을 완성하시오(어형 변형 가능). (총 20점)

Beyond the _____ understanding of the purpose and goal of an organization, the leader should get members to feel that their _____ values and those of the group are _____.

[1] 밑줄에 알맞은 어휘를 채우며, [대괄호] 안에서 알맞은 표현을 고르고 문법 출제의도를 쓰세요. (각 3점씩 20문제, 총 60점)

① In the door-in-the-face 1) t_____, a large, 2) [reasonable / unreasonable] request is 3) [making / made], 4) [which / what / that] is turned down; this is followed by a smaller more reasonable request.

'면전에서 문 닫기 기법'에서는, 크고 불합리한 요청이 이루어지고, 그것이 거절되며, 이것이 더 작으면서 더 합리적인 요청으로 이어진다.

② (❶) People are more likely to 5) [agree / agreeing] to this smaller second request when it is 6) [placing / placed] in the context of the more unreasonable request than if it 7) [was / had been] placed at the outset.

사람들은 이 더 작은 두 번째 요청이 처음부터 이루어진 경우보다 더 불합리한 요청이라는 맥락 속에서 이루어질 때 그것에 동의할 가능성이 더 크다.

③ (❷) The success of this technique may be related to the reciprocity social 8) n_____, the rule that we should pay back in kind 9) [that / what] we receive from 10) [other / others].

이 기법의 성공은 '호혜적 사회 규범', 즉 우리가 다른 사람들로부터 받는 것을 동일하게 갚아야 한다는 규칙과 관련이 있을 것이다.

④ (❸) The person 11) [asking / asked] for our support or 12) a_____, 13) [appears / appearing] to 14) [had made / have made] a concession by giving up their initial request, for a much smaller one.

우리의 지원이나 도움을 요청하는 사람은 훨씬 더 작은 요청을 위해 자신의 처음 요청을 포기함으로써 양보를 한 것처럼 보인다.

⑤ (❹ As a result, we feel 15) [compelling / compelled] to reciprocate and agree to the smaller request.)

그 결과, 우리는 더 작은 요청에 화답하고 동의해야 한다고 느낀다.

⑥ A common 16) a_____ of door-in-the-face is when teens ask their parents for a large request (attending an out-of-town concert) and then when the 17) p_____ is denied, 18) [asks / asking / asked] them for something smaller (attending a local concert).

면전에서 문 닫기 기법이 흔히 응용되는 것은 십 대들이 자기 부모에게 큰 요청(다른 도시에서 하는 콘서트에 참석하기)을 한 뒤 허락이 거부되면 그들에게 더 작은 것(지역 콘서트에 참석하기)을 요청하는 경우이다.

⑦ (❺) Having 19) [denied / been denied] the larger request 20) [increases / decreases] the likelihood that parents will acquiesce in the later, smaller request.

더 큰 요청을 거부한 것은 부모가 그 뒤의 더 작은 요청을 묵인할 가능성을 높인다.

* reciprocate: 화답하다 ** concession: 양보 *** acquiesce: 묵인하다

글의 전개방식	통념과 반박	문제와 해결	연구·실험	비교·대조	예시	비유	시간적 흐름	스토리텔링	기타

개요도	서론		본론		결론	
	글감 제시		분석 진행		사례 제시	
	성공적인 조직의 리더는 개인의 목표와 조직의 가치를 감정적으로 연관 짓는 데 성공한다.		호혜적 사회 규범 덕에 이 기법이 성공하는데, 마치 처음 요청을 포기함으로써 '양보'를 한 것처럼 보이기 때문이다.		십 대들이 큰 요청을 한 뒤 거부되면 더 작은 요청을 연달아 하는 상황을 떠올릴 수 있다.	

[2] 우리말과 일치하도록 주어진 단어를 바르게 배열하여 〈주제 및 제목〉을 쓰시오. (각 10점씩 2문제, 총 20점)	
한글	면전에서 문 닫기 기법이 작동하는 방식
영어	door-in-the-face / works / technique / how / the
정답	
한글	규범적 측면에서의 면전에서 문 닫기 기법
영어	From / The / Door-In-The-Face / Perspective / A / Normative / Technique
정답	

[3] 위 지문에 있는 단어만을 활용하여 다음 〈요약문〉을 완성하시오(어형 변형 가능). (총 20점)

Because of the reciprocity social _____ where we should pay back what we receive, the door-in-the-face technique works as it seems like a _____ of giving up the initial _____.

[1] 밑줄에 알맞은 어휘를 채우며, [대괄호] 안에서 알맞은 표현을 고르고 문법 출제의도를 쓰세요. (각 3점씩 20문제, 총 60점)

① "Capitalism" is generally **1)** [understanding / understood] as a market-based, economic system **2)** [governing / governed] by capital — that is, the **3)** w_____ of an individual or an establishment accumulated by or employed in **4)** [its / their] business activities.

일반적으로 '자본주의'는 자본, 즉 사업 활동에 의해 축적되거나 그에 사용되는 개인이나 회사의 재산에 의해 지배되는 시장 기반의 경제 체제로 이해된다.

② Entrepreneurs and the institutions they **5)** [create / creating] **6)** [generate / generating] the capital **7)** [which / with which / what / whose] businesses provide goods, services, and **8)** p_____s to workers.

기업가와 그들이 만드는 기관은 기업이 상품, 서비스, 노동자의 임금을 제공하는 데 사용하는 자본을 창출한다.

③ Defenders of capitalism argue **9)** [which / what / that] this system maximally **10)** d_____s social freedoms and desirable resources, **11)** [results / resulting] in the best economic outcomes for everyone in society.

자본주의 옹호자들은 이 체제가 사회적 자유와 가치 있는 자원을 최대한 배분하여 사회의 모든 사람에게 최상의 경제적 결과를 낸다고 주장한다.

④ On this view, business's only social responsibilities are to **12)** [maximize / minimize] **13)** [legal / legally] generated profits.

이러한 관점에서는, 기업의 유일한 사회적 책임은 합법적으로 창출되는 이윤을 최대화하는 것이다.

⑤ **14)** [However / For instance / Moreover], over the past several decades there has been a **15)** s_____ reaction against this view.

그러나 지난 수십 년간에 걸쳐 이 견해에 대한 상당한 반발이 있었다.

⑥ It is argued **16)** [which / what / that] businesses have responsibilities far beyond following the law and profit making.

기업은 법을 따르고 이윤을 창출하는 것을 훨씬 넘어서는 그 이상의 책임이 있다는 주장이 제기된다.

⑦ When society accepts **17)** c_____, this view holds, it need not also **18)** [accept / accepted] the view that economic **19)** f_____ always has priority over competing conceptions of the collection and **20)** d_____ of social goods, or of other responsibilities owed to employees, customers, society, and the environment.

이 견해가 주장하는 바는, 사회가 자본주의를 받아들일 때 경제적 자유가 사회적 재화의 축적과 분배, 혹은 직원, 고객, 사회, 그리고 환경에 빚진 여타의 책임이라는 대립하는 개념보다 항상 우선한다는 관점 또한 받아들일 필요는 없다는 것이다.

* entrepreneur: 기업가

글의 전개방식	통념과 반박	문제와 해결	연구·실험	비교·대조	예시	비유	시간적 흐름	스토리텔링	기타

개요도	서론	본론	결론
	개념 소개	견해 소개	상반되는 견해 소개
	자본주의란 자본에 의해 운영되는 시장 기반 경제 체제로 이해된다.	찬성론자들은 최상의 경제 결과가 모두에게 나온다는 점을 강조한다.	사업은 단순히 법을 지켜 이윤을 만드는 것이 아니라, 특정 사회적 책임이 있다는 견해도 존재한다.

[2] 우리말과 일치하도록 주어진 단어를 바르게 배열하여 〈주제 및 제목〉을 쓰시오. (각 10점씩 2문제, 총 20점)

한글	자본주의를 둘러싼 상반된 관점들
영어	contrasting / surrounding / capitalism / perspectives
정답	
한글	자본주의와 기업의 사회적 책임
영어	and / Capitalism / of / Responsibilities / Social / Businesses
정답	

[3] 위 지문에 있는 단어만을 활용하여 다음 〈요약문〉을 완성하시오(어형 변형 가능). (총 20점)

Though defenders of capitalism argue that capitalism results in the best economic _____ for everyone, this view has been challenged by an argument that emphasizes the social _____ of business.

[1] 밑줄에 알맞은 어휘를 채우며, [대괄호] 안에서 알맞은 표현을 고르고 문법 출제의도를 쓰세요. (각 3점씩 20문제, 총 60점)

① The relationship between 1) c_____ and social change 2) [is / are / being] a bit like the relationship between a 3) r_____ and a mudslide.

위기와 사회 변화의 관계는 호우와 진흙 사태의 관계와 다소 비슷하다.

② The rain doesn't 4) [give / give to] the mudslide its power — that comes from the weight of earth, 5) [building / built] up over decades.

비가 진흙 사태에 그것의 힘을 가하는 것이 아니라, 그것은 수십 년 동안 쌓인 흙의 무게에서 비롯되는 것이다.

③ 6) [That / What] the rain can do 7) [is / are / being] 8) [loosen / tighten] things up, 9) [creates / creating] the conditions for change.

비가 '할 수' 있는 것은 상태를 느슨하게 만들어, 변화를 위한 여건을 만드는 것이다.

④ Britain's post-Second World War 10) s_____ didn't solve the problems of the war: it addressed the pent-up problems of the 1930s, and its 11) i_____ ingredients dated back further, to the opening years of the 1900s.

영국의 제2차 세계 대전 이후 합의는 전쟁의 문제들을 해결한 것이 아니었다. 그것은 1930년대의 억눌려 있던 문제를 다루었고, 그것의 지적 요소들은 역사가 1900년대 초반까지 더 거슬러 올라갔다.

⑤ 12) [Likewise / Otherwise / Nevertheless], America's New Deal of the 1930s was 13) [triggering / triggered] by the Great Depression, but the issues 14) [it / they] addressed and the approaches it applied 15) [emerging / emerged / were emerged] decades before, in the 16) p_____ and populist movements of the 1890s and 1900s.

마찬가지로, 1930년대의 미국의 뉴딜 정책은 대공황에 의해 촉발되었지만, 그것이 다룬 문제와 그것이 사용한 접근 방식은 수십 년 전, 1890년대와 1900년대의 진보 운동과 인민주의 운동에서 나타났다.

⑥ So, 17) [if / unless] the 2020 pandemic does 18) [lead / leading] to a radical social renewal, then the main elements of that 19) r_____ will be 20) [visible / visibly] already today.

따라서 만약 2020년의 전 세계적인 유행병이 진정 급격한 사회 개선을 가져온다면, 그러면 그 개선의 주요 요소들은 오늘날 이미 눈에 보일 것이다.

* pent-up: 억눌려 있는

글의 전개방식	통념과 반박	문제와 해결	연구·실험	비교·대조	예시	비유	시간적 흐름	스토리텔링	기타

	서론	본론	결론
개요도	주장의 집약적 제시 위기와 사회적 변화 사이의 관계는 호우와 진흙 사태의 관계와 비슷하다.	사례 제시 영국의 제2차대전 후 합의와 뉴딜 정책은 모두 위기가 사회적 변화에 대한 여건을 만든다는 것을 보여준다.	부연 설명 마찬가지로 2020년 판데믹 위기가 사회적 변화를 이끈다면, 그 사회적 변화의 구성요소는 이미 눈에 보일 것이다.

[2] 우리말과 일치하도록 주어진 단어를 바르게 배열하여 〈주제 및 제목〉을 쓰시오. (각 10점씩 2문제, 총 20점)

한글	위기가 사회 변화에 미치는 영향
영어	on / social / influence / change / of / crisis / the
정답	
한글	위기가 사회 변화에 실제로 미치는 영향에 대한 통찰
영어	For / Actually / What / A / Change / Social / On / A / Does / Insight / An / Crisis
정답	

[3] 위 지문에 있는 단어만을 활용하여 다음 〈요약문〉을 완성하시오(어형 변형 가능). (총 20점)

A _____ itself does not give any power to a social change, but it outlines _____ for a series of _____ to occur.

[1] 밑줄에 알맞은 어휘를 채우며, [대괄호] 안에서 알맞은 표현을 고르고 문법 출제의도를 쓰세요. (각 3점씩 20문제, 총 60점)

① The 1) c_____s of an agricultural society affected its long-run growth pattern prior to the Industrial Revolution, 2) [while / during] self-sufficiency and land 3) [dependency / independency] limited the 4) m_____ to increase the yield.

농업 사회의 특징은 산업 혁명 이전에 그것의 장기적인 성장 패턴에 영향을 미친 한편, 자급자족과 토지 의존은 수확량을 증가시키려는 의욕을 제한했다.

② ❶ 5) [Even though / Despite / In spite] some attempts were 6) [making / made] to reform agricultural production, the low level of technologies 7) [available / unavailable] could not 8) c_____ on the effect of those attempts.

비록 농업 생산을 개혁하려는 몇차례의 시도가 있었지만, 가용할 수 있는 기술 수준이 낮아 그러한 시도의 효과를 이용할 수 없었다.

③ ❷ 9) [Moreover / Instead / Thus], 10) [elasticity / inelasticity] in demand, instability in supply, and price divergence 11) [preventing / prevented] the capital accumulation 12) [needing / needed] for reinvestment in agricultural technologies.

게다가, 수요의 비탄력성, 공급의 불안정성, 그리고 가격 격차는 농업 기술 재투자에 필요한 자본의 축적을 방해했다.

④ ❸ All of these factors 13) [created / were created] a 14) v_____ circle such that agricultural 15) p_____ could not 16) [boom / be boomed].

이 모든 요인들이 악순환을 만들어 농업 생산은 크게 증가할 수 없었다.

⑤ ❹ As a result, the 17) a_____ society 18) [showed / showing] a long-term 19) d_____ growth 20) p_____ in history.

결과적으로, 농업 사회는 역사적으로 장기간 둔화하는 성장 패턴을 보였다.

* inelasticity: 비탄력성 ** divergence: 격차, 차이 *** decelerate: 둔화하다

글의 전개방식	통념과 반박	문제와 해결	연구·실험	비교·대조	예시	비유	시간적 흐름	스토리텔링	기타

개요도	서론		본론		결론	
	글감 제시		분석 진행		논의 마무리	
	농경 사회의 특성은 그것의 장기적 성장 패턴에 영향을 주었다.		낮은 수준의 기술, 수요의 비탄력성,, 공급 불안정성 등이 자본의 축적을 막아 악순환을 만들었다.		농경 사회는 장기적으로 둔화하는 성장 패턴을 보인다.	

[2] 우리말과 일치하도록 주어진 단어를 바르게 배열하여 <주제 및 제목>을 쓰시오. (각 10점씩 2문제, 총 20점)

한글	장기적인 성장을 방해하는 농업 사회의 특성
영어	of / that / long-term / prevent / growth / society / agricultural / characteristics
정답	
한글	농업사회의 감속성장 패턴에 관한 분석
영어	Pattern / Analysis / Growth / of / Agricultural / Decelerated / Society / on / An
정답	

[3] 위 지문에 있는 단어만을 활용하여 다음 <요약문>을 완성하시오(어형 변형 가능). (총 20점)

Several factors such as _____ demand, unstable _____ and divergent prices did make the long-term growth pattern of agricultural society _____.

[1] 밑줄에 알맞은 어휘를 채우며, [대괄호] 안에서 알맞은 표현을 고르고 문법 출제의도를 쓰세요. (각 3점씩 20문제, 총 60점)

① It is 1) e_____ 2) [**that / what / which**] self-esteem has a significant effect on health — both directly and indirectly.
자존감이 건강에 큰 영향을 미치는 것은 분명한데, 직접적으로든 간접적으로든 모두 그렇다.

② 3) [**However / Thus / For instance**], self-esteem is 4) [**typical / typically**] considered a key feature of mental health and therefore worth 5) [**pursue / to pursue / pursuing**] in its own 6) r_____.
예를 들면, 자존감은 일반적으로 정신 건강의 주요 특징으로 여겨지므로 그 자체만으로 추구할 가치가 있다.

③ It may also have an 7) [**direct / indirect**] influence through 8) [**its / their**] 9) c_____ to intentions to undertake healthy or unhealthy actions.
그것은 또한 건강에 좋거나 건강에 좋지 않은 행동을 시도하려는 의도에 원인을 제공함으로써 간접적인 영향을 미칠 수도 있다.

④ For instance, at a commonsense level, individuals who respect and value themselves will, other things 10) [**being / are**] equal, seek to look after themselves by 11) [**adopting / adapting**] courses of action 12) [**what / that**] prevent disease.
예를 들면, 상식적인 수준에서 자신을 존중하고 중시하는 사람은 다른 것이 같은 조건이라면, 질병을 막는 행동 방침을 채택함으로써 자신을 돌보려고 할 것이다.

⑤ Less obviously perhaps, there is strong evidence that people enjoying high self-esteem are 13) [**more / less**] willing to 14) [**tolerate / tolerating**] dissonance and more likely to take rational action to reduce that dissonance, by, for example, 15) [**reject / rejects / rejecting**] unhealthy behaviour.
아마 덜 분명하기는 하겠지만, 높은 자존감을 누리는 사람은 부조화를 덜 용인하려 하고 그러한 부조화를 줄이기 위해, 예컨대 건강에 좋지 않은 행동을 거부함으로써, 이성적인 행동을 할 가능성이 더 크다는 강력한 증거가 있다.

⑥ Those having low self-esteem are more likely to conform to interpersonal pressures than those enjoying high self-esteem with unfortunate 16) c_____s when such social pressure results 17) [**from / in**] 'unhealthy behaviour'.
자존감이 낮은 사람들은 높은 자존감을 누리는 사람들보다 대인 관계에서 오는 압박에 반대하여 (→ 순응하여) 그러한 사회적 압박이 '건강에 좋지 않은 행동'으로 귀결될 때의 불행한 결과를 맞이할 가능성이 더 크다.

⑦ In terms of empowerment, 18) [**despite / though**], any unthinking yielding to social 19) p_____ would be considered 20) [**healthy / unhealthy**]!
하지만 자율권의 측면에서는 사회적 압박에 경솔하게 굴복하는 것은 무엇이든 건강에 좋지 않은 것으로 여겨질 것이다!

* dissonance: 부조화 ** empowerment: 자율권

글의 전개방식	통념과 반박	문제와 해결	연구·실험	비교·대조	예시	비유	시간적 흐름	스토리텔링	기타

개요도	서론		본론		결론	
	주장 제시		근거 제시		근거 확장	
	자존감이 건강에 큰 영향을 미치는 것은 분명한데, 직/간접적으로 모두 그렇다.		자존감은 정신 건강의 주요 특징이므로 그 자체만으로 건강과 관련 있다.		높은 자존감을 가진 사람은 부조화를 줄이기 위해 이성적인 행동을 할 가능성이 더 크다.	

[2] 우리말과 일치하도록 주어진 단어를 바르게 배열하여 〈주제 및 제목〉을 쓰시오. (각 10점씩 2문제, 총 20점)

한글	건강에 대한 자존감의 영향
영어	health / the / on / of / self-esteem / influence
정답	
한글	자존감이 건강에 미치는 직간접적 영향
영어	Self-Esteem / Health / Indirect / of / and / on / Effects / Direct
정답	

[3] 위 지문에 있는 단어만을 활용하여 다음 〈요약문〉을 완성하시오(어형 변형 가능). (총 20점)

Self-esteem can positively affect _____ both directly and indirectly because individuals with high self-esteem will take _____ action to reduce _____.

[1] 밑줄에 알맞은 어휘를 채우며, [대괄호] 안에서 알맞은 표현을 고르고 문법 출제의도를 쓰세요. (각 3점씩 20문제, 총 60점)

① In recent years, researchers have been trying to understand the changes 1) [what / that] occur in the brain during 2) a_____.
최근 몇 년 동안, 연구자들은 사춘기에 뇌에서 일어나는 변화를 알기 위해 노력해 오고 있다.

② Structural brain imaging studies over the past decade have 3) [challenged / been challenged] the belief that structural brain development ends in early childhood, 4) [reveals / revealed / revealing] that changes 5) o_____ through early adulthood.
지난 십 년에 걸친 뇌 구조 영상 연구는 뇌 구조 발달이 유아기에 끝난다는 믿음에 이의를 제기하며 변화는 성인기 초기 내내 일어난다는 것을 밝혔다.

③ 6) [In addition / However / Otherwise], these studies provide an 7) i_____ into the biological basis for understanding adolescent thinking and behavior.
그뿐만 아니라, 이러한 연구들은 사춘기의 사고와 행동을 이해하기 위한 생물학적 근거에 대한 통찰을 제공한다.

④ For example, the ventromedial prefrontal cortex of the brain is 8) r_____ for evaluating risk and reward to help 9) [guide / guided] the person to make a 10) d_____.
예를 들면, 뇌의 복내측 시상하핵 전전두엽 피질은 사람이 결정을 내리도록 이끄는 데 도움이 되도록 위험과 보상을 평가하는 것을 담당한다.

⑤ Imaging studies have 11) [shown / been shown] that this part of the brain is the last to 12) m_____ in adolescents, 13) [which / what / when / that] supports behavioral studies that show adolescents take greater risks than adults in activities such as substance abuse.
영상 연구는 뇌의 이 부분이 청소년에게 있어서 가장 마지막으로 발달한다는 것을 보여 주었는데, 이것은 성인보다 청소년이 약물 남용과 같은 행동에서 더 큰 위험을 감수한다는 것을 보여 주는 행동 연구들을 뒷받침한다.

⑥ Adolescents tend to 14) [engage / engaging] in more reckless behaviors 15) [because / because of] the area of the brain that assesses risk and benefits has not 16) [complete / completely] developed yet.
청소년은 더 무모한 행동을 하는 경향이 있는데, 위험과 이득을 평가하는 뇌의 영역이 아직 완전히 발달하지는 않았기 때문이다.

⑦ These findings, along with other studies 17) [examining / examined] the 18) m_____ of other regions of the prefrontal cortex during adolescence, suggest 19) [what / that / which] the spontaneity, short-sightedness, and risk-taking behaviors associated with adolescence could be partially 20) [biological / biologically] in nature.
사춘기의 전전두엽 피질의 다른 부위의 발달을 조사하는 다른 연구와 함께, 이러한 연구 결과는 청소년기와 연관된 즉흥성, 짧은 생각 및 모험을 감수하는 행동이 사실상 부분적으로 생물학적일 수 있다는 것을 시사한다.

* ventromedial prefrontal cortex: 복내측시상하핵 전전두엽 피질
** reckless: 무모한. 무분별한 *** spontaneity: 즉흥성

글의 전개방식	통념과 반박	문제와 해결	연구·실험	비교·대조	예시	비유	시간적 흐름	스토리텔링	기타

	서론	본론	결론
	글감 제시	연구 소개	함의 제시
개요도	뇌 구조 영상 연구를 통해 뇌 구조 발달이 성인기 초기 내내 일어난다는 것을 밝혔다.	복내측시상하핵 전전두엽 피질이 덜 발달하여, 청소년은 더 무모하고 위험한 행동을 한다는 연구가 있다.	연구 결과는 즉흥성이 사실상 부분적으로 생물학적인 이유가 있음을 시사한다.

[2] 우리말과 일치하도록 주어진 단어를 바르게 배열하여 〈주제 및 제목〉을 쓰시오. (각 10점씩 2문제, 총 20점)

한글	뇌의 발달 구조에 대한 분석
영어	an / on / the / of / analysis / developmental / structure / the / brain
정답	
한글	청소년들이 위험을 감수하는 이유에 대한 생물학적 접근
영어	to / Are / Approach / Biological / Why / Adolescents / Risk-Takers
정답	

[3] 위 지문에 있는 단어만을 활용하여 다음 〈요약문〉을 완성하시오(어형 변형 가능). (총 20점)

The spontaneity and short-sightedness of adolescence can be partially attributed to biological reasons beca use a part of the brain that is _____ for _____ risk is still being _____.

[1] 밑줄에 알맞은 어휘를 채우며, [대괄호] 안에서 알맞은 표현을 고르고 문법 출제의도를 쓰세요. (각 3점씩 20문제, 총 60점)

① Both 1) p_____ and over-the-counter drugs are 2) [**subject** / **object**] to strict control by the FDA, 3) [**includes** / **including**] the regulation of manufacturing processes, specific 4) r_____s for the demonstration of safety and efficacy, 5) [**as well** / **as well as**] well-defined limits on advertising and labeling claims.

　처방이 필요한 약과 처방전 없이 살 수 있는 약 모두 FDA의 엄격한 통제를 받는데, 광고와 라벨의 설명 문구에 대한 명확한 제한과 아울러, 제조 과정의 규제, 안전과 효능의 입증에 대한 특정 요건이 포함된다.

② (C) Such controls provide assurances to consumers and health care professionals about the quality of the products and contribute to their 6) a_____ as "legitimate" treatments.

　(C) 그러한 통제는 소비자와 보건 전문가에게 제품의 질에 대한 확신을 주며, '적법한' 치료제로 그것을 받아들이는 데 기여한다.

③ The exemption of dietary 7) s_____s from these specific regulatory controls may impact their 8) c_____ as "legitimate".

　건강 보조 식품에서 이러한 특정한 규제적 통제를 면제하는 것은 그것이 '적법한' 것으로 여겨지는 데 영향을 줄 수도 있다.

④ (B) 9) [**If** / **Unless**] health care professionals feel 10) [**that** / **what** / **which**] the quality of dietary supplement products 11) [**is** / **are** / **being**] lacking, and if they consider dietary supplements outside the scope of "prevailing" medical or pharmacy practice, then physicians and pharmacists will have a low level of 12) c_____ in recommending these products to their patients for fear of legal action.

　(B) 보건 전문가가 건강 보조 식품의 질이 부족하다고 느낀다면, 그리고 그들이 건강 보조 식품을 '널리 행하여지는' 의료나 약제 업무 영역을 벗어난다고 간주한다면, 그러면 의사와 약사는 소송을 두려워해서 이러한 제품을 자신의 환자에게 추천하는 데 낮은 수준의 확신을 가질 것이다.

⑤ (A) Physicians and pharmacists cannot, 13) [**however** / **in addition** / **therefore**], 14) s_____ 15) [**them** / **themselves**] from the use of dietary supplements.

　(A) 그러나 의사와 약사는 건강 보조 식품의 사용에서 자신을 떼어 놓고 생각할 수 없다.

⑥ With more than 29,000 dietary supplements on the market, consumers have broad access to and 16) [**are** / **being**] using these products.

　29,000개가 넘는 건강 보조 식품이 시장에 나와 있으며, 소비자들은 이러한 제품에 폭넓게 접근할 수 있고 이용하고 있다.

⑦ 17) [**In fact** / **Otherwise** / **For instance**], a survey of consumers has suggested 18) [**what** / **that** / **in which** / **which**] approximately 42% of American consumers 19) [**being** / **were**] using complementary and 20) a_____ therapies, with 24% of consumers using plant-based dietary supplements on a regular basis.

　사실, 소비자 설문 조사는 미국 소비자의 대략 42퍼센트가 보완 요법과 대체 요법을 이용하고 있고, 소비자의 24퍼센트는 정기적으로 식물성 건강 보조 식품을 이용하고 있다는 것을 보여주었다.

* efficacy: 효능, 효험 ** legitimate: 적법한. 정당한 *** exemption: 면제

글의 전개방식	통념과 반박	문제와 해결	연구·실험	비교·대조	예시	비유	시간적 흐름	스토리텔링	기타

개요도	서론		본론		결론	
	배경 제시		문제 제기		부연 설명	
	의약품은 모두 FDA의 엄격한 통제를 받는데, 제조 과정은 물론 광고나 설명 문구 등 전반을 포함한다.		건강 보조 식품에서 특정 규제를 면제하는 것은 적법성 문제에 영향을 줄 수 있다.		의사와 약사는 건강 보조 식품과 떼어낼 수 없고, 시중에 많은 종류의 건강 보조 식품과 소비자가 있다.	

[2] 우리말과 일치하도록 주어진 단어를 바르게 배열하여 〈주제 및 제목〉을 쓰시오. (각 10점씩 2문제, 총 20점)

한글	규제를 벗어난 건강 보조 식품
영어	dietary / regulatory / supplements / control / out / of
정답	
한글	건강보조식품에 대한 확고한 규제 부재의 문제화
영어	Absence / Supplements / Regulation / of / Firm / on / Problematizing / The / Dietary
정답	

[3] 위 지문에 있는 단어만을 활용하여 다음 〈요약문〉을 완성하시오(어형 변형 가능). (총 20점)

Despite the fact that there are many dietary _____ and consumers, there are not enough _____ controls that make them _____.

Part III
변형문제

[①어법] 다음 글을 읽고, 어법상 틀린 부분의 개수를 찾고 틀린 부분을 바르게 고치시오.

Leo Lionni, an internationally known designer, illustrator, and graphic artist, being born in Holland and lived in Italy until he came to the United States in 1939. As a little boy, he would go into the museums in Amsterdam, and that's how he taught himself how to draw. He got into writing and illustrating children's books almost by accident. Lionni tore out bits of paper from a magazine and used it as characters and made up a story to entertain his grandchildren on a train ride. This story became what we now know as the children's book titled Little Blue and Little Yellow. He became the first children's author/ illustrator to use collage as the main medium for his illustrations. Lionni wrote and illustrated more than 40 children's books. In 1982, Lionni was diagnosed with Parkinson's disease, but he kept work in drawing, illustrating and teaching. He passed away in October 1999 in Italy.

① 1개　　② 2개　　③ 3개　　④ 4개　　⑤ 5개

ⓐ : _____ → _____　　　ⓑ : _____ → _____

ⓒ : _____ → _____　　　ⓓ : _____ → _____

ⓔ : _____ → _____

[②요약 서술형] 글의 요약문을 본문의 단어를 활용하여 서술하시오. (어형 변화 가능)

한글

조건　　　　　　　　　　　요약문 없음

정답

[③주제 서술형] 글의 주제를 조건과 한글 의미와 일치하도록 쓰시오.

한글
조건　　　　　　　　　　　주제 없음
정답

[④제목 서술형] 글의 제목을 조건과 한글 의미와 일치하도록 쓰시오.

한글
단어　　　　　　　　　　　제목 없음
정답

[⑤주요문장 서술형] 빈칸에 알맞은 말을 <조건>에 맞게 영작하시오. [Tip! 주요 문장 3가지는 시험 직전 꼭 암기하세요!]

한글　어린 소년이었을 때 그는 암스테르담의 박물관에 들어가곤 했는데, 그것이 그가 그림 그리는 법을 독학한 방법이다.

영어　As a little boy, he would go into the museums in Amsterdam, and _____.

조건　① 관계부사와 재귀대명사를 활용할 것
② [teach / draw / that]을 활용할 것
③ 총 8단어로 쓸 것 (필요시 주어진 단어 변형 가능)

정답

한글　이 이야기가 우리가 현재 Little Blue and Little Yellow라는 제목의 아동 도서로 알고 있는 것이 되었다.

영어　This story _____.

조건　① 목적격 관계대명사와 과거분사를 활용할 것
② [know / title / become]을 활용할 것
③ 총 15단어로 쓸 것 (필요시 주어진 단어 변형 가능)

정답

한글　1982년, Lionni는 파킨슨병을 진단받았지만, 그는 그리기, 삽화 그리기, 그리고 가르치는 일을 계속했다.

영어　In 1982, Lionni was diagnosed with Parkinson's disease, but _____.

조건　① keep -ing 구문을 활용할 것
② [illustrating / work / drawing / teaching]을 활용할 것
③ 총 8단어로 쓸 것 (필요시 주어진 단어 변형 가능)

정답

[①어법] 다음 글을 읽고, 어법상 틀린 부분의 개수를 찾고 틀린 부분을 바르게 고치시오.

Thomas Jefferson's knowledge of and passion for all things agricultural were truly extraordinary. Driving by a desire to see the South freed from its reliance on cotton, he was always on the lookout for crops that could replace it. While touring the south of France in 1787, Jefferson discovered that Italian rice was preferred to the American import grown in the Carolinas. Intent on discovering why this might do so, he took a detour into the Italian region of Lombardy on a mission of rice reconnaissance (a journey that, because it required crossing the Alps, was extremely dangerous at the time). There he discovered what the good folks of Lombardy were growing a superior strain of crop — whose export for planting outside of Italy was a crime punishable by death. Undaunted, Jefferson sent a small packet of the rice grain to his good friend James Madison and members of the South Carolina delegation. Later, he was stuffed his pockets with some of the rice grains, and "walked it" out of the country. The rice is grown in parts of the United States to this day.

① 1개　　② 2개　　③ 3개　　④ 4개　　⑤ 5개

ⓐ : _____ → _____　　　ⓑ : _____ → _____

ⓒ : _____ → _____　　　ⓓ : _____ → _____

ⓔ : _____ → _____

[②요약 서술형] 글의 요약문을 본문의 단어를 활용하여 서술하시오. (어형 변화 가능)

한글	더 좋은 품종을 재배하기 위해 이탈리아 쌀을 본국에 들여옴으로써 Thomas Jefferson은 사형을 당할 위험을 감수했다.
조건	1. the death penalty / grow / strain / run / introduce / Italian rice / home country / face를 활용할 것 (필요 시 변형 가능) 2. 동명사와 in order to 구문을 활용할 것 3. 총 25단어 이내로 작성할 것
정답	

[③주제 서술형] 글의 주제를 조건과 한글 의미와 일치하도록 쓰시오.

한글	Jefferson과 이탈리아 쌀 이야기
조건	story 를 활용하고 필요한 단어를 추가하여 총 7단어로 작성할 것
정답	

[④제목 서술형] 글의 제목을 조건과 한글 의미와 일치하도록 쓰시오.

한글	이탈리아 쌀을 위한 Jefferson의 노력
단어	Efforts 를 활용하고 필요한 단어를 추가하여 총 5단어로 작성할 것
정답	

[⑤주요문장 서술형] 빈칸에 알맞은 말을 <조건>에 맞게 영작하시오. [Tip! 주요 문장 3가지는 시험 직전 꼭 암기하세요!]

한글	농업적인 모든 것에 대한 Thomas Jefferson의 지식과 열정은 정말 대단했다.
영어	_____ were truly extraordinary.
조건	① 병렬구조를 활용할 것 ② [passion / knowledge / agricultural]을 활용할 것 ③ 총 10단어로 쓸 것 (필요시 주어진 단어 변형 가능)
정답	
한글	면화에 대한 의존에서 해방되는 (미국) 남부를 보고 싶은 욕망에 이끌려, 그는 늘 그것을 대체할 수 있는 농작물을 찾고 있었다.
영어	_____ he was always on the lookout for crops that could replace it.
조건	① 분사 구문을 활용할 것 ② [reliance / drive / cotton / desire]을 활용할 것 ③ 총 14단어로 쓸 것 (필요시 주어진 단어 변형 가능)
정답	
한글	그곳에서 그는 Lombardy의 선량한 사람들이 우수한 품종의 농작물을 재배하고 있고, 이탈리아 이외의 지역에서 재배하기 위한 수출은 사형에 처할 수 있는 범죄라는 것을 알게 되었다.
영어	There he discovered that the good folks of Lombardy were growing a superior strain of crop — _____
조건	① 소유격 관계대명사를 활용할 것 ② [punishable / plant / export / crime / plant]을 활용할 것 ③ 총 13단어로 쓸 것 (필요시 주어진 단어 변형 가능)
정답	

[①어법] 다음 글을 읽고, 어법상 틀린 부분의 개수를 찾고 틀린 부분을 바르게 고치시오.

It's the late 1800s. Anesthesia has just been introduced. Surgeries are on the rise, but a disturbing number of patients are dying due to infection. Joseph Lister is determined figuring out why and what can be done about it. After much research and thought, he concludes that Pasteur's controversial germ theory holds the key to the mystery. Killing germs in wounds with heat isn't an option, however — a completely new method is required. Lister guesses that there may be a chemical solution, and later that year, he reads in a newspaper that the treatment of sewage with a chemical called carbolic acid reduced the incidence of disease among the people and cattle of a nearby small English town. Lister follows the lead and, in 1865, develops a successful method of applying carbolic acid to wounds to prevent infection. He continues to work along this line and establishes antisepsis as a basic principle of surgery. Thanks to his discoveries and innovations, amputations become less frequent, deaths due to infection drop sharp, and new surgeries previously considered impossible are being routinely planned and executed.

① 1개   ② 2개   ③ 3개   ④ 4개   ⑤ 5개

ⓐ : _____ → _____   ⓑ : _____ → _____

ⓒ : _____ → _____   ⓓ : _____ → _____

ⓔ : _____ → _____

[②요약 서술형] 글의 요약문을 본문의 단어를 활용하여 서술하시오. (어형 변화 가능)

한글	많은 사람들이 감염으로 죽고 있었기 때문에, Joseph Lister는 소독법을 확립하기 위해 석탄산을 사용하는 혁신적인 아이디어를 생각해냈다.
조건	1. antisepsis / come up with / carbolic acid / die / infection / since / innovative를 활용할 것 (필요 시 변형 가능) 2. 과거 진행형과 동명사, to 부정사를 활용할 것 3. 총 23단어 이내로 작성할 것
정답	

[③주제 서술형] 글의 주제를 조건과 한글 의미와 일치하도록 쓰시오.

한글	수술을 위해 석탄산을 사용하는 방법의 개발
조건	developing / carbolic acid 를 활용하고 필요한 단어를 추가하여 총 9단어로 작성할 것
정답	

[④제목 서술형] 글의 제목을 조건과 한글 의미와 일치하도록 쓰시오.

한글	소독법에 석탄산을 사용하는 것에 대한 Joseph Lister의 통찰
단어	Insight / Antisepsis 를 활용하고 필요한 단어를 추가하여 총 9단어로 작성할 것
정답	

[⑤주요문장 서술형] 빈칸에 알맞은 말을 <조건>에 맞게 영작하시오. [Tip! 주요 문장 3가지는 시험 직전 꼭 암기하세요!]

한글	Joseph Lister는 그 원인과 대처 방안을 알아내기로 결심한다.
영어	Joseph Lister is determined to _____.
조건	① 간접의문문과 조동사 수동태를 활용할 것 ② [do / figure / about]을 활용할 것 ③ 총 10단어로 쓸 것 (필요시 주어진 단어 변형 가능)
정답	
한글	Lister는 화학적 해결책이 있을 수도 있다고 추측하고, 그해 말, 석탄산이라고 불리는 화학 물질로 하수를 처리한 것이 근처의 작은 영국 마을의 사람들과 소들 사이에서 질병 발생률을 감소시켰다는 것을 신문에서 읽는다.
영어	Lister guesses that there may be a chemical solution, and later that year, he reads in a newspaper that _____ among the people and cattle of a nearby small English town.
조건	① 과거분사를 활용할 것 ② [carbolic acid / disease / sewage / treatment / incidence / reduce]을 활용할 것 ③ 총 15단어로 쓸 것 (필요시 주어진 단어 변형 가능)
정답	
한글	그의 발견과 혁신 덕분에, 절단 수술의 횟수가 줄어들고, 감염으로 인한 사망이 급격히 감소하며, 이전에는 불가능하다고 여겨졌던 새로운 수술들이 일상적으로 계획되고 실행되고 있다.
영어	Thanks to his discoveries and innovations, amputations become less frequent, deaths due to infection drop sharply, and _____
조건	① 과거분사와 현재진행 수동태를 활용할 것 ② [consider / surgery / execute / routinely / impossible / previously]을 활용할 것 ③ 총 11단어로 쓸 것 (필요시 주어진 단어 변형 가능)
정답	

[①어법] 다음 글을 읽고, 어법상 틀린 부분의 개수를 찾고 틀린 부분을 바르게 고치시오.

While both history and geography could serve to develop nationalistic sentiments, the relative position of these two subjects in the educational system largely came to depend on the degree which either seemed more useful in building up the idea of a national identity. In Germany, with its long history of shifting borders and divisions into small states, geographical patterns associated with the German-speaking lands seemed very significant, and so geography was seen as very importantly. Norway, on the other hand, had developed its educational system during the union of the crowns with Sweden (1814-1905) and it had no disputed borders. Under these circumstances, Norway's national awakening was fostering by teaching about the glorious history of Viking times and about the precious liberal constitution of 1814. Hence, history predominated over geography. Finland, however, which had also experienced a union of crowns (in this case with Tsarist Russia), lacked a clearly discernible glorious past and so geography developed as a relatively more important subject. A pioneering research work of great political importance in the Finnish liberation process, the Atlas of Finland, stressed the uniqueness of the Finnish lands.

① 1개　　② 2개　　③ 3개　　④ 4개　　⑤ 5개

ⓐ : _____ → _____　　　ⓑ : _____ → _____
ⓒ : _____ → _____　　　ⓓ : _____ → _____
ⓔ : _____ → _____

[②요약 서술형] 글의 요약문을 본문의 단어를 활용하여 서술하시오. (어형 변화 가능)

한글	교육 시스템에서 역사와 지리는 모두 민족주의적 정서를 형성하는 역할을 하며, 그 유용성에 따라 상대적 위치가 달라질 수 있다.
조건	1. the educational system / build / relative / usefulness / nationalistic sentiment를 활용할 것 (필요 시 변형 가능) 2. both A and B 구문과 to 부정사, 소유격 관계대명사를 활용할 것 3. 총 22단어 이내로 작성할 것
정답	

[③주제 서술형] 글의 주제를 조건과 한글 의미와 일치하도록 쓰시오.

한글	국가 정체성을 발전시키기 위한 교육에서 역사와 지리의 상대적 위치
조건	relative / education / identity 를 활용하고 필요한 단어를 추가하여 총 **12단어**로 작성할 것
정답	

[④제목 서술형] 글의 제목을 조건과 한글 의미와 일치하도록 쓰시오.

한글	민족주의 정서 형성을 위한 역사와 지리에 대한 강조의 지역적 차이 탐색
단어	Exploring / Emphasis / Nationalistic 를 활용하고 필요한 단어를 추가하여 총 **13단어**로 작성할 것
정답	

[⑤주요문장 서술형] 빈칸에 알맞은 말을 <조건>에 맞게 영작하시오. [Tip! 주요 문장 3가지는 시험 직전 꼭 암기하세요!]

한글	역사학과 지리학 모두 국가주의적 정서를 발달시키는 데 도움이 될 수 있었지만, 교육 제도에서 이 두 과목의 상대적 위치는 국가 정체성의 개념을 형성하는 데 어느 쪽이 더 유용해 보이는지의 정도에 따라 대체로 달라지게 되었다.
영어	While both history and geography could serve to develop nationalistic sentiments, the relative position of these two subjects in the educational system largely _____ in building up the idea of a national identity.
조건	① 전치사 + 관계대명사 구문을 활용할 것 ② [useful / seem / degree / depend]을 활용할 것 ③ 총 12단어로 쓸 것 (필요시 주어진 단어 변형 가능)
정답	
한글	독일에서는, 변경되는 국경과 소국으로 분할되는 오랜 역사를 가지고 있어, 독일어권 영토와 관련된 지리적 양상이 매우 중요해 보였고, 따라서 지리학이 매우 중요하게 여겨졌다.
영어	In Germany, with its long history of shifting borders and divisions into small states, _____, and so geography was seen as very important.
조건	① 과거분사를 활용할 것 ② [German-speaking / significant / geographical / pattern / associate / land]을 활용할 것 ③ 총 10단어로 쓸 것 (필요시 주어진 단어 변형 가능)
정답	
한글	그러나 마찬가지로 왕위 통합을 경험했었던 핀란드는 명백하게 뚜렷한 영광스러운 과거를 가지지 못했고, 그래서 지리학이 상대적으로 더 중요한 과목으로 발전했다.
영어	Finland, however, _____, lacked a clearly discernible glorious past and so geography developed as a relatively more important subject.
조건	① 주격 관계대명사를 활용할 것 ② [union / experience / crown]을 활용할 것 ③ 총 8단어로 쓸 것 (필요시 주어진 단어 변형 가능)
정답	

[①어법] 다음 글을 읽고, 어법상 틀린 부분의 개수를 찾고 틀린 부분을 바르게 고치시오.

One dimension of ethical theory that needs mentioning is the issue of autonomy of ethics in relation to religion. Many ethical works are written from a religious point of view, and many concrete moral judgments are influenced by religion. A question in ethical theory is whether ethics have some kind of evidential dependence on religion. Consider the question whether moral knowledge — say, that lying is (with certain exceptions) wrong — requiring knowing any religious truth. This does not seem so. To say this is not to claim (as some would) that we can know moral truths even if there are no theological or religious truths. The point is theologically neutral on this matter. It is which knowledge of moral truths does not depend on knowledge of God or of religious truths. This view that moral knowledge is possible independently of religion is not antireligious, and indeed it has often been holding by religiously committed philosophers and by theologians.

① 1개   ② 2개   ③ 3개   ④ 4개   ⑤ 5개

ⓐ : _____ → _____   ⓑ : _____ → _____

ⓒ : _____ → _____   ⓓ : _____ → _____

ⓔ : _____ → _____

[②요약 서술형] 글의 요약문을 본문의 단어를 활용하여 서술하시오. (어형 변화 가능)

한글	많은 윤리적인 작품들이 종교적인 관점에서 쓰여지지만, 도덕적 진실에 대한 지식은 신학적 진실과 독립적인 것으로 보인다.
조건	1. independent / theological / perspective / moral / ethical works / though를 활용할 것 (필요 시 변형 가능) 2. 수동태와 it seems ~ 구문을 활용할 것 3. 총 22단어 이내로 작성할 것
정답	

[③주제 서술형] 글의 주제를 조건과 한글 의미와 일치하도록 쓰시오.

한글	신학적 진실과 도덕적 지식의 중립성
조건	theological / neutrality 를 활용하고 필요한 단어를 추가하여 총 **7단어**로 작성할 것
정답	

[④제목 서술형] 글의 제목을 조건과 한글 의미와 일치하도록 쓰시오.

한글	도덕적 진실을 찾기 위해 우리는 종교적이어야 할까?
단어	Religious / Moral 를 활용하고 필요한 단어를 추가하여 총 **8단어**로 작성할 것
정답	

[⑤주요문장 서술형] 빈칸에 알맞은 말을 〈조건〉에 맞게 영작하시오. [Tip! 주요 문장 3가지는 시험 직전 꼭 암기하세요!]

한글	언급할 필요가 있는 윤리 이론의 한 가지 측면은 종교와 관련한 윤리의 자율성 문제이다.
영어	_____ is the issue of autonomy of ethics in relation to religion.
조건	① 주격 관계대명사를 활용할 것 ② [mentioning / ethical / dimension]을 활용할 것 ③ 총 8단어로 쓸 것 (필요시 주어진 단어 변형 가능)
정답	
한글	윤리 이론에서의 한 가지 문제는, 윤리가 종교에 대해 일종의 증거적 의존성을 가지고 있느냐이다.
영어	A question in ethical theory is _____.
조건	① whether 절을 활용할 것 ② [dependence / religion / ethics]을 활용할 것 ③ 총 10단어로 쓸 것 (필요시 주어진 단어 변형 가능)
정답	
한글	도덕적 지식은 종교와 관계없이 가능하다는 이 견해는 종교에 반하는 것이 아니며, 사실상 그것은 종교적으로 헌신적인 철학자들과 신학자들이 흔히 품어 왔던 것이었다.
영어	_____, and indeed it has often been held by religiously committed philosophers and by theologians.
조건	① 동격의 that을 활용할 것 ② [possible / antireligious / moral / independently]을 활용할 것 ③ 총 13단어로 쓸 것 (필요시 주어진 단어 변형 가능)
정답	

[①어법] 다음 글을 읽고, 어법상 틀린 부분의 개수를 찾고 틀린 부분을 바르게 고치시오.

Several factors have identified as influences on the development of moral identity, some individual and some contextual. At the individual level, things such as personality, cognitive development, attitudes and values, and broader self and identity development can impact moral identity development. For example, those more advanced in cognitive and identity development have greater capacities for moral identity development. Also, greater appreciation for moral values might facilitate their subsequent integration into identity. At the contextual level, one important factor is the person's social structure, including neighborhood, school, family, and institutions such as religious, youth, or community organizations. For example, a caring and supportive family environment can facilitate the development of morality and identity, as well as the integration of the two into moral identity. Additionally, involvement in religious and youth organizations can provide not only moral beliefs systems but also opportunities to act on those beliefs (e.g., through community involvement), which can aid their integration into identity.

① 1개　　② 2개　　③ 3개　　④ 4개　　⑤ 5개

ⓐ : _____ → _____　　　ⓑ : _____ → _____

ⓒ : _____ → _____　　　ⓓ : _____ → _____

ⓔ : _____ → _____

[②요약 서술형] 글의 요약문을 본문의 단어를 활용하여 서술하시오. (어형 변화 가능)

한글	도덕적 정체성의 발달에는 몇 가지 요인이 영향을 미치는데, 그 중 일부는 개인적인 것이고 다른 일부는 맥락적인 것이다.
조건	1. factors / moral / individual / contextual / influence / the development / while를 활용할 것 (필요 시 변형 가능) 2. 관계대명사의 계속적 용법을 활용할 것 3. 총 17단어 이내로 작성할 것
정답	

[③주제 서술형] 글의 주제를 조건과 한글 의미와 일치하도록 쓰시오.

한글	도덕적 정체성의 발달을 위한 개인적이고 맥락적인 요소들
조건	contextual / development 를 활용하고 필요한 단어를 추가하여 총 10단어로 작성할 것
정답	

[④제목 서술형] 글의 제목을 조건과 한글 의미와 일치하도록 쓰시오.

한글	도덕적 정체성 발달에 영향을 미치는 요인의 분류
단어	Categorization / Factors / Identity 를 활용하고 필요한 단어를 추가하여 총 10단어로 작성할 것
정답	

[⑤주요문장 서술형] 빈칸에 알맞은 말을 <조건>에 맞게 영작하시오. [Tip! 주요 문장 3가지는 시험 직전 꼭 암기하세요!]

한글	여러 가지 요인들이 도덕적 정체성 발달에 영향을 미치는 것으로 밝혀졌는데, 어떤 것은 개인적이고, 어떤 것은 상황적이다.
영어	Several factors have been identified _____.
조건	① 전치사구를 활용할 것 ② [individual / contextual / moral / influence / development]을 활용할 것 ③ 총 13단어로 쓸 것 (필요시 주어진 단어 변형 가능)
정답	
한글	예를 들어, 인지 및 정체성 발달에서 더 뛰어난 사람들은 도덕적 정체성 발달에 대한 능력이 더 뛰어나다.
영어	For example, _____ have greater capacities for moral identity development.
조건	① those 후치 수식구문을 활용할 것 ② [cognitive / advance / development / identity]을 활용할 것 ③ 총 8단어로 쓸 것 (필요시 주어진 단어 변형 가능)
정답	
한글	게다가, 종교 단체 및 청소년 단체에 참여하는 것은 도덕적 신념 체계뿐만 아니라, (예를 들어, 지역 사회 참여를 통해) 그러한 신념에 따라 행동할 기회도 제공할 수 있으며, 이는 그것이 정체성으로 통합되는 것을 도울 수 있다.
영어	Additionally, involvement in religious and youth organizations can provide not only moral beliefs systems but also opportunities to act on those beliefs (e.g., through community involvement), _____.
조건	① 관계대명사의 계속적 용법을 활용할 것 ② [integration / identity / aid]을 활용할 것 ③ 총 7단어로 쓸 것 (필요시 주어진 단어 변형 가능)
정답	

[①어법] 다음 글을 읽고, 어법상 틀린 부분의 개수를 찾고 틀린 부분을 바르게 고치시오.

Today we are using some 400 million plus tonnes of paper per annum in a global population of about seven billion, but if we look at the anticipated population figure in 2045 of nine billion, just on that basis alone paper production will need to increase by 30 per cent. On top of that within our current population not everybody being able to get a newspaper or has a book to read, or has enough exercise books to write on at school. As their percentage increases the demand for paper will also increase. We have limited land and a limited number of trees, and if we don't recycle we will not be able to supply the 400 million tonnes we need today or meet the demands of an increasing population. Remember of course that within the 400 million tonnes we use today about 200 million tonnes of waste paper is used in their manufacturing; 200 million tonnes of waste paper generates rough 160 million tonnes of recycled paper. Therefore if we didn't recycle we would only have 240 million tonnes of paper so there would be a shortfall or we would have to use more pulp.

① 1개　　② 2개　　③ 3개　　④ 4개　　⑤ 5개

ⓐ : ＿＿＿＿＿ → ＿＿＿＿＿　　　　ⓑ : ＿＿＿＿＿ → ＿＿＿＿＿

ⓒ : ＿＿＿＿＿ → ＿＿＿＿＿　　　　ⓓ : ＿＿＿＿＿ → ＿＿＿＿＿

ⓔ : ＿＿＿＿＿ → ＿＿＿＿＿

[②요약 서술형] 글의 요약문을 본문의 단어를 활용하여 서술하시오. (어형 변화 가능)

한글	만약 우리가 종이를 재활용하지 않는다면, 증가하는 인구 규모를 고려할 때 가까운 미래에 종이에 대한 수요가 충족되지 못할 수도 있다.
조건	1. satisfy / growing / the population / near / consider / may를 활용할 것 (필요 시 변형 가능) 2. 조동사 수동태와 분사구문을 활용할 것 3. 총 15단어 이내로 작성할 것 (빈칸 부분만)
정답	If we do not recycle paper, the demand for paper ＿＿＿＿＿＿＿＿＿＿＿.

[③주제 서술형] 글의 주제를 조건과 한글 의미와 일치하도록 쓰시오.

한글	증가하는 수요에 대한 종이 재활용의 중요성
조건	importance / recycling / increasing 를 활용하고 필요한 단어를 추가하여 총 9단어로 작성할 것
정답	

[④제목 서술형] 글의 제목을 조건과 한글 의미와 일치하도록 쓰시오.

한글	비상: 종이가 부족할 수 있다
단어	Run 를 활용하고 필요한 단어를 추가하여 총 7단어로 작성할 것
정답	

[⑤주요문장 서술형] 빈칸에 알맞은 말을 <조건>에 맞게 영작하시오. [Tip! 주요 문장 3가지는 시험 직전 꼭 암기하세요!]

한글	오늘날 우리는 약 70억 명의 전 세계 인구 내에서 1년에 약 4억 톤 이상의 종이를 사용하고 있지만, 만약 우리가 2045년에 90억명으로 예상되는 인구 수치를 본다면, 단지 그것에만 근거해도 종이 생산량을 30퍼센트 늘려야 할 것이다.
영어	Today we are using some 400 million plus tonnes of paper per annum in a global population of about seven billion, but ＿＿＿＿＿＿＿＿＿＿, just on that basis alone paper production will need to increase by 30 per cent.
조건	① 과거분사를 활용할 것 ② [anticipate / figure / population]을 활용할 것 ③ 총 13단어로 쓸 것 (필요시 주어진 단어 변형 가능)
정답	
한글	우리는 제한된 땅과 제한된 수의 나무를 가지고 있으며, 만약 우리가 재활용을 하지 않는다면 우리는 오늘날 필요로 하는 4억 톤의 종이를 공급하거나 늘어나는 인구의 수요를 충족시킬 수 없을 것이다.
영어	We have limited land and a limited number of trees, and if we don't recycle we will not be able to ＿＿＿＿＿＿＿＿.
조건	① 목적격 관계대명사 생략 구조와 병렬 구조를 활용할 것 ② [demand / supply / tonne / meet / population]을 활용할 것 ③ 총 16단어로 쓸 것 (필요시 주어진 단어 변형 가능)
정답	
한글	오늘날 우리가 사용하는 4억 톤의 종이 내에서 그것을 제조하는 데 약 2억 톤의 폐지가 사용되는데, 2억 톤의 폐지는 대략 1억 6천만 톤의 재생지를 만들어 낸다는 것을 물론 명심하라.
영어	Remember of course that ＿＿＿＿＿＿＿＿＿; 200 million tonnes of waste paper generates roughly 160 million tonnes of recycled paper.
조건	① 목적격 관계대명사 생략 구조와 수동태를 활용할 것 ② [manufacturing / tonnes / waste / use]을 활용할 것 ③ 총 20단어로 쓸 것 (필요시 주어진 단어 변형 가능)
정답	

[①어법] 다음 글을 읽고, 어법상 틀린 부분의 개수를 찾고 틀린 부분을 바르게 고치시오.

For years, companies and countries took their rare metal supply lines for granted, unaware of the material makeup of their products. In fact, in 2011, Congress forced the U.S. military to research its supply chains because the Pentagon was having difficulty determining whose advanced metals it needed. As the materials that make up product components to have become more varied and complex, those who rely on sophisticated hardware can no longer afford to remain in the dark. Now, corporate and government leaders are realizing how important rare metals are. Indeed, efforts to secure rare metals have been sparked a war over the periodic table. In offices from Tokyo to Washington, D.C., in research and development labs from Cambridge, Massachusetts, to Baotou, China, and in strategic command centers the world over, new policies and the launching of research programs are ensuring which nations have access. The struggle for minor metals isn't imminent; it's already here and is shaping the relationship between countries as conflicts over other resources were in the past.

① 1개   ② 2개   ③ 3개   ④ 4개   ⑤ 5개

ⓐ : _____ → _____   ⓑ : _____ → _____

ⓒ : _____ → _____   ⓓ : _____ → _____

ⓔ : _____ → _____

[②요약 서술형] 글의 요약문을 본문의 단어를 활용하여 서술하시오. (어형 변화 가능)

한글	기업과 국가들은 수년간 당연하게 여겨온 희귀금속 공급선이 이제는 확실하게 확보돼야 한다는 것을 깨달았다.
조건	1. realize / firmly / metal supply lines / granted / secure / should를 활용할 것 (필요 시 변형 가능) 2. 접속사 that과 목적격 관계대명사, 조동사 수동태를 활용할 것 3. 총 22단어 이내로 작성할 것
정답	

[③주제 서술형] 글의 주제를 조건과 한글 의미와 일치하도록 쓰시오.

한글	기업과 정부의 희귀 금속 확보 노력
조건	**efforts / secure / rare**를 활용하고 필요한 단어를 추가하여 총 **9단어**로 작성할 것
정답	

[④제목 서술형] 글의 제목을 조건과 한글 의미와 일치하도록 쓰시오.

한글	희귀금속 공급선 문제화 및 확보
단어	**Problematizing / Supply** 를 활용하고 필요한 단어를 추가하여 총 **8단어**로 작성할 것
정답	

[⑤주요문장 서술형] 빈칸에 알맞은 말을 〈조건〉에 맞게 영작하시오. [Tip! 주요 문장 3가지는 시험 직전 꼭 암기하세요!]

한글	실은, 2011년, 미 의회는 미국 군대에 그것의 공급망을 연구하도록 강제했는데, 그 이유는 펜타곤(미국 국방부)이 그것에 어떤 첨단 금속이 필요한지 결정하는 데 어려움을 겪고 있었기 때문이다.
영어	In fact, in 2011, Congress forced the U.S. military to research its supply chains because the Pentagon _____.
조건	① 간접의문문을 활용할 것 ② [metal / determine / difficulty / need]을 활용할 것 ③ 총 9단어로 쓸 것 (필요시 주어진 단어 변형 가능)
정답	
한글	이제, 기업과 정부 지도자들은 희금속이 얼마나 중요한지 깨닫고 있다.
영어	Now, corporate and government leaders _____.
조건	① 간접의문문을 활용할 것 ② [metal / important / realize]을 활용할 것 ③ 총 7단어로 쓸 것 (필요시 주어진 단어 변형 가능)
정답	
한글	비주류 금속을 위한 경쟁은 곧 닥쳐올 듯한 것이 아니라 이미 여기 있으며, 과거에 다른 자원을 둘러싼 분쟁이 그랬던 것처럼 국가 간의 관계를 형성하고 있다.
영어	The struggle for minor metals isn't imminent; it's already here and is shaping the relationship between countries _____.
조건	① 대동사를 활용할 것 ② [past / conflict / resource]을 활용할 것 ③ 총 9단어로 쓸 것 (필요시 주어진 단어 변형 가능)
정답	

[①어법] 다음 글을 읽고, 어법상 틀린 부분의 개수를 찾고 틀린 부분을 바르게 고치시오.

The effects of climate change will fall most heavy upon the poor of the world. Regions such as Africa could face severely compromised food production and water shortages, while coastal areas in South, East, and Southeast Asia will be at great risk of flooding. Tropical Latin America will see damage to forests and agricultural areas due to drier climate, while in South America changes in precipitation patterns and the disappearance of glaciers will significantly be affected water availability. While the richer countries may have the economic resources to adapt to many of the effects of climate change, without significant aid poorer countries will be unable to implement preventive measures, especially those that rely on the newest technologies. This raises fundamental issues of environmental justice in relation to the impact of economic and political power on environmental policy on a global scale. The concept of climate justice is a term used for framing global warming as an ethical and political issue, rather than one that is pure environmental or physical in nature. The principles of climate justice imply an equitable sharing both of the burdens of climate change and the costs of developing policy responses.

① 1개   ② 2개   ③ 3개   ④ 4개   ⑤ 5개

ⓐ : _____ → _____   ⓑ : _____ → _____

ⓒ : _____ → _____   ⓓ : _____ → _____

ⓔ : _____ → _____

[②요약 서술형] 글의 요약문을 본문의 단어를 활용하여 서술하시오. (어형 변화 가능)

한글	형평성 문제를 해결하기 위해, 기후 정의의 개념은 환경 문제를 윤리적, 정치적 문제로 표현하는 것과 관련이 있다.
조건	1. concerned / frame / political / justice / ethical를 활용할 것 (필요 시 변형 가능) 2. 동명사를 활용할 것 3. 총 18단어 이내로 작성할 것 (빈칸 부분만)
정답	_____, in order to address equity issues.

[③주제 서술형] 글의 주제를 조건과 한글 의미와 일치하도록 쓰시오.

한글	기후 변화의 불균일한 영향과 환경 정의
조건	uneven / climate / environmental 를 활용하고 필요한 단어를 추가하여 총 8단어로 작성할 것
정답	

[④제목 서술형] 글의 제목을 조건과 한글 의미와 일치하도록 쓰시오.

한글	기후 정의: 지구 온난화에 대한 윤리적, 정치적 접근법
단어	Ethical / Political / Global 를 활용하고 필요한 단어를 추가하여 총 10단어로 작성할 것
정답	

[⑤주요문장 서술형] 빈칸에 알맞은 말을 〈조건〉에 맞게 영작하시오. [Tip! 주요 문장 3가지는 시험 직전 꼭 암기하세요!]

한글	더 부유한 나라들은 기후 변화의 많은 영향에 적응하기 위한 경제적 자원을 가지고 있을 수도 있지만, 상당한 원조가 없을 경우 더 가난한 나라들은 예방조치, 특히 최신 기술에 의존하는 조치를 시행할 수 없을 것이다.
영어	While the richer countries may have the economic resources to adapt to many of the effects of climate change, without significant aid poorer countries will be unable to _____.
조건	① 주격 관계대명사를 활용할 것 ② [rely / especially / technology / preventive / implement / measure]을 활용할 것 ③ 총 11단어로 쓸 것 (필요시 주어진 단어 변형 가능)
정답	
한글	이는 세계적인 규모로 경제력 및 정치력이 환경 정책에 미치는 영향과 관련하여 환경 정의라는 근본적인 문제를 제기한다.
영어	This raises fundamental issues of environmental justice _____.
조건	① the impact of A on B 구문을 활용할 것 ② [political / global / power / economic / impact / relation / environmental]을 활용할 것 ③ 총 17단어로 쓸 것 (필요시 주어진 단어 변형 가능)
정답	
한글	기후 정의라는 개념은 지구 온난화를 본질적으로 순전히 환경적이거나 물리적인 것이라기보다는, 윤리적이고 정치적인 문제로 만들기 위해 사용되는 용어이다.
영어	The concept of climate justice is a term used for framing global warming as an ethical and political issue, rather than _____.
조건	① 주격 관계대명사와 부정대명사를 활용할 것 ② [physical / environmental / purely / nature]을 활용할 것 ③ 총 9단어로 쓸 것 (필요시 주어진 단어 변형 가능)
정답	

[①어법] 다음 글을 읽고, 어법상 틀린 부분의 개수를 찾고 틀린 부분을 바르게 고치시오.

Organic chemistry is the part of chemistry what is concerned with the compounds of carbon. That one element can command a whole division being evidence of carbon's pregnant mediocrity. Carbon lies at the midpoint of the Periodic Table, the chemist's map of chemical properties of the elements, and is largely indifferent to the relationships it enters into. In particular, it is content to bond to itself. As a result of its mild and unaggressive character, it is able to form chains and rings of startling complexity. Startling complexity is exactly what organisms need if they are to be regarded as being alive, and thus the compounds of carbon are the structural and reactive infrastructure of life. So extensively are the compounds of carbon, currently numbering in the millions, that it is not surprised that a whole branch of chemistry has evolved for their study and has developed special techniques, systems of nomenclature, and attitudes.

① 1개   ② 2개   ③ 3개   ④ 4개   ⑤ 5개

ⓐ : _____ → _____   ⓑ : _____ → _____

ⓒ : _____ → _____   ⓓ : _____ → _____

ⓔ : _____ → _____

[②요약 서술형] 글의 요약문을 본문의 단어를 활용하여 서술하시오. (어형 변화 가능)

한글	화학의 일부로서, 유기화학은 탄소의 다양한 화합물을 연구하는데, 탄소의 온화한 특성은 복잡한 사슬을 형성할 수 있게 한다.
조건	1. character / the formation / various / mild / allow for / chains를 활용할 것 (필요 시 변형 가능) 2. 소유격 관계대명사를 활용할 것 3. 총 17단어 이내로 작성할 것 (빈칸 부분만)
정답	As a branch of chemistry, _____ _____.

[③주제 서술형] 글의 주제를 조건과 한글 의미와 일치하도록 쓰시오.

한글	유기화학과 탄소화합물의 평범함
조건	organic / mediocrity 를 활용하고 필요한 단어를 추가하여 총 8단어로 작성할 것
정답	

[④제목 서술형] 글의 제목을 조건과 한글 의미와 일치하도록 쓰시오.

한글	유기화학: 개념과 설명
단어	Concept 를 활용하고 필요한 단어를 추가하여 총 5단어로 작성할 것
정답	

[⑤주요문장 서술형] 빈칸에 알맞은 말을 〈조건〉에 맞게 영작하시오. [Tip! 주요 문장 3가지는 시험 직전 꼭 암기하세요!]

한글	하나의 원소가 한 분야 전체를 차지할 수 있다는 사실은 탄소의 풍요한 범용성에 대한 증거이다.
영어	_____.
조건	① 접속사 that을 활용할 것 ② [division / pregnant / mediocrity / evidence / command]을 활용할 것 ③ 총 14단어로 쓸 것 (필요시 주어진 단어 변형 가능)
정답	
한글	놀라울 정도의 복잡성은 바로 유기체가 살아 있는 것으로 여겨지려면 필요로 하는 것이고, 따라서 탄소 화합물은 생명체의 구조적이고 반응적인 하부 구조이다.
영어	
조건	① what 명사절과 be to 용법, 수동태를 활용할 것 ② [alive / organism / regard]을 활용할 것 ③ 총 12단어로 쓸 것 (필요시 주어진 단어 변형 가능)
정답	
한글	현재 그 수가 수백만 개에 달하는 탄소 화합물은 매우 광범위해서, 화학의 한 분야 전체가 그것의 연구를 위해 발전해 왔고 특별한 기술, 명명법의 체계, 사고방식을 발전시켜 온 것은 놀라운 일이 아니다.
영어	So _____.
조건	① 형용사 도치와 so ~ that ... 구문, 가주어 진주어 구문, 현재완료, 병렬 구조를 활용할 것 ② [nomenclature / attitude / branch / compound / extensive / chemistry / technique / carbon]을 활용할 것 ③ 총 37단어로 쓸 것 (필요시 주어진 단어 변형 가능)
정답	

[①어법] 다음 글을 읽고, 어법상 틀린 부분의 개수를 찾고 틀린 부분을 바르게 고치시오.

Humans have been used borax for more than four thousand years. Since the 1800s, it has been mined near Death Valley, California. Dirt cheap, borax has many industrial uses, but in the home it is used as a natural laundry-cleaning booster, multipurpose cleaner, fungicide, herbicide, and disinfectant. Off-white, odorless, and alkaline, borax crystals can be mixed with other cleaning agents for added power. Despite you certainly wouldn't want to eat it, borax is relatively safe and is quite effective without being toxic. It is useful in a lot of the ways that baking soda does, but it's stronger and disinfects more, so it's good for mold, mildew, and deeper dirt. In general, use baking soda first and use borax only in situations which something stronger is needed. It will enable you to get even stubborn stains clean without resorting to toxic chemicals. Borax should not be used where it might get into food, and it should be safely stored out of the reach of children and pets.

① 1개   ② 2개   ③ 3개   ④ 4개   ⑤ 5개

ⓐ : _____ → _____   ⓑ : _____ → _____

ⓒ : _____ → _____   ⓓ : _____ → _____

ⓔ : _____ → _____

[②요약 서술형] 글의 요약문을 본문의 단어를 활용하여 서술하시오. (어형 변화 가능)

한글	
조건	요약문 없음
정답	

[③주제 서술형] 글의 주제를 조건과 한글 의미와 일치하도록 쓰시오.

한글	
조건	주제 없음
정답	

[④제목 서술형] 글의 제목을 조건과 한글 의미와 일치하도록 쓰시오.

한글	
단어	제목 없음
정답	

[⑤주요문장 서술형] 빈칸에 알맞은 말을 〈조건〉에 맞게 영작하시오. [Tip! 주요 문장 3가지는 시험 직전 꼭 암기하세요!]

한글	회색을 띤 백색이고, 냄새가 없으며, 알칼리성인 붕사 결정은 효능을 더하기 위해 다른 세정제와 혼합될 수 있다.
영어	Off-white, odorless, and alkaline, borax crystals _____.
조건	① 수동태를 활용할 것 ② [add / clean / mix / agent]을 활용할 것 ③ 총 10단어로 쓸 것 (필요시 주어진 단어 변형 가능)
정답	
한글	그것은 베이킹 소다가 유용하게 사용되는 방식 중의 많은 방식에서 유용하지만, 더 강력하고 더 많이 소독되므로 곰팡이, 흰곰팡이, 찌든 때에 효과적이다.
영어	It is useful in a lot of _____.
조건	① 관계부사와 비교급을 활용할 것 ② [mildew / baking soda / disinfect / dirt]을 활용할 것 ③ 총 21단어로 쓸 것 (필요시 주어진 단어 변형 가능)
정답	
한글	그것으로 독성이 있는 화학 물질에 의존하지 않고 지우기 힘든 얼룩까지도 깨끗하게 할 수 있을 것이다.
영어	It _____ without resorting to toxic chemicals.
조건	① enable A to B 구문을 활용할 것 ② [stubborn / enable / clean]을 활용할 것 ③ 총 9단어로 쓸 것 (필요시 주어진 단어 변형 가능)
정답	

[①어법] 다음 글을 읽고, 어법상 틀린 부분의 개수를 찾고 틀린 부분을 바르게 고치시오.

There would be much less to say did it not for space probes that have visited the giant planets and their moons. Exploration began with fly-bys (missions that flew past the planet) but has moved on to the stage of orbital tours in the case of Jupiter and Saturn, that have each had a mission that orbited the planet for several years and that was able to make repeated close fly-bys of at least the regular satellites. Close fly-bys of moons enable detailed imaging, and usually take the probe close enough to see how the moon affects the strong magnetic field surrounds the planet and to detect whether the moon also has its own magnetic field. The size of the slight deflection to a probe's trajectory as it passes close to a moon enables the moon's mass to be determined. Knowing the moon's size, it is then easy to work out its density.

① 1개   ② 2개   ③ 3개   ④ 4개   ⑤ 5개

ⓐ : _____ → _____	ⓑ : _____ → _____
ⓒ : _____ → _____	ⓓ : _____ → _____
ⓔ : _____ → _____	

[②요약 서술형] 글의 요약문을 본문의 단어를 활용하여 서술하시오. (어형 변화 가능)

한글	플라이바이는 사람들이 거대한 행성과 그 위성의 상세한 이미지를 가질 수 있게 해주었고, 자기장을 감지하고 행성의 크기와 밀도를 측정할 수 있게 해주었다.
조건	1. measure / giant / detailed / density / moons / detect를 활용할 것 (필요 시 변형 가능) 2. allow A to V 구문과 병렬구조를 활용할 것 3. 총 24단어 이내로 작성할 것
정답	

[③주제 서술형] 글의 주제를 조건과 한글 의미와 일치하도록 쓰시오.

한글	거대 행성과 그 위성 탐사를 위한 근접 비행(플라이바이)
조건	**fly-bys / explorations** 를 활용하고 필요한 단어를 추가하여 총 **9단어**로 작성할 것
정답	

[④제목 서술형] 글의 제목을 조건과 한글 의미와 일치하도록 쓰시오.

한글	플라이바이를 통한 다른 행성으로의 탐험
단어	**Expedition** 를 활용하고 필요한 단어를 추가하여 총 **7단어**로 작성할 것
정답	

[⑤주요문장 서술형] 빈칸에 알맞은 말을 〈조건〉에 맞게 영작하시오. [Tip! 주요 문장 3가지는 시험 직전 꼭 암기하세요!]

한글	만약 거대 행성과 그것들의 위성을 방문한 무인 우주 탐사선이 없다면 할 말이 훨씬 더 적을 것이다.
영어	There would be much less to say _____.
조건	① 가정법 도치를 활용할 것 ② [planet / probe / visit / giant / moon / space]을 활용할 것 ③ 총 15단어로 쓸 것 (필요시 주어진 단어 변형 가능)
정답	
한글	위성에 대한 가까운 플라이바이는 상세한 영상 촬영을 가능하게 하며, 일반적으로, 위성이 행성을 둘러싸고 있는 강한 자기장에 어떤 영향을 미치는지 보고 그리고 그 위성 또한 자체의 자기장을 가지는지 탐지할 만큼 가깝게 무인 우주 탐사선을 접근시킨다.
영어	Close fly-bys of moons enable detailed imaging, and usually take the probe close enough _____ and to detect whether the moon also has its own magnetic field.
조건	① 간접의문문을 활용할 것 ② [surround / magnetic / moon / affect]을 활용할 것 ③ 총 13단어로 쓸 것 (필요시 주어진 단어 변형 가능)
정답	
한글	위성의 크기를 알면, 그것의 밀도를 쉽게 계산할 수 있다.
영어	_____.
조건	① 가주어 진주어 구문과 분사 구문을 활용할 것 ② [size / density / know / work out]을 활용할 것 ③ 총 13단어로 쓸 것 (필요시 주어진 단어 변형 가능)
정답	

[①어법] 다음 글을 읽고, 어법상 틀린 부분의 개수를 찾고 틀린 부분을 바르게 고치시오.

The term common pool resources refers to resources that are available to all, but owning by no one. Nature-based examples include forests, oceans, and vistas, whereas common pool cultural resources can include a community's song, dance, and traditions. Many tourism products and experiences rely on common pool resources. The extent and accessibility of these resources has led McKean to suggest that common pool resources, in addition to be available to anyone, are difficult to protect and easy to deplete. Hardin presented the initial illustration of this concept in his influential article titled "The Tragedy of the Commons." In this article, he described a community that thrives on the growth of its cattle, what graze on communal pastureland. As demand grows, residents are inclined to maximize their benefits by ignoring the cumulative effect of each person grazing an additional head of cattle on the communal lands. Hardin asserted that the ignorance of individuals using common pool resources will lead to eventual depletion of the resource. The potential combined impact of individual use of common pool resources is an important element of tourism's sustainable development.

① 1개　　② 2개　　③ 3개　　④ 4개　　⑤ 5개

ⓐ : ＿＿＿＿＿＿＿ → ＿＿＿＿＿＿＿　　　　ⓑ : ＿＿＿＿＿＿＿ → ＿＿＿＿＿＿＿

ⓒ : ＿＿＿＿＿＿＿ → ＿＿＿＿＿＿＿　　　　ⓓ : ＿＿＿＿＿＿＿ → ＿＿＿＿＿＿＿

ⓔ : ＿＿＿＿＿＿＿ → ＿＿＿＿＿＿＿

[②요약 서술형] 글의 요약문을 본문의 단어를 활용하여 서술하시오. (어형 변화 가능)

한글	Hardin이 유명하게 개념화한 것처럼, 모든 사람이 사용할 수 있지만 아무도 소유하지 않는 자원은 각 사용의 잠재적 영향에 대한 무지로 인해 쉽게 고갈될 수 있다.
조건	1. deplete / easy / own / resources / conceptualize / available / famously를 활용할 것 (필요 시 변형 가능) 2. 접속사와 주격 관계대명사, 병렬구조, 조동사 수동태를 활용할 것 3. 총 19단어 이내로 작성할 것 (빈칸 부분만)
정답	＿＿＿＿＿＿＿＿＿＿＿＿＿＿＿＿＿＿＿＿＿＿＿＿＿＿＿＿＿＿＿＿ because of ignorance of the potential influence of each use.

[③주제 서술형] 글의 주제를 조건과 한글 의미와 일치하도록 쓰시오.

한글	공유 자원의 개념과 공유지의 비극
조건	concept / resources 를 활용하고 필요한 단어를 추가하여 총 11단어로 작성할 것
정답	

[④제목 서술형] 글의 제목을 조건과 한글 의미와 일치하도록 쓰시오.

한글	공유지의 자원이 고갈되는 방식
단어	Commons / Depleted 를 활용하고 필요한 단어를 추가하여 총 8단어로 작성할 것
정답	

[⑤주요문장 서술형] 빈칸에 알맞은 말을 〈조건〉에 맞게 영작하시오. [Tip! 주요 문장 3가지는 시험 직전 꼭 암기하세요!]

한글	'공유 자원'이라는 용어는 모든 사람이 사용할 수 있지만, 아무도 소유하지 않은 자원을 말한다.
영어	The term *common pool resources* refers to ＿＿＿＿＿＿＿＿＿＿＿＿＿＿＿＿.
조건	① 주격 관계대명사를 활용할 것 ② [own / available / resource]을 활용할 것 ③ 총 10단어로 쓸 것 (필요시 주어진 단어 변형 가능)
정답	
한글	수요가 늘면서, 주민들은 각자가 공유지에서 소 한 마리씩을 추가로 방목하는 행위의 누적 결과를 무시함으로써 자신들의 이익을 극대화하고 싶어 한다.
영어	As demand grows, residents are inclined to maximize their benefits ＿＿＿＿＿＿＿＿＿＿＿＿＿＿＿＿.
조건	① 동명사와 현재분사를 활용할 것 ② [cumulative / additional / graze / communal / ignore / cattle]을 활용할 것 ③ 총 18단어로 쓸 것 (필요시 주어진 단어 변형 가능)
정답	
한글	Hardin은 개인들이 공유 자원을 사용하는 것에 대한 무지는 결국 자원의 고갈을 초래하게 된다고 주장했다.
영어	Hardin asserted that the ＿＿＿＿＿＿＿＿＿＿＿＿＿＿＿＿.
조건	① 현재분사를 활용할 것 ② [depletion / resource / ignorance / common / individual / eventual]을 활용할 것 ③ 총 15단어로 쓸 것 (필요시 주어진 단어 변형 가능)
정답	

[①어법] 다음 글을 읽고, 어법상 틀린 부분의 개수를 찾고 틀린 부분을 바르게 고치시오.

If part of the attraction of the community to outsiders are its cultural heritage and traditions, that will likely change over time and frequently not for the better. Symbols of a historic culture may be pervasive, but only in a make-believe form. Tourist shops on small Pacific islands may sell replicas of native art — all turned out in huge quantities by manufacturers in other parts of the world. Plastic Black Forest clocks and Swiss music boxes are offered to tourists that are mass-produced in Taiwan or China. A commitment to craftsmanship and true local heritage vanishing. These false symbols of earlier times contribute to an overly commercial feeling at destinations and a sense that nothing seems real now, and perhaps never was. A danger lies in the loss of a sense of personal identity by residents and a feeling of being disconnected from their past. Their heritage and culture now seem less significant or important. It serves primarily as a commercial front for visitors who buy cheap trinkets and watch professionally staged shows that attempt to recreate cultural practices or historic events.

① 1개　　② 2개　　③ 3개　　④ 4개　　⑤ 5개

ⓐ : _____ → _____　　　ⓑ : _____ → _____

ⓒ : _____ → _____　　　ⓓ : _____ → _____

ⓔ : _____ → _____

[②요약 서술형] 글의 요약문을 본문의 단어를 활용하여 서술하시오. (어형 변화 가능)

한글	대량생산과 상업적 정서는 관광지의 문화유산과 전통을 크게 변화시켜 정체성 상실로 이어질 수 있다.
조건	1. heritage / a tourist spot / mass / lead / commercial / the loss를 활용할 것 (필요 시 변형 가능) 2. 관계대명사의 계속적 용법을 활용할 것 3. 총 25단어 이내로 작성할 것
정답	

[③주제 서술형] 글의 주제를 조건과 한글 의미와 일치하도록 쓰시오.

한글	전통 유산의 상업화와 그 위협
조건	commercialization / heritage 를 활용하고 필요한 단어를 추가하여 총 7단어로 작성할 것
정답	

[④제목 서술형] 글의 제목을 조건과 한글 의미와 일치하도록 쓰시오.

한글	관광의 역학: 문화유산과 전통이 바뀔 수 있는 방식
단어	Dynamics / Tradition / Change 를 활용하고 필요한 단어를 추가하여 총 11단어로 작성할 것
정답	

[⑤주요문장 서술형] 빈칸에 알맞은 말을 〈조건〉에 맞게 영작하시오. [Tip! 주요 문장 3가지는 시험 직전 꼭 암기하세요!]

한글	이러한 이전 시대의 가짜 상징물은 여행지에서의 지나치게 상업적인 느낌과, 이제는 어떤 것도 진짜처럼 보이지 않고 아마도 진짜인 적도 없었다는 느낌의 원인이 된다.
영어	These false symbols of earlier times _____.
조건	① 동격의 that과 병렬 구조를 활용할 것 ② [commercial / contribute / overly / destination / seem / perhaps]을 활용할 것 ③ 총 20단어로 쓸 것 (필요시 주어진 단어 변형 가능)
정답	

한글	위험은 주민들의 개인 정체성 상실과 자신들의 과거로부터 단절됐다는 느낌에 있다.
영어	A danger lies in the _____.
조건	① 병렬구조를 활용할 것 ② [identity / feeling / disconnect / past / resident / personal]을 활용할 것 ③ 총 18단어로 쓸 것 (필요시 주어진 단어 변형 가능)
정답	

한글	그것은 값싼 장신구를 구매하고 문화적 관습이나 역사적 사건을 재현하려는 전문적으로 연출된 쇼를 보는 방문객들에게 주로 상업의 첨병 역할을 한다.
영어	It serves primarily as a commercial front for visitors _____.
조건	① 주격 관계대명사와 to 부정사를 활용할 것 ② [professionally / trinket / practice / historic / cultural / recreate / attempt]을 활용할 것 ③ 총 18단어로 쓸 것 (필요시 주어진 단어 변형 가능)
정답	

[①어법] 다음 글을 읽고, 어법상 틀린 부분의 개수를 찾고 틀린 부분을 바르게 고치시오.

Physical contests and games in Greek culture influenced art, philosophy and the everyday lives of people wealthy enough to train, hiring professionals and travel to events. However, Greek contests and games were different from the organized competitive sports of today. First, they were grounded in religion; second, they lacked complex administrative structures; third, they did not involve measurements and record keeping from event to. However, there is one major similarity: they often reproduced dominant patterns of social relations in society as a whole. The power and advantages that went with being wealthy, male, young and able-bodied in Greek society shaped the games and contests in ways what limited the participation of most people. Even the definitions of excellence used to evaluate performance reflected the abilities of young males. This meant that the abilities of others were substandard by definition — if you could not do it as a young, able-bodied Greek man did it, you were doing it the wrong way. This legitimized and preserved the privilege enjoyed by a select group of men in Greek society.

① 1개　　② 2개　　③ 3개　　④ 4개　　⑤ 5개

ⓐ : _____ → _____　　ⓑ : _____ → _____

ⓒ : _____ → _____　　ⓓ : _____ → _____

ⓔ : _____ → _____

[②요약 서술형] 글의 요약문을 본문의 단어를 활용하여 서술하시오. (어형 변화 가능)

한글	그리스 문화에서 신체적 경쟁과 오늘날 스포츠의 주요한 유사점 중 하나는 사회적 관계의 지배적인 패턴을 재현하는 기능이다.
조건	1. dominant / similarity / reproduce / social relations / sports of today를 활용할 것 (필요 시 변형 가능) 2. 동명사를 활용할 것 3. 총 23단어 이내로 작성할 것
정답	

[③주제 서술형] 글의 주제를 조건과 한글 의미와 일치하도록 쓰시오.

한글	다양한 시간 설정에서 스포츠의 기능에 대한 교차 조사
조건	functions / settings 를 활용하고 필요한 단어를 추가하여 총 **9단어**로 작성할 것
정답	

[④제목 서술형] 글의 제목을 조건과 한글 의미와 일치하도록 쓰시오.

한글	그리스 문화의 체육 대회와 오늘날 스포츠의 비교
단어	Physical / Culture / Today 를 활용하고 필요한 단어를 추가하여 총 **10단어**로 작성할 것
정답	

[⑤주요문장 서술형] 빈칸에 알맞은 말을 <조건>에 맞게 영작하시오. [Tip! 주요 문장 3가지는 시험 직전 꼭 암기하세요!]

한글	그러나 한 가지 주요한 유사점이 있다. 즉 그것은 흔히 사회 전반의 사회적 관계의 지배적인 패턴을 재현했다.
영어	However, Greek contests and games _____.
조건	① 과거분사를 활용할 것 ② [competitive / organize / different]을 활용할 것 ③ 총 9단어로 쓸 것 (필요시 주어진 단어 변형 가능)
정답	
한글	그리스 사회에서 부유하고, 남성이며, 젊고 신체 건강한 것과 병행하는 권력과 이점은 대부분의 사람들의 참여를 제한하는 방식으로 경기와 대회의 모습을 만들었다.
영어	The power and advantages that went with being wealthy, male, young and able-bodied in Greek society shaped the games and contests _____.
조건	① 주격 관계대명사를 활용할 것 ② [participation / limit / way]을 활용할 것 ③ 총 9단어로 쓸 것 (필요시 주어진 단어 변형 가능)
정답	
한글	이것은 그리스 사회에서 선택된 남성 집단이 누리는 특권을 정당화하고 보호했다.
영어	This legitimized and preserved the privilege _____.
조건	① 과거 분사를 활용할 것 ② [Greek / select / enjoy]을 활용할 것 ③ 총 10단어로 쓸 것 (필요시 주어진 단어 변형 가능)
정답	

[①어법] 다음 글을 읽고, 어법상 틀린 부분의 개수를 찾고 틀린 부분을 바르게 고치시오.

In the field of musical expertise, there is a dichotomy of thinking. On the one hand, there is a widespread perception in the general population what expert musicians have innate talent, or giftedness, beyond ordinary abilities. Talent, as part of the vernacular in the field of music, is usually assuming to be a stable trait — one is either born with musical talent or not. Music aptitude tests popular in the early to mid-twentieth century, such as the Seashore Tests of Musical Talent and the Music Aptitude Profile, attempted to find children who had this musical talent. On the other hand, there is a very real feeling that ability in music comes from a disciplined work ethic. It would be unacceptable, even for that considered talented, not to practice. In fact, those who are considered talented being expected to practice all the more.

① 1개   ② 2개   ③ 3개   ④ 4개   ⑤ 5개

ⓐ : _____ → _____   ⓑ : _____ → _____

ⓒ : _____ → _____   ⓓ : _____ → _____

ⓔ : _____ → _____

[②요약 서술형] 글의 요약문을 본문의 단어를 활용하여 서술하시오. (어형 변화 가능)

한글	음악 분야에는 사람들이 위대한 음악적 능력을 타고난 재능이나 훈련된 직업 윤리로 돌리는 이분법적 사고가 있다.
조건	1. disciplined / attribute / innate / work ethic를 활용할 것 (필요 시 변형 가능) 2. 전치사+관계대명사 구조와 either A or B 구문을 활용할 것 3. 총 17단어 이내로 작성할 것 (빈칸 부분만)
정답	There is a dichotomy of thinking in the field of music, _____.

[③주제 서술형] 글의 주제를 조건과 한글 의미와 일치하도록 쓰시오.

한글	음악 분야에서의 사고의 이분법
조건	dichotomy / field 를 활용하고 필요한 단어를 추가하여 총 9단어로 작성할 것
정답	

[④제목 서술형] 글의 제목을 조건과 한글 의미와 일치하도록 쓰시오.

한글	타고난 재능 또는 훈련된 관행: 음악 속 흑백 사고에 대해 배우기
단어	Innate / Disciplined / Thinking / Black-and-White 를 활용하고 필요한 단어를 추가하여 총 12단어로 작성할 것
정답	

[⑤주요문장 서술형] 빈칸에 알맞은 말을 <조건>에 맞게 영작하시오. [Tip! 주요 문장 3가지는 시험 직전 꼭 암기하세요!]

한글	재능은, 음악 분야에서 사용되는 말의 일부로, 주로 불변의 특성으로 간주되는데, 사람은 음악적 재능을 타고났거나, 그렇지 않다는 것이다.
영어	_____ one is either born with musical talent or not.
조건	① 수동태를 활용할 것 ② [assume / trait / vernacular / stable / field]을 활용할 것 ③ 총 19단어로 쓸 것 (필요시 주어진 단어 변형 가능)
정답	
한글	재능이 있다고 여겨지는 사람들에게 조차도 연습하지 않는 것은 용납될 수 없을 것이다.
영어	_____.
조건	① 가주어/진주어 구문과 과거분사를 활용할 것 ② [unacceptable / consider / practice / talent]을 활용할 것 ③ 총 12단어로 쓸 것 (필요시 주어진 단어 변형 가능)
정답	
한글	사실상, 재능이 있다고 여겨지는 사람들은 그만큼 더 연습해야 한다.
영어	_____.
조건	① 5형식 수동태와 주격 관계대명사를 활용할 것 ② [expect / practice / consider / talent]을 활용할 것 ③ 총 14단어로 쓸 것 (필요시 주어진 단어 변형 가능)
정답	

[①어법] 다음 글을 읽고, 어법상 틀린 부분의 개수를 찾고 틀린 부분을 바르게 고치시오.

For a long time photographs were understood to be visible traces, as irrefutable evidence of the existence of the presented, its "it has been." Therefore, photographs were initially classified as documents, whether using in the media, in the family album, in books, archives or collections. As digitization began to feed into the realm of photography, and the end of the photographic era was proclaimed, it was its documentary qualities, its "ontology" as a chemical-physical symbol, that suddenly lost its persuasive powers. But even if the sting of digital doubt seems deep ingrained within the photographic authenticity and evidence, many of its tasks and uses have hardly changed. When we look at a family album created with digital images, closely inspect the X-rays of a broken foot together with the doctor, or view the image of the finish of the 100-meter finals at the Olympic Games, our trust in photography remains. If we trust the use of the images, or more precisely, if we assign it persuasive powers via their use, it does not matter whether they are analog or   digital. In other words: We doubt photography, but still use certain photographs to dispel doubt and produce evidence.

① 1개　　② 2개　　③ 3개　　④ 4개　　⑤ 5개

ⓐ : ＿＿＿＿＿＿ → ＿＿＿＿＿＿　　　　ⓑ : ＿＿＿＿＿＿ → ＿＿＿＿＿＿

ⓒ : ＿＿＿＿＿＿ → ＿＿＿＿＿＿　　　　ⓓ : ＿＿＿＿＿＿ → ＿＿＿＿＿＿

ⓔ : ＿＿＿＿＿＿ → ＿＿＿＿＿＿

[②요약 서술형] 글의 요약문을 본문의 단어를 활용하여 서술하시오. (어형 변화 가능)

한글	디지털화가 마치 사진 시대의 종말을 알리는 것처럼 보일 수 있지만, 우리는 여전히 증거와 설득의 원천으로서 사진에 특정 기능과 가치를 부여한다.
조건	1. endow / mark / the photographic era / digitization를 활용할 것 (필요 시 변형 가능) 2. 접속사와 as if 구문을 활용할 것 3. 총 23단어 이내로 작성할 것 (빈칸 부분만)
정답	＿＿＿＿＿＿＿＿＿＿＿＿＿＿＿＿＿＿ ＿＿＿＿＿＿＿＿＿＿＿＿ as a source of evidence and persuasion.

[③주제 서술형] 글의 주제를 조건과 한글 의미와 일치하도록 쓰시오.

한글	디지털화 및 사진에 대한 인식 변화
조건	changing / perception 를 활용하고 필요한 단어를 추가하여 총 **6단어**로 작성할 것
정답	

[④제목 서술형] 글의 제목을 조건과 한글 의미와 일치하도록 쓰시오.

한글	사진의 증거력은 여전히 강력하다
단어	Evidential / Photographs 를 활용하고 필요한 단어를 추가하여 총 **8단어**로 작성할 것
정답	

[⑤주요문장 서술형] 빈칸에 알맞은 말을 <조건>에 맞게 영작하시오. [Tip! 주요 문장 3가지는 시험 직전 꼭 암기하세요!]

한글	디지털화가 사진 영역에 영향을 미치기 시작하고, 사진 시대의 끝이 선포되었을 때, 돌연 그것의 설득력을 잃은 것은 바로 그것의 사실을 기록하는 본질, 즉 화학적, 물리적 상징으로서의 그것의 '존재론'이었다.
영어	As digitization began to feed into the realm of photography, and the end of the photographic era was proclaimed, ＿＿＿＿＿＿＿＿＿＿.
조건	① It that 강조구문을 활용할 것 ② [documentary / persuasive / chemical-physical / ontology / quality]을 활용할 것 ③ 총 17단어로 쓸 것 (필요시 주어진 단어 변형 가능)
정답	
한글	우리가 이미지의 사용을 신뢰하거나, 더 정확하게는, 우리가 그것의 사용을 통해 그것에 설득력을 부여한다면, 그것이 아날로그인지, 디지털인지는 중요하지 않다.
영어	If we trust the use of the images, or more precisely, if we assign them persuasive powers via their use, ＿＿＿＿＿＿＿＿＿＿.
조건	① whether 명사절을 활용할 것 ② [analog / matter / digital]을 활용할 것 ③ 총 10단어로 쓸 것 (필요시 주어진 단어 변형 가능)
정답	
한글	다시 말해서, 우리는 사진을 불신하지만, 불신을 떨쳐 버리고 명백성을 제시하기 위해 특정한 사진을 여전히 사용한다.
영어	In other words: We doubt photography, but still use certain photographs ＿＿＿＿＿＿＿＿＿＿.
조건	① 병렬 구조를 활용할 것 ② [evidence / produce / dispel]을 활용할 것 ③ 총 6단어로 쓸 것 (필요시 주어진 단어 변형 가능)
정답	

[①어법] 다음 글을 읽고, 어법상 틀린 부분의 개수를 찾고 틀린 부분을 바르게 고치시오.

Predicting whether a movie will be a success is perhaps the "Holy Grail" of most film-makers and especially the big movie studios. While critical acclaim is always welcome, in the end it is important that a movie makes money. For the big studios — now increasingly owned by massive global corporations — making movies that deliver wide profit margins are the ultimate metric of performance. Movies increasingly depend on non-theatrical sources for revenues. This fact does not diminish the continuing significance of solid box office performance. When a movie hits top spot at the box office, not only is this deliver direct revenue yield, it can further promote other income sources over time. A high public profile means not only that its potential as an attractive choice for repeat viewing on other platforms increases but that its potential to yield sequels might increase, too. In the end, nothing breeds success like success. This maxim is probably the main reason why the major movie studios really like making sequels to highly successful movies and really like to hire star actors with a track record of appearing in blockbuster films that generally do good at the box office.

① 1개 ② 2개 ③ 3개 ④ 4개 ⑤ 5개

ⓐ : _____ → _____   ⓑ : _____ → _____

ⓒ : _____ → _____   ⓓ : _____ → _____

ⓔ : _____ → _____

[②요약 서술형] 글의 요약문을 본문의 단어를 활용하여 서술하시오. (어형 변화 가능)

한글	비록 영화 산업이 수익을 내기 위해 비극장적인 자원을 점점 더 많이 활용하고 있지만, 매표소 흥행의 중요성은 여전히 확고하다.
조건	1. industries / solid / non-theatrical / utilize / box office success / remain / make profits를 활용할 것 (필요 시 변형 가능) 2. 현재 진행형과 동명사를 활용할 것 3. 총 20단어 이내로 작성할 것
정답	

[③주제 서술형] 글의 주제를 조건과 한글 의미와 일치하도록 쓰시오.

한글	큰 수익률을 위한 매표소 흥행의 중요성
조건	importance / success / wide 를 활용하고 필요한 단어를 추가하여 총 **10단어**로 작성할 것
정답	

[④제목 서술형] 글의 제목을 조건과 한글 의미와 일치하도록 쓰시오.

한글	성공은 성공을 가져온다: 영화산업의 성공을 위해 박스오피스가 중심이 되는 이유
단어	Centered / Success / Movie를 활용하고 필요한 단어를 추가하여 총 **14단어**로 작성할 것
정답	

[⑥주요문장 서술형] 빈칸에 알맞은 말을 <조건>에 맞게 영작하시오. [Tip! 주요 문장 3가지는 시험 직전 꼭 암기하세요!]

한글	비평가의 찬사는 늘 반가운 것이지만, 결국 영화는 돈을 버는 것이 중요하다.
영어	While critical acclaim is always welcome, in the end _____.
조건	① 가주어 진주어 구문을 활용할 것 ② [make money / important]를 활용할 것 ③ 총 8단어로 쓸 것 (필요시 주어진 단어 변형 가능)
정답	
한글	영화가 박스 오피스에서 정상을 차지하면, 이것은 직접적인 수익 산출을 낼 뿐만 아니라, 시간이 지나면서 다른 수입원을 더욱더 활성화할 수 있다.
영어	When a movie hits top spot at the box office, _____.
조건	① 도치 구문을 활용할 것 ② [sources / income / revenue yield / promote / deliver]을 활용할 것 ③ 총 17단어로 쓸 것 (필요시 주어진 단어 변형 가능)
정답	
한글	높은 대중의 관심은 다른 플랫폼에서 반복 시청을 위한 매력적인 선택으로서 그것의 잠재적 가능성이 증가한다는 것뿐만 아니라, 속편을 제작할 가능성도 증가할 수 있다는 것을 의미한다.
영어	A high public profile means not only that its potential as an attractive choice for repeat viewing on other platforms increases _____.
조건	① to 부정사를 활용할 것 ② [yield / potential / sequels]을 활용할 것 ③ 총 10단어로 쓸 것 (필요시 주어진 단어 변형 가능)
정답	

[①어법] 다음 글을 읽고, 어법상 틀린 부분의 개수를 찾고 틀린 부분을 바르게 고치시오.

Learners can improve the effectiveness of their attributions through training. In a pioneering study, Carol Susan Dweck, an American psychologist, was provided students who demonstrated learned helplessness with both successful and unsuccessful experiences. When the students were unsuccessful, the experimenter specifically stated that the failure was caused by lack of effort or ineffective strategies. Comparable students were given similar experiences but no training. After 25 sessions, the learners who were counseled about their effort and strategies responded more appropriate to failure by persisting longer and adapting their strategies more effectively. Additional research has corroborated Dweck's findings. Strategy instruction was most effective for students who believed that they were already trying hard. This research suggests that teachers can increase students' motivation to learn by teaching them learning strategies and encouraging them to attribute successes to effort.

① 1개　　② 2개　　③ 3개　　④ 4개　　⑤ 5개

ⓐ : _____ → _____　　　ⓑ : _____ → _____

ⓒ : _____ → _____　　　ⓓ : _____ → _____

ⓔ : _____ → _____

[②요약 서술형] 글의 요약문을 본문의 단어를 활용하여 서술하시오. (어형 변화 가능)

한글	한 실험은 학생들이 그들의 학습을 그들 자신에게 돌릴 때 더 오래 지속되고 더 전략적으로 된다는 것을 보여주었다.
조건	1. attribute / reveal / persist / strategic를 활용할 것 (필요 시 변형 가능) 2. 접속사 that과 재귀대명사를 활용할 것 3. 총 18단어 이내로 작성할 것
정답	

[③주제 서술형] 글의 주제를 조건과 한글 의미와 일치하도록 쓰시오.

한글	학습자의 귀인의 효과성 향상
조건	improving / attribution 를 활용하고 필요한 단어를 추가하여 총 **6단어**로 작성할 것
정답	

[④제목 서술형] 글의 제목을 조건과 한글 의미와 일치하도록 쓰시오.

한글	귀인효과를 통한 학생의 학습동기 부여
단어	Motivating / Effect 를 활용하고 필요한 단어를 추가하여 총 **6단어**로 작성할 것
정답	

[⑤주요문장 서술형] 빈칸에 알맞은 말을 〈조건〉에 맞게 영작하시오. [Tip! 주요 문장 3가지는 시험 직전 꼭 암기하세요!]

한글	선구적인 한 연구에서, 미국 심리학자인 Carol Susan Dweck은 학습된 무력감을 보이는 학생들에게 성공한 경험과 성공하지 못한 경험 모두를 제공했다.
영어	In a pioneering study, Carol Susan Dweck, an American psychologist, _____.
조건	① 주격 관계대명사와 both A and B 구문을 활용할 것 ② [successful / provide / demonstrate / experience / helplessness]을 활용할 것 ③ 총 12단어로 쓸 것 (필요시 주어진 단어 변형 가능)
정답	
한글	전략 교육은 이미 자신이 열심히 노력하고 있다고 믿는 학생들에게 가장 효과적이었다.
영어	_____.
조건	① 주격 관계대명사와 접속사 that, 과거진행형을 활용할 것 ② [try / believe / instruction / strategy / effective]을 활용할 것 ③ 총 15단어로 쓸 것 (필요시 주어진 단어 변형 가능)
정답	
한글	이 연구는 교사들이 학생들에게 학습 전략을 가르치고 성공을 노력 덕분으로 생각하도록 고무함으로써 학생들의 학습 동기를 향상할 수 있다는 것을 보여준다.
영어	_____.
조건	① 접속사 that과 동명사, 병렬구조를 활용할 것 ② [increase / suggest / encourage / success / attribute / motivation]을 활용할 것 ③ 총 24단어로 쓸 것 (필요시 주어진 단어 변형 가능)
정답	

[①어법] 다음 글을 읽고, 어법상 틀린 부분의 개수를 찾고 틀린 부분을 바르게 고치시오.

A lot of research discusses what leads to relatively permanent acquisition of new knowledge or skills. You won't be surprising to hear that active learning works far better than passive learning. In other words, sitting still in a classroom for more than a half hour at a time (no matter how interesting the material) isn't nearly as potently as having opportunities to engage actively with the concepts through discussion, group interaction, practice, immersion, or some other form of direct experience. Likewise, it is absolutely critical for retaining new knowledge and skills that all your senses are engaged. It is great to simulate your intellect, but even better if you can become involved emotionally, physically, and interpersonally. In other words, it isn't enough to merely read this material in a book or hear an instructor talk about them in class. You must also have opportunities to practicing the skills and make the ideas your own.

① 1개   ② 2개   ③ 3개   ④ 4개   ⑤ 5개

ⓐ : _____ → _____   ⓑ : _____ → _____

ⓒ : _____ → _____   ⓓ : _____ → _____

ⓔ : _____ → _____

[②요약 서술형] 글의 요약문을 본문의 단어를 활용하여 서술하시오. (어형 변화 가능)

한글	칠판을 응시하는 것보다 학습자가 적극적으로 교재에 참여하고 아이디어를 자신의 것으로 만들 수 있는 기회를 가질 때 학습효과가 훨씬 강하다.
조건	1. strong / the material / opportunities / own / effect / engage를 활용할 것 (필요 시 변형 가능) 2. 비교급 강조표현과 병렬구조, to 부정사를 활용할 것 3. 총 22단어 이내로 작성할 것 (빈칸 부분만)
정답	Rather than staring at a blackboard, _____ _____.

[③주제 서술형] 글의 주제를 조건과 한글 의미와 일치하도록 쓰시오.

한글	지식 습득을 위한 능동적 학습의 효과
조건	active / aquisition 를 활용하고 필요한 단어를 추가하여 총 9단어로 작성할 것
정답	

[④제목 서술형] 글의 제목을 조건과 한글 의미와 일치하도록 쓰시오.

한글	능동적 학습의 힘
단어	Power 를 활용하고 필요한 단어를 추가하여 총 5단어로 작성할 것
정답	

[⑤주요문장 서술형] 빈칸에 알맞은 말을 <조건>에 맞게 영작하시오. [Tip! 주요 문장 3가지는 시험 직전 꼭 암기하세요!]

한글	많은 연구는 무엇이 새로운 지식이나 기술을 비교적 영구적으로 습득할 수 있게 하는가에 관해 논한다.
영어	_____.
조건	① 관계대명사 what을 활용할 것 ② [acquisition / relatively / permanent / knowledge / discuss]을 활용할 것 ③ 총 16단어로 쓸 것 (필요시 주어진 단어 변형 가능)
정답	
한글	마찬가지로, 새로운 지식과 기술을 유지하기 위해서는 여러분의 '모든' 감각이 관여하는 것이 절대적으로 중요하다.
영어	Likewise, _____.
조건	① 가주어/진주어 구문과 동명사를 활용할 것 ② [knowledge / absolutely / engage / critical / retain]을 활용할 것 ③ 총 16단어로 쓸 것 (필요시 주어진 단어 변형 가능)
정답	
한글	다시 말해서, 단순히 책에 있는 이 자료를 읽거나 수업 시간에 교사가 그것에 관해 말하는 것을 듣는 것만으로는 충분하지 않다.
영어	In other words, _____.
조건	① 가주어/진주어 구문과 지각동사를 활용할 것 ② [material / instructor / merely / hear]을 활용할 것 ③ 총 20단어로 쓸 것 (필요시 주어진 단어 변형 가능)
정답	

[①어법] 다음 글을 읽고, 어법상 틀린 부분의 개수를 찾고 틀린 부분을 바르게 고치시오.

According to Piaget, organizing, assimilating, and accommodating can be viewed as a kind of complex balancing act. In his theory, the actual changes in thinking take place through the process of equilibration — the act of searching for a balance. Piaget assumed that people continually test the adequacy of their thinking processes in order to achieve that balance. Briefly, the process of equilibration works like this: If we apply a particular scheme to an event or situation and the scheme working, then equilibrium exists. If the scheme does not produce a satisfying result, then disequilibrium exists, and we become uncomfortable. This motivates us to keep searched for a solution through assimilation and accommodation, and thus our thinking changes and moves ahead. Of course, the level of disequilibrium must be just right or optimal — too little and we aren't interested in changing, too much and we may be discouraged or anxious and not changed.

① 1개　　② 2개　　③ 3개　　④ 4개　　⑤ 5개

ⓐ : ＿＿＿＿＿＿ → ＿＿＿＿＿＿　　　ⓑ : ＿＿＿＿＿＿ → ＿＿＿＿＿＿

ⓒ : ＿＿＿＿＿＿ → ＿＿＿＿＿＿　　　ⓓ : ＿＿＿＿＿＿ → ＿＿＿＿＿＿

ⓔ : ＿＿＿＿＿＿ → ＿＿＿＿＿＿

[②요약 서술형] 글의 요약문을 본문의 단어를 활용하여 서술하시오. (어형 변화 가능)

한글	Piaget는 사고란 특정한 체계가 문맥에 지속적으로 적용되고 수정되는 균형의 과정과 같다고 믿었다.
조건	1. revise / scheme / contexts / equilibration / constant / apply를 활용할 것 (필요 시 변형 가능) 2. 접속사 that과 전치사+관계대명사 구조, 수동태, 병렬구조를 활용할 것 3. 총 22단어 이내로 작성할 것
정답	

[③주제 서술형] 글의 주제를 조건과 한글 의미와 일치하도록 쓰시오.

한글	균형을 찾는 과정으로서의 사고
조건	thinking / equilibrium 를 활용하고 필요한 단어를 추가하여 총 **7단어**로 작성할 것
정답	

[④제목 서술형] 글의 제목을 조건과 한글 의미와 일치하도록 쓰시오.

한글	생각이 변화하고 앞으로 나아가는 방식에 대한 Piaget의 설명
단어	**Account / Moves** 를 활용하고 필요한 단어를 추가하여 총 **9단어**로 작성할 것
정답	

[⑤주요문장 서술형] 빈칸에 알맞은 말을 〈조건〉에 맞게 영작하시오. [Tip! 주요 문장 3가지는 시험 직전 꼭 암기하세요!]

한글	Piaget에 따르면, 조직하기, 동화하기, 그리고 조절하기는 일종의 복잡한 균형 잡기 행위로 여겨질 수 있다.
영어	According to Piaget, ＿＿＿＿＿＿＿＿＿＿＿＿＿＿＿＿.
조건	① 조동사 수동태를 활용할 것 ② [assimilating / balancing / view / accommodating / complex]을 활용할 것 ③ 총 14단어로 쓸 것 (필요시 주어진 단어 변형 가능)
정답	
한글	간단히 말해서, 평형 과정은 다음과 같이 작동한다. 만약 우리가 어떤 사건이나 상황에 특정한 도식을 적용하고 그 도식이 작동하면 평형이 나타난다.
영어	Briefly, the process of equilibration works like this: ＿＿＿＿＿＿＿＿＿＿＿＿＿＿.
조건	① If 조건절을 활용할 것 ② [apply / equilibrium / exist / scheme]을 활용할 것 ③ 총 18단어로 쓸 것 (필요시 주어진 단어 변형 가능)
정답	
한글	이것은 우리가 동화와 조절을 통해 해결책을 계속 찾도록 동기를 부여하고, 따라서 우리의 사고는 변화하며 앞으로 나아간다.
영어	＿＿＿＿＿＿＿＿＿＿＿＿＿＿, and thus our thinking changes and moves ahead.
조건	① 동명사와 5형식 문장 구조를 활용할 것 ② [motivate / assimilation / accommodation / search for]을 활용할 것 ③ 총 13단어로 쓸 것 (필요시 주어진 단어 변형 가능)
정답	

[①어법] 다음 글을 읽고, 어법상 틀린 부분의 개수를 찾고 틀린 부분을 바르게 고치시오.

In many ways it's difficult to imagine communicating without any emotion whatsoever. What would communication stripped of its nonverbal components even look like? Perhaps messaging technology can give us a clue. After all, who hasn't experienced a misunderstanding with someone when exchanged text messages? While there can be a number of reasons for this, many misinterpretations are in fact because the lack of nonverbal cues and tone of voice in these communications. Numerous studies of text messaging and email support this. A 2005 paper, "Egocentrism Over E-Mail: Can We Communicate as Well as We Think?" cites studies that showed participants had a 50 percent chance of correctly distinguishing whether the tone in an email being sarcastic or not. If our ability to correctly deduce such information is no better than chance, it's small wonder texting often leading to misunderstandings.

① 1개　　② 2개　　③ 3개　　④ 4개　　⑤ 5개

ⓐ : _____ → _____　　　ⓑ : _____ → _____

ⓒ : _____ → _____　　　ⓓ : _____ → _____

ⓔ : _____ → _____

[②요약 서술형] 글의 요약문을 본문의 단어를 활용하여 서술하시오. (어형 변화 가능)

한글	수많은 연구들은 우리가 문자 메시지를 오해하는 이유가 비언어적인 신호와 목소리 톤의 부족 때문이라는 사실을 지적한다.
조건	1. tone / the lack / point to / numerous / nonverbal / due to를 활용할 것 (필요 시 변형 가능) 2. 동격의 that과 관계부사, 병렬구조를 활용할 것 3. 총 26단어 이내로 작성할 것
정답	

[③주제 서술형] 글의 주제를 조건과 한글 의미와 일치하도록 쓰시오.

한글	오해 없는 의사소통을 위한 비언어적 신호의 중요성
조건	nonverbal / misunderstanding 를 활용하고 필요한 단어를 추가하여 총 9단어로 작성할 것
정답	

[④제목 서술형] 글의 제목을 조건과 한글 의미와 일치하도록 쓰시오.

한글	우리가 가끔 문자 메시지를 잘못 해석하는 이유
단어	Misinterpret / Text 를 활용하고 필요한 단어를 추가하여 총 6단어로 작성할 것
정답	

[⑤주요문장 서술형] 빈칸에 알맞은 말을 〈조건〉에 맞게 영작하시오. [Tip! 주요 문장 3가지는 시험 직전 꼭 암기하세요!]

한글	여러 가지 면에서 전혀 아무 감정도 없이 의사소통하는 것은 상상하기 어렵다.
영어	_____ .
조건	① 가주어/진주어 구문과 동명사를 활용할 것 ② [emotion / difficult / communicate / imagine]을 활용할 것 ③ 총 12단어로 쓸 것 (필요시 주어진 단어 변형 가능)
정답	
한글	비언어적 요소가 제거된 의사소통은 심지어 어떤 모습일까?
영어	_____ .
조건	① 과거분사를 활용할 것 ② [nonverbal / communication / strip / component]을 활용할 것 ③ 총 11단어로 쓸 것 (필요시 주어진 단어 변형 가능)
정답	
한글	만약 그러한 정보를 정확하게 추론하는 우리의 능력이 우연보다 나을 것이 없다면, 문자 메시지가 자주 오해를 불러일으키는 것은 별로 놀라운 일이 아니다.
영어	_____ .
조건	① 가주어/진주어 구문과 to 부정사를 활용할 것 ② [information / correctly / wonder / misunderstanding / chance / deduce]을 활용할 것 ③ 총 21~22단어로 쓸 것 (필요시 주어진 단어 변형 가능)
정답	

[①어법] 다음 글을 읽고, 어법상 틀린 부분의 개수를 찾고 틀린 부분을 바르게 고치시오.

Social validation means that certain beliefs and values are confirming only by the shared social experience of a group. For example, any given culture cannot prove that its religion and moral system are superior to another culture's religion and moral system, but if the members reinforce each other's beliefs and values, they come to be taken for granted. Those who fail to accept such beliefs and values run the risk of "excommunication," of throwing out of the group. The test of whether they work or not is how comfortable and anxiety-free members are when they abide by it. In these realms, the group learns that certain beliefs and values, as initially promulgated by prophets, founders, and leaders, "work" in the sense of reducing uncertainty in critical areas of the group's functioning. Moreover, as they continue to provide meaning and comfort to group members, they also become transforming into non-discussible assumptions even though they may not be correlated with actual performance.

① 1개　　② 2개　　③ 3개　　④ 4개　　⑤ 5개

ⓐ : _____ → _____　　　ⓑ : _____ → _____

ⓒ : _____ → _____　　　ⓓ : _____ → _____

ⓔ : _____ → _____

[②요약 서술형] 글의 요약문을 본문의 단어를 활용하여 서술하시오. (어형 변화 가능)

한글	특정 신념과 가치는 집단의 공유된 사회적 경험에 의해서만 확인되기 때문에, 사회적 확인은 집단의 기능 과정에 크게 영향을 미친다.
조건	1. certain / confirm / affect / share / social validation / great를 활용할 것 (필요 시 변형 가능) 2. with 분사구문과 과거분사를 활용할 것 3. 총 20단어 이내로 작성할 것 (빈칸 부분만)
정답	_____ _____ the course of the group's functioning.

[③주제 서술형] 글의 주제를 조건과 한글 의미와 일치하도록 쓰시오.

한글	사회적 검증의 개념과 작동 방식
조건	concept / validation 를 활용하고 필요한 단어를 추가하여 총 **9단어**로 작성할 것
정답	

[④제목 서술형] 글의 제목을 조건과 한글 의미와 일치하도록 쓰시오.

한글	사회적 확인: 특정 신념이 그룹 내에서 확인되는 방식
단어	**Certain / Confirmed** 를 활용하고 필요한 단어를 추가하여 총 **10단어**로 작성할 것
정답	

[⑤주요문장 서술형] 빈칸에 알맞은 말을 〈조건〉에 맞게 영작하시오. [Tip! 주요 문장 3가지는 시험 직전 꼭 암기하세요!]

한글	'사회적 확인'이란 특정 신념과 가치가 한 집단의 공유된 사회적 경험에 의해서만 확인된다는 것을 의미한다.
영어	_____.
조건	① 접속사 that 과 수동태, 과거분사를 활용할 것 ② [validation / experience / confirm / belief / value / social]을 활용할 것 ③ 총 19단어로 쓸 것 (필요시 주어진 단어 변형 가능)
정답	
한글	그것들(신념과 가치)이 효과가 있는지 없는지에 대한 시험은 구성원들이 그것들을 준수할 때 얼마나 편안하고 불안함이 없는가 하는 것이다.
영어	_____.
조건	① 간접의문문을 활용할 것 ② [comfortable / abide / anxiety-free / work]을 활용할 것 ③ 총 20단어로 쓸 것 (필요시 주어진 단어 변형 가능)
정답	
한글	더욱이, 그것들이 집단 구성원들에게 의미와 편안함을 계속 제공함에 따라, 그것들은 또한 실제의 행위와 서로 상관관계가 없을 수 있을지라도 논할 수 없는 전제로 변형된다.
영어	Moreover, as they continue to provide meaning and comfort to group members, _____
조건	① 과거분사와 조동사 수동태를 활용할 것 ② [correlate / assumption / non-discussible / performance / transform]을 활용할 것 ③ 총 17단어로 쓸 것 (필요시 주어진 단어 변형 가능)
정답	

[①어법] 다음 글을 읽고, 어법상 틀린 부분의 개수를 찾고 틀린 부분을 바르게 고치시오.

Socio-cultural behaviors arise from the exchange of information between individuals and, therefore, they are close linked to how the information flows among the population. In particular, the social ties built and maintained in the local neighborhood are useful for solving concrete local problems and affect the spread of information and behaviors, play a key role in integrating social groups at higher scales. Residential segregation directly impacts how these social ties of physical nearness are displayed, drawing boundaries on the structure of information flows. We can think of the segregation process as a dynamical formation of echo-chambers: social fragmentation over the residential space encourages individual within a group to interact only with their peers. In this case, the collective behaviors of the socio-cultural space that emerge could clash at higher scales, as polarized positions may arise.

① 1개　　② 2개　　③ 3개　　④ 4개　　⑤ 5개

ⓐ : _____ → _____　　　ⓑ : _____ → _____

ⓒ : _____ → _____　　　ⓓ : _____ → _____

ⓔ : _____ → _____

[②요약 서술형] 글의 요약문을 본문의 단어를 활용하여 서술하시오. (어형 변화 가능)

한글	사회문화적 행동이 개인 간의 정보 교환에서 발생한다는 사실의 시사점은 사회적 유대가 더 높은 규모의 사회집단을 통합하는 데 핵심적인 역할을 할 수 있다는 것이다.
조건	1. social ties / integrate / at higher scales / socio-cultural behaviors / the implication / arise / the exchange / individuals / a key role를 활용할 것 (필요 시 변형 가능) 2. 동격의 that과 접속사 that, 동명사를 활용할 것 3. 총 32단어 이내로 작성할 것
정답	

[③주제 서술형] 글의 주제를 조건과 한글 의미와 일치하도록 쓰시오.

한글	개인 간의 정보 교환이 사회 문화적 행동에 미치는 영향
조건	exchanges / individuals / behaviors 를 활용하고 필요한 단어를 추가하여 총 11단어로 작성할 것
정답	

[④제목 서술형] 글의 제목을 조건과 한글 의미와 일치하도록 쓰시오.

한글	정보 흐름의 구조와 사회문화적 행동
단어	Structure / Sociocultural 를 활용하고 필요한 단어를 추가하여 총 7단어로 작성할 것
정답	

[⑤주요문장 서술형] 빈칸에 알맞은 말을 <조건>에 맞게 영작하시오. [Tip! 주요 문장 3가지는 시험 직전 꼭 암기하세요!]

한글	특히 지역 사회에서 구축되고 유지되는 사회적 유대는 구체적인 지역 문제를 해결하는 데 유용하며 정보와 행동의 확산에 영향을 미쳐, 더 높은 수준에서 사회 집단을 통합하는 데 핵심적인 역할을 한다.
영어	In particular, _____, playing a key role in integrating social groups at higher scales.
조건	① 과거분사와 동명사, 병렬 구조를 활용할 것 ② [neighborhood / maintain / spread / behavior / concrete / tie]을 활용할 것 ③ 총 25단어로 쓸 것 (필요시 주어진 단어 변형 가능)
정답	
한글	거주지 분리는 이러한 물리적 근접성의 사회적 유대가 어떻게 나타나는지에 직접적인 영향을 미쳐, 정보 흐름의 구조에 경계를 짓는다.
영어	_____.
조건	① 간접의문문과 수동태, 분사구문을 활용할 것 ② [segregation / boundary / information / nearness / physical / draw / structure / information flows]을 활용할 것 ③ 총 21단어로 쓸 것 (필요시 주어진 단어 변형 가능)
정답	
한글	이러한 경우에, 새로이 생겨나는, 사회문화적 공간의 집단행동이 더 높은 수준에서 충돌할 수도 있을 터인데, 이는 양극화된 입장이 생길 수도 있기 때문이다.
영어	In this case, _____.
조건	① 주격 관계대명사와 과거분사를 활용할 것 ② [emerge / collective / polarize / socio-cultural / arise / behavior]을 활용할 것 ③ 총 19단어로 쓸 것 (필요시 주어진 단어 변형 가능)
정답	

[①어법] 다음 글을 읽고, 어법상 틀린 부분의 개수를 찾고 틀린 부분을 바르게 고치시오.

Connecting the current offline population will be a difficult undertaking. Many of the remaining unserved areas are geographically challenging to reach due to rough terrain or remote location, thus raising providers' costs and pushing broadband services further out of reach of low-income households. However, more affordable and accessible Internet is becoming a reality in parts of the world, thanks to satellite technologies emerged as an alternative to expanding access at lower costs to remote locations across the planet. For example, a network of orbital satellites operated by an American spacecraft manufacturer has launched 1,735 satellites into orbit since 2019. According to the company: "The satellite network is ideally suited for areas of the globe which connectivity has typically been a challenge. Unbounded by traditional ground infrastructure, the network can deliver high-speed broadband Internet to locations where access has been unreliable or completely unavailable."

① 1개   ② 2개   ③ 3개   ④ 4개   ⑤ 5개

ⓐ : _____ → _____   ⓑ : _____ → _____

ⓒ : _____ → _____   ⓓ : _____ → _____

ⓔ : _____ → _____

[②요약 서술형] 글의 요약문을 본문의 단어를 활용하여 서술하시오. (어형 변화 가능)

한글	위성 기술 덕분에, 지리적으로 어려운 지역에 인터넷 서비스를 제공하는 것이 가능해졌다.
조건	1. thanks to / geographically / possible / provide / challenging를 활용할 것 (필요 시 변형 가능) 2. 가주어 진주어 구문을 활용할 것 3. 총 15단어 이내로 작성할 것
정답	

[③주제 서술형] 글의 주제를 조건과 한글 의미와 일치하도록 쓰시오.

한글	지리적으로 어려운 지역에 인터넷 서비스를 제공하는 위성 기술
조건	satellite / supply / geographically 를 활용하고 필요한 단어를 추가하여 총 10단어로 작성할 것
정답	

[④제목 서술형] 글의 제목을 조건과 한글 의미와 일치하도록 쓰시오.

한글	세계를 연결하는 궤도 위성들
단어	Orbital / Connecting 를 활용하고 필요한 단어를 추가하여 총 6단어로 작성할 것
정답	

[⑤주요문장 서술형] 빈칸에 알맞은 말을 <조건>에 맞게 영작하시오. [Tip! 주요 문장 3가지는 시험 직전 꼭 암기하세요!]

한글	예를 들어, 한 미국 우주선 제조업체가 운영하는 궤도 위성망은 2019년 이래로 1,735개의 인공위성을 궤도로 쏘아 올려 왔다.
영어	For example, _____.
조건	① 과거분사와 현재완료를 활용할 것 ② [satellite / manufacturer / launch / spacecraft / orbital]을 활용할 것 ③ 총 19단어로 쓸 것 (필요시 주어진 단어 변형 가능)
정답	
한글	그 회사에 따르면 "그 위성망은 (인터넷) 접속성이 대체로 난제였던 지구의 여러 지역에 이상적으로 적합합니다.
영어	According to the company: _____.
조건	① 관계부사와 현재완료를 활용할 것 ② [suit / connectivity / typically / challenge / satellite]을 활용할 것 ③ 총 18단어로 쓸 것 (필요시 주어진 단어 변형 가능)
정답	
한글	그 위성망은, 기존의 지상 기반 시설에 구애되지 않으므로, (인터넷) 접속을 믿을 수 없었거나 전적으로 이용할 수 없었던 지역에 고속 광대역 인터넷을 제공할 수 있습니다."
영어	Unbounded by traditional ground infrastructure, _____.
조건	① 관계부사와 현재완료를 활용할 것 ② [broadband / high-speed / access / unavailable / unreliable / location]을 활용할 것 ③ 총 17단어로 쓸 것 (필요시 주어진 단어 변형 가능)
정답	

[①어법] 다음 글을 읽고, 어법상 틀린 부분의 개수를 찾고 틀린 부분을 바르게 고치시오.

Data will be generated from everywhere. Cars, smartphones, bodies, minds, homes, and cities will be sources of massive amounts of information what will grow exponentially and flow at an unprecedented speed over the internet. In the years ahead, the expression "less is more" will have a greater level of importance as to how you integrate the ocean of insights coming your way and will aid you to understand the world around you. The amount of information and media surrounding us will be impracticable to process and retrieve; you can leave those for the machines, which can process data faster and more accurate than we can. Your job will be to focus on what matters most to you. The key to an easy digital future is not so much accessing a tsunami of data but how you comprehend and translate it into new contexts, scenarios, and ideas.

① 1개　　② 2개　　③ 3개　　④ 4개　　⑤ 5개

ⓐ : _____ → _____　　　ⓑ : _____ → _____

ⓒ : _____ → _____　　　ⓓ : _____ → _____

ⓔ : _____ → _____

[②요약 서술형] 글의 요약문을 본문의 단어를 활용하여 서술하시오. (어형 변화 가능)

한글	모든 곳에서 데이터가 생성되고 그 양이 기하급수적으로 증가하기 때문에, 우리는 데이터를 이해하고 가치 있는 아이디어로 번역할 수 있어야 한다.
조건	1. generate / valuable / comprehend / exponentially / translate / grow / able를 활용할 것 (필요 시 변형 가능) 2. 수동태와 병렬 구조를 활용할 것 3. 총 23단어 이내로 작성할 것
정답	

[③주제 서술형] 글의 주제를 조건과 한글 의미와 일치하도록 쓰시오.

한글	늘어나는 데이터와 인간의 역할
조건	amount / data 를 활용하고 필요한 단어를 추가하여 총 8단어로 작성할 것
정답	

[④제목 서술형] 글의 제목을 조건과 한글 의미와 일치하도록 쓰시오.

한글	데이터 쓰나미 속에서 헤엄치기 위해 해야 할 일
단어	Swim / Tsunami 를 활용하고 필요한 단어를 추가하여 총 11단어로 작성할 것
정답	

[⑤주요문장 서술형] 빈칸에 알맞은 말을 <조건>에 맞게 영작하시오. [Tip! 주요 문장 3가지는 시험 직전 꼭 암기하세요!]

한글	앞으로는, "더 적은 것이 더 많은 것이다"라는 표현이 여러분이 어떻게 자신에게 닥쳐오는 수많은 식견을 통합하는지에 관해 더 큰 정도의 중요성을 가질 것이고, 여러분이 주변 세상을 이해하도록 도움을 줄 것이다.
영어	In the years ahead, the expression "less is more" will have a greater level of importance _____
조건	① 간접의문문과 현재분사, 병렬구조를 활용할 것 ② [integrate / understand / aid / insight / world]을 활용할 것 ③ 총 22단어로 쓸 것 (필요시 주어진 단어 변형 가능)
정답	
한글	우리를 둘러싸고 있는 정보와 매체의 양은 처리하고 기억하기가 거의 불가능할 것이어서, 여러분은 그것을 기계에 맡길 수 있는데, 그것(기계)은 우리가 할 수 있는 것보다 더 빠르고 더 정확하게 데이터를 처리할 수 있다.
영어	The amount of information and media surrounding us will be impracticable to process and retrieve; _____ .
조건	① 관계대명사의 계속적 용법과 비교급, 병렬 구조를 활용할 것 ② [leave / accurately / process / machine / data]을 활용할 것 ③ 총 18단어로 쓸 것 (필요시 주어진 단어 변형 가능)
정답	
한글	안락한 디지털 미래의 비결은 쓰나미처럼 밀려오는 데이터에 접근하는 것이라기보다는 오히려 어떻게 그것을 이해해서 새로운 맥락, 시나리오, 아이디어로 바꾸는가이다.
영어	The key to an easy digital future is _____ .
조건	① 병렬구조와 간접의문문, not so much A but B 구문을 활용할 것 ② [comprehend / translate / access / context / tsunami]을 활용할 것 ③ 총 21단어로 쓸 것 (필요시 주어진 단어 변형 가능)
정답	

[①어법] 다음 글을 읽고, 어법상 틀린 부분의 개수를 찾고 틀린 부분을 바르게 고치시오.

Unless you're one of those lucky people who only drive new cars, on at least one occasion you've probably experienced the painful realization that your car is too old and no longer worth repaired any more. As a car ages, more and more things can go wrong and need fixing. At some point, the owner needs to decide: is it worth getting this latest issue looked at or is it time to give up on this car and find another? The problem is that a lot of money has already been spent on the car, and scrapping them makes it seem as if that money has just been wasted, which makes it very difficult to choose the best option. It's a problem known as entrapment, when a person gets trapping into making the wrong decision just because they've previously invested so much.

① 1개　　② 2개　　③ 3개　　④ 4개　　⑤ 5개

ⓐ : _____ → _____　　　ⓑ : _____ → _____

ⓒ : _____ → _____　　　ⓓ : _____ → _____

ⓔ : _____ → _____

[②요약 서술형] 글의 요약문을 본문의 단어를 활용하여 서술하시오. (어형 변화 가능)	
한글	속박감이라고 알려진 개념은 우리가 단지 이전의 투자 때문에 때때로 잘못된 결정을 한다는 것을 나타낸다.
조건	1. entrapment / previous / just / make / decision / indicate를 활용할 것 (필요 시 변형 가능) 2. 과거분사와 접속사 that을 활용할 것 3. 총 18단어 이내로 작성할 것
정답	

[③주제 서술형] 글의 주제를 조건과 한글 의미와 일치하도록 쓰시오.	
한글	속박감의 개념과 사례
조건	entrapment / example 를 활용하고 필요한 단어를 추가하여 총 8단어로 작성할 것
정답	

[④제목 서술형] 글의 제목을 조건과 한글 의미와 일치하도록 쓰시오.	
한글	속박감: 당신이 여전히 매몰 비용을 신경쓰는 이유
단어	Care / Sunk 를 활용하고 필요한 단어를 추가하여 총 9단어로 작성할 것
정답	

[⑤주요문장 서술형] 빈칸에 알맞은 말을 〈조건〉에 맞게 영작하시오. [Tip! 주요 문장 3가지는 시험 직전 꼭 암기하세요!]	
한글	어떤 시점에서는, 소유자가 결정을 내려야 하는데, 이 최근 문제를 살펴보게 하는 것이 가치가 있는가, 아니면 이 차를 포기하고 다른 차를 구해서 얻을 때인가?
영어	At some point, the owner needs to decide: _____ or is it time to give up on this car and find another?
조건	① worth -ing 구문과 목적격 보어를 활용할 것 ② [get / look / issue]을 활용할 것 ③ 총 9단어로 쓸 것 (필요시 주어진 단어 변형 가능)
정답	
한글	문제는 이미 그 차에 많은 돈이 들어갔고 폐차하는 것이 그 돈이 그저 헛되이 쓰인 것처럼 보이게 하는데, 그것이 선택할 수 있는 최선의 것을 고르는 것을 매우 어렵게 만든다는 것이다.
영어	The problem is that a lot of money has already been spent on the car, and _____.
조건	① 관계대명사의 계속적 용법과 가목적어 진목적어 구문, 현재완료 수동태를 활용할 것 ② [waste / difficult / scrap / option]을 활용할 것 ③ 총 23단어로 쓸 것 (필요시 주어진 단어 변형 가능)
정답	
한글	그것은 '속박감'이라고 알려진 문제인데, 어떤 사람이 단지 이전에 매우 많이 투자했다는 이유만으로 잘못된 결정을 내리는 함정에 빠지는 경우이다.
영어	It's a problem known as entrapment, _____.
조건	① 동명사와 과거 분사, 현재완료를 활용할 것 ② [trap / decision / invest / previously]을 활용할 것 ③ 총 17~18단어로 쓸 것 (필요시 주어진 단어 변형 가능)
정답	

[①어법] 다음 글을 읽고, 어법상 틀린 부분의 개수를 찾고 틀린 부분을 바르게 고치시오.

Teams and organizations also have a 'mental life'. Most leaders work hard to get alignment — getting everybody on the same thinking wavelength. But to help organizations and teams flourished, leaders must also work equally hard on getting attunement —— getting people on the same feeling wavelength, getting the purpose of the organization and the meaning of the work to resonate with people in a felt way. 'Felt' is the important word here. That is relatively easy to explain the purpose and goals of an organization in a cognitive way. But to function at our best, we have to feel the connection between what we are asking to do and some larger purpose of the group. Leaders of flourishing organizations succeed in making strong feeling connections between the personal goals and values of the people working there and those of the organization, or even the larger society. The tighter the links in the chain, a happier the people and the better the results.

① 1개　　② 2개　　③ 3개　　④ 4개　　⑤ 5개

ⓐ : _____ → _____　　　ⓑ : _____ → _____

ⓒ : _____ → _____　　　ⓓ : _____ → _____

ⓔ : _____ → _____

[②요약 서술형] 글의 요약문을 본문의 단어를 활용하여 서술하시오. (어형 변화 가능)

한글	조직의 목적과 목표에 대한 인지적 이해를 넘어, 리더는 구성원들이 자신의 개인적 가치와 집단의 가치가 연결되었다고 느끼도록 해야 한다.
조건	1. personal / connected를 활용할 것 (필요 시 변형 가능) 2. 준사역동사 get과 접속사 that, 지시대명사 those를 활용할 것 3. 총 18단어 이내로 작성할 것 (빈칸 부분만)
정답	Beyond the cognitive understanding of the purpose and goal of an organization, _____

[③주제 서술형] 글의 주제를 조건과 한글 의미와 일치하도록 쓰시오.

한글	리더가 그룹 구성원들 사이에서 (감정적)조화를 이루는 것의 중요성
조건	significance / attunement / members 를 활용하고 필요한 단어를 추가하여 총 9단어로 작성할 것
정답	

[④제목 서술형] 글의 제목을 조건과 한글 의미와 일치하도록 쓰시오.

한글	조직의 성공 비결: 사람들의 마음을 조율하기
단어	Key / Attuned 를 활용하고 필요한 단어를 추가하여 총 9단어로 작성할 것
정답	

[⑤주요문장 서술형] 빈칸에 알맞은 말을 〈조건〉에 맞게 영작하시오. [Tip! 주요 문장 3가지는 시험 직전 꼭 암기하세요!]

한글	조직의 목적과 목표를 인지적인 방식으로 설명하는 것은 비교적 쉽다.
영어	_____ of an organization in a cognitive way.
조건	① 가주어/진주어 구문을 활용할 것 ② [goal / relatively / purpose / explain]을 활용할 것 ③ 총 10단어로 쓸 것 (필요시 주어진 단어 변형 가능)
정답	
한글	하지만 우리가 최상의 상태에서 기능하기 위해서, 우리는 하라는 요구를 받고 있는 것과 집단의 어떤 더 큰 목적 사이의 연관성을 '느껴야' 한다.
영어	But to function at our best, we have to feel _____.
조건	① between A and B 구문과 관계대명사 what 절, 현재진행 수동태을 활용할 것 ② [purpose / connection / ask / group]을 활용할 것 ③ 총 17단어로 쓸 것 (필요시 주어진 단어 변형 가능)
정답	
한글	그 사슬의 고리가 단단할수록, 그 (조직의) 사람들은 더 행복하고, 결과는 더 좋다.
영어	_____ and the better the results.
조건	① the 비교급, the 비교급 구문을 활용할 것 ② [people / tight / link / chain]을 활용할 것 ③ 총 11단어로 쓸 것 (필요시 주어진 단어 변형 가능)
정답	

[①어법] 다음 글을 읽고, 어법상 틀린 부분의 개수를 찾고 틀린 부분을 바르게 고치시오.

In the door-in-the-face technique, a large, unreasonable request is made, that is turned down; this is followed by a smaller more reasonable request. People are more likely to agree to this smaller second request when it is placing in the context of the more unreasonable request than if it had been placed at the outset. The success of this technique may be related to the reciprocity social norm, the rule that we should pay back in kind what we receive from others. The person asking for our support or assistance, appears to make a concession by giving up their initial request, for a much smaller one. As a result, we feel compelled to reciprocate and agree to the smaller request. A common application of door-in-the-face is when teens ask their parents for a large request (attending an out-of-town concert) and then when the permission is denied, asks them for something smaller (attending a local concert). Having been denied the larger request increases the likelihood that parents will acquiesce in the later, smaller request.

① 1개   ② 2개   ③ 3개   ④ 4개   ⑤ 5개

ⓐ : _____ → _____   ⓑ : _____ → _____

ⓒ : _____ → _____   ⓓ : _____ → _____

ⓔ : _____ → _____

[②요약 서술형] 글의 요약문을 본문의 단어를 활용하여 서술하시오. (어형 변화 가능)

한글	받은 것을 갚아야 하는 호혜적 사회규범 때문에, '면전에서 문 닫기 기법'이 효과가 있는데, 이는 처음의 요구를 포기하여 양보하는 것처럼 보이기 때문이다.
조건	1. a concession / the door-in-the-face technique / request / give up / the reciprocity social norm / receive를 활용할 것 (필요 시 변형 가능) 2. 관계부사와 관계대명사 what, 동명사를 활용할 것 3. 총 30단어 이내로 작성할 것
정답	

[③주제 서술형] 글의 주제를 조건과 한글 의미와 일치하도록 쓰시오.

한글	면전에서 문 닫기 기법이 작동하는 방식
조건	technique 를 활용하고 필요한 단어를 추가하여 총 **5단어**로 작성할 것
정답	

[④제목 서술형] 글의 제목을 조건과 한글 의미와 일치하도록 쓰시오.

한글	규범적 측면에서의 면전에서 문 닫기 기법
단어	**Normative** 를 활용하고 필요한 단어를 추가하여 총 **7단어**로 작성할 것
정답	

[⑤주요문장 서술형] 빈칸에 알맞은 말을 〈조건〉에 맞게 영작하시오. [Tip! 주요 문장 3가지는 시험 직전 꼭 암기하세요!]

한글	사람들은 이 더 작은 두 번째 요청이 처음부터 이루어진 경우보다 더 불합리한 요청이라는 맥락 속에서 이루어질 때 그것에 동의할 가능성이 더 크다.
영어	People are more likely to agree to this smaller second request when it is placed in the context of the more unreasonable request _____.
조건	① 비교급 접속사 than과 과거완료 수동태를 활용할 것 ② [place / outset]을 활용할 것 ③ 총 9단어로 쓸 것 (필요시 주어진 단어 변형 가능)
정답	
한글	우리의 지원이나 도움을 요청하는 사람은 훨씬 더 작은 요청을 위해 자신의 처음 요청을 포기함으로써 양보를 한 것처럼 보인다.
영어	The person asking for our support or assistance, _____, for a much smaller one.
조건	① to 부정사의 완료 시제와 동명사를 활용할 것 ② [concession / appear / initial / request]을 활용할 것 ③ 총 12단어로 쓸 것 (필요시 주어진 단어 변형 가능)
정답	
한글	더 큰 요청을 거부한 것은 부모가 그 뒤의 더 작은 요청을 묵인할 가능성을 높인다.
영어	_____ in the later, smaller request.
조건	① 동명사와 동격의 that을 활용할 것 ② [increase / deny / acquiesce / likelihood / request]을 활용할 것 ③ 총 12단어로 쓸 것 (필요시 주어진 단어 변형 가능)
정답	

[①어법] 다음 글을 읽고, 어법상 틀린 부분의 개수를 찾고 틀린 부분을 바르게 고치시오.

"Capitalism" is generally understood as a market-based, economic system governing by capital — that is, the wealth of an individual or an establishment accumulated by or employed in its business activities. Entrepreneurs and the institutions they create generate the capital which businesses provide goods, services, and payments to workers. Defenders of capitalism argue that this system maximally distributes social freedoms and desirable resources, resulting in the best economic outcomes for everyone in society. On this view, business's only social responsibilities are to maximize legally generated profits. However, over the past several decades there has been a significant reaction against this view. It is argued that businesses have responsibilities far beyond following the law and profit making. When society accepts capitalism, this view holds, it need not also accepted the view that economic freedom always has priority over competing conceptions of the collection and distribution of social goods, or of other responsibilities owed to employees, customers, society, and the environment.

① 1개　　② 2개　　③ 3개　　④ 4개　　⑤ 5개

ⓐ : _____ → _____　　　　ⓑ : _____ → _____

ⓒ : _____ → _____　　　　ⓓ : _____ → _____

ⓔ : _____ → _____

[②요약 서술형] 글의 요약문을 본문의 단어를 활용하여 서술하시오. (어형 변화 가능)

한글	자본주의의 옹호자들은 자본주의가 모든 사람들에게 최고의 경제적 결과를 가져다 준다고 주장하지만, 이러한 관점은 사업의 사회적 책임을 강조하는 주장에 의해 도전을 받아왔다.
조건	1. defenders / outcomes / challenge / capitalism / emphasize / an argument / responsibilities를 활용할 것 (필요 시 변형 가능) 2. 접속사 that과 현재완료 수동태, 주격 관계대명사를 활용할 것 3. 총 30단어 이내로 작성할 것
정답	

[③주제 서술형] 글의 주제를 조건과 한글 의미와 일치하도록 쓰시오.

한글	자본주의를 둘러싼 상반된 관점들
조건	contrasting / surrounding 를 활용하고 필요한 단어를 추가하여 총 4단어로 작성할 것
정답	

[④제목 서술형] 글의 제목을 조건과 한글 의미와 일치하도록 쓰시오.

한글	자본주의와 기업의 사회적 책임
단어	Responsibilities 를 활용하고 필요한 단어를 추가하여 총 6단어로 작성할 것
정답	

[⑤주요문장 서술형] 빈칸에 알맞은 말을 <조건>에 맞게 영작하시오. [Tip! 주요 문장 3가지는 시험 직전 꼭 암기하세요!]

한글	기업가와 그들이 만드는 기관은 기업이 상품, 서비스, 노동자의 임금을 제공하는 데 사용하는 자본을 창출한다.
영어	Entrepreneurs and _____ goods, services, and payments to workers.
조건	① 목적격 관계대명사의 생략 구조와 전치사+관계대명사 구조를 활용할 것 ② [generate / business / provide / capital]을 활용할 것 ③ 총 11단어로 쓸 것 (필요시 주어진 단어 변형 가능)
정답	
한글	자본주의 옹호자들은 이 체제가 사회적 자유와 가치 있는 자원을 최대한 배분하여 사회의 모든 사람에게 최상의 경제적 결과를 낸다고 주장한다.
영어	Defenders of capitalism argue that this system maximally distributes social freedoms and desirable resources, _____.
조건	① 분사구문을 활용할 것 ② [outcome / result / economic]을 활용할 것 ③ 총 10단어로 쓸 것 (필요시 주어진 단어 변형 가능)
정답	
한글	기업은 법을 따르고 이윤을 창출하는 것을 훨씬 넘어서는 그 이상의 책임이 있다는 주장이 제기된다.
영어	_____ and profit making.
조건	① 가주어/진주어 구문과 접속사 that, 동명사를 활용할 것 ② [responsibility / follow / argue / business]을 활용할 것 ③ 총 12단어로 쓸 것 (필요시 주어진 단어 변형 가능)
정답	

[①어법] 다음 글을 읽고, 어법상 틀린 부분의 개수를 찾고 틀린 부분을 바르게 고치시오.

The relationship between crisis and social change is a bit like the relationship between a rainstorm and a mudslide. The rain doesn't give the mudslide its power — that comes from the weight of earth, building up over decades. What the rain can do are loosen things up, creating the conditions for change. Britain's post-Second World War settlement didn't solve the problems of the war: it addressed the pent-up problems of the 1930s, and its intellectual ingredients dated back further, to the opening years of the 1900s. Likewise, America's New Deal of the 1930s was triggered by the Great Depression, but the issues they addressed and the approaches it applied emerged decades before, in the progressive and populist movements of the 1890s and 1900s. So, if the 2020 pandemic does lead to a radical social renewal, then the main elements of that renewal will be visible already today.

① 1개　　② 2개　　③ 3개　　④ 4개　　⑤ 5개

ⓐ : _____ → _____　　ⓑ : _____ → _____

ⓒ : _____ → _____　　ⓓ : _____ → _____

ⓔ : _____ → _____

[②요약 서술형] 글의 요약문을 본문의 단어를 활용하여 서술하시오. (어형 변화 가능)

한글	위기 자체가 사회 변화에 어떤 힘을 주는 것은 아니지만, 그것은 일련의 변화가 일어날 수 있는 조건의 윤곽을 그린다.
조건	1. crisis / occur / a series of / outline / renewals를 활용할 것 (필요 시 변형 가능) 2. 재귀대명사와 의미상 주어 for, to 부정사를 활용할 것 3. 총 23단어 이내로 작성할 것
정답	

[③주제 서술형] 글의 주제를 조건과 한글 의미와 일치하도록 쓰시오.

한글	위기가 사회 변화에 미치는 영향
조건	influence / social 를 활용하고 필요한 단어를 추가하여 총 **7단어**로 작성할 것
정답	

[④제목 서술형] 글의 제목을 조건과 한글 의미와 일치하도록 쓰시오.

한글	위기가 사회 변화에 실제로 미치는 영향에 대한 통찰
단어	Insight / Does 를 활용하고 필요한 단어를 추가하여 총 **12단어**로 작성할 것
정답	

[⑤주요문장 서술형] 빈칸에 알맞은 말을 <조건>에 맞게 영작하시오. [Tip! 주요 문장 3가지는 시험 직전 꼭 암기하세요!]

한글	비가 '할 수' 있는 것은 상태를 느슨하게 만들어, 변화를 위한 여건을 만드는 것이다.
영어	_____, creating the conditions for change.
조건	① 관계대명사 what을 활용할 것 ② [things / loosen / rain]을 활용할 것 ③ 총 9단어로 쓸 것 (필요시 주어진 단어 변형 가능)
정답	
한글	마찬가지로, 1930년대의 미국의 뉴딜 정책은 대공황에 의해 촉발되었지만, 그것이 다룬 문제와 그것이 사용한 접근 방식은 수십 년 전, 1890년대와 1900년대의 진보 운동과 인민주의 운동에서 나타났다.
영어	Likewise, America's New Deal of the 1930s was triggered by the Great Depression, but _____, in the progressive and populist movements of the 1890s and 1900s.
조건	① 목적격 관계대명사의 생략 구조를 활용할 것 ② [approach / issue / address / emerge / apply]을 활용할 것 ③ 총 12단어로 쓸 것 (필요시 주어진 단어 변형 가능)
정답	
한글	따라서 만약 2020년의 전 세계적인 유행병이 진정 급격한 사회 개선을 가져온다면, 그러면 그 개선의 주요 요소들은 오늘날 이미 눈에 보일 것이다.
영어	So, _____, then the main elements of that renewal will be visible already today.
조건	① do 강조를 활용할 것 ② [radical / pandemic / renewal]을 활용할 것 ③ 총 11단어로 쓸 것 (필요시 주어진 단어 변형 가능)
정답	

[①어법] 다음 글을 읽고, 어법상 틀린 부분의 개수를 찾고 틀린 부분을 바르게 고치시오.

The characteristics of an agricultural society affected its long-run growth pattern prior to the Industrial Revolution, while self-sufficiency and land dependency limited the motivation to increase the yield. In spite of some attempts were made to reform agricultural production, the low level of technologies available could not capitalize on the effect of those attempts. Moreover, inelasticity in demand, instability in supply, and price divergence prevented the capital accumulation needing for reinvestment in agricultural technologies. All of these factors created a vicious circle such that agricultural production could not boom. As a result, the agricultural society showed a long-term decelerating growth pattern in history.

① 1개　　② 2개　　③ 3개　　④ 4개　　⑤ 5개

ⓐ : _____ → _____ ⓑ : _____ → _____

ⓒ : _____ → _____ ⓓ : _____ → _____

ⓔ : _____ → _____

[②요약 서술형] 글의 요약문을 본문의 단어를 활용하여 서술하시오. (어형 변화 가능)

한글	비탄력적인 수요, 불안정한 공급, 가격 차이와 같은 몇 가지 요인들이 농업 사회의 장기적인 성장 패턴이 둔화되도록 만들었다.
조건	1. inelastic / divergent / growth / decelerate를 활용할 것 (필요 시 변형 가능) 2. 5형식 문장 구조와 do 강조구문을 활용할 것 3. 총 21단어 이내로 작성할 것
정답	

[③주제 서술형] 글의 주제를 조건과 한글 의미와 일치하도록 쓰시오.

한글	장기적인 성장을 방해하는 농업 사회의 특성
조건	agricultural / prevent / growth 를 활용하고 필요한 단어를 추가하여 총 8단어로 작성할 것
정답	

[④제목 서술형] 글의 제목을 조건과 한글 의미와 일치하도록 쓰시오.

한글	농업사회의 감속성장 패턴에 관한 분석
단어	Analysis / Decelerated / Agricultural 를 활용하고 필요한 단어를 추가하여 총 9단어로 작성할 것
정답	

[⑤주요문장 서술형] 빈칸에 알맞은 말을 <조건>에 맞게 영작하시오. [Tip! 주요 문장 3가지는 시험 직전 꼭 암기하세요!]

한글	비록 농업 생산을 개혁하려는 몇차례의 시도가 있었지만, 가용할 수 있는 기술 수준이 낮아 그러한 시도의 효과를 이용할 수 없었다.
영어	Even though _____, the low level of technologies available could not capitalize on the effect of those attempts.
조건	① 5형식 수동태를 활용할 것 ② [reform / agricultural / attempt / production]을 활용할 것 ③ 총 8단어로 쓸 것 (필요시 주어진 단어 변형 가능)
정답	
한글	게다가, 수요의 비탄력성, 공급의 불안정성, 그리고 가격 격차는 농업 기술 재투자에 필요한 자본의 축적을 방해했다.
영어	Moreover, inelasticity in demand, instability in supply, and price divergence _____.
조건	① 과거분사를 활용할 것 ② [accumulation / prevent / agricultural / investment / technology]을 활용할 것 ③ 총 10단어로 쓸 것 (필요시 주어진 단어 변형 가능)
정답	
한글	이 모든 요인들이 악순환을 만들어 농업 생산은 크게 증가할 수 없었다.
영어	All of these factors created _____.
조건	① such that 구문을 활용할 것 ② [agricultural / boom / production / vicious]을 활용할 것 ③ 총 10단어로 쓸 것 (필요시 주어진 단어 변형 가능)
정답	

[①어법] 다음 글을 읽고, 어법상 틀린 부분의 개수를 찾고 틀린 부분을 바르게 고치시오.

It is evident that self-esteem has a significant effect on health — both directly and indirectly. For instance, self-esteem is typically considered a key feature of mental health and therefore worth pursue in its own right. It may also have an indirect influence through its contribution to intentions to undertake healthy or unhealthy actions. For instance, at a commonsense level, individuals who respect and value themselves will, other things are equal, seek to look after themselves by adopting courses of action that prevent disease. Less obviously perhaps, there is strong evidence that people enjoying high self-esteem are less willing to tolerate dissonance and more likely to take rational action to reduce that dissonance, by, for example, rejects unhealthy behaviour. Those having low self-esteem are more likely to conform to interpersonal pressures than those enjoying high self-esteem with unfortunate consequences when such social pressure results in 'unhealthy behaviour'. In terms of empowerment, though, any unthinking yielding to social pressure would be considered unhealthy!

① 1개　　② 2개　　③ 3개　　④ 4개　　⑤ 5개

ⓐ : ＿＿＿＿＿＿ → ＿＿＿＿＿＿　　　ⓑ : ＿＿＿＿＿＿ → ＿＿＿＿＿＿

ⓒ : ＿＿＿＿＿＿ → ＿＿＿＿＿＿　　　ⓓ : ＿＿＿＿＿＿ → ＿＿＿＿＿＿

ⓔ : ＿＿＿＿＿＿ → ＿＿＿＿＿＿

[②요약 서술형] 글의 요약문을 본문의 단어를 활용하여 서술하시오. (어형 변화 가능)

한글	자존감은 직간접적으로 건강에 긍정적인 영향을 미칠 수 있는데, 이는 자존감이 높은 사람들이 부조화를 줄이기 위해 이성적인 행동을 취할 것이기 때문이다.
조건	1. reduce / direct / positive / affect / self-esteem / rational / dissonance를 활용할 것 (필요 시 변형 가능) 2. 병렬 구조와 접속사, to 부정사를 활용할 것 3. 총 21단어 이내로 작성할 것
정답	

[③주제 서술형] 글의 주제를 조건과 한글 의미와 일치하도록 쓰시오.

한글	건강에 대한 자존감의 영향
조건	influence / self-esteem 를 활용하고 필요한 단어를 추가하여 총 6단어로 작성할 것
정답	

[④제목 서술형] 글의 제목을 조건과 한글 의미와 일치하도록 쓰시오.

한글	자존감이 건강에 미치는 직간접적 영향
단어	Effects / Health 를 활용하고 필요한 단어를 추가하여 총 8단어로 작성할 것
정답	

[⑤주요문장 서술형] 빈칸에 알맞은 말을 〈조건〉에 맞게 영작하시오. [Tip! 주요 문장 3가지는 시험 직전 꼭 암기하세요!]

한글	그것은 또한 건강에 좋거나 건강에 좋지 않은 행동을 시도하려는 의도에 원인을 제공함으로써 간접적인 영향을 미칠 수도 있다.
영어	＿＿＿＿＿＿＿＿＿＿＿＿＿＿＿＿＿＿＿ — both directly and indirectly.
조건	① 가주어/진주어 구문을 활용할 것 ② [self-esteem / evident / significant / health]을 활용할 것 ③ 총 11단어로 쓸 것 (필요시 주어진 단어 변형 가능)
정답	
한글	아마 덜 분명하기는 하겠지만, 높은 자존감을 누리는 사람은 부조화를 덜 용인하려 하고 그러한 부조화를 줄이기 위해, 예컨대 건강에 좋지 않은 행동을 거부함으로써, 이성적인 행동을 할 가능성이 더 크다는 강력한 증거가 있다.
영어	Less obviously perhaps, there is ＿＿＿＿＿＿＿＿＿＿＿＿＿＿＿ and more likely to take rational action to reduce that dissonance, by, for example, rejecting unhealthy behaviour.
조건	① 동격의 that과 be willing to V 구문, 현재분사를 활용할 것 ② [dissonance / evidence / self-esteem / tolerate]을 활용할 것 ③ 총 13단어로 쓸 것 (필요시 주어진 단어 변형 가능)
정답	
한글	자존감이 낮은 사람들은 높은 자존감을 누리는 사람들보다 대인 관계에서 오는 압박에 반대하여 (→ 순응하여) 그러한 사회적 압박이 '건강에 좋지 않은 행동'으로 귀결될 때의 불행한 결과를 맞이할 가능성이 더 크다.
영어	Those having low self-esteem ＿＿＿＿＿＿＿＿＿＿＿＿＿＿＿ with unfortunate consequences when such social pressure results in unhealthy behaviour'.
조건	① be likely to V 구문과 비교급, 현재분사를 활용할 것 ② [conform / enjoy / interpersonal / pressure]을 활용할 것 ③ 총 13단어로 쓸 것 (필요시 주어진 단어 변형 가능)
정답	

[①어법] 다음 글을 읽고, 어법상 틀린 부분의 개수를 찾고 틀린 부분을 바르게 고치시오.

In recent years, researchers have been trying to understand the changes that occur in the brain during adolescence. Structural brain imaging studies over the past decade have challenged the belief that structural brain development ends in early childhood, reveals that changes occur through early adulthood. In addition, these studies provide an insight into the biological basis for understanding adolescent thinking and behavior. For example, the ventromedial prefrontal cortex of the brain is responsible for evaluating risk and reward to help guided the person to make a decision. Imaging studies have shown that this part of the brain is the last to mature in adolescents, which supports behavioral studies that show adolescents take greater risks than adults in activities such as substance abuse. Adolescents tend to engage in more reckless behaviors because the area of the brain that assesses risk and benefits has not completely developed yet. These findings, along with other studies examining the maturation of other regions of the prefrontal cortex during adolescence, suggest that the spontaneity, short-sightedness, and risk-taking behaviors associated with adolescence could be partially biological in nature.

① 1개　　② 2개　　③ 3개　　④ 4개　　⑤ 5개

ⓐ : ＿＿＿＿＿＿＿ → ＿＿＿＿＿＿＿　　　　ⓑ : ＿＿＿＿＿＿＿ → ＿＿＿＿＿＿＿

ⓒ : ＿＿＿＿＿＿＿ → ＿＿＿＿＿＿＿　　　　ⓓ : ＿＿＿＿＿＿＿ → ＿＿＿＿＿＿＿

ⓔ : ＿＿＿＿＿＿＿ → ＿＿＿＿＿＿＿

[②요약 서술형] 글의 요약문을 본문의 단어를 활용하여 서술하시오. (어형 변화 가능)

한글	청소년기의 자발성과 근시안적 사고는 위험을 평가하는 뇌의 한 부분이 여전히 개발되고 있기 때문에 생물학적인 이유에 부분적으로 기인할 수 있다.
조건	1. develop / partially / responsible / biological / evaluate / attribute를 활용할 것 (필요 시 변형 가능) 2. 조동사 수동태와 주격 관계대명사, 현재진행 수동태을 활용할 것 3. 총 23단어 이내로 작성할 것 (빈칸 부분만)
정답	The spontaneity and short-sightedness of adolescence ＿＿＿＿＿＿＿＿＿＿＿＿＿＿＿＿＿＿＿＿＿＿＿＿＿＿＿＿＿＿＿＿＿＿＿＿＿.

[③주제 서술형] 글의 주제를 조건과 한글 의미와 일치하도록 쓰시오.

한글	뇌의 발달 구조에 대한 분석
조건	developmental / brain 를 활용하고 필요한 단어를 추가하여 총 9단어로 작성할 것
정답	

[④제목 서술형] 글의 제목을 조건과 한글 의미와 일치하도록 쓰시오.

한글	청소년들이 위험을 감수하는 이유에 대한 생물학적 접근
단어	Biological / Adolescents / Risk-Takers 를 활용하고 필요한 단어를 추가하여 총 7단어로 작성할 것
정답	

[⑤주요문장 서술형] 빈칸에 알맞은 말을 〈조건〉에 맞게 영작하시오. [Tip! 주요 문장 3가지는 시험 직전 꼭 암기하세요!]

한글	지난 십 년에 걸친 뇌 구조 영상 연구는 뇌 구조 발달이 유아기에 끝난다는 믿음에 이의를 제기하며 변화는 성인기 초기 내내 일어난다는 것을 밝혔다.
영어	Structural brain imaging studies over the past decade have challenged the belief that structural brain development ends in early childhood, ＿＿＿＿＿＿＿＿＿＿＿＿＿＿＿＿＿＿＿＿＿＿＿＿＿＿＿＿＿＿.
조건	① 분사구문과 접속사 that을 활용할 것 ② [adulthood / occur / reveal]을 활용할 것 ③ 총 7단어로 쓸 것 (필요시 주어진 단어 변형 가능)
정답	
한글	예를 들면, 뇌의 복내측 시상하핵 전전두엽 피질은 사람이 결정을 내리도록 이끄는 데 도움이 되도록 위험과 보상을 평가하는 것을 담당한다.
영어	For example, the ventromedial prefrontal cortex of the brain is ＿＿＿＿＿＿＿＿＿＿＿＿＿＿＿＿＿＿＿＿＿＿＿＿＿＿＿.
조건	① to 부정사의 부사적 용법과 동명사, 5형식 문장 구조를 활용할 것 ② [reward / decision / evaluate / responsible / guide]을 활용할 것 ③ 총 15단어로 쓸 것 (필요시 주어진 단어 변형 가능)
정답	
한글	영상 연구는 뇌의 이 부분이 청소년에게 있어서 가장 마지막으로 발달한다는 것을 보여 주었는데, 이것은 성인보다 청소년이 약물 남용과 같은 행동에서 더 큰 위험을 감수한다는 것을 보여 주는 행동 연구들을 뒷받침한다.
영어	Imaging studies have shown that this part of the brain is the last to mature in adolescents, ＿＿＿＿＿＿＿＿＿＿＿＿＿＿＿＿＿＿＿ in activities such as substance abuse.
조건	① 주격 관계대명사를 활용할 것 ② [adolescent / support / behavioral / risk]을 활용할 것 ③ 총 12단어로 쓸 것 (필요시 주어진 단어 변형 가능)
정답	

[①어법] 다음 글을 읽고, 어법상 틀린 부분의 개수를 찾고 틀린 부분을 바르게 고치시오.

Both prescription and over-the-counter drugs are subject to strict control by the FDA, includes the regulation of manufacturing processes, specific requirements for the demonstration of safety and efficacy, as well as well-defined limits on advertising and labeling claims. Such controls provide assurances to consumers and health care professionals about the quality of the products and contribute to their acceptance as "legitimate" treatments. The exemption of dietary supplements from these specific regulatory controls may impact their consideration as "legitimate". If health care professionals feel that the quality of dietary supplement products being lacking, and if they consider dietary supplements outside the scope of "prevailing" medical or pharmacy practice, then physicians and pharmacists will have a low level of confidence in recommending these products to their patients for fear of legal action. Physicians and pharmacists cannot, however, separate themselves from the use of dietary supplements. With more than 29,000 dietary supplements on the market, consumers have broad access to and are using these products. In fact, a survey of consumers has suggested which approximately 42% of American consumers were using complementary and alternative therapies, with 24% of consumers using plant-based dietary supplements on a regular basis.

① 1개   ② 2개   ③ 3개   ④ 4개   ⑤ 5개

ⓐ : _____ → _____   ⓑ : _____ → _____

ⓒ : _____ → _____   ⓓ : _____ → _____

ⓔ : _____ → _____

[②요약 서술형] 글의 요약문을 본문의 단어를 활용하여 서술하시오. (어형 변화 가능)

한글	건강보조식품과 소비자가 많은데도 이를 적법한 것으로 만드는 규제가 충분하지 않다.
조건	1. legitimate / regulatory controls / there / despite / dietary supplements를 활용할 것 (필요 시 변형 가능) 2. 동격의 that과 주격 관계대명사를 활용할 것 3. 총 21단어 이내로 작성할 것
정답	

[③주제 서술형] 글의 주제를 조건과 한글 의미와 일치하도록 쓰시오.

한글	규제를 벗어난 건강 보조 식품
조건	dietary / regulatory 를 활용하고 필요한 단어를 추가하여 총 **6단어**로 작성할 것
정답	

[④제목 서술형] 글의 제목을 조건과 한글 의미와 일치하도록 쓰시오.

한글	건강보조식품에 대한 확고한 규제 부재의 문제화
단어	Absence / Regulation 를 활용하고 필요한 단어를 추가하여 총 **9단어**로 작성할 것
정답	

[⑤주요문장 서술형] 빈칸에 알맞은 말을 〈조건〉에 맞게 영작하시오. [Tip! 주요 문장 3가지는 시험 직전 꼭 암기하세요!]

한글	처방이 필요한 약과 처방전 없이 살 수 있는 약 모두 FDA의 엄격한 통제를 받는데, 광고와 라벨의 설명 문구에 대한 명확한 제한과 아울러, 제조 과정의 규제, 안전과 효능의 입증에 대한 특정 요건이 포함된다.
영어	Both prescription and over-the-counter drugs _____ of manufacturing processes, specific requirements for the demonstration of safety and efficacy, as well as well-defined limits on advertising and labeling claims.
조건	① be subject to V 구문과 분사 구문을 활용할 것 ② [include / regulation / strict / control]을 활용할 것 ③ 총 11단어로 쓸 것 (필요시 주어진 단어 변형 가능)
정답	

한글	그러나 의사와 약사는 건강 보조 식품의 사용에서 자신을 떼어 놓고 생각할 수 없다.
영어	Physicians and pharmacists cannot, however, _____.
조건	① 재귀대명사를 활용할 것 ② [supplement / separate / use / dietary]을 활용할 것 ③ 총 8단어로 쓸 것 (필요시 주어진 단어 변형 가능)
정답	

한글	사실, 소비자 설문 조사는 미국 소비자의 대략 42퍼센트가 보완 요법과 대체 요법을 이용하고 있고, 소비자의 24퍼센트는 정기적으로 식물성 건강 보조 식품을 이용하고 있다는 것을 보여주었다.
영어	In fact, a survey of consumers has suggested that approximately 42% of American consumers were using complementary and alternative therapies, _____
조건	① with 분사구문을 활용할 것 ② [dietary / supplements / regular / consumer]을 활용할 것 ③ 총 12단어로 쓸 것 (필요시 주어진 단어 변형 가능)
정답	

Teacher's day

Now Playing

수능 날 1시 10분,
그 1시간 10분을 너의 시간으로

01:10   11:16

구매인증 남기고
1등급 비밀자료
GET!

— SCAN ME! —

정답 및 해설

EBS 수능특강 영어 주제 소재편 20~31강

2024학년도 수능·내신대비교재

EBS 수능특강 영어 「1시 10분」

스승의날
Teachers Day Publisher

Part I 손필기 분석지 & Ⓢhorts

20강 1번

Ⓢhorts Ⓕlow

1) -

Ⓢhorts Ⓞverview

2) -

3) -

Ⓢhorts Ⓓetails

1. F / Lionni가 네덜란드에서 태어나 1939년 미국에 올 때까지 이탈리아에서 살았다고 했으므로, 1939년이 되어서야 네덜란드가 아닌 다른 나라에 처음으로 살았다는 표현은 틀림. not until 구문 활용, other than (-외에) 구문 정리할 것.

2. T / Lionni가 기차를 타고 가면서 잡지에서 종잇조각을 뜯어내어 그것을 캐릭터로 사용하여 이야기를 구성했다고 했으며, 바로 앞 문장에서 우연히 아동 도서를 쓰고 삽화를 그리게 되었다고 했으므로 즉흥적으로 했다는 표현은 맞음.

3. T / Lionni가 콜라주를 사용한 최초의 아동 도서 작가이자 삽화가가 되었다고 했으므로. <name A B> 5형식 수동태 구문 정리할 것.

4. F / Lionni는 파킨슨병을 진단받았지만, 그는 그리기와 가르치는 일을 계속했다고 했으므로. keep A from -ing ⇔ keep -ing 정리할 것.

Ⓢhorts Ⓖrammar

was / taught / them / what / working

20강 2번

Ⓢhorts Ⓕlow

1) A-B-C

Ⓢhorts Ⓞverview

2) the story of Jefferson and Italian rice

3) Jefferson's Efforts for Italian Rice

Ⓢhorts Ⓓetails

1. T / Jefferson이 면화에 대한 의존에서 해방되는 남부를 보고 싶은 욕망에 대체할 수 있는 농작물을 찾고 있다고 했으므로, 한 작물에 의존하지 않고 독립하는 것을 원해서 대체 작물을 찾았다는 표현은 맞음. 분사구문(desiring~)과 resort to=depend on=rely on 정리할 것.

2. F / Jefferson이 이탈리아 쌀이 캐롤라이나의 미국산 수입품보다 더 선호된다는 것을 발견했다고 했으므로, 어떠한 쌀도 캐롤라이나의 수입품보다 선호되지 않았다는 표현은 틀림. 비교급에서 사용되는 지시대명사 that의 용법을 정리할 것.

3. F / Lombardy의 우수한 품종의 농작물을 이탈리아 이외의 지역에서 재배하기 위해 수출하는 것은 범죄라는 것을 알았음에도 불구하고 멋대로 가져갔다고 했으므로, 불법적으로 수출하지 않는 방법을 찾았다는 표현은 틀림. not 과 il- 부정어구가 두 곳이 사용 되어서 긍정의 의미로 해석되는 것에 주의. 분사구문, 가주어 진주어 구문 정리할 것.

Ⓢhorts Ⓖrammar

were / Driven / it / whose / stuffed

20강 3번

Ⓢhorts Ⓕlow

1) A-C-B

Ⓢhorts Ⓞverview

2) developing a method of applying carbolic acid for surgeries

3) Joseph Lister's Insight Into Using Carbolic Acid for Antisepsis

Ⓢhorts Ⓓetails

1. F / 마취법이 도입되었고 수술은 증가추세라고 했으므로, 수술 건수는 거의 증가하지 않았다는 표현은 틀림. hardly=rarely=scarcely=seldom 부정어구 정리할 것.

2. F / Lister는 석탄산이라고 불리는 화학 물질로 하수를 처리한 것이 질병 발생률을 감소시켰다고 했으므로, 석탄산이라고 불리는 질병을 한 화학물질이 감소시켰다는 표현은 틀림.

3. T / 소독을 수술의 기본 원칙으로 확립 하였고 이 덕분에 절단 수술의 횟수가 줄었다고 했으므로.

Ⓢhorts Ⓖrammar

due to / what / required / prevent / sharply / are being

21강 1번

Ⓢhorts Ⓕlow

1) B-A-C

Ⓢhorts Ⓞverview

2) relative position of history and geography in education for developing national identity

3) Exploring Regional Differences of Emphasis on History and Geography for Building Nationalistic Sentiment

Ⓢhorts Ⓓetails

1. T / 교육 제도에서 이 두 과목의 상대적 위치는 국가 정체성의 개념을 형성하는데 더 유용해 보이는 정도에 따라 달라진다고 했으므로, 항상 동일하게 중요하게 여겨지진 않았다는 표현은 맞음.

2. T / 독일에서는 독일어권 영토와 관련된 지리적 양상이 중요했기에 지리학이 매우 중요하게 여겨졌고, 노르웨이는 분쟁 중인 국경이 없고 바이킹 시대의 영광스러운 역사에 대한 교육에 의해 국가적 자각이 촉진되어 역사학이 우위를 차지한다고 했으므로. former(전자), latter(후자), 부정대명사 one 정리할 것.

3. T / 핀란드는 노르웨이와 마찬가지로 왕위 통합을 경험했지만, 영광스러운 과거를 가지지 못했기 때문에 지리학이 상대적으로 중요한 과목으로 발전했다고 했으므로.

Ⓢhorts Ⓖrammar

While / to which / useful / fostered / had

21강 2번

Ⓢhorts Ⓕlow

1) C-B-A

Ⓢhorts Ⓞverview

2) theological truth and neutrality of moral knowledge
3) Should We Be Religious To Find Moral Truths?

Ⓢhorts Ⓓetails

1. F / 윤리가 종교에 대해 일종의 증거적 의존성을 가지고 있느냐가 윤리 이론에서 한 가지 문제라고 했고, 거짓말이 잘못된 것이라는 것은 종교적 진리를 알아야 할 필요가 있는 것은 아니라고 주장하므로, 종교가 도덕적 판단의 기초라는 생각에 동의한다는 표현은 틀림. 동격의 that 정리할 것.

2. F / 도덕적 지식은 종교와 관계없이 가능하다는 이 견해는 종교적으로 헌신적인 신학자들이 흔히 품어왔던 것이라고 했으므로, 어떠한 신학자들도 그것을 주장한 적이 없다는 표현은 틀림.

Ⓢhorts Ⓖrammar

is / whether / requires / even if / independently / held

21강 3번

Ⓢhorts Ⓕlow

1) C-B-A

Ⓢhorts Ⓞverview

2) individual and contextual factors for the development of moral identity
3) Categorization of Influential Factors for the Development of Moral Identity

Ⓢhorts Ⓓetails

1. F / 개인적이고 상황적인 차원에서의 요인들이 도덕적 정체성 발달에 영향을 미친다고 했으므로, 개인적 차원이 아닌 상황적 차원에서의 요인들만이 영향을 미친다는 표현은 틀림. not A but B 구문을 it~that 강조 구문으로 사용하였고, 최근에 강조 구문에서 but 이하 부분을 뒤로 빼는 경우가 많으므로 형태를 익힐 것.

2. T / 인지 및 정체성 발달에서 더 뛰어난 사람들은 도덕적 정체성 발달에 대한 능력이 더 뛰어나다고 했으므로. the 비교급, the 비교급 구문 정리할 것.

3. T / 도덕적 가치관에 대한 더 많은 이해는 그것이 정체성으로 통합되는 것을 촉진할 수 있다고 했으므로, 더 잘 통합된다고 한 표현은 맞음. 5형식 문장, 가목적어, 의미상 주어, 진목적어 구문 정리할 것.

4. F / 개인이 속한 단체에 참여하는 것은 도덕적 신념 체계뿐만 아니라 그러한 신념에 따라 행동할 기회도 제공할 수 있다고 했으므로, 신념 체계가 아닌 행동할 기회만을 제공한다는 표현을 틀림. 전치사 + 관계대명사 구문 정리할 것.

Ⓢhorts Ⓖrammar

been identified / including / which

22강 1번

Ⓢhorts Ⓕlow

1) A-C-B

Ⓢhorts Ⓞverview

2) the importance of paper recycling for the increasing demand
3) Emergency: We May Run Out Of Paper

Ⓢhorts Ⓓetails

1. T / 현재 70억 명의 인구가 1년에 약 4억 톤 이상의 종이를 사용한다고 했고, 90억 명이 되는 2045년에는 종이 생산량이 30퍼센트 늘어난다고 했으므로, 약 5억2천 톤 정도의 종이를 사용한다는 표현은 맞음. 가주어 진주어 구문 정리할 것.

2. T / 현재 우리의 인구 내에서 모든 사람이 신문을 구할 수 있거나 읽을 책을 가지고 있는 것은 아니고 그들의 비율이 늘어남에 따라 종이에 대한 수요 역시 늘어난다고 했으므로, 더 많은 사람들이 책을 사고 소유할수록 종이에 대한 수요도 또한 증가한다는 표현은 맞음. the 비교급, the 비교급 구문 정리할 것.

3. T / 2억 톤의 폐지는 대략 1억 6천만 톤의 재생지를 만들어 낸다고 했으므로, 4억 톤의 재생지를 만들기 위해서는 5억 톤의 폐지가 필요하다고 말할 수 있음.

Ⓢhorts Ⓖrammar

if / is / limited / that / its / use

22강 2번

Ⓢhorts Ⓕlow

1) B-A-C

Ⓢhorts Ⓞverview

2) efforts to secure rare metals by companies and governments
3) Problematizing and Securing Supply Lines for Rare Metals

Ⓢhorts Ⓓetails

1. F / 제품의 부품을 구성하는 재료가 더 다양해짐에 따라 정교한 하드웨어에 의존하는 사람들은 더 이상 아무것도 모르는 상태로 있을 여유가 없다고 했으므로, 알 필요가 없다는 표현은 틀림.

2. T / 기업과 정부 지도자들은 희금속이 얼마나 중요한지 깨닫고 있으며 실제로 희금속을 확보하기 위한 노력이 주기율표를 둘러싼 전쟁을 촉발시켰다고 했으므로. given의 의미, 가주어 진주어 구문 정리할 것.

3. F / 비주류 금속을 위한 경쟁은 곧 닥쳐올 듯한 것이 아니라 이미 여기 있다고 했으므로, 먼 미래에 겪을 문제라고 한 표현은 틀림.

Ⓢhorts Ⓖrammar

because / determining / it needed / have become / important / sparked / did

22강 3번

Ⓢhorts Ⓕlow

1) C-B-A

Ⓢhorts Ⓞverview

2) uneven effect of climate change and environmental justice

3) Climate Justice: an Ethical and Political Approach to Global Warming

Ⓢhorts Ⓓetails

1. T / 기후 변화의 영향은 세계의 가난한 사람들을 가장 크게 덮칠 것이라고 했으므로, 그 해로운 영향이 부자들과 가난한 사람들 모두에게 같은 크기는 아니므로.

2. T / 가난한 나라들은 최신 기술에 의존하는 조치를 시행할 수 없을 것이라고 했으므로, 그 나라가 얼마나 부유한지에 따라 달라질 수 있다는 표현은 맞음. it that 강조 구문 정리할 것.

3. F / 기후 정의라는 개념은 지구 온난화를 순전히 환경적이라기보다는 정치적인 문제로 만들기 위해 사용되는 용어라고 했으므로, 정치적으로 중립적이라는 표현은 틀림. 5형식 문장 구조 정리할 것.

Ⓢhorts Ⓖrammar

heavily / due to / raises / purely

23강 1번

Ⓢhorts Ⓕlow

1) A-B-C

Ⓢhorts Ⓞverview

2) organic chemistry and the mediocrity of carbonic compounds

3) Concept and Explanation of Organic Chemistry

Ⓢhorts Ⓓetails

1. T / 하나의 원소가 한 분야 전체를 차지할 수 있다는 사실은 탄소의 풍부한 범용성에 대한 증거라고 했으므로, 유기 화학이 탄소 화합물과 관련된 분야라는 사실이 탄소가 얼마나 널리 사용되는지를 보여준다는 것은 맞음.

2. T / 탄소는 놀라울 정도의 복잡성을 가진 사슬을 형성할 수 있고 이러한 복잡성이 유기체가 살아있는 것으로 여기게 만드는 것이고, 그렇기에 탄소 화합물이 생명체(유기체)의 하부 구조라고 했으므로. 만약 탄소가 복잡성을 갖지 못하면 (유기체가 살아 있는 것으로 여겨지지 못하므로) 생명체의 하부 구조라고 볼 수 없다는 표현은 맞음.

3. F / 탄소 화합물은 매우 광범위해서 화학의 한 분야 전체가 그것의 연구를 위해 발전해 왔다고 했으므로, 너무 광범위해서 화학의 한 분야 전체가 발전할 수 없었다는 표현은 틀림. too~to 구문 정리할 것.

Ⓢhorts Ⓖrammar

that / is / itself / what / be regarded / extensive / evolved

23강 2번

Ⓢhorts Ⓕlow

1) -

Ⓢhorts Ⓞverview

2) -

3) -

Ⓢhorts Ⓓetails

1. T / 붕사는 값이 매우 싸므로 공업용으로 많이 사용되고 가정에서도 여러 가지로 사용된다고 했으므로, 경제적인 이점 때문에 사용한다는 표현은 맞음.

2. F / 붕사 결정은 효능을 더하기 위해 다른 세정제와 혼합할 수 있다고 했으므로, 세정제의 기능을 약화시킨다는 표현은 틀림. lead to = result in = cause 정리할 것.

3. F / 베이킹 소다를 먼저 사용하고 더 강한 것이 필요한 상황에서 붕사를 사용하는 것은 맞지만, 본문에서 독성이 있는 화학물질에 의존하지 않는다고 했으므로, 붕산이 도움이 되는 것은 독성이 있는 화학물질 때문이라는 표현은 틀림. 관계 대명사의 계속적 용법, attribute A to B 구문 정리할 것.

Ⓢhorts Ⓖrammar

been mined / it / effective / is / where / to get / stored

23강 3번

Ⓢhorts Ⓕlow

1) C-A-B

Ⓢhorts Ⓞverview

2) fly-bys for explorations of giant planets and their moons

3) An Expedition to Other Planets Via Fly-Bys

Ⓢhorts Ⓓetails

1. F / 탐사는 플라이 바이로 시작되었고 목성의 경우 궤도 선회의 단계로 넘어갔다고 했으므로, 궤도 선회를 하고 나서야 플라이 바이를 시작할 수 있었다는 표현은 틀림. not ~ until 구문을 it ~ that 강조 구문으로 강조한 문장의 형태와 의미 정리할 것.

2. F / 위성이 행성을 둘러싸고 있는 강한 자기장에 어떤 영향을 미치는지 보고 위성 자체의 자기장을 가지는지 탐지할 만큼 가깝게 탐사선을 접근시킨다고 했으므로, 위성 자체의 자기장에 대한 정보를 얻을 수 없다는 표현은 틀림.

3. T / 우주 탐사선이 위성에 근접하여 지날 때의 궤적에 대한 편차의 크기로 위성의 질량을 알아낼 수 있다고 했으므로, 직접 착륙하지 않고도 질량을 알아낼 수 있다는 표현은 맞음.

Ⓢhorts Ⓖrammar

much / were / have / which / close enough / be determined

24강 1번

Ⓢhorts Ⓕlow

1) A-B-C

Ⓢhorts Ⓞverview

2) the concept of common pool resources and the tragedy of commons
3) How Resources of the Commons End Up Depleted

Ⓢhorts Ⓓetails

1. F / 공유 자원은 모든 사람이 사용할 수 있지만 아무도 소유하지 않는 자원을 말한다고 했으므로, 모든 사람이 소유하고 누구도 이용할 수 없다는 표현은 틀림.

2. F / 공유자원은 누구라도 이용 가능한 것에 덧붙여 보호하기는 어렵다고 했으므로, 자원들의 지속가능성을 극대화 시킨다는 표현은 틀림.

3. F / 사람들 자신들의 이익을 극대화 하고 싶어 하고 그러한 무지가 결국 자원의 고갈을 초래한다고 했으므로, 자원의 고갈이 이익을 극대화 하고자 하는 열망을 이끈다는 표현은 틀림. result from <-> result in = lead to 정리할 것.

Ⓢhorts Ⓖrammar

owned / being / are / which / grazing / is

24강 2번

Ⓢhorts Ⓕlow

1) C-B-A

Ⓢhorts Ⓞverview

2) commercialization of traditional heritage and its threat
3) Dynamics of Tourism: How Cultural Heritage and Tradition Can Be Changed

Ⓢhorts Ⓓetails

1. T / 외부인에게 지역 사회의 매력 중 일부가 문화적 유산이라면 유서 깊은 문화의 상징물이 넘칠지 모르나(양적인 측면), 진짜가 아닌 형태로만 그럴 뿐(질적인 측면)이라고 했으므로.

2. F / 이전 시대의 가짜 상징물이 어떤 것도 진짜처럼 보이지 않는 느낌의 원인이 된다고 했으므로, 그 느낌이 가짜 상징물이 넘쳐나는 결과를 낳는다는 표현은 틀림.

3. T / 위험은 주민들의 개인 정체성 상실과 자신들의 과거로부터 단절됐다는 느낌에 있다고 했으므로, 가짜 상징물이 만연하면 그런 느낌을 겪게 될 가능성이 커진다는 표현은 맞음.

Ⓢhorts Ⓖrammar

is / frequently / that / was / significant / primarily / who

24강 3번

Ⓢhorts Ⓕlow

1) C-A-B

Ⓢhorts Ⓞverview

2) cross-examination on functions of sports in different time settings
3) Comparing Physical Contests in Greek Culture and Sports of Today

Ⓢhorts Ⓓetails

1. T / 그리스의 대회와 경기는 오늘날의 체계화된 경쟁 스포츠와는 달랐다고 했으므로, 고대 그리스 대회가 오늘날의 대회보다 더 조직적이라고 말할 수 없다는 표현은 맞음.

2. T / 사회 전반의 사회적 관계의 지배적인 패턴을 재현했다고 했으므로, 고대 그리스 시대의 운동 경기의 특징들은 그 당시 사회 구조의 특징들과 모순이 없었다는 표현은 맞음.

3. T / 그리스 사회에서 남성이고 젊고 건강한 것과 병행하는 권력과 이점은, 심지어 경기력을 평가하기 위해 사용된 탁월함의 정의도 젊은 남성의 능력을 반영한 대회의 모습을 만들었다고 했으므로. 분사구문, 조동사 + have pp 구문, 가주어 진주어 구문 정리할 것.

Ⓢhorts Ⓖrammar

wealthy enough / that / it

25강 1번

Ⓢhorts Ⓕlow

1) B-A-C

Ⓢhorts Ⓞverview

2) the dichotomy of thinking in the field of music
3) Innate Talent or Disciplined Practice: Learning About the Black-and-White Thinking in Music

Ⓢhorts Ⓓetails

1. F / 음악의 분야에서는 영재성이 있다는 인식뿐만 아니라 능력은 훈련된 근면 정신에서 비롯되는 것이라는 생각으로 양분되어 있다고 했으므로, 재능이 가장 중요하다는 생각만 있다는 표현은 틀림. it ~ that 강조, 동격의 that 구문 정리할 것.

2. F / 재능이 중요하다는 주장에서, 재능은 주로 불변의 특성으로 간주되며 타고 나는 것으로 여긴다고 했으므로, 원하는 사람에게 모두 가능하다는 표현은 틀림.

3. T / 음악에서의 능력은 근면 정신에서 비롯된다는 주장에서 재능이 있다고 여겨지는 사람들은 그만큼 더 연습해야 한다고 했으므로. the 비교급, the 비교급 구문 정리할 것.

Ⓢhorts Ⓖrammar

that / assumed / popular / attempted / that / to practice / are

25강 2번

Ⓢhorts Ⓕlow

1) B-C-A

Ⓢhorts Ⓞverview

2) digitization and changing perception on photographs
3) The Evidential Power of Photographs Still Remains Strong

Ⓢhorts Ⓓetails

1. T / 디지털화가 사진 영역에 영향을 미치기 시작하면서 설득력을 잃은 것이 사실을 기록하는 본질이라고 했으므로, 그 이전에는 기록하는 본질을 지녔다는 것을 알 수 있으며, 사진을 처음에는 문서로 분류했다고 했으므로.

2. F / 디지털 불신의 아픔이 사진의 신뢰성에 배어든 것 같지만 사진의 임무와 용도 가운데 많은 것들은 거의 변한 적이 없다고 했으므로, 거의 모든 임무가 이전과 바뀌고 있다는 표현은 틀림. with + N + 분사 [부대상황 분사 구문] 정리할 것.

3. T / 우리가 이미지의 사용을 통해 설득력을 부여한다면 그것이 아날로그인지, 디지털인지는 중요하지 않다고 했으므로.

Ⓢhorts Ⓖrammar

understood / initially / was / even if / deeply / inspect / precisely / them

25강 3번

Ⓢhorts Ⓕlow

1) C-A-B

Ⓢhorts Ⓞverview

2) the importance of box office success for wide profit margin
3) Success Brings Success: Why Box Office Is Centered For the Success of Movie Industry

Ⓢhorts Ⓓetails

1. T / 영화는 점점 더 영화관 외의 수입원에 의존하긴 하지만, 이러한 사실이 견실한 박스 오피스 성과의 중요성을 깎아내리지 않는다고 했으므로.

2. T / 비평가의 찬사는 늘 반가운 것이지만 결국 영화는 돈을 버는 것이 중요하다고 했으므로. valuable = invaluable = priceless 정리할 것.

3. T / 영화가 정상을 차지하면 직접적인 수익 산출을 내고 다른 수입원을 활성화 한다고 했으므로. not only A but (also) B 구문 정리할 것.

Ⓢhorts Ⓖrammar

is / increasingly / is / does / why / highly / well

26강 1번

Ⓢhorts Ⓕlow

1) A-C-B

Ⓢhorts Ⓞverview

2) improving the effectiveness of learner's attribution
3) Motivating Student's Learning Through Attribution Effect

Ⓢhorts Ⓓetails

1. T / 추가적인 연구가 Dweck의 연구결과를 입증했으며, 이러한 전략 교육은 이미 자신이 열심히 노력하고 있다고 믿는 학생들에게 가장 효과적이라고 했으므로. 유의어 정리, 관계대명사 계속적 용법 정리할 것.

2. F / 비교 가능한 학생들에게 훈련이 주어지지 않은 경우보다 상담 받은 학습자들이 실패에 더 적절하게 대응했다고 했으므로 같은 반응을 보였다는 표현은 틀림.

3. F / 전략 교육은 자신이 열심히 노력하고 있다고 믿는 학생들에게 효과적이라고 했으므로, 자신이 열심히 하고 있다는 믿음과 관련 없다는 표현은 틀림.

Ⓢhorts Ⓖrammar

provided / that / given / appropriately / hard / to attribute

26강 2번

Ⓢhorts Ⓕlow

1) A-B-C

Ⓢhorts Ⓞverview

2) effectiveness of active learning for the acquisition of knowledge
3) The Power of Active Learning

Ⓢhorts Ⓓetails

1. F / 새로운 지식과 기술을 유지하기 위해서는 모든 감각이 관여하는 것이 절대적으로 중요하다고 했으므로, 하나의 감각을 이용한 학습이 충분하다는 표현은 틀림. 관계대명사 계속적 용법 정리할 것.

2. T / 능동적인 학습이 수동적인 학습보다 훨씬 효과가 있다는 말을 들어도 놀라지 않을 것이라고 했으므로. 비교급 구문 정리할 것.

3. T / 기술을 연습하고 아이디어를 자신의 것으로 만들 기회를 가져야 한다고 했으므로, 그러한 기회를 갖는 것이 필수적이라는 표현은 맞음. 가주어 진주어 구문 정리할 것.

Ⓢhorts Ⓖrammar

what / surprised / far / actively / engaged

26강 3번

Ⓢhorts Ⓕlow

1) C-B-A

Ⓢhorts Ⓞverview

2) thinking as a process of finding equilibrium
3) Piaget's Account on How Thinking Changes and Moves Ahead

Ⓢhorts Ⓓetails

1. T / 자신의 사고 과정의 적절성을 끊임없이 시험하고 비평형 상태가 생기면 불편해지고 이러한 것을 해결하기 위해 동기를 부여하고 우리의 사고는 변화하며 앞으로 나아간다고 했으므로, 새로운 정보가 들어올 때 인지적 갈등(비평형 상태)이 생기고 학습자가 해결책을 찾으려는 동기가 생긴다는 표현은 맞음.

2. F / 우리가 동화와 조절을 통해 해결책을 계속 찾도록 동기를 부여하고, 따라서 우리의 사고는 변화하며 앞으로 나아간다고 했으므로, 정적이고 고정적인 상태라는 표현은 틀림.

3. T / 사람들이 균형을 이루기 위해 자신의 사고 과정의 적절성을 끊임없이 시험한다고 했으므로 되풀이 하는 과정이라는 표현은 맞음.

Ⓢhorts Ⓖrammar

be viewed / that / exists / uncomfortable / searching

27강 1번

Ⓢhorts Ⓕlow

1) C-A-B

Ⓢhorts Ⓞverview

2) the importance of nonverbal cues for communication without misunderstanding
3) Why We Sometimes Misinterpret Text Messages

Ⓢhorts Ⓓetails

1. T / 문자 메시지와 이메일에 대한 수많은 연구가 많은 오해가 의사소통에서 비언어적 단서와 목소리의 어조가 부족하기 때문이라고 했으므로. 가목적어 진목적어 구문 정리할 것.

2. F / 참가자들이 이메일의 어조가 비꼬는 것인지 아닌지를 정확하게 구별할 수 있는 가능성이 50퍼센트라는 했고, 문자 메시지가 자주 오해를 불러일으키는 것은 놀라운 일도 아니라고 했으므로, 이메일과 같은 소통은 대면 소통보다 효율적이라는 표현은 틀림.

Ⓢhorts Ⓖrammar

its / give / exchanging / due to / was / leads

27강 2번

Ⓢhorts Ⓕlow

1) B-C-A

Ⓢhorts Ⓞverview

2) the concept of social validation and how it works
3) Social Validation: How Certain Beliefs Are Confirmed Within A Group

Ⓢhorts Ⓓetails

1. F / 어떤 특정한 문화도 자신의 종교와 도덕 체계가 다른 문화의 그것들보다 우월하다는 것을 증명할 수는 없다고 했으므로, 입증하는 것이 가능하다는 표현은 틀림. 가주어 진주어 구문 정리할 것.

2. T / 한 집단은 특정한 믿음과 신념이 집단의 기능 중 중요한 영역에서 불확실성을 감소시킨다는 의미에서 효과가 있다는 것을 배운다고 했으므로, 의심을 줄이는데 효과적이라는 표현은 맞음.

3. F / 사회적 확인이란 구성원들이 서로의 신념과 가치를 강화한다면 자신들의 문화의 우월성을 당연하게 받아들인다고 했으므로, 자신의 신념과 가치에 대해서 의심하는 과정이라는 표현은 틀림.

Ⓢhorts Ⓖrammar

confirmed / be taken / is / them / transformed

27강 3번

Ⓢhorts Ⓕlow

1) B-A-C

Ⓢhorts Ⓞverview

2) the influence of exchanges of information between individuals on socio-cultural behaviors
3) Structure of Information Flows and Sociocultural Behaviors

Ⓢhorts Ⓓetails

1. F / 사회 문화적 행동은 개인 간의 정보 교환에서 발생한다고 했으므로, 사회 문화적 행동이 정보 교환과 독립적이라는 표현은 틀림.

2. T / 지역 사회에서 구축되는 사회적 유대는 지역 문제를 해결하는데 유용하며 더 높은 수준에서 사회 집단을 통합하는데 핵심적인 역할을 한다고 했으므로.

3. T / 거주지 분리는 집단 내의 개인들이 자신들의 동료들과만 상호 작용을 하도록 조장해서 양극화된 입장이 생길 수 있다고 했으므로, 그들과 유사한 사람들과만 상호작용 하고 그 결과 강력한 의견을 가진 고립된 집단을 만들게 된다는 표현은 맞음.

Ⓢhorts Ⓖrammar

closely / playing / how / arise

28강 1번

Shorts Flow

1) B-A-C

Shorts Overview

2) satellite technology for supplying internet service to geographically challenging areas
3) Orbital Satellites For Connecting the World

Shorts Details

1. F / 서비스가 제공되지 않는 지역들 중 많은 곳이 지리적으로 도달하기 어렵고 공급자의 비용을 높여 저소득 가구가 서비스를 이용할 수 없게 한다고 했으므로, 지리적으로 도달하기 쉽고 저소득 가구에 낮은 가격으로 서비스를 제공하게 한다는 표현은 틀림. 분사구문, 가목적어 진목적어 구문 정리할 것.

2. T / 지구 도처의 외딴 지역에 더 저렴한 비용으로 인터넷 접속을 확장하는 것에 대한 대안인 인공위성 기술 덕분에 저렴하고 이용하기 쉬운 인터넷이 현실이 되고 있다고 했으므로.

3. T / 한 미국 우주선 제조업체가 2019년 이래로 1735개의 인공위성을 궤도로 쏘아 올렸고, 인터넷 접속성이 난제였던 여러 지역에 이상적으로 적합하다고 했으므로, 인공위성을 쏘아 올렸고 그 결과 이전에는 인터넷 접속이 어려웠던 지역에 인터넷을 가능하게 하기위한 네트워크를 만들었다는 표현은 맞음.

Shorts Grammar

due to / emerging / has / where / completely

28강 2번

Shorts Flow

1) C-A-B

Shorts Overview

2) the growing amount of data and human's job
3) What Should Be Done To Swim In The Tsunami of Data

Shorts Details

1. T / 우리를 둘러싸고 있는 정보의 양은 처리하고 기억하기 거의 불가능해서 기계에게 그것을 맡길 수 있다고 했으므로. 가목적어 진목적어 의미상 주어 구문, 관계 대명사의 계속적 용법 정리할 것.

2. F / 안락한 디지털 미래의 비결은 쓰나미처럼 밀려오는 데이터에 접근하는 것이라기보다는 어떻게 그것을 이해해서 새로운 맥락, 아이디어로 바꾸는지 라고 했으므로, 모든 정보를 처리하는 것이 관련성과 관계없이 중요하다는 표현은 틀림. 가주어 진주어 구문 정리할 것.

3. T / 기계는 우리가 할 수 있는 것보다 더 빠르고 정확하게 데이터를 처리할 수 있다고 했으므로.

Shorts Grammar

be generated / that / coming / which / it

29강 1번

Shorts Flow

1) A-C-B

Shorts Overview

2) the concept of entrapment and an example case
3) Entrapment: Why You Still Care About the Sunk Cost

Shorts Details

1. T / 어떤 사람이 단지 이전에 매우 많이 투자했다는 이유만으로 잘못된 결정을 내리는 함정에 빠지는 경우가 있다고 했으므로. 가목적어 진목적어 구문 정리할 것.

2. F / 어떤 시점에서 수리를 하는 것이 가치가 있는가 아니면 다른 차를 구해서 얻을 때인가를 결정을 내려야 하고, 이전에 그 차에 많은 돈이 들어갔다는 사실이 최선의 것을 고르는 것을 어렵게 한다고 했으므로, 결정하는 것은 항상 쉽다는 표현은 틀림. 가주어 진주어 구문 정리할 것.

Shorts Grammar

Unless / repairing / that / been spent / as if / as / trapped / invested

29강 2번

Shorts Flow

1) B-A-C

Shorts Overview

2) the significance of leader's getting attunement within group members
3) A Key to an Organization's Success: Getting People Attuned

Shorts Details

1. T / 사고의 일치를 얻기 위해서 열심히 노력하지만 또한 동조를 얻는 데도 똑같이 열심히 노력해야 한다고 했으며, 이것이 사람들에게 반향을 불러일으키도록 하는 것이라고 했으므로. strive for 의미, not only A but also B 구문, 분사 구문 정리할 것.

2. F / 그 집단의 사슬의 고리가 단단할수록 그 사람들은 더 행복하고 결과는 좋다고 했으므로, 분열된 감정이 더 행복한 노동력으로 이어진다는 표현은 틀림.

3. T / 번창하는 조직의 리더는 그곳에서 일하는 사람들의 개인적인 목표와 가치를 더 큰 집단의 목표와 가치를 강력하게 연관 짓는데 성공한다고 했으므로, 직원들의 개인적인 목표와 가치 사이의 강한 유대감을 우선시하는 조직은 직원들의 만족도와 더 나은 결과를 달성한다는 표현은 맞음.

Shorts Grammar

equally / to explain / being asked / The

29강 3번

Ⓢhorts Ⓕlow

1) A-C-B

Ⓢhorts Ⓞverview

2) how the door-in-the-face technique works
3) The Door-In-The-Face Technique From A Normative Perspective

Ⓢhorts Ⓓetails

1. T / 면전에서 문 닫기 기법에서는 크고 불합리한 요청이 이루어지고 그것이 거절되며, 이것이 더 작으면서 합리적인 요청으로 이어진다고 했으므로. 관계 대명사의 계속적 용법과 지문과의 유의어 표현 정리할 것.

2. F / 면전에서 문 닫기 기법을 사용하는 사람은 더 작은 요청을 위해 자신의 처음 요청을 포기함으로써 양보를 한 것처럼 보이고 이것이 더 작은 요청에 화답하고 동의해야 한다고 느낀다고 했으므로, 부담을 덜 느끼게 한다는 표현은 틀림. 분사 구문 정리할 것.

3. T / 이 기법의 성공은 호혜적 사회 규범, 즉 우리가 다른 사람들로부터 받는 것을 동일하게 갚아야 한다는 규칙과 관련이 있다고 했으므로, 이 기법의 효과는 상호주의 규범에 기인한다는 표현은 맞음. attribute A to B 표현, 관계 대명사의 계속적 용법 정리할 것.

Ⓢhorts Ⓖrammar

which / agree / had been / others / have made / compelled / asking / denied

30강 1번

Ⓢhorts Ⓕlow

1) A-C-B

Ⓢhorts Ⓞverview

2) contrasting perspectives surrounding capitalism
3) Capitalism and Social Responsibilities of Businesses

Ⓢhorts Ⓓetails

1. T / 자본주의 옹호자들은 이 체제가 사회적 자유와 가치 있는 자원을 최대한 배분하여 사회의 모든 사람에게 최상의 경제적 결과를 낸다고 주장하므로. 분사 구문 정리할 것

2. F / 기업의 유일한 사회적 책임은 합법적으로 창출되는 이윤을 최대화하는 것이라는 견해에 대한 상당한 반발이 있었다고 했으므로, 지금까지 완전하다고 하는 표현은 틀림.

3. F / 사회가 자본주의를 받아들일 때 경제적 자유가 항상 우선한다는 관점을 받아들일 필요는 없다고 했으므로, 항상 경제적 자유의 우선순위를 의미한다는 표현은 틀림.

Ⓢhorts Ⓖrammar

governed / generate / with which / resulting / legally / that / accept /

30강 2번

Ⓢhorts Ⓕlow

1) B-C-A

Ⓢhorts Ⓞverview

2) the influence of crisis on social change
3) An Insight On What A Crisis Actually Does For A Social Change

Ⓢhorts Ⓓetails

1. F / 만약 2020년의 전 세계적인 유행병이 급격한 사회 개선을 가져온다면, 그 개선의 주요 요소들은 오늘날 이미 눈에 보일 것이라고 했으므로, 대유행이 끝난 후에야 볼 수 있다는 표현은 틀림.

2. T / 비가 진흙 사태에 그것의 힘을 가하는 것이 아니라, 그것은 수십 년 동안 쌓인 흙의 무게에서 비롯되는 것이라고 했으므로, 역사의 초기시기로 거슬러 올라간다는 표현은 맞음.

3. F / 뉴딜정책과 2차 세계 대전 이후 합의는 그 이전 시대의 사건들과 관련이 있다고 했으므로, 완전히 단절되었다는 표현은 틀림.

Ⓢhorts Ⓖrammar

built / is / it / emerged / visible

30강 3번

Ⓢhorts Ⓕlow

1) A-B-C

Ⓢhorts Ⓞverview

2) characteristics of agricultural society that prevent long-term growth
3) An Analysis on Decelerated Growth Pattern of Agricultural Society

Ⓢhorts Ⓓetails

1. T / 농업 사회는 역사적으로 장기간 둔화하는 성장 패턴을 보였다고 했으므로, 산업 혁명 이전의 농업 사회의 장기적인 성장 패턴은 감속하고 있었다는 표현은 맞음.

2. F / 자급자족과 토지 의존은 수확량을 증가시키려는 의욕을 제한했다고 했으므로, 수확량을 증가시키려는 동기가 강했다는 표현은 틀림.

3. F / 가용할 수 있는 기술 수준이 낮아 농업 생산을 개혁하려는 시도의 효과를 이용할 수 없었고, 가격 격차가 농업 기술 재투자에 필요한 자본의 축적을 방해했다고 하므로, 농업 기술이 고도로 발달하여 재투자를 위해 자본 축적이 필요하지 않았다는 표현은 틀림.

Ⓢhorts Ⓖrammar

while / made / created / has

31강 1번

Ⓢhorts Ⓕlow

1) B-C-A

Ⓢhorts Ⓞverview

2) the influence of self-esteem on health
3) Direct and Indirect Effects of Self-Esteem on Health

Ⓢhorts Ⓓetails

1. F / 자존감이 낮은 사람들은 대인 관계에서 오는 압박에 순응하여 그러한 사회적 압박이 건강에 좋지 않은 행동으로 귀결될 때의 불행한 결과를 맞이할 가능성이 더 크다고 하므로, 자존감이 낮은 사람들은 사회적 압력에 저항하고 건강한 행동을 할 가능성이 더 높다는 것은 틀림.

2. T / 높은 자존감을 누리는 사람은 부조화를 덜 용인하려 하고 그러한 부조화를 줄이기 위해 이성적인 행동을 할 가능성이 더 크다는 강력한 증거가 있다고 하므로, 자존감이 높은 사람들은 부조화에 덜 관대하고 그것을 최소화하기 위해 이성적인 행동을 할 가능성이 더 높다는 표현은 맞음.

3. F / 자신을 존중하고 중시하는 사람은 질병을 막는 행동 방침을 채택함으로써 자신을 돌보려고 한다고 했으므로, 자신을 더 존중할수록 질병을 예방하기 위한 조치를 취할 가능성이 줄어든다는 표현은 틀림.

Ⓢhorts Ⓖrammar

that / typically / pursuing / its / being / tolerate / in / though

31강 2번

Ⓢhorts Ⓕlow

1) A-C-B

Ⓢhorts Ⓞverview

2) an analysis on the developmental structure of the brain
3) Biological Approach to Why Adolescents Are Risk-Takers

Ⓢhorts Ⓓetails

1. T / 뇌의 전전두엽 피질은 사람이 결정을 내리도록 이끄는 데 도움이 되도록 위험과 보상을 평가하는 것을 담당하며 뇌의 이 부분이 청소년에 있어서 가장 마지막으로 발달하는 것을 보여준다고 하므로, 청소년들에 계속 발달하고 있으며 그렇기 때문에 성숙한 의사결정을 하는데 어려움을 겪는다는 표현은 맞음.

2. F / 연구 결과 뇌의 발달에 따라 위험을 감수하는 행동을 한다고 하므로, 환경적인 요인에만 기인할 수 있다는 표현은 틀림.

Ⓢhorts Ⓖrammar

that / challenged / revealing / guide / shown / which / because / biological

31강 3번

Ⓢhorts Ⓕlow

1) C-B-A

Ⓢhorts Ⓞverview

2) dietary supplements out of regulatory control
3) Problematizing The Absence of Firm Regulation on Dietary Supplements

Ⓢhorts Ⓓetails

1. T / 건강 보조 식품에서 특정한 규제적 통제를 면제하는 것은 그것이 적법한 것으로 여겨지는데 영향을 줄 수도 있고 의사와 약사는 소송을 두려워해서 이러한 제품을 환자에게 추천하는 데 낮은 수준의 확신을 갖는다고 하므로, 통제가 부족하기 때문에 추천하는 것에 대한 신뢰도가 낮을 수 있다는 표현은 맞음.

2. F / 처방이 필요한 약과 처방전 없이 살 수 있는 약 모두 FDA의 엄격한 통제를 받는다고 했고 건강 보조 식품에서 이러한 특정한 통제를 면제하는 것이 적법한 여겨지는 데 영향을 준다고 하므로, 건강 보조 식품이 더 엄격한 통제를 받는다는 표현은 틀림.

Ⓢhorts Ⓖrammar

including / is / themselves / using / were

Part II 컴팩트

Compact 20강 1번

1)	known	2)	illustrator	3)	was
4)	until	5)	how	6)	taught
7)	accident	8)	them	9)	entertain
10)	what	11)	know	12)	titled
13)	use	14)	collage	15)	medium
16)	more	17)	diagnosed	18)	disease
19)	working	20)	pass		
21)	-				
22)	-				
23)	-				

Compact 20강 2번

1)	passion	2)	agricultural	3)	were
4)	extraordinary	5)	Driven	6)	reliance
7)	that	8)	it	9)	that
10)	to	11)	be	12)	detour
13)	extremely	14)	that	15)	superior
16)	whose	17)	punishable	18)	delegation
19)	stuffed	20)	grown		
21)	the story of Jefferson and Italian rice				
22)	Jefferson's Efforts for Italian Rice				
23)	By introducing Italian rice to his home country in order to **grow** a better strain, Thomas Jefferson ran the risk of facing the **death** penalty. 더 좋은 품종을 재배하기 위해 이탈리아 쌀을 본국에 들여옴으로써 Thomas Jefferson은 사형을 당할 위험을 감수했다.				

Compact 20강 3번

1)	been introduced	2)	rise	3)	due to
4)	infection	5)	to figure	6)	what
7)	it	8)	controversial	9)	holds
10)	required	11)	that	12)	sewage
13)	chemical	14)	incidence	15)	successful
16)	principle	17)	innovation	18)	less
19)	sharply	20)	are being		
21)	developing a method of applying carbolic acid for surgeries				
22)	Joseph Lister's Insight Into Using Carbolic Acid for Antisepsis				
23)	Since many people were dying due to **infection**, Joseph Lister came up with an **innovative** idea of using carbolic acid to establish antisepsis. 많은 사람들이 감염으로 죽었기 때문에, Joseph Lister는 소독법을 확립하기 위해 석탄산을 사용하는 혁신적인 아이디어를 생각해냈다.				

Compact 21강 1번

1)	While	2)	nationalistic	3)	to which
4)	useful	5)	division	6)	associated
7)	important	8)	on the other hand	9)	had
10)	circumstance	11)	fostered	12)	glorious
13)	constitution	14)	predominate	15)	however
16)	had	17)	lacked	18)	more
19)	pioneering	20)	uniqueness		
21)	relative position of history and geography in education for developing national identity				
22)	Exploring Regional Differences of Emphasis on History and Geography for Building Nationalistic Sentiment				
23)	Both history and geography in the **educational** system serve to build nationalistic **sentiment**, whose relative position may change according to their **usefulness**. 교육 시스템에서 역사와 지리는 모두 민족주의적 정서를 형성하는 역할을 하며, 그 유용성에 따라 상대적 위치가 달라질 수 있다.				

Compact 21강 2번

1)	dimension	2)	is	3)	autonomy
4)	ethical	5)	written	6)	concrete
7)	whether	8)	has	9)	dependence
10)	Consider	11)	whether	12)	requires
13)	moral	14)	even if	15)	theological
16)	neutral	17)	that	18)	is
19)	independently	20)	held		
21)	theological truth and neutrality of moral knowledge				
22)	Should We Be Religious To Find Moral Truths?				
23)	Though many ethical works are written from a **religious** perspective, it seems that knowledge of moral truth is in **dependent** of **theological** truth. 많은 윤리적인 작품들이 종교적인 관점에서 쓰여지지만, 도덕적 진실에 대한 지식은 신학적 진실과 독립적인 것으로 보인다.				

Compact 21강 3번

1)	been identified	2)	identity	3)	cognitive
4)	For example	5)	more	6)	appreciation
7)	facilitate	8)	subsequent	9)	integration
10)	structure	11)	including	12)	For example
13)	supportive	14)	facilitate	15)	morality
16)	as well as	17)	involvement	18)	act
19)	belief	20)	which		
21)	individual and contextual factors for the development of moral identity				
22)	Categorization of Influential Factors for the Development of Moral Identity				
23)	Several **factors** influence the development of moral **identity**, some of which are individual while others are **contextual**. 도덕적 정체성의 발달에는 몇 가지 요인이 영향을 미치는데, 그 중 일부는 개인적인 것이고 다른 일부는 맥락적인 것이다.				

Compact 22강 1번

1)	if	2)	anticipate	3)	production
4)	increase	5)	is	6)	get
7)	increases	8)	limited	9)	supply
10)	demand	11)	Remember	12)	that
13)	use	14)	its	15)	generates
16)	roughly	17)	if	18)	recycle
19)	shortfall	20)	use		
21)	the importance of paper recycling for the increasing demand				
22)	Emergency: We May Run Out Of Paper				
23)	If we do not **recycle** paper, the demand for paper may not be satisfied in the near future considering the growing size of the **population**. 만약 우리가 종이를 재활용하지 않는다면, 증가하는 인구 규모를 고려할 때 가까운 미래에 종이에 대한 수요가 충족되지 못할 수도 있다.				

Compact 22강 2번

1)	unaware	2)	makeup	3)	its
4)	because	5)	determining	6)	which
7)	it needed	8)	component	9)	have become
10)	sophisticated	11)	to remain	12)	corporate
13)	important	14)	sparked	15)	strategic
16)	that	17)	struggle	18)	shaping
19)	conflict	20)	did		
21)	efforts to secure rare metals by companies and governments				
22)	Problematizing and Securing Supply Lines for Rare Metals				
23)	Companies and countries **realized** that rare metal supply lines that they **took for granted** for several years should now be firmly secured. 기업과 국가들은 수년간 당연하게 여겨온 희귀금속 공급선이 이제는 확실하게 확보돼야 한다는 것을 깨달았다.				

Compact 22강 3번

1)	fall	2)	heavily	3)	severely
4)	shortage	5)	agricultural	6)	due to
7)	while	8)	disappearance	9)	affect
10)	availability	11)	unable	12)	implement
13)	raises	14)	relation	15)	scale
16)	used	17)	purely	18)	imply
19)	equitable	20)	burden		
21)	uneven effect of climate change and environmental justice				
22)	Climate Justice: an Ethical and Political Approach to Global Warming				
23)	The concept of climate **justice** is concerned with **framing** an environmental problem as an **ethical** and political concern, in order to address equity issues. 형평성 문제를 해결하기 위해, 기후 정의의 개념은 환경 문제를 윤리적, 정치적 문제로 표현하는 것과 관련이 있다.				

Compact 23강 1번

1)	that	2)	concerned	3)	compound
4)	command	5)	is	6)	indifferent
7)	it enters	8)	content	9)	itself
10)	unaggressive	11)	complexity	12)	what
13)	if	14)	be regarded	15)	reactive
16)	extensive	17)	currently	18)	surprising
19)	evolved	20)	technique		
21)	organic chemistry and the mediocrity of carbonic compounds				
22)	Concept and Explanation of Organic Chemistry				
23)	As a branch of chemistry, organic chemistry studies various **compounds** of carbon, whose mild **character** allows for the formation of **complex** chains. 화학의 일부로서, 유기화학은 탄소의 다양한 화합물을 연구하는데, 탄소의 온화한 특성은 복잡한 사슬을 형성할 수 있게 한다.				

Compact 23강 2번

1)	used	2)	been mined	3)	industrial
4)	used	5)	be mixed	6)	Although
7)	it	8)	effective	9)	without
10)	useful	11)	is	12)	situation
13)	where	14)	to get	15)	stubborn
16)	resort	17)	where	18)	safely
19)	stored	20)	reach		
21)	-				
22)	-				
23)	-				

Compact 23강 3번

1)	much	2)	were	3)	visited
4)	Exploration	5)	which	6)	mission
7)	close enough	8)	how	9)	magnetic
10)	surrounding	11)	detect	12)	whether
13)	its	14)	slight	15)	passes
16)	mass	17)	be determined	18)	Knowing
19)	to work	20)	density		
21)	fly-bys for explorations of giant planets and their moons				
22)	An Expedition to Other Planets Via Fly-Bys				
23)	**Fly-bys** allowed people to have detailed images of giant planets and their **moons**, detect magnetic fields, and measure the size and **density** of planets. 플라이바이는 사람들이 거대한 행성과 그 위성의 상세한 이미지를 가질 수 있게 해주었고, 자기장을 감지하고 행성의 크기와 밀도를 측정할 수 있게 해주었다.				

Compact 24강 1번

1)	available	2)	owned	3)	cultural
4)	accessibility	5)	led	6)	suggest
7)	being	8)	are	9)	initial
10)	community	11)	which	12)	maximize
13)	grazing	14)	that	15)	ignorance
16)	using	17)	depletion	18)	potential
19)	is	20)	sustainable		

21) the concept of common pool resources and the tragedy of commons

22) How Resources of the Commons End Up Depleted

23) As Hardin famously conceptualized, resources that are **available** to everyone but owned by no one can be easily depleted because of the **ignorance** on the **potential** influence of each use.
Hardin 유명하게 개념화한 것처럼, 모든 사람이 사용할 수 있지만 아무도 소유하지 않는 자원은 각 사용의 잠재적 영향에 대한 무지로 인해 쉽게 고갈될 수 있다.

Compact 24강 2번

1)	is	2)	change	3)	frequently
4)	pervasive	5)	turned	6)	offered
7)	that	8)	commitment	9)	heritage
10)	vanishes	11)	destination	12)	was
13)	resident	14)	being disconnected	15)	less
16)	significant	17)	primarily	18)	commercial
19)	who	20)	to recreate		

21) commercialization of traditional heritage and its threat

22) Dynamics of Tourism: How Cultural Heritage and Tradition Can Be Changed

23) Mass production and **commercial** sentiment can greatly change the cultural **heritage** and tradition of a tourist spot, which can lead to the loss of **identity**.
대량생산과 상업적 정서는 관광지의 문화유산과 전통을 크게 변화시켜 정체성 상실로 이어질 수 있다.

Compact 24강 3번

1)	philosophy	2)	wealthy enough	3)	hire
4)	However	5)	competitive	6)	administrative
7)	measurement	8)	However	9)	similarity
10)	dominant	11)	that	12)	that
13)	limited	14)	participation	15)	used
16)	evaluate	17)	that	18)	it
19)	preserve	20)	privilege		

21) cross-examination on functions of sports in different time settings

22) Comparing Physical Contests in Greek Culture with Sports of Today

23) One major **similarity** between physical contests in Greek culture and sports of today is the function of reproducing **dominant** patterns of social relations.
그리스 문화에서 신체적 경쟁과 오늘날 스포츠의 주요한 유사점 중 하나는 사회적 관계의 지배적인 패턴을 재현하는 기능이다.

Compact 25강 1번

1)	expertise	2)	On the other hand	3)	perception
4)	that	5)	innate	6)	ordinary
7)	Talent	8)	assumed	9)	trait
10)	either	11)	popular	12)	attempted
13)	that	14)	unacceptable	15)	those
16)	to practice	17)	In fact	18)	considered
19)	are	20)	to practice		

21) the dichotomy of thinking in the field of music

22) Innate Talent or Disciplined Practice: Learning About the Black-and-White Thinking in Music

23) There is a **dichotomy** of thinking in the field of music, in which people attribute great musical **ability** to either an innate **talent** or a disciplined work ethic.
음악 분야에는 사람들이 위대한 음악적 능력을 타고난 재능이나 훈련된 직업 윤리로 돌리는 이분법적 사고가 있다.

Compact 25강 2번

1)	understood	2)	visible	3)	initially
4)	used	5)	realm	6)	was
7)	its	8)	even if	9)	deeply
10)	authenticity	11)	hardly	12)	created
13)	closely	14)	inspect	15)	remains
16)	precisely	17)	assign	18)	them
19)	whether	20)	evidence		

21) digitization and changing perception on photographs

22) The Evidential Power of Photographs Still Remains Strong

23) Though digitization may seem as if it marked the end of the **photographic** era, we still endow certain functions and values on photographs as a source of **evidence** and **persuasion**.
디지털화가 마치 사진 시대의 종말을 알리는 것처럼 보일 수 있지만, 우리는 여전히 증거와 설득의 원천으로서 사진에 특정 기능과 가치를 부여한다.

Compact 25강 3번

1)	is	2)	that	3)	increasingly
4)	massive	5)	is	6)	performance
7)	revenue	8)	diminish	9)	significance
10)	does	11)	promote	12)	high
13)	its	14)	attractive	15)	potential
16)	breed	17)	why	18)	highly
19)	successful	20)	well		

21) the importance of box office success for wide profit margin

22) Success Brings Success: Why Box Office Is Centered For the Success of Movie Industry

23) Even though movie industries are increasingly utilizing non-theatrical sources for making **profits**, the importance of box office **success** remains **solid**.
비록 영화 산업이 수익을 내기 위해 비극장적인 자원을 점점 더 많이 활용하고 있지만, 매표소 흥행의 중요성은 여전히 확고하다.

Compact 26강 1번

1)	effectiveness	2)	provided	3)	who
4)	helplessness	5)	unsuccessful	6)	that
7)	ineffective	8)	Comparable	9)	given
10)	appropriately	11)	persist	12)	adapting
13)	effectively	14)	Additional	15)	that
16)	hard	17)	that	18)	increase
19)	motivation	20)	to attribute		
21)	improving the effectiveness of learner's attribution				
22)	Motivating Student's Learning Through Attribution Effect				
23)	An experiment revealed that students **persist** longer and get more **strategic** when they **attribute** their learning to themselves. 한 실험은 학생들이 그들의 학습을 그들 자신에게 돌릴 때 더 오래 지속되고 더 전략적이 된다는 것을 보여주었다.				

Compact 26강 2번

1)	what	2)	relatively	3)	acquisition
4)	surprised	5)	that	6)	far
7)	In other words	8)	potent	9)	having
10)	actively	11)	interaction	12)	Likewise
13)	engaged	14)	It	15)	intellect
16)	if	17)	emotionally	18)	merely
19)	it	20)	practice		
21)	effectiveness of active learning for the acquisition of knowledge				
22)	The Power of Active Learning				
23)	Rather than staring at a blackboard, the learning effect is much stronger when learners actively **engage** with the material and have **opportunities** to make the ideas their own. 칠판을 응시하는 것보다 학습자가 적극적으로 교재에 참여하고 아이디어를 자신의 것으로 만들 수 있는 기회를 가질 때 학습효과가 훨씬 강하다.				

Compact 26강 3번

1)	be viewed	2)	complex	3)	take
4)	process	5)	assumed	6)	that
7)	adequacy	8)	achieve	9)	Briefly
10)	scheme	11)	works	12)	exists
13)	satisfying	14)	uncomfortable	15)	searching
16)	optimal	17)	interested	18)	discouraged
19)	anxious	20)	change		
21)	thinking as a process of finding equilibrium				
22)	Piaget's Account on How Thinking Changes and Moves Ahead				
23)	Piaget believed that thinking is like the process of **equilibration** in which a particular **scheme** is **constantly** applied to contexts and revised. Piaget는 사고란 특정한 체계가 문맥에 지속적으로 적용되고 수정되는 균형의 과정과 같다고 믿었다.				

Compact 27강 1번

1)	to imagine	2)	without	3)	its
4)	component	5)	give	6)	clue
7)	experienced	8)	exchanging	9)	While
10)	a	11)	misinterpretation	12)	due to
13)	Numerous	14)	that	15)	correctly
16)	was	17)	sarcastic	18)	correctly
19)	texting	20)	leads		
21)	the importance of nonverbal cues for communication without misunderstanding				
22)	Why We Sometimes Misinterpret Text Messages				
23)	Numerous studies point to the fact that the reason why we **misunderstand** text messages is due to the lack of **nonverbal** cues and tone of voice. 많은 연구들은 우리가 문자 메시지를 오해하는 이유가 비언어적인 신호와 목소리 톤의 부족 때문이라는 사실을 지적한다.				

Compact 27강 2번

1)	validation	2)	confirmed	3)	For example
4)	superior	5)	reinforce	6)	be taken
7)	who	8)	accept	9)	being thrown
10)	is	11)	abide	12)	them
13)	that	14)	initially	15)	uncertainty
16)	critical	17)	Moreover	18)	transformed
19)	even though	20)	performance		
21)	the concept of social validation and how it works				
22)	Social Validation: How Certain Beliefs Are Confirmed Within A Group				
23)	With certain beliefs and values being **confirmed** only by the shared social **experience** of a group, social validation greatly affects the course of the group's functioning. 특정 신념과 가치는 집단의 공유된 사회적 경험에 의해서만 확인되기 때문에, 사회적 확인은 집단의 기능 과정에 큰 영향을 미친다.				

Compact 27강 3번

1)	exchange	2)	therefore	3)	closely
4)	flows	5)	are	6)	useful
7)	concrete	8)	playing	9)	Residential
10)	directly	11)	how	12)	displayed
13)	structure	14)	dynamical	15)	to interact
16)	collective	17)	that	18)	emerge
19)	polarize	20)	arise		
21)	the influence of exchanges of information between individuals on socio-cultural behaviors				
22)	Structure of Information Flows and Sociocultural Behaviors				
23)	The implication of the fact that socio-cultural behaviors arise from the **exchange** of information between **individuals** is that social ties can play a key role in **integrating** social groups at higher scales. 사회문화적 행동이 개인 간의 정보 교환에서 발생한다는 사실의 시사점은 사회적 유대가 더 높은 규모의 사회집단을 통합하는 데 핵심적인 역할을 할 수 있다는 것이다.				

Compact 28강 1번

1)	population	2)	geographically	3)	due to
4)	raising	5)	However	6)	affordable
7)	emerging	8)	alternative	9)	expanding
10)	For example	11)	has	12)	suited
13)	where	14)	typically	15)	Unbounded
16)	where	17)	has	18)	unreliable
19)	completely	20)	unavailable		
21)	satellite technology for supplying internet service to geographically challenging areas				
22)	Orbital Satellites For Connecting the World				
23)	Thanks to **satellite** technologies, it became possible to provide internet service to **geographically** challenging areas. 위성 기술 덕분에, 지리적으로 어려운 지역에 인터넷 서비스를 제공하는 것이 가능해졌다.				

Compact 28강 2번

1)	be generated	2)	massive	3)	that
4)	unprecedented	5)	more	6)	importance
7)	integrate	8)	insight	9)	coming
10)	aid	11)	surrounding	12)	that
13)	which	14)	accurately	15)	what
16)	is	17)	accessing	18)	how
19)	comprehend	20)	it		
21)	the growing amount of data and human's job				
22)	What Should Be Done To Swim In The Tsunami of Data				
23)	Since data is **generated** from everywhere and the amount grows **exponentially**, we should be able to **comprehend** and translate data into valuable ideas. 모든 곳에서 데이터가 생성되고 그 양이 기하급수적으로 증가하기 때문에, 우리는 데이터를 이해하고 가치 있는 아이디어로 번역할 수 있어야 한다.				

Compact 29강 1번

1)	Unless	2)	who	3)	occasion
4)	experienced	5)	realization	6)	repairing
7)	wrong	8)	looked	9)	that
10)	been spent	11)	it	12)	as if
13)	which	14)	difficult	15)	choose
16)	as	17)	entrapment	18)	trapped
19)	decision	20)	invested		
21)	the concept of entrapment and an example case				
22)	Entrapment: Why You Still Care About the Sunk Cost				
23)	A concept known as entrapment indicates that we sometimes make a wrong **decision** just because of previous **investments**. 속박감이라고 알려진 개념은 우리가 단지 이전의 투자 때문에 때때로 잘못된 결정을 한다는 것을 나타낸다.				

Compact 29강 2번

1)	organization	2)	hard	3)	wavelength
4)	to flourish	5)	equally	6)	purpose
7)	resonate	8)	It	9)	relatively
10)	to explain	11)	cognitive	12)	feel
13)	connection	14)	what	15)	being asked
16)	succeed	17)	personal	18)	those
19)	chain	20)	the		
21)	the significance of leader's getting attunement within group members				
22)	A Key to an Organization's Success: Getting People Attuned				
23)	Beyond the **cognitive** understanding of the purpose and goal of an organization, the leader should get members to feel that their **personal** values and those of the group are **connected**. 조직의 목적과 목표에 대한 인지적 이해를 넘어. 리더는 구성원들이 자신의 개인적 가치와 집단의 가치가 연결되었다고 느끼도록 해야 한다.				

Compact 29강 3번

1)	technique	2)	unreasonable	3)	made
4)	which	5)	agree	6)	placed
7)	had been	8)	norm	9)	what
10)	others	11)	asking	12)	assistance
13)	appears	14)	have made	15)	compelled
16)	application	17)	permission	18)	asking
19)	denied	20)	increases		
21)	how the door-in-the-face technique works				
22)	The Door-In-The-Face Technique From A Normative Perspective				
23)	Because of the reciprocity social **norm** where we should pay back what we receive, the door-in-the-face technique works as it seems like a **concession** of giving up the initial **request**. 받은 것을 갚아야 하는 호혜적 사회규범 때문에, 처음 요구한 것을 양보하는 것처럼 보이는 '면전에서 문 닫기 기법'이 작동한다.				

Compact 30강 1번

1)	understood	2)	governed	3)	wealth
4)	its	5)	create	6)	generate
7)	with which	8)	payment	9)	that
10)	distribute	11)	resulting	12)	maximize
13)	legally	14)	However	15)	significant
16)	that	17)	capitalism	18)	accept
19)	freedom	20)	distribution		
21)	contrasting perspectives surrounding capitalism				
22)	Capitalism and Social Responsibilities of Businesses				
23)	Though defenders of capitalism argue that capitalism results in the best economic **outcomes** for everyone, this view has been challenged by an argument that emphasizes the social **responsibilities** of business. 자본주의의 옹호자들은 자본주의가 모든 사람들에게 최고의 경제적 결과를 가져다 준다고 주장하지만, 이러한 관점은 사업의 사회적 책임을 강조하는 주장에 의해 도전을 받아왔다.				

Compact 30강 2번

1)	crisis	2)	is	3)	rainstorm
4)	give	5)	built	6)	What
7)	is	8)	loosen	9)	creating
10)	settlement	11)	intellectual	12)	Likewise
13)	triggered	14)	it	15)	emerged
16)	progressive	17)	if	18)	lead
19)	renewal	20)	visible		
21)	the influence of crisis on social change				
22)	An Insight On What A Crisis Actually Does For A Social Change				
23)	A **crisis** itself does not give any power to a social change, but it outlines **conditions** for a series of **renewals** to occur. 위기 자체가 사회 변화에 어떤 힘을 주는 것은 아니지만, 그것은 일련의 변화가 일어날 수 있는 조건의 윤곽을 그린다.				

Compact 30강 3번

1)	characteristic	2)	while	3)	dependency
4)	motivation	5)	Even though	6)	made
7)	available	8)	capitalize	9)	Moreover
10)	inelasticity	11)	prevented	12)	needed
13)	created	14)	vicious	15)	production
16)	boom	17)	agricultural	18)	showed
19)	decelerating	20)	pattern		
21)	characteristics of agricultural society that prevent long-term growth				
22)	An Analysis on Decelerated Growth Pattern of Agricultural Society				
23)	Several factors such as **inelastic** demand, unstable **supply**, and divergent prices did make the long-term growth pattern of agricultural society **decelerated**. 비탄력적인 수요, 불안정한 공급, 가격 차이와 같은 몇 가지 요인들이 농업 사회의 장기적인 성장 패턴이 둔화되도록 만들었다.				

Compact 31강 1번

1)	evident	2)	that	3)	For instance
4)	typically	5)	pursuing	6)	right
7)	indirect	8)	its	9)	contribution
10)	being	11)	adopting	12)	that
13)	less	14)	tolerate	15)	rejecting
16)	consequence	17)	in	18)	though
19)	pressure	20)	unhealthy		
21)	the influence of self-esteem on health				
22)	Direct and Indirect Effects of Self-Esteem on Health				
23)	Self-esteem can positively affect **health** both directly and indirectly because individuals with high self-esteem will take **rational** action to reduce **dissonance**. 자존감은 직간접적으로 건강에 긍정적인 영향을 미칠 수 있는데, 이는 자존감이 높은 사람들이 부조화를 줄이기 위해 이성적인 행동을 취할 것이기 때문이다.				

Compact 31강 2번

1)	that	2)	adolescence	3)	challenged
4)	revealing	5)	occur	6)	In addition
7)	insight	8)	responsible	9)	guide
10)	decision	11)	shown	12)	mature
13)	which	14)	engage	15)	because
16)	completely	17)	examining	18)	maturation
19)	that	20)	biological		
21)	an analysis on the developmental structure of the brain				
22)	Biological Approach to Why Adolescents Are Risk-Takers				
23)	The spontaneity and short-sightedness of adolescence can be partially attributed to biological reasons because a part of the brain that is **responsible** for **evaluating** risk is still being **developed**. 청소년기의 자발성과 근시안적 사고는 위험을 평가하는 뇌의 한 부분이 여전히 개발되고 있기 때문에 생물학적인 이유에 부분적으로 기인할 수 있다.				

Compact 31강 3번

1)	prescription	2)	subject	3)	including
4)	requirement	5)	as well as	6)	acceptance
7)	supplement	8)	consideration	9)	If
10)	that	11)	is	12)	confidence
13)	however	14)	separate	15)	themselves
16)	are	17)	In fact	18)	that
19)	were	20)	alternative		
21)	dietary supplements out of regulatory control				
22)	Problematizing The Absence of Firm Regulation on Dietary Supplements				
23)	Despite the fassct that there are many dietary **supplements** and consumers, there are not enough **regulatory** controls that make them **legitimate**. 건강보조식품과 소비자가 많은데도 이를 적법한 것으로 만드는 규제가 충분하지 않다.				

Part III 변형문제

20강 1번

① ③

Leo Lionni, an internationally known designer, illustrator, and graphic artist, ⓐ**being → was** born in Holland and lived in Italy until he came to the United States in 1939. As a little boy, he would go into the museums in Amsterdam, and that's how he taught himself how to draw. He got into writing and illustrating children's books almost by accident. Lionni tore out bits of paper from a magazine and used ⓑ**it → them** as characters and made up a story to entertain his grandchildren on a train ride. This story became what we now know as the children's book titled Little Blue and Little Yellow. He became the first children's author/ illustrator to use collage as the main medium for his illustrations. Lionni wrote and illustrated more than 40 children's books. In 1982, Lionni was diagnosed with Parkinson's disease, but he kept ⓒ**work → working** in drawing, illustrating and teaching. He passed away in October 1999 in Italy.

② 요약문 정답

-

③ 주제 정답

-

④ 제목 정답

-

⑤ 주요문장 정답

1. As a little boy, he would go into the museums in Amsterdam, and <u>that's how he taught himself how to draw.</u>

2. This story <u>became what we now know as the children's book titled Little Blue and Little Yellow.</u>

3. In 1982, Lionni was diagnosed with Parkinson's disease, but <u>he kept working in drawing, illustrating and teaching.</u>

20강 2번

① ④

Thomas Jefferson's knowledge of and passion for all things agricultural were truly extraordinary. ⓐ**Driving → Driven** by a desire to see the South freed from its reliance on cotton, he was always on the lookout for crops that could replace it. While touring the south of France in 1787, Jefferson discovered that Italian rice was preferred to the American import grown in the Carolinas. Intent on discovering why this might ⓑ**do → be** so, he took a detour into the Italian region of Lombardy on a mission of rice reconnaissance (a journey that, because it required crossing the Alps, was extremely dangerous at the time). There he discovered ⓒ**what → that** the good folks of Lombardy were growing a superior strain of crop — whose export for planting outside of Italy was a crime punishable by death. Undaunted, Jefferson sent a small packet of the rice grain to his good friend James Madison and members of the South Carolina delegation. Later, he ⓓ**was stuffed → stuffed** his pockets with some of the rice grains, and "walked it" out of the country. The rice is grown in parts of the United States to this day.

② 요약문 정답

By introducing Italian rice to his home country in order to grow a better strain, Thomas Jefferson ran the risk of facing the death penalty.

③ 주제 정답

the story of Jefferson and Italian rice

④ 제목 정답

Jefferson's Efforts for Italian Rice

⑤ 주요문장 정답

1. <u>Thomas Jefferson's knowledge of and passion for all things agricultural</u> were truly extraordinary.

2. <u>Driven by a desire to see the South freed from its reliance on cotton,</u> he was always on the lookout for crops that could replace it.

3. There he discovered that the good folks of Lombardy were growing a superior strain of crop — <u>whose export for planting outside of Italy was a crime punishable by death.</u>

① ②

It's the late 1800s. Anesthesia has just been introduced. Surgeries are on the rise, but a disturbing number of patients are dying due to infection. Joseph Lister is determined @**figuring →** **to figure** out why and what can be done about it. After much research and thought, he concludes that Pasteur's controversial germ theory holds the key to the mystery. Killing germs in wounds with heat isn't an option, however — a completely new method is required. Lister guesses that there may be a chemical solution, and later that year, he reads in a newspaper that the treatment of sewage with a chemical called carbolic acid reduced the incidence of disease among the people and cattle of a nearby small English town. Lister follows the lead and, in 1865, develops a successful method of applying carbolic acid to wounds to prevent infection. He continues to work along this line and establishes antisepsis as a basic principle of surgery. Thanks to his discoveries and innovations, amputations become less frequent, deaths due to infection drop ⓑ**sharp → sharply**, and new surgeries previously considered impossible are being routinely planned and executed.

② 요약문 정답

Since many people were dying due to infection, Joseph Lister came up with an innovative idea of using carbolic acid to establish antisepsis.

③ 주제 정답

developing a method of applying carbolic acid for surgeries

④ 제목 정답

Joseph Lister's Insight Into Using Carbolic Acid for Antisepsis

⑤ 주요문장 정답

1. Joseph Lister is determined to <u>figure out why and what can be done about it</u>.

2. Lister guesses that there may be a chemical solution, and later that year, he reads in a newspaper that <u>the treatment of sewage with a chemical called carbolic acid reduced the incidence of disease</u> among the people and cattle of a nearby small English town.

3. Thanks to his discoveries and innovations, amputations become less frequent, deaths due to infection drop sharply, and <u>new surgeries previously considered impossible are being routinely planned and executed</u>.

① ③

While both history and geography could serve to develop nationalistic sentiments, the relative position of these two subjects in the educational system largely came to depend on the degree @**which →** **to which** either seemed more useful in building up the idea of a national identity. In Germany, with its long history of shifting borders and divisions into small states, geographical patterns associated with the German-speaking lands seemed very significant, and so geography was seen as very ⓑ**importantly →** **important**. Norway, on the other hand, had developed its educational system during the union of the crowns with Sweden (1814-1905) and it had no disputed borders. Under these circumstances, Norway's national awakening was ⓒ**fostering →** **fostered** by teaching about the glorious history of Viking times and about the precious liberal constitution of 1814. Hence, history predominated over geography. Finland, however, which had also experienced a union of crowns (in this case with Tsarist Russia), lacked a clearly discernible glorious past and so geography developed as a relatively more important subject. A pioneering research work of great political importance in the Finnish liberation process, the Atlas of Finland, stressed the uniqueness of the Finnish lands.

② 요약문 정답

Both history and geography in the educational system serve to build nationalistic sentiment, whose relative position may change according to their usefulness.

③ 주제 정답

relative position of history and geography in education for developing national identity

④ 제목 정답

Exploring Regional Differences of Emphasis on History and Geography for Building Nationalistic Sentiment

⑤ 주요문장 정답

1. While both history and geography could serve to develop nationalistic sentiments, the relative position of these two subjects in the educational system largely <u>came to depend on the degree to which either seemed more useful</u> in building up the idea of a national identity.

2. In Germany, with its long history of shifting borders and divisions into small states, <u>geographical patterns associated with the German-speaking lands seemed very significant</u>, and so geography was seen as very important.

3. Finland, however, <u>which had also experienced a union of crowns</u>, lacked a clearly discernible glorious past and so geography developed as a relatively more important subject.

21강 2번

① ④

One dimension of ethical theory that needs mentioning is the issue of autonomy of ethics in relation to religion. Many ethical works are written from a religious point of view, and many concrete moral judgments are influenced by religion. A question in ethical theory is whether ethics ⓐhave → has some kind of evidential dependence on religion. Consider the question whether moral knowledge — say, that lying is (with certain exceptions) wrong — ⓑrequiring → requires knowing any religious truth. This does not seem so. To say this is not to claim (as some would) that we can know moral truths even if there are no theological or religious truths. The point is theologically neutral on this matter. It is ⓒwhich → that knowledge of moral truths does not depend on knowledge of God or of religious truths. This view that moral knowledge is possible independently of religion is not antireligious, and indeed it has often been ⓓholding → held by religiously committed philosophers and by theologians.

② 요약문 정답

Though many ethical works are written from a religious perspective, it seems that knowledge of moral truth is independent of theological truth.

③ 주제 정답

theological truth and neutrality of moral knowledge

④ 제목 정답

Should We Be Religious To Find Moral Truths?

⑤ 주요문장 정답

1. One dimension of ethical theory that needs mentioning is the issue of autonomy of ethics in relation to religion.

2. A question in ethical theory is whether ethics has some kind of evidential dependence on religion.

3. This view that moral knowledge is possible independently of religion is not antireligious, and indeed it has often been held by religiously committed philosophers and by theologians.

21강 3번

① ①

Several factors have ⓐidentified → been identified as influences on the development of moral identity, some individual and some contextual. At the individual level, things such as personality, cognitive development, attitudes and values, and broader self and identity development can impact moral identity development. For example, those more advanced in cognitive and identity development have greater capacities for moral identity development. Also, greater appreciation for moral values might facilitate their subsequent integration into identity. At the contextual level, one important factor is the person's social structure, including neighborhood, school, family, and institutions such as religious, youth, or community organizations. For example, a caring and supportive family environment can facilitate the development of morality and identity, as well as the integration of the two into moral identity. Additionally, involvement in religious and youth organizations can provide not only moral beliefs systems but also opportunities to act on those beliefs (e.g., through community involvement), which can aid their integration into identity.

② 요약문 정답

Several factors influence the development of moral identity, some of which are individual while others are contextual.

③ 주제 정답

individual and contextual factors for the development of moral identity

④ 제목 정답

Categorization of Influential Factors for the Development of Moral Identity

⑤ 주요문장 정답

1. Several factors have been identified as influences on the development of moral identity, some individual and some contextual.

2. For example, those more advanced in cognitive and identity development have greater capacities for moral identity development.

3. Additionally, involvement in religious and youth organizations can provide not only moral beliefs systems but also opportunities to act on those beliefs (e.g., through community involvement), which can aid their integration into identity.

① ③

Today we are using some 400 million plus tonnes of paper per annum in a global population of about seven billion, but if we look at the anticipated population figure in 2045 of nine billion, just on that basis alone paper production will need to increase by 30 per cent. On top of that within our current population not everybody ⓐbeing → is able to get a newspaper or has a book to read, or has enough exercise books to write on at school. As their percentage increases the demand for paper will also increase. We have limited land and a limited number of trees, and if we don't recycle we will not be able to supply the 400 million tonnes we need today or meet the demands of an increasing population. Remember of course that within the 400 million tonnes we use today about 200 million tonnes of waste paper is used in ⓑtheir → its manufacturing; 200 million tonnes of waste paper generates ⓒrough → roughly 160 million tonnes of recycled paper. Therefore if we didn't recycle we would only have 240 million tonnes of paper so there would be a shortfall or we would have to use more pulp.

② 요약문 정답

If we do not recycle paper, the demand for paper may not be satisfied in the near future considering the growing size of the population.

③ 주제 정답

the importance of paper recycling for the increasing demand

④ 제목 정답

Emergency: We May Run Out Of Paper

⑤ 주요문장 정답

1. Today we are using some 400 million plus tonnes of paper per annum in a global population of about seven billion, but if we look at the anticipated population figure in 2045 of nine billion, just on that basis alone paper production will need to increase by 30 per cent.

2. We have limited land and a limited number of trees, and if we don't recycle we will not be able to supply the 400 million tonnes we need today or meet the demands of an increasing population.

3. Remember of course that within the 400 million tonnes we use today about 200 million tonnes of waste paper is used in its manufacturing; 200 million tonnes of waste paper generates roughly 160 million tonnes of recycled paper.

① ⑤

For years, companies and countries took their rare metal supply lines for granted, unaware of the material makeup of their products. In fact, in 2011, Congress forced the U.S. military to research its supply chains because the Pentagon was having difficulty determining ⓐwhose → which advanced metals it needed. As the materials that make up product components ⓑto have become → have become more varied and complex, those who rely on sophisticated hardware can no longer afford to remain in the dark. Now, corporate and government leaders are realizing how important rare metals are. Indeed, efforts to secure rare metals have ⓒbeen sparked → sparked a war over the periodic table. In offices from Tokyo to Washington, D.C., in research and development labs from Cambridge, Massachusetts, to Baotou, China, and in strategic command centers the world over, new policies and the launching of research programs are ensuring ⓓwhich → that nations have access. The struggle for minor metals isn't imminent; it's already here and is shaping the relationship between countries as conflicts over other resources ⓔwere → did in the past.

② 요약문 정답

Companies and countries realized that rare metal supply lines that they took for granted for several years should now be firmly secured.

③ 주제 정답

efforts to secure rare metals by companies and governments

④ 제목 정답

Problematizing and Securing Supply Lines for Rare Metals

⑤ 주요문장 정답

1. In fact, in 2011, Congress forced the U.S. military to research its supply chains because the Pentagon was having difficulty determining which advanced metals it needed.

2. Now, corporate and government leaders are realizing how important rare metals are.

3. The struggle for minor metals isn't imminent; it's already here and is shaping the relationship between countries as conflicts over other resources did in the past.

① ③

The effects of climate change will fall most ⓐ**heavy → heavily** upon the poor of the world. Regions such as Africa could face severely compromised food production and water shortages, while coastal areas in South, East, and Southeast Asia will be at great risk of flooding. Tropical Latin America will see damage to forests and agricultural areas due to drier climate, while in South America changes in precipitation patterns and the disappearance of glaciers will significantly ⓑ**be affected → affect** water availability. While the richer countries may have the economic resources to adapt to many of the effects of climate change, without significant aid poorer countries will be unable to implement preventive measures, especially those that rely on the newest technologies. This raises fundamental issues of environmental justice in relation to the impact of economic and political power on environmental policy on a global scale. The concept of climate justice is a term used for framing global warming as an ethical and political issue, rather than one that is ⓒ**pure → purely** environmental or physical in nature. The principles of climate justice imply an equitable sharing both of the burdens of climate change and the costs of developing policy responses.

② 요약문 정답

The concept of climate justice is concerned with framing an environmental problem as an ethical and political concern, in order to address equity issues.

③ 주제 정답

uneven effect of climate change and environmental justice

④ 제목 정답

Climate Justice: an Ethical and Political Approach to Global Warming

⑤ 주요문장 정답

1. While the richer countries may have the economic resources to adapt to many of the effects of climate change, without significant aid poorer countries will be unable to implement preventive measures, especially those that rely on the newest technologies.

2. This raises fundamental issues of environmental justice in relation to the impact of economic and political power on environmental policy on a global scale.

3. The concept of climate justice is a term used for framing global warming as an ethical and political issue, rather than one that is purely environmental or physical in nature.

① ④

Organic chemistry is the part of chemistry ⓐ**what → that** is concerned with the compounds of carbon. That one element can command a whole division ⓑ**being → is** evidence of carbon's pregnant mediocrity. Carbon lies at the midpoint of the Periodic Table, the chemist's map of chemical properties of the elements, and is largely indifferent to the relationships it enters into. In particular, it is content to bond to itself. As a result of its mild and unaggressive character, it is able to form chains and rings of startling complexity. Startling complexity is exactly what organisms need if they are to be regarded as being alive, and thus the compounds of carbon are the structural and reactive infrastructure of life. So ⓒ**extensively → extensive** are the compounds of carbon, currently numbering in the millions, that it is not ⓓ**surprised → surprising** that a whole branch of chemistry has evolved for their study and has developed special techniques, systems of nomenclature, and attitudes.

② 요약문 정답

As a branch of chemistry, organic chemistry studies various compounds of carbon, whose mild character allows for the formation of complex chains.

③ 주제 정답

organic chemistry and the mediocrity of carbonic compounds

④ 제목 정답

Concept and Explanation of Organic Chemistry

⑤ 주요문장 정답

1. That one element can command a whole division is evidence of carbon's pregnant mediocrity.

2. Startling complexity is exactly what organisms need if they are to be regarded as being alive, and thus the compounds of carbon are the structural and reactive infrastructure of life.

3. So extensive are the compounds of carbon, currently numbering in the millions, that it is not surprising that a whole branch of chemistry has evolved for their study and has developed special techniques, systems of nomenclature, and attitudes.

① ④

Humans have ⓐ**been used → used** borax for more than four thousand years. Since the 1800s, it has been mined near Death Valley, California. Dirt cheap, borax has many industrial uses, but in the home it is used as a natural laundry-cleaning booster, multipurpose cleaner, fungicide, herbicide, and disinfectant. Off-white, odorless, and alkaline, borax crystals can be mixed with other cleaning agents for added power. ⓑ**Despite → Although** you certainly wouldn't want to eat it, borax is relatively safe and is quite effective without being toxic. It is useful in a lot of the ways that baking soda ⓒ**does → is**, but it's stronger and disinfects more, so it's good for mold, mildew, and deeper dirt. In general, use baking soda first and use borax only in situations ⓓ**which → where** something stronger is needed. It will enable you to get even stubborn stains clean without resorting to toxic chemicals. Borax should not be used where it might get into food, and it should be safely stored out of the reach of children and pets.

② 요약문 정답

-

③ 주제 정답

-

④ 제목 정답

-

⑤ 주요문장 정답

1. Off-white, odorless, and alkaline, borax crystals <u>can be mixed with other cleaning agents for added power.</u>

2. It is useful in a lot of <u>the ways that baking soda is, but it's stronger and disinfects more, so it's good for mold, mildew, and deeper dirt.</u>

3. It <u>will enable you to get even stubborn stains clean</u> without resorting to toxic chemicals.

---

① ③

There would be much less to say ⓐ**did → were** it not for space probes that have visited the giant planets and their moons. Exploration began with fly-bys (missions that flew past the planet) but has moved on to the stage of orbital tours in the case of Jupiter and Saturn, ⓑ**that → which** have each had a mission that orbited the planet for several years and that was able to make repeated close fly-bys of at least the regular satellites. Close fly-bys of moons enable detailed imaging, and usually take the probe close enough to see how the moon affects the strong magnetic field ⓒ**surrounds → surrounding** the planet and to detect whether the moon also has its own magnetic field. The size of the slight deflection to a probe's trajectory as it passes close to a moon enables the moon's mass to be determined. Knowing the moon's size, it is then easy to work out its density.

② 요약문 정답

Fly-bys allowed people to have detailed images of giant planets and their moons, detect magnetic fields, and measure the size and density of planets.

③ 주제 정답

fly-bys for explorations of giant planets and their moons

④ 제목 정답

An Expedition to Other Planets Via Fly-Bys

⑤ 주요문장 정답

1. There would be much less to say <u>were it not for space probes that have visited the giant planets and their moons.</u>

2. Close fly-bys of moons enable detailed imaging, and usually take the probe close enough <u>to see how the moon affects the strong magnetic field surrounding the planet</u> and to detect whether the moon also has its own magnetic field.

3. <u>Knowing the moon's size, it is then easy to work out its density.</u>

24강 1번

① ③

The term common pool resources refers to resources that are available to all, but ⓐowning → owned by no one. Nature-based examples include forests, oceans, and vistas, whereas common pool cultural resources can include a community's song, dance, and traditions. Many tourism products and experiences rely on common pool resources. The extent and accessibility of these resources has led McKean to suggest that common pool resources, in addition to ⓑbe → being available to anyone, are difficult to protect and easy to deplete. Hardin presented the initial illustration of this concept in his influential article titled "The Tragedy of the Commons." In this article, he described a community that thrives on the growth of its cattle, ⓒwhat → which graze on communal pastureland. As demand grows, residents are inclined to maximize their benefits by ignoring the cumulative effect of each person grazing an additional head of cattle on the communal lands. Hardin asserted that the ignorance of individuals using common pool resources will lead to eventual depletion of the resource. The potential combined impact of individual use of common pool resources is an important element of tourism's sustainable development.

② 요약문 정답

As Hardin famously conceptualized, resources that are available to everyone but owned by no one can be easily depleted because of ignorance of the potential influence of each use.

③ 주제 정답

the concept of common pool resources and the tragedy of commons

④ 제목 정답

How Resources of the Commons End Up Depleted

⑤ 주요문장 정답

1. The term *common pool resources* refers to resources that are available to all, but owned by no one.

2. As demand grows, residents are inclined to maximize their benefits by ignoring the cumulative effect of each person grazing an additional head of cattle on the communal lands.

3. Hardin asserted that the ignorance of individuals using common pool resources will lead to eventual depletion of the resource.

24강 2번

① ②

If part of the attraction of the community to outsiders ⓐare → is its cultural heritage and traditions, that will likely change over time and frequently not for the better. Symbols of a historic culture may be pervasive, but only in a make-believe form. Tourist shops on small Pacific islands may sell replicas of native art — all turned out in huge quantities by manufacturers in other parts of the world. Plastic Black Forest clocks and Swiss music boxes are offered to tourists that are mass-produced in Taiwan or China. A commitment to craftsmanship and true local heritage ⓑvanishing → vanishes. These false symbols of earlier times contribute to an overly commercial feeling at destinations and a sense that nothing seems real now, and perhaps never was. A danger lies in the loss of a sense of personal identity by residents and a feeling of being disconnected from their past. Their heritage and culture now seem less significant or important. It serves primarily as a commercial front for visitors who buy cheap trinkets and watch professionally staged shows that attempt to recreate cultural practices or historic events.

② 요약문 정답

Mass production and commercial sentiment can greatly change the cultural heritage and tradition of a tourist spot, which can lead to the loss of identity.

③ 주제 정답

commercialization of traditional heritage and its threat

④ 제목 정답

Dynamics of Tourism: How Cultural Heritage and Tradition Can Be Changed

⑤ 주요문장 정답

1. These false symbols of earlier times contribute to an overly commercial feeling at destinations and a sense that nothing seems real now, and perhaps never was.

2. A danger lies in the loss of a sense of personal identity by residents and a feeling of being disconnected from their past.

3. It serves primarily as a commercial front for visitors who buy cheap trinkets and watch professionally staged shows that attempt to recreate cultural practices or historic events.

① ②

Physical contests and games in Greek culture influenced art, philosophy and the everyday lives of people wealthy enough to train, ⓐhiring → hire professionals and travel to events. However, Greek contests and games were different from the organized competitive sports of today. First, they were grounded in religion; second, they lacked complex administrative structures; third, they did not involve measurements and record keeping from event to. However, there is one major similarity: they often reproduced dominant patterns of social relations in society as a whole. The power and advantages that went with being wealthy, male, young and able-bodied in Greek society shaped the games and contests in ways ⓑwhat → that limited the participation of most people. Even the definitions of excellence used to evaluate performance reflected the abilities of young males. This meant that the abilities of others were substandard by definition — if you could not do it as a young, able-bodied Greek man did it, you were doing it the wrong way. This legitimized and preserved the privilege enjoyed by a select group of men in Greek society.

② 요약문 정답

One major similarity between physical contests in Greek culture and sports of today is the function of reproducing dominant patterns of social relations.

③ 주제 정답

cross-examination on functions of sports in different time settings

④ 제목 정답

Comparing Physical Contests in Greek Culture with Sports of Today

⑤ 주요문장 정답

1. However, Greek contests and games were different from the organized competitive sports of today.

2. The power and advantages that went with being wealthy, male, young and able-bodied in Greek society shaped the games and contests in ways that limited the participation of most people.

3. This legitimized and preserved the privilege enjoyed by a select group of men in Greek society.

① ④

In the field of musical expertise, there is a dichotomy of thinking. On the one hand, there is a widespread perception in the general population ⓐwhat → that expert musicians have innate talent, or giftedness, beyond ordinary abilities. Talent, as part of the vernacular in the field of music, is usually ⓑassuming → assumed to be a stable trait — one is either born with musical talent or not. Music aptitude tests popular in the early to mid-twentieth century, such as the Seashore Tests of Musical Talent and the Music Aptitude Profile, attempted to find children who had this musical talent. On the other hand, there is a very real feeling that ability in music comes from a disciplined work ethic. It would be unacceptable, even for ⓒthat → those considered talented, not to practice. In fact, those who are considered talented ⓓbeing → are expected to practice all the more.

② 요약문 정답

There is a dichotomy of thinking in the field of music, in which people attribute great musical ability to either an innate talent or a disciplined work ethic.

③ 주제 정답

the dichotomy of thinking in the field of music

④ 제목 정답

Innate Talent or Disciplined Practice: Learning About the Black-and-White Thinking in Music

⑤ 주요문장 정답

1. Talent, as part of the vernacular in the field of music, is usually assumed to be a stable trait — one is either born with musical talent or not.

2. It would be unacceptable, even for those considered talented, not to practice.

3. In fact, those who are considered talented are expected to practice all the more.

① ③

For a long time photographs were understood to be visible traces, as irrefutable evidence of the existence of the presented, its "it has been." Therefore, photographs were initially classified as documents, whether @using → used in the media, in the family album, in books, archives or collections. As digitization began to feed into the realm of photography, and the end of the photographic era was proclaimed, it was its documentary qualities, its "ontology" as a chemical-physical symbol, that suddenly lost its persuasive powers. But even if the sting of digital doubt seems ⓑdeep → deeply ingrained within the photographic authenticity and evidence, many of its tasks and uses have hardly changed. When we look at a family album created with digital images, closely inspect the X-rays of a broken foot together with the doctor, or view the image of the finish of the 100-meter finals at the Olympic Games, our trust in photography remains. If we trust the use of the images, or more precisely, if we assign ©it → them persuasive powers via their use, it does not matter whether they are analog or digital. In other words: We doubt photography, but still use certain photographs to dispel doubt and produce evidence.

② 요약문 정답
Though digitization may seem as if it marked the end of the photographic era, we still endow certain functions and values on photographs as a source of evidence and persuasion.

③ 주제 정답
digitization and changing perception on photographs

④ 제목 정답
The Evidential Power of Photographs Still Remains Strong

⑤ 주요문장 정답

1. As digitization began to feed into the realm of photography, and the end of the photographic era was proclaimed, it was its documentary qualities, its "ontology" as a chemical-physical symbol, that suddenly lost its persuasive powers.

2. If we trust the use of the images, or more precisely, if we assign them persuasive powers via their use, it does not matter whether they are analog or digital.

3. In other words: We doubt photography, but still use certain photographs to dispel doubt and produce evidence.

① ③

Predicting whether a movie will be a success is perhaps the "Holy Grail" of most film-makers and especially the big movie studios. While critical acclaim is always welcome, in the end it is important that a movie makes money. For the big studios — now increasingly owned by massive global corporations — making movies that deliver wide profit margins @are → is the ultimate metric of performance. Movies increasingly depend on non-theatrical sources for revenues. This fact does not diminish the continuing significance of solid box office performance. When a movie hits top spot at the box office, not only ⓑis → does this deliver direct revenue yield, it can further promote other income sources over time. A high public profile means not only that its potential as an attractive choice for repeat viewing on other platforms increases but that its potential to yield sequels might increase, too. In the end, nothing breeds success like success. This maxim is probably the main reason why the major movie studios really like making sequels to highly successful movies and really like to hire star actors with a track record of appearing in blockbuster films that generally do © good → well at the box office.

② 요약문 정답
Even though movie industries are increasingly utilizing non-theatrical sources for making profits, the importance of box office success remains solid.

③ 주제 정답
the importance of box office success for wide profit margin

④ 제목 정답
Success Brings Success: Why Box Office Is Centered For the Success of Movie Industry

⑤ 주요문장 정답

1. While critical acclaim is always welcome, in the end it is important that a movie makes money.

2. When a movie hits top spot at the box office, not only does this deliver direct revenue yield, it can further promote other income sources over time.

3. A high public profile means not only that its potential as an attractive choice for repeat viewing on other platforms increases but that its potential to yield sequels might increase, too.

26강 1번

① ②

Learners can improve the effectiveness of their attributions through training. In a pioneering study, Carol Susan Dweck, an American psychologist, ⓐ **was provided → provided** students who demonstrated learned helplessness with both successful and unsuccessful experiences. When the students were unsuccessful, the experimenter specifically stated that the failure was caused by lack of effort or ineffective strategies. Comparable students were given similar experiences but no training. After 25 sessions, the learners who were counseled about their effort and strategies responded more ⓑ **appropriate → appropriately** to failure by persisting longer and adapting their strategies more effectively. Additional research has corroborated Dweck's findings. Strategy instruction was most effective for students who believed that they were already trying hard. This research suggests that teachers can increase students' motivation to learn by teaching them learning strategies and encouraging them to attribute successes to effort.

② 요약문 정답

An experiment revealed that students persist longer and get more strategic when they attribute their learning to themselves.

③ 주제 정답

improving the effectiveness of learner's attribution

④ 제목 정답

Motivating Student's Learning Through Attribution Effect

⑤ 주요문장 정답

1. In a pioneering study, Carol Susan Dweck, an American psychologist, provided students who demonstrated learned helplessness with both successful and unsuccessful experiences.

2. Strategy instruction was most effective for students who believed that they were already trying hard.

3. This research suggests that teachers can increase students' motivation to learn by teaching them learning strategies and encouraging them to attribute successes to effort.

26강 2번

① ④

A lot of research discusses what leads to relatively permanent acquisition of new knowledge or skills. You won't be ⓐ<u>surprising → **surprised**</u> to hear that active learning works far better than passive learning. In other words, sitting still in a classroom for more than a half hour at a time (no matter how interesting the material) isn't nearly as ⓑ **potently → potent** as having opportunities to engage actively with the concepts through discussion, group interaction, practice, immersion, or some other form of direct experience. Likewise, it is absolutely critical for retaining new knowledge and skills that all your senses are engaged. It is great to simulate your intellect, but even better if you can become involved emotionally, physically, and interpersonally. In other words, it isn't enough to merely read this material in a book or hear an instructor talk about ⓒ<u>them → **it**</u> in class. You must also have opportunities to ⓓ<u>practicing → **practice**</u> the skills and make the ideas your own.

② 요약문 정답

Rather than staring at a blackboard, <u>the learning effect is much stronger when learners actively engage with the material and have opportunities to make the ideas their own.</u>

③ 주제 정답

effectiveness of active learning for the acquisition of knowledge

④ 제목 정답

The Power of Active Learning

⑤ 주요문장 정답

1. <u>A lot of research discusses what leads to relatively permanent acquisition of new knowledge or skills.</u>

2. Likewise, <u>it is absolutely critical for retaining new knowledge and skills that all your senses are engaged.</u>

3. In other words, <u>it isn't enough to merely read this material in a book or hear an instructor talk about it in class.</u>

26강 3번

① ③

According to Piaget, organizing, assimilating, and accommodating can be viewed as a kind of complex balancing act. In his theory, the actual changes in thinking take place through the process of equilibration — the act of searching for a balance. Piaget assumed that people continually test the adequacy of their thinking processes in order to achieve that balance. Briefly, the process of equilibration works like this: If we apply a particular scheme to an event or situation and the scheme ⓐ working → works, then equilibrium exists. If the scheme does not produce a satisfying result, then disequilibrium exists, and we become uncomfortable. This motivates us to keep ⓑsearched → searching for a solution through assimilation and accommodation, and thus our thinking changes and moves ahead. Of course, the level of disequilibrium must be just right or optimal — too little and we aren't interested in changing, too much and we may be discouraged or anxious and not ⓒchanged → change.

② 요약문 정답

Piaget believed that thinking is like the process of equilibration in which a particular scheme is constantly applied to contexts and revised.

③ 주제 정답

thinking as a process of finding equilibrium

④ 제목 정답

Piaget's Account on How Thinking Changes and Moves Ahead

⑤ 주요문장 정답

1. According to Piaget, organizing, assimilating, and accommodating can be viewed as a kind of complex balancing act.

2. Briefly, the process of equilibration works like this: If we apply a particular scheme to an event or situation and the scheme works, then equilibrium exists.

3. This motivates us to keep searching for a solution through assimilation and accommodation, and thus our thinking changes and moves ahead.

27강 1번

① ④

In many ways it's difficult to imagine communicating without any emotion whatsoever. What would communication stripped of its nonverbal components even look like? Perhaps messaging technology can give us a clue. After all, who hasn't experienced a misunderstanding with someone when ⓐexchanged → exchanging text messages? While there can be a number of reasons for this, many misinterpretations are in fact ⓑ because → due to the lack of nonverbal cues and tone of voice in these communications. Numerous studies of text messaging and email support this. A 2005 paper, "Egocentrism Over E-Mail: Can We Communicate as Well as We Think?" cites studies that showed participants had a 50 percent chance of correctly distinguishing whether the tone in an email ⓒbeing → was sarcastic or not. If our ability to correctly deduce such information is no better than chance, it's small wonder texting often ⓓ leading → leads to misunderstandings.

② 요약문 정답

Numerous studies point to the fact that the reason why we misunderstand text messages is due to the lack of nonverbal cues and tone of voice.

③ 주제 정답

the importance of nonverbal cues for communication without misunderstanding

④ 제목 정답

Why We Sometimes Misinterpret Text Messages

⑤ 주요문장 정답

1. In many ways it's difficult to imagine communicating without any emotion whatsoever.

2. What would communication stripped of its nonverbal components even look like?

3. If our ability to correctly deduce such information is no better than chance, it's small wonder texting often leads to misunderstandings.

27강 2번

① ④

Social validation means that certain beliefs and values are ⓐconfirming → **confirmed** only by the shared social experience of a group. For example, any given culture cannot prove that its religion and moral system are superior to another culture's religion and moral system, but if the members reinforce each other's beliefs and values, they come to be taken for granted. Those who fail to accept such beliefs and values run the risk of "excommunication," of ⓑthrowing → **being thrown** out of the group. The test of whether they work or not is how comfortable and anxiety-free members are when they abide by ⓒit → **them**. In these realms, the group learns that certain beliefs and values, as initially promulgated by prophets, founders, and leaders, "work" in the sense of reducing uncertainty in critical areas of the group's functioning. Moreover, as they continue to provide meaning and comfort to group members, they also become ⓓtransforming → **transformed** into non-discussible assumptions even though they may not be correlated with actual performance.

② 요약문 정답

With certain beliefs and values being confirmed only by the shared social experience of a group, social validation greatly affects the course of the group's functioning.

③ 주제 정답

the concept of social validation and how it works

④ 제목 정답

Social Validation: How Certain Beliefs Are Confirmed Within A Group

⑤ 주요문장 정답

1. Social validation means that certain beliefs and values are confirmed only by the shared social experience of a group.

2. The test of whether they work or not is how comfortable and anxiety-free members are when they abide by them.

3. Moreover, as they continue to provide meaning and comfort to group members, they also become transformed into non-discussible assumptions even though they may not be correlated with actual performance.

27강 3번

① ②

Socio-cultural behaviors arise from the exchange of information between individuals and, therefore, they are ⓐclose → **closely** linked to how the information flows among the population. In particular, the social ties built and maintained in the local neighborhood are useful for solving concrete local problems and affect the spread of information and behaviors, ⓑplay → **playing** a key role in integrating social groups at higher scales. Residential segregation directly impacts how these social ties of physical nearness are displayed, drawing boundaries on the structure of information flows. We can think of the segregation process as a dynamical formation of echo-chambers: social fragmentation over the residential space encourages individual within a group to interact only with their peers. In this case, the collective behaviors of the socio-cultural space that emerge could clash at higher scales, as polarized positions may arise.

② 요약문 정답

The implication of the fact that socio-cultural behaviors arise from the exchange of information between individuals is that social ties can play a key role in integrating social groups at higher scales.

③ 주제 정답

the influence of exchanges of information between individuals on socio-cultural behaviors

④ 제목 정답

Structure of Information Flows and Sociocultural Behaviors

⑤ 주요문장 정답

1. In particular, the social ties built and maintained in the local neighborhood are useful for solving concrete local problems and affect the spread of information and behaviors, playing a key role in integrating social groups at higher scales.

2. Residential segregation directly impacts how these social ties of physical nearness are displayed, drawing boundaries on the structure of information flows.

3. In this case, the collective behaviors of the socio-cultural space that emerge could clash at higher scales, as polarized positions may arise.

① ②

Connecting the current offline population will be a difficult undertaking. Many of the remaining unserved areas are geographically challenging to reach due to rough terrain or remote location, thus raising providers' costs and pushing broadband services further out of reach of low-income households. However, more affordable and accessible Internet is becoming a reality in parts of the world, thanks to satellite technologies ⓐ emerged → emerging as an alternative to expanding access at lower costs to remote locations across the planet. For example, a network of orbital satellites operated by an American spacecraft manufacturer has launched 1,735 satellites into orbit since 2019. According to the company: "The satellite network is ideally suited for areas of the globe ⓑwhich → where connectivity has typically been a challenge. Unbounded by traditional ground infrastructure, the network can deliver high-speed broadband Internet to locations where access has been unreliable or completely unavailable."

② 요약문 정답

Thanks to satellite technologies, it became possible to provide internet service to geographically challenging areas.

③ 주제 정답

satellite technology for supplying internet service to geographically challenging areas

④ 제목 정답

Orbital Satellites For Connecting the World

⑤ 주요문장 정답

1. For example, a network of orbital satellites operated by an American spacecraft manufacturer has launched 1,735 satellites into orbit since 2019.

2. According to the company: "The satellite network is ideally suited for areas of the globe where connectivity has typically been a challenge.

3. Unbounded by traditional ground infrastructure, the network can deliver high-speed broadband Internet to locations where access has been unreliable or completely unavailable."

① ③

Data will be generated from everywhere. Cars, smartphones, bodies, minds, homes, and cities will be sources of massive amounts of information ⓐ what → that will grow exponentially and flow at an unprecedented speed over the internet. In the years ahead, the expression "less is more" will have a greater level of importance as to how you integrate the ocean of insights coming your way and will aid you to understand the world around you. The amount of information and media surrounding us will be impracticable to process and retrieve; you can leave ⓑthose → that for the machines, which can process data faster and more ⓒaccurate → accurately than we can. Your job will be to focus on what matters most to you. The key to an easy digital future is not so much accessing a tsunami of data but how you comprehend and translate it into new contexts, scenarios, and ideas.

② 요약문 정답

Since data is generated from everywhere and the amount grows exponentially, we should be able to comprehend and translate data into valuable ideas.

③ 주제 정답

the growing amount of data and human's job

④ 제목 정답

What Should Be Done To Swim In The Tsunami of Data

⑤ 주요문장 정답

1. In the years ahead, the expression "less is more" will have a greater level of importance as to how you integrate the ocean of insights coming your way and will aid you to understand the world around you.

2. The amount of information and media surrounding us will be impracticable to process and retrieve; you can leave that for the machines, which can process data faster and more accurately than we can.

3. The key to an easy digital future is not so much accessing a tsunami of data but how you comprehend and translate it into new contexts, scenarios, and ideas.

① ③

Unless you're one of those lucky people who only drive new cars, on at least one occasion you've probably experienced the painful realization that your car is too old and no longer worth ⓐ<u>repaired → repairing</u> any more. As a car ages, more and more things can go wrong and need fixing. At some point, the owner needs to decide: is it worth getting this latest issue looked at or is it time to give up on this car and find another? The problem is that a lot of money has already been spent on the car, and scrapping ⓑ<u>them → it</u> makes it seem as if that money has just been wasted, which makes it very difficult to choose the best option. It's a problem known as entrapment, when a person gets ⓒ<u>trapping → trapped</u> into making the wrong decision just because they've previously invested so much.

② 요약문 정답

A concept known as entrapment indicates that we sometimes make a wrong decision just because of previous investments.

③ 주제 정답

the concept of entrapment and an example case

④ 제목 정답

Entrapment: Why You Still Care About the Sunk Cost

⑤ 주요문장 정답

1. At some point, the owner needs to decide: <u>is it worth getting this latest issue looked at</u> or is it time to give up on this car and find another?

2. The problem is that a lot of money has already been spent on the car, and <u>scrapping it makes it seem as if that money has just been wasted, which makes it very difficult to choose the best option.</u>

3. It's a problem known as entrapment, <u>when a person gets trapped into making the wrong decision just because they've previously invested so much.</u>

① ④

Teams and organizations also have a 'mental life'. Most leaders work hard to get alignment — getting everybody on the same thinking wavelength. But to help organizations and teams ⓐ<u>flourished → to flourish</u>, leaders must also work equally hard on getting attunement —— getting people on the same feeling wavelength, getting the purpose of the organization and the meaning of the work to resonate with people in a felt way. 'Felt' is the important word here. ⓑ<u>That → It</u> is relatively easy to explain the purpose and goals of an organization in a cognitive way. But to function at our best, we have to feel the connection between what we are ⓒ<u>asking → being asked</u> to do and some larger purpose of the group. Leaders of flourishing organizations succeed in making strong feeling connections between the personal goals and values of the people working there and those of the organization, or even the larger society. The tighter the links in the chain, ⓓ<u>a → the</u> happier the people and the better the results.

② 요약문 정답

Beyond the cognitive understanding of the purpose and goal of an organization, <u>the leader should get members to feel that their personal values and those of the group are connected</u>.

③ 주제 정답

the significance of leader's getting attunement within group members

④ 제목 정답

A Key to an Organization's Success: Getting People Attuned

⑤ 주요문장 정답

1. <u>It is relatively easy to explain the purpose and goals</u> of an organization in a cognitive way.

2. But to function at our best, we have to feel <u>the connection between what we are being asked to do and some larger purpose of the group.</u>

3. <u>The tighter the links in the chain, the happier the people</u> and the better the results.

29강 3번

① ⑤

In the door-in-the-face technique, a large, unreasonable request is made, ⓐthat → **which** is turned down; this is followed by a smaller more reasonable request. People are more likely to agree to this smaller second request when it is ⓑplacing → **placed** in the context of the more unreasonable request than if it had been placed at the outset. The success of this technique may be related to the reciprocity social norm, the rule that we should pay back in kind what we receive from others. The person asking for our support or assistance, appears to ⓒmake → **have made** a concession by giving up their initial request, for a much smaller one. As a result, we feel compelled to reciprocate and agree to the smaller request. A common application of door-in-the-face is when teens ask their parents for a large request (attending an out-of-town concert) and then when the permission is denied, ⓓasks → **asking** them for something smaller (attending a local concert) . Having ⓔbeen denied → **denied** the larger request increases the likelihood that parents will acquiesce in the later, smaller request.

② 요약문 정답

Because of the reciprocity social norm where we should pay back what we receive,
the door-in-the-face technique works as it seems like a concession of giving up the initial request.

③ 주제 정답

how the door-in-the-face technique works

④ 제목 정답

The Door-In-The-Face Technique From A Normative Perspective

⑤ 주요문장 정답

1. People are more likely to agree to this smaller second request when it is placed in the context of the more unreasonable request <u>than if it had been placed at the outset.</u>

2. The person asking for our support or assistance, <u>appears to have made a concession by giving up their initial request</u>, for a much smaller one.

3. <u>Having denied the larger request increases the likelihood that parents will acquiesce</u> in the later, smaller request.

30강 1번

① ③

"Capitalism" is generally understood as a market-based, economic system ⓐgoverning → **governed** by capital — that is, the wealth of an individual or an establishment accumulated by or employed in its business activities. Entrepreneurs and the institutions they create generate the capital ⓑwhich → **with which** businesses provide goods, services, and payments to workers. Defenders of capitalism argue that this system maximally distributes social freedoms and desirable resources, resulting in the best economic outcomes for everyone in society. On this view, business's only social responsibilities are to maximize legally generated profits. However, over the past several decades there has been a significant reaction against this view. It is argued that businesses have responsibilities far beyond following the law and profit making. When society accepts capitalism, this view holds, it need not also ⓒaccepted → **accept** the view that economic freedom always has priority over competing conceptions of the collection and distribution of social goods, or of other responsibilities owed to employees, customers, society, and the environment.

② 요약문 정답

Though defenders of capitalism argue that capitalism results in the best economic outcomes for everyone, this view has been challenged by an argument that emphasizes the social responsibilities of business.

③ 주제 정답

contrasting perspectives surrounding capitalism

④ 제목 정답

Capitalism and Social Responsibilities of Businesses

⑤ 주요문장 정답

1. Entrepreneurs and <u>the institutions they create generate the capital with which businesses provide</u> goods, services, and payments to workers.

2. Defenders of capitalism argue that this system maximally distributes social freedoms and desirable resources, <u>resulting in the best economic outcomes for everyone in society.</u>

3. <u>It is argued that businesses have responsibilities far beyond following the law</u> and profit making.

30강 2번

① ③

The relationship between crisis and social change is a bit like the relationship between a rainstorm and a mudslide. The rain doesn't give the mudslide its power — that comes from the weight of earth, ⓐ building → built up over decades. What the rain can do ⓑare → is loosen things up, creating the conditions for change. Britain's post-Second World War settlement didn't solve the problems of the war: it addressed the pent-up problems of the 1930s, and its intellectual ingredients dated back further, to the opening years of the 1900s. Likewise, America's New Deal of the 1930s was triggered by the Great Depression, but the issues ⓒ they → it addressed and the approaches it applied emerged decades before, in the progressive and populist movements of the 1890s and 1900s. So, if the 2020 pandemic does lead to a radical social renewal, then the main elements of that renewal will be visible already today.

② 요약문 정답

A crisis itself does not give any power to a social change, but it outlines conditions for a series of renewals to occur.

③ 주제 정답

the influence of crisis on social change

④ 제목 정답

An Insight On What A Crisis Actually Does For A Social Change

⑤ 주요문장 정답

1. What the rain can do is loosen things up, creating the conditions for change.

2. Likewise, America's New Deal of the 1930s was triggered by the Great Depression, but the issues it addressed and the approaches it applied emerged decades before, in the progressive and populist movements of the 1890s and 1900s.

3. So, if the 2020 pandemic does lead to a radical social renewal, then the main elements of that renewal will be visible already today.

30강 3번

① ②

The characteristics of an agricultural society affected its long-run growth pattern prior to the Industrial Revolution, while self-sufficiency and land dependency limited the motivation to increase the yield. ⓐIn spite of → Even though some attempts were made to reform agricultural production, the low level of technologies available could not capitalize on the effect of those attempts. Moreover, inelasticity in demand, instability in supply, and price divergence prevented the capital accumulation ⓑneeding → needed for reinvestment in agricultural technologies. All of these factors created a vicious circle such that agricultural production could not boom. As a result, the agricultural society showed a long-term decelerating growth pattern in history.

② 요약문 정답

Several factors such as inelastic demand, unstable supply, and divergent prices did make the long-term growth pattern of agricultural society decelerated.

③ 주제 정답

characteristics of agricultural society that prevent long-term growth

④ 제목 정답

An Analysis on Decelerated Growth Pattern of Agricultural Society

⑤ 주요문장 정답

1. Even though some attempts were made to reform agricultural production, the low level of technologies available could not capitalize on the effect of those attempts.

2. Moreover, inelasticity in demand, instability in supply, and price divergence prevented the capital accumulation needed for reinvestment in agricultural technologies.

3. All of these factors created a vicious circle such that agricultural production could not boom.

① ③

It is evident that self-esteem has a significant effect on health — both directly and indirectly. For instance, self-esteem is typically considered a key feature of mental health and therefore worth ⓐ pursue → **pursuing** in its own right. It may also have an indirect influence through its contribution to intentions to undertake healthy or unhealthy actions. For instance, at a commonsense level, individuals who respect and value themselves will, other things ⓑ are → **being** equal, seek to look after themselves by adopting courses of action that prevent disease. Less obviously perhaps, there is strong evidence that people enjoying high self-esteem are less willing to tolerate dissonance and more likely to take rational action to reduce that dissonance, by, for example, ⓒ rejects → **rejecting** unhealthy behaviour. Those having low self-esteem are more likely to conform to interpersonal pressures than those enjoying high self-esteem with unfortunate consequences when such social pressure results in 'unhealthy behaviour'. In terms of empowerment, though, any unthinking yielding to social pressure would be considered unhealthy!

② 요약문 정답
Self-esteem can positively affect health both directly and indirectly because individuals with high self-esteem will take rational action to reduce dissonance.

③ 주제 정답
the influence of self-esteem on health

④ 제목 정답
Direct and Indirect Effects of Self-Esteem on Health

⑤ 주요문장 정답

1. It is evident that self-esteem has a significant effect on health — both directly and indirectly.

2. Less obviously perhaps, there is strong evidence that people enjoying high self-esteem are less willing to tolerate dissonance and more likely to take rational action to reduce that dissonance, by, for example, rejecting unhealthy behaviour.

3. Those having low self-esteem are more likely to conform to interpersonal pressures than those enjoying high self-esteem with unfortunate consequences when such social pressure results in unhealthy behaviour'.

---

① ②

In recent years, researchers have been trying to understand the changes that occur in the brain during adolescence. Structural brain imaging studies over the past decade have challenged the belief that structural brain development ends in early childhood, ⓐ reveals → **revealing** that changes occur through early adulthood. In addition, these studies provide an insight into the biological basis for understanding adolescent thinking and behavior. For example, the ventromedial prefrontal cortex of the brain is responsible for evaluating risk and reward to help ⓑ guided → **guide** the person to make a decision. Imaging studies have shown that this part of the brain is the last to mature in adolescents, which supports behavioral studies that show adolescents take greater risks than adults in activities such as substance abuse. Adolescents tend to engage in more reckless behaviors because the area of the brain that assesses risk and benefits has not completely developed yet. These findings, along with other studies examining the maturation of other regions of the prefrontal cortex during adolescence, suggest that the spontaneity, short-sightedness, and risk-taking behaviors associated with adolescence could be partially biological in nature.

② 요약문 정답
The spontaneity and short-sightedness of adolescence can be partially attributed to biological reasons because a part of the brain that is responsible for evaluating risk is still being developed.

③ 주제 정답
an analysis on the developmental structure of the brain

④ 제목 정답
Biological Approach to Why Adolescents Are Risk-Takers

⑤ 주요문장 정답

1. Structural brain imaging studies over the past decade have challenged the belief that structural brain development ends in early childhood, revealing that changes occur through early adulthood.

2. For example, the ventromedial prefrontal cortex of the brain is responsible for evaluating risk and reward to help guide the person to make a decision.

3. Imaging studies have shown that this part of the brain is the last to mature in adolescents, which supports behavioral studies that show adolescents take greater risks than adults in activities such as substance abuse.

① ③

Both prescription and over-the-counter drugs are subject to strict control by the FDA, ⓐincludes → **including** the regulation of manufacturing processes, specific requirements for the demonstration of safety and efficacy, as well as well-defined limits on advertising and labeling claims. Such controls provide assurances to consumers and health care professionals about the quality of the products and contribute to their acceptance as "legitimate" treatments. The exemption of dietary supplements from these specific regulatory controls may impact their consideration as "legitimate". If health care professionals feel that the quality of dietary supplement products ⓑbeing → **is** lacking, and if they consider dietary supplements outside the scope of "prevailing" medical or pharmacy practice, then physicians and pharmacists will have a low level of confidence in recommending these products to their patients for fear of legal action. Physicians and pharmacists cannot, however, separate themselves from the use of dietary supplements. With more than 29,000 dietary supplements on the market, consumers have broad access to and are using these products. In fact, a survey of consumers has suggested ⓒwhich → **that** approximately 42% of American consumers were using complementary and alternative therapies, with 24% of consumers using plant-based dietary supplements on a regular basis.

② 요약문 정답

Despite the fact that there are many dietary supplements and consumers, there are not enough regulatory controls that make them legitimate.

③ 주제 정답

dietary supplements out of regulatory control

④ 제목 정답

Problematizing The Absence of Firm Regulation on Dietary Supplements

⑤ 주요문장 정답

1. Both prescription and over-the-counter drugs <u>are subject to strict control by the FDA, including the regulation</u> of manufacturing processes, specific requirements for the demonstration of safety and efficacy, as well as well-defined limits on advertising and labeling claims.

2. Physicians and pharmacists cannot, however, <u>separate themselves from the use of dietary supplements</u>.

3. In fact, a survey of consumers has suggested that approximately 42% of American consumers were using complementary and alternative therapies, <u>with 24% of consumers using plant-based dietary supplements on a regular basis</u>.